Hybrid Hate

Hybrid Hate

*Conflations of Antisemitism and
Anti-Black Racism from the Renaissance to
the Third Reich*

TUDOR PARFITT

Oxford University Press is a department of the University of Oxford. It furthers the University's objective of excellence in research, scholarship, and education by publishing worldwide. Oxford is a registered trade mark of Oxford University Press in the UK and certain other countries.

Published in the United States of America by Oxford University Press
198 Madison Avenue, New York, NY 10016, United States of America.

© Oxford University Press 2020

All rights reserved. No part of this publication may be reproduced, stored in a retrieval system, or transmitted, in any form or by any means, without the prior permission in writing of Oxford University Press, or as expressly permitted by law, by license, or under terms agreed with the appropriate reproduction rights organization. Inquiries concerning reproduction outside the scope of the above should be sent to the Rights Department, Oxford University Press, at the address above.

You must not circulate this work in any other form
and you must impose this same condition on any acquirer.

Library of Congress Cataloging-in-Publication Data
Names: Parfitt, Tudor, author.
Title: Hybrid Hate : Conflations of Antisemitism and Anti-Black Racism
from the Renaissance to the Third Reich / Tudor Parfitt.
Description: New York, NY, United States of America : Oxford University Press, 2020. |
Includes bibliographical references and index.
Identifiers: LCCN 2020016025 (print) | LCCN 2020016026 (ebook) |
ISBN 9780190083335 (hardback) | ISBN 9780197529294 (epub) |
ISBN 9780190083342 (updf) | ISBN 9780190083366 (online)
Subjects: LCSH: Racism—Religious aspects—Christianity—History. |
Antisemitism—History. | Jews—History. | Black Jews—History. |
Blacks—History. | African Americans—History. |
African American Jews—History.
Classification: LCC BT734 .P37 2020 (print) |
LCC BT734 (ebook) | DDC 261.8/3—dc23
LC record available at https://lccn.loc.gov/2020016025
LC ebook record available at https://lccn.loc.gov/2020016026

For my mother

The most striking circumstance . . . was that of the change of the Jews to black.
> Joseph Barnard Davis (1801–1881)

I do not believe in a pure black Jew.
> Sir Richard Francis Burton (1821–1890)

The Semites belong to the mulatto class, a transition stage between black and white.
> Friedrich Ratzel (1844–1904)

And the shoe of the eternal Jew performs a negro dance on my nerves.
> George Grosz (1893–1959)

The Jew is a negro.
> Louis-Ferdinand Céline (1894–1961)

Jews . . . these negroid parasites in our national body.
> Adolf Hitler (1889–1945)

The problem wouldn't arise if Jews had blue skin.
> François Truffaut (1932–1984)

Contents

Prologue   ix

1. "The Truth of the Origination of the World and Mankind"   1
2. Blacks and Jews in the Western Imaginaire   31
3. All Africa and Her Prodigies   56
4. The Loango Turn   64
5. "The Most Striking Circumstance": Black Jews and Sustaining the Doctrine of the Unity of Mankind   76
6. Polygenists, Black Jews, and the Proofs for the Disunity of Man   99
7. The Racial Face   133
8. The Black/Jew   156
9. The Black/Jew in the Racial State   177
10. *Rassenwahn*   206

Notes   229
Bibliography   249
Index   273

Prologue

The study of Western racism has tended to concentrate either on the hatred, persecution, and murder of Jews or the hatred, murder, and enslavement of black people. Scholars engaged in the field of antisemitism are rarely engaged in the field of anti-black racism, yet the connections between the two are intimate and instructive. In *Towards the Final Solution* (1979), George Lachmann Mosse (1918–1999), the distinguished American historian, noted that the two racisms exist in separate geographical spheres. In Great Britain, with its great overseas empire, there was a good deal of hatred of blacks but little hatred of Jews, about whom little was known. In parts of Europe such as Germany, the Hapsburg Empire, or Russia, where blacks were relatively unknown, Jews were hated but no one bothered too much about blacks (Mosse.1979; MacMaster.2000).

Similarly, one of the greatest writers on antisemitism, the French historian Léon Poliakov (1910–1997), correctly observed that Enlightenment and nineteenth-century race theorists were concerned predominantly with Jews and blacks. However, he considered that the hatreds of Jews and blacks occupied different psychological spheres, had little if anything in common, and were expressed by completely different people and for different reasons (Poliakov.1971).

This book argues that Western thinking about race, from the time of Paracelsus to the period of the Third Reich, was indeed mainly concerned with Jews and blacks. During the race wars against blacks and Jews that spanned these five centuries, blacks and Jews were regularly twinned, through a range of metrics and historical and theological theories and legerdemain. Even the most fanatical, tunnel-visioned advocates for the denigration of Jews would, more often than not, have similar or identical views on blacks, while the most hardened anti-black bigots would hold similar views about Jews. Racial constructions about Jews and blacks during the period covered by this book were often of the same order, and frequently fused or alloyed together as one. In the complicated history of racial thinking, blacks and Jews were linked as the main objects, as well as the main victims.

One literal fusion of black and Jew came about through the discovery of the phenomenon of black Jews. One such group had a particularly powerful impact on the development of race theory. My own interest in this group started in 2015, when I came across a few lines in a German book by Christian Georg Andreas Oldendorp, published in 1777, which mentioned, almost in passing, the existence of a community of black Jews in the west African kingdom of Loango. I discovered that the natural scientists and race theorists of the late Enlightenment period and later, in Germany, France, the United States, and Great Britain, were intrigued and troubled by the existence of these black Jews, who would be a focus of racial discussions for the following century.

It was the theoretical and polemical importance of such hybrids, and the epistemic wealth of the notion of "black Jew" in the context of evolving racial hierarchies and racial difference, that piqued my interest. As I studied the Enlightenment reactions to the discovery of this remote community, it became clear to me that the key concept of hybridity in current cultural theory was of equally great significance for earlier generations of scholars and played an important role in the precision of theories of difference. It was also clear that the reactions of scholars and theorists to this community and other black hybrids were both historically significant and pointed toward wider intellectual horizons.

I began to see that the construction of the complex difference of the hybrid black Jew, as this image developed, involved a bricolage between visions of Jews and blacks, rooted in cultural as well as perceived racial difference, over many centuries. Moreover, hybrid black Jews, as will become apparent, became crucial in one side or the other of the centuries-long debate between the supporters and opponents of the doctrine of the unity of humankind.[1] But what was perhaps even more important was that the establishment of a much-discussed color spectrum for Jews, which started with the discovery of this group, contributed in some part to an eventual conflation of racial ideas about Jews and blacks, which emerged around the middle of the nineteenth century. This development constitutes the main matter of this book.

Many ideas about blacks and Jews that emerged during the race debates of the nineteenth century had been foreshadowed by medieval prejudice. The slowly evolving Western structures of race that were forged in the long years of persecution of Jews and blacks, viewed from the perspective of *la longue durée*, present a continuity. From the period of the Renaissance to the first half of the twentieth century, the words gradually changed, but the sentiments and often the metaphors stayed the same.

The new vocabulary of race, which eschewed earlier models rooted in the Judeo-Christian tradition, was enlisted to fight ongoing battles that never failed to be centered on the unitary or multiple origins of humankind. Out of this dogmatic struggle emerged a fusion of ideas about Jews and blacks that found its most complete and deadly form in Fascist Italy, Vichy France, and the Third Reich. Common archetypes and conflations joined together and fortified the two fundamental racisms of the West.

1
"The Truth of the Origination of the World and Mankind"

The study of racism is tantamount to a study of the struggle between the theory that humankind had diverse beginnings, which is known as polygenesis, and the theory that there was but one founding event, that which took place in the verdant Garden of Eden. Monogenesis, the traditional and ancient belief of the Abrahamic faiths that the whole of humankind descended from Adam and Eve, obviously implied kinship between all peoples. Acts 17:26 explained that God "made from one, every nation of men to live on all the face of the earth."

In *The City of God* Augustine of Hippo (354–430), the theologian and philosopher from what is today Algeria, accepted that the seventy-two nations that were thought to make up the world's population were descended from Eve and Adam. But he wondered if and under what circumstances other creatures, including the so-called monstrous races, should be considered human. Using the analogy of a child born with an extra finger, he argued that in the same way that such a child was evidently human, so monstrous races were fully part of humankind, notwithstanding the radical differences they displayed.

Augustine was from the ancient Numidian city of Thagaste, today's Souq Ahras in northeastern Algeria. A great center of Berber culture, Thagaste was also at the crossroads of Roman and African civilizations. He was aware of the many kinds of people who flocked to the markets of Thagaste both from the far-flung Roman Empire and from sub-Saharan Africa, famous in the geographical literature available to him for its monstrous races.

In *The City of God* (16:8) he noted that there were other such races, some of which were said to have one eye in the middle of the forehead, others had feet pointing backward, others yet a double set of sexual equipment, male and female; some had no mouth and had to breathe only through the nose, others were only a cubit high and were called by the Greeks "Pygmies." There were also tales of a particular race with two feet but only one leg, who could not bend the knee but could run very fast—these were called *Skiopodes*. On a hot day they would lie on their back and shade themselves with their feet. There were others with no head, but with eyes in their shoulders. According to some widely believed medieval forgeries, Augustine himself had seen such creatures with his own eyes (Boodts.2019).

In fact, Augustine would not be drawn into this polemical area. He believed that whatever differences might theoretically exist between man and monster, "whoever is anywhere born a man, that is, a rational mortal animal, no matter what unusual appearance he presents in color, movement, sound, nor how peculiar he is in some power, part, or quality of his nature, no Christian can doubt that he springs from that first man, Adam" (Boodts.2019 n.pag). This remarkable passage foreshadows a good deal of the discussion about race for the following fifteen hundred years.

For followers of the Abrahamic faiths, all men and women were descended from Adam and Eve. Jews subscribed to the monogenist principle, on the grounds, according to a Rabbinic source, that the story of Adam was intended to prevent anyone from boasting that "my father is greater than yours." The Adam story, moreover, testified to the greatness of God, who miraculously was able to bring about the extraordinary diversity of mankind from just one prototype.

According to the Bible, once the Flood had destroyed nearly all the world's people, it was repopulated through the efforts of the few survivors—Japhet, Ham, and Shem, the sons of Noah. From late medieval times there was a consensus that Noah's three sons were responsible for founding the populations of the three parts of the world: Europe, Africa, and Asia. Medieval maps such as the *orbis terrarum* chart, where a T was inserted into the O of the globe, presented the world and the origins of its peoples in this tripartite way. Bishop Isidore of Seville's famous *Etymologiae*, which was the most widely used medieval textbook, explained the world's divisions in a similar way.

According to the succinct account in the influential biblical dictionary of the French Benedictine monk Antoine Augustin Calmet (1672–1757)

> Ham, son of Noah, brother to Shem and Japheth, is believed to have been Noah's youngest son. One day when Noah had drank wine, Ham perceived his venerable ancestor lying in his tent, exposed indecently, at which he ridiculed. Noah, when he awoke, said "Cursed be Canaan; a servant of servants shall he be to his brethren." From these words it is conjectured, that Canaan gave his father Ham intelligence of Noah's nakedness. . . .

It is believed he had Africa for his inheritance, and that he peopled it. (Calmet.1812 n.pag)

This belief was widespread in medieval and early modern Europe and would persist into modern times. The English sailor and explorer George Best (d.1584) explained in *A True Discourse of the Late Voyages of Discoverie* (1578) that as a result of Ham's crime, his descendants through the line of Cush would always be loathsome and black and that all the "blacke Moores" in Africa were descended from the cursed Cush. However, he also added a secular, medical spin by explaining that this "blacknesse proceedeth [from an] infection in the *bloud*" (Shelford.2013 p.75).

For hundreds of years, barely anyone in the Judeo-Christian world doubted the biblical account of the creation of man in the Garden of Eden. The vast majority of Europeans until the nineteenth century and beyond would have accepted the fervent and beautiful creed of Reverend Samuel Purchas (1577?–1626), the Anglican clergyman and compiler of travelers' tales. In *Purchas His Pilgrimage* (1614), the great chronicler declared in ringing tones his conviction that the

> incomprehensible unities, which the Angels with covered faces in their Holy, holy, holy-hymns resound, and Lauds in Trinity, hath pleased in this varietie to diversify his works, all serving one humane nature, infinitely multiplied in persons, exceedingly varied in accidents, that wee also might serve that One-most God: tawney Moore, Negro, duskie Libyan, ash-colored Indian, olive-colored American should with the whiter European become *one sheep-fold,* under *one great Sheepheard, till this mortalitie being swallowed up of Life,* wee may all *be one, as he and the father are one*; and (all of this varietie swallowed up into an ineffable unitie) only the language of Canaan be heard, only the father's name written in their foreheads, the lamb's song in their mouths, the victorious Palmes in their hands and their long robes, *being made white in the blood of the Lamb,* where they follow whithersoever hee goeth, filling Heaven and Earth with their everlasting Halleluiah without any more distinction of Color, Nation, Language, Sex, Condition, all may bee One in him that is One. (Purchas.1614 p.656)

The longstanding certainties about the "incomprehensible unities" of mankind started to crumble during the Age of Discovery, as new lands and peoples in Africa and the Americas had to be accounted for. It was not obvious how the Americas could fit into the usual tripartite division of the world or how their strange-looking populations could be connected to the sons of Noah, who as far as anyone knew had been fully engaged in the Old World. Out of the growing uncertainties arose new scientific discourses that marked the beginning of modern racism.

As Native Americans, such as the four "Mohawk Kings" who journeyed to London in 1710, and Africans started being seen in Europe, as private citizens or captives or in well-publicized official delegations, this issue was brought back from the colonial frontier to the capitals of Europe and became a matter of interest for thinking people. These newly discovered populations challenged the all-embracing Augustinian model, and questions about the origins of these people provoked a debate between traditional and more progressive interpretations of the Bible and eventually between the Bible and the scientific ideas of the day, as Renaissance anthropologists tried to wrest the study of humanity from theology.

Two of the more influential heterodox, theological arguments to emerge from this debate were pre-Adamism and polygenesis. Both theories were considered at best eccentric, and at worst heretical, until the first half of the nineteenth century. Proponents of these views were often the most radical and contrarian thinkers of their day. They were courageous, often brilliant, and frequently argumentative.

One of the first defenders of polygenesis was the iconoclastic Swiss scholar and physician Paracelsus (Philippus Aureolus Theophrastus Bombastus von Hohenheim) (1493–1541), known by his contemporaries as "the Luther of Medicine," who traveled widely and studied in a number of Italian universities, without taking a degree in any of them. Denounced by one of his students in Basel as an "impious sot," he was often obscene, "personally unbearable," and quarrelsome.

His most famous book was *Das Buch Paragranum* (The Against the Grain Book), and indeed he was against many of the received ideas of his time and was ready to take on anyone, including the ecclesiastical establishment. Between 1480 and 1520 more geographical discoveries had been made about the world and its inhabitants than in the previous thousand years. Contemplating these marvelous new lands in 1520, he invoked Augustine's concern for people of distant islands, noting skeptically that there was no good reason to believe that the sons of Adam had taken off for distant, out-of-the way islands. He speculated that the populations that descended directly from Adam were to be found only in a very restricted part of the earth but that because God did not like the idea of leaving the rest of the world empty He created the negroes,[1] native Americans, and other odd people to fill it up.

These people originated from another being that had been created apart from the creation of Adam. Richard Popkin maintained that Paracelsus cannot truly be counted among polygenesis theorists, since he included in his list of groups not descended from Adam salamanders, nymphs, sirens, and sylphs. Thus, Popkin argued that their distinct creation from that of human beings fails to constitute a polygenenetic theory, as it does not apply to humans. However, the all-embracing Augustinian model, which was at the heart of Christian monogenesis, had included all manner of creatures, at least theoretically, and when Paracelsus set himself against this model, he was attacking the unity of mankind. Unsurprisingly, the controversial scholar got into trouble, for this and other things, and was forced to leave Basel in 1528, eventually dying, either as a result of a drunken excess or having been pushed, perhaps by envious colleagues, down a steep path. In any event Paracelsus mounted a tiger that was destined to roam the world for centuries, bringing untold suffering and genocide in its wake (Popkin.1987; Simmons.2002; Brace.2005; Smith.2015).

The doctrine of multiple creations, which appeared to proffer the answer to some basic questions around human difference, was soon to be taken up by others. Perhaps the most important was the brilliant philosopher Giordano Bruno (1548–1600), who was brought up in Nola, a town on the slopes of Vesuvius. At the age of fifteen, Bruno joined the Dominican order in Naples.

This teeming metropolis, the fifth biggest city in the world, was full of fishermen, prostitutes, street vendors, carpenters, blacksmiths, slaves, and water sellers who went barefoot and lived mainly on figs and bread (Rowland.2008). Jews had been forced to leave Naples in 1541 (and would not be allowed to settle there until 1735), but the city was full of slaves, 80 percent of whom were black Africans. Bruno lived just off Via Duomo in the heart of this vibrant, opinionated city, in the wealthy monastery attached to the church of San Domenico Maggiore, the mother church of the Dominican order and former seat of the University of Naples.[2] In 1576, shortly after saying his first Mass, tipped off that the Inquisition was after him, he fled Naples and embarked on fifteen years of travel throughout Europe. Awarded a doctorate at the University of Toulouse, he went on to Paris where, on the basis of a few scintillating lectures, he was offered a chair at the Sorbonne. This enabled him to stay in Paris long enough to write *De Umbris Idearum*

(On the Shadows of Ideas), in which he broached the topic of the unity of the Universe (Charlton.2012). Everything throughout the universe, he explained, could be reduced to atoms; it was the love of God that bound them together and unified them.[3] Having tackled the unity of the universe, in 1591 he went on to address the unity of mankind. He explored the idea of parallel Adams in different parts of the earth, and in different worlds, and developed a theory that is consistent with his larger, astoundingly accurate vision of an infinity of worlds.

As far as the earth was concerned, it was clear to him that its different kinds of humans, which he subdivided on a color scheme, could not be the product of an original man. Directly contradicting Augustine and Christian orthodoxy and including many of the same ideas as Paracelsus, in *De innumerabilibus, immenso, et infigurabili* (Of the innumerable, the immense and the unfigurable) (1591) he explained that:

> There are many different species of men, the black generation
> Of Ethiopians, and the tawny ones, such as America produces,
> And the wet beings hidden away, living in the caves of the sea,
> And the Pygmies passing the ages in ever-inaccessible places
> And the citizens of the veins of the Earth, who stand guard
> At the Mines, and the giant monsters of the South:
> Nor indeed do they hark back to the same origin. (quoted in Smith. 2015 p.97)

As Justin Smith rightly observes: "For Bruno, all of the types of being on this list were equally real, and they were for him all literally 'races of men.' The fact that Ethiopians and Americans occur on the same list as pygmies and giants shows the limited extent to which, in the Renaissance, non-European peoples had begun to be incorporated into the European imagination" (Smith.2015 p.97). Finally, echoing Paracelsus and again taking issue with Augustine, Bruno addressed the enigma of populations found on distant inaccessible islands. Augustine had argued that somehow people had reached these remote places on boats. But Bruno thought that imagining such long journeys was to miss the point: Life could be generated, independently, anywhere. He maintained that "every island everywhere can give a beginning to things, although the same form is not preserved everywhere the same, for one species flourishes in one place, another in another."

Then there were the problems inherent in a literal reading of the Hebrew bible. He wrote:

> It is said in the Prophets, and is well known among the same people [the Jews] that all races of men are to be traced to one first father, or to three, as I learn and firmly believe from the Hebrew remains, of which some trace the only superior race, that is, the Jews, to one protoplast, and the other races to the two first, which were created two days before.

Bruno was referring to the fact that in the first chapter of Genesis we read: "God created mankind in his own image . . . male and female he created them." It is not until the second chapter that we hear anything about the particular man, Adam, and his consort Eve, in the Garden of Eden: "And the Lord God formed man of the dust of the ground, and breathed into his nostrils the breath of life; and man became a living soul. And the Lord God planted a garden eastward in Eden; and there he put the man whom he had formed." Bruno declared that the *only* race to derive from this man, Adam, formed "from the dust of the ground," was the Jewish race. The other two races—the white race and the black race—had different origins: "And the three races had three Patriarchs . . . first Enoch, then Leviathan, and the third Adam . . . from whom alone was descended the sacred race" (Bendyshe.1865 p.379). There were, then, three races: whites, blacks, and Jews. This ejected the Jews and blacks from the common European heritage, as understood by Bruno, as surely as the Jews had been ejected from Naples, the tumultuous town in which he had studied.

One seemingly gratuitous line foreshadowed later racist writing. "No one of sound judgment," he sneered, "can refer the Ethiopian race to that first human being" (Smith.2015 p.97). To publicly attribute a separate origin for Jews, blacks, or, indeed, anyone else, and to deny what Purchas would refer to as the "incomprehensible unitie" of man was still at the end of the sixteenth century both heterodox and hazardous. After years of inquisitorial interrogation Bruno was accused of being an "impenitent, pertinacious, and obstinate heretic."

Bruno was never inhibited by discretion. One of the witnesses at his lengthy trial denounced the excitable little Neapolitan for bragging, as he was lolling in a Venetian gondola, that he had figured out how Jesus had performed his miracles and was all set to perform them himself. It was too much for the Holy Office. On Ash Wednesday, 1600, he was taken to Rome's *Campo de' Fiori*, close to where his imposing statue stands today. He was naked, his tongue in a gag (or spiked) to prevent him from addressing the vast crowd, which included many pilgrims who had flocked to Rome for the jubilee of the pope, Clement VIII. He was burned alive at the stake (not specifically for his polygenism but, among other things, for the crime of positing the notion of an infinite cosmos and claiming that the Holy Spirit was the soul of the world). Three years later his works were placed on the *Index Librorum Prohibitorum*.[4]

Sixteen years after the burning of Bruno, Julius Caesar Vanini, otherwise known as Lucilio Vanini (1585–1619),[5] another southern Italian (he was born in Apulia and studied in Naples), got into the kind of trouble he had spent a lifetime trying to avoid. In *De Admirandis Naturae Reginae Deaeque Mortalium Arcanis* (On the Wonderful Secrets of Nature, the Queen and Goddess of Mortals) (Paris, 1616), very cautiously, but not cautiously enough, Vanini used the risky but widespread literary conceit of putting dangerous ideas into the mouth of a random speaker in a dialogue:

> Others have dreamed that the first man has taken his origin from mud, putrified by the corruption of certain monkeys, swine, and frogs, and thence (they say) proceeds the great resemblance there is betwixt our flesh and propensions, and that of those creatures. Other atheists, more mild, have thought that *none but the Ethiopians* are produced from a race of monkeys, because the same degree of heat is found in both ... Atheists cry out to us continually, that the first men went upon all four as other beasts, and 'tis by education only they have changed this custom, which, nevertheless, in their old age, returns to them. (Bendyshe.1865 p.355)

This tentative Renaissance evolutionary theory, foreshadowing Darwin, perhaps shows that Vanini's out-and-out serious "atheists" assumed not only that black Africans but everyone descended from apes.[6] However, "mild" or "gentle" atheists, less problematically, explained that the only section of humanity that descended from apes was the blacks. In this way, Vanini, like Bruno, singled out blacks for special comment. It was blacks whom Vanini had his character associate with monkeys, and it was blacks that Bruno declared very specifically could have nothing to do with the first two humans in the Garden of Eden.

Bruno's cruel fate befell Vanini. His punishment was meted out in Toulouse, a self-satisfied city then and now, never partial to heresy. His tormentors tied a placard around his neck: *Atéiste et blasphémateur du nom de Dieu* (atheist and blasphemer of the name of God) and he was taken to the Place du Salin, where his blaspheming tongue was pulled out with pincers. He was garroted and his corpse burned. A nondescript little plaque, set into a cracked pavement, now records the event (Levy.1995; Smith.2015).

Despite the warning provided by these gruesome spectacles, throughout the seventeenth century occasional doubts about the Genesis story continued to surface. However, in general, barely anyone dared publicly to proclaim any kind of pre-Adamite theory or any form of polygenesis. An important exception was the eccentric French Calvinist theologian Isaac La Peyrère (1596–1676). Born in Bordeaux to wealthy Calvinist parents of Portuguese Jewish origins, La Peyrère, like Bruno and Vanini, dared to go down forbidden paths. Driven by a desire to explain the origins of humankind within a scriptural framework, he contrived to publish some of the most outrageous and scandalous views imaginable for his time and place.

The first sixty years of the seventeenth century had been marked by a deepening interest in Judeo-centric Christian eschatology, particularly in England and the Dutch Republic, and some of La Peyrère's theological musings can be viewed as an extension of this body of writing. In *Rapell des Juifs* (1643) he had explained that with the imminent End of Days the Jews would be "recalled" to France. From France they would be led by *le roi universel*—the king of France—to Jerusalem. From the rebuilt Holy City, the French king would rule over the entire earth. Jews and Christians would unite in a worldwide, Judeo-Christian church and with the return of Jesus, the king of France, along with the son of God and the Christian Jews, would administer the glorious Messianic age. First of all, he urged the French, who were not fond of Jews, to desist from all anti-Jewish discrimination, "even though Christians may find Jews repulsive" as Stephen Greenblatt put it, and immediately readmit Jews into the kingdom.

Despite his Jewish origins, La Peyrère did not find Jews very appealing either, although he dedicated his most famous book to "all the Synagogues of the Jews dispersed over the face of the EARTH." Any unpleasant characteristics Jews might have would disappear once they converted to Christianity. Jews, it had to be recognized, were black and smelly. But the blackness of their skin and their disagreeable smell would vanish the moment they embraced the Christian faith. On this happy day their previously black faces would shine like "the breast of a pigeon (an exceeding white one at that)" and they would smell like "musk and amber."

La Peyrère's views on the origins of man were unusual for the time. In his day it took a brave man to pin his flag either to the mast of pre-Adamism or polygenesis, or indeed to state that the Bible was wrong. With the publication of *Prae-Adamitae* (1655) La Peyrère did all three. Prudently published in the more tolerant Dutch Republic, in Latin, in its first year *Prae-Adamitae* was reissued three times; it came out in English as *Men Before Adam* the following year in two editions, and in 1661 in Dutch. In this famous book he set out his belief in the creation of Adam, as described in Genesis, but refused to accept that Genesis could account for all peoples.

Like Bruno, he thought that Adam should be considered the progenitor not of the human race, but only of the Jews. Moreover, it was only Jews who were drowned in the Flood; the rest of humankind was unaffected. Undoubtedly La Peyrère was a sort of reluctant philo-Semite, conceivably proud of his Jewish heritage, and his underlying desire may have been in some way to acknowledge the major role Jews occupied in the sacred history of the West.

However, there were unintended consequences. Jews were not, according to La Peyrère, "made of the same stuff as everybody else" as Popkin claims. They originated from clay, whereas the rest of humankind was created in a different way, in the image of God. Livingstone rightly stresses La Peyrère's "concern to separate out the Jewish experience from the rest of world history ... the pre-Adamite theory was designed to cut a deep gorge between the Jews and the gentiles" (Livingstone.2008 p.35). La Peyrère's thinking was affected by his long-lived fascination with the Genesis story. In the first chapter of Genesis, he pointed out, as had Bruno sixty years before, there was one creation of men and women, created in the likeness of God, followed in the second chapter by the creation of Adam of the dust of the ground. Instead of granting a little poetic license and taking these two narratives as differing accounts of the same event, La Peyrère, like Bruno, understood them as distinct chapters of human history. In defense of his reading of the text he pointed to various biblical hints that there must have been humans in the vicinity of the Garden of Eden long before Adam.

Paul's letter to the Romans asserted that there was already sin (and therefore presumably sinners) in the world when Adam was created. In addition, the Bible tells us that "Abel was a keeper of sheep" and "Cain was a tiller of the ground." Why would Abel bother to keep sheep if there were no other people around to buy them? Did Cain's calling as a farmer not imply that there were other people, such as "artificers," already well established in the world who could sell him agricultural implements such as plowshares? Without such craftsmen he would have been impossibly busy, digging mines for ore and making furnaces and forges in order to be able to fashion the tools he needed. Moreover, the fact that Adam and Eve covered themselves with garments once they were made aware of their nakedness similarly suggested that shoemakers, skinners, and others were already laboring in their respective trades long before Adam came on the scene (Greenblatt.2017).

This was all very well, but to propose that Adam was the biological father not of humankind, but only of the Jews, created a major theological problem. Orthodox Christian doctrine from the time of Augustine had maintained that original sin was transmitted biologically by Adam to the whole of humankind. La Peyrère argued that sin, as well as technology, must have existed before Adam, and if Adam transmitted sin biologically, it was only to the Jews. Gentiles acquired biologically transmitted sin from pre-Adamic men and women (Morrow.2016).

A few brave spirits, such as the famous and influential Dutch-Portuguese writer, mystic, publisher, and rabbi, Menasseh ben Israel (1604–1657), admitted to being quite intrigued by this scandalous thesis. Indeed, for Jews, La Peyrère's treatment of the Christian doctrine of original sin was less explosive. Outside Jewish circles, however, it was soon clear which way the wind was blowing, and the attacks against *Prae-Adamitae* started to proliferate. True, the book came out anonymously, but its authorship was almost immediately detected, and book and author were swiftly denounced. Nobody liked it.

Shortly after its publication it was decreed a godless work against the public interest by the President and Council of Holland and Zeeland in The Hague. Copies of the unwelcome book were burned. In Paris the burning was carried out by the public hangman. The Paris *parlement* weighed in against it. One of the first to denounce him, the bishop of Namur, in the Spanish Netherlands, in which town La Peyrère was living at the time, used the Christmas Mass of 1655 to attack him from the beautifully ornate carved wooden pulpit of Namur cathedral "as a Calvinist and as a Jew."[7] La Peyrère was no doubt alarmed. However, his powerful patron, the prince of Condé, Louis II de Bourbon (1621–1686), the famous French general, was only thirty-five miles away, in Brussels, and it was to Brussels, therefore, that he took himself in haste.

The prince does not appear to have stirred himself for his faithful secretary, and in 1656, on the order of the Archbishop of Mechelen, a town a little to the north of Brussels, thirty armed men stormed into La Peyrère's Brussels lodgings and hauled him to prison, charged with being "*un hérétique détestable*." Under interrogation, at first he stuck to his guns, but it soon dawned on him that he was in mortal danger.

It was suggested that were he to convert to Catholicism, apologize to the pope, and publicly recant, all would be forgiven. However, he persisted in pointing out that his theory served some useful purposes for everyone, including the Catholic Church, and in fact could and should be viewed as a godsend. As he obsessively put it: "By this hypothesis all the disputes which have raged about the origin of the peoples discovered over the last two centuries by our forebears have been resolved."

Pope Alexander VII chuckled when he met the eccentric theologian in Rome: "[L]et us embrace this man who is before Adam," he said, good-naturedly patting him on the back, and later he had a good laugh with the general of the Jesuits over La Peyrère's ridiculous book. The Pope invited him to stay on in Rome, but after a discreet interval he slipped away and returned to Paris, where he was again taken under the wing of the prince of Condé, this time as a librarian. Any shame he might have felt as a result of his opportunistic conversion was deflected by the publication in 1658 of his *Lettre à Philotine*. Always labile in his loyalty, La Peyrère tried to explain that his sudden conversion was simply part of a cunning plan, a much bigger project—the unification of the faiths that was now to be brought about, not by the king of France, as he had originally proposed, but by Pope Alexander VII.

Ten years after the publication of *Prae-Adamitae* La Peyrère retired, as a lay brother, to the Oratorian seminary in Aubervilliers, now a scruffy suburb of Paris, where he stayed, entirely convinced of the truth of his theory, until his death in 1676. If he was convinced, few others were, and dozens of refutations of *Prae-Adamitae* came out, including a book by the German theologian Antonius Hulsius (1615–1685) with the irresistible title *Non-existent pre-Adamite, or, a confutation of a certain somebody's vain and Socinianizing dream, by which an anonymous author, using the Holy Scriptures as a pretext, endeavored not long ago to expound to the imprudent that there were men in the world before the first Adam.*

In his doctoral thesis Johann Andreas Fabricius (1696–1769), who went on to be a philosopher at the University of Jena, and spent his life looking for new proofs of Christian revelation, noted another thirty-seven works attacking the idea of polygenism that had appeared in the meantime. But the ripples made by *Prae-Adamitae* were not restricted to Europe. Just four years after La Peyrère's death Morgan Grenfell, an Anglican clergyman from Gloucestershire who worked as a vicar in the colonial town of Middle Plantation[8] in British Virginia, gave a telling example of how useful pre-Adamism could be in the modern racist business of justifying slavery and the segregation of blacks.

An opponent of slavery and colonial arrogance, Grenfell wrote an explosive book, *The Negro's and Indians Advocate*,[9] which explained that slaveowners, eager to assert that Africans were outside the family of man, were very taken with La Peyrère's idea, which they preferred to the older slur connecting blacks with the curse of Ham: "The Pre-Adamite whimsey," he wrote laconically, "is preferred above the Curse." The slaveowners preferred the doctrine of pre-Adamism, according to him, because it was "exceedingly useful to undermine the Bible and Religion" and because they considered it "invincible" (Grenfell.1680).

Within a few years other contrarian voices swelled the polygenist chorus. One belonged to Louis-Armand de Lom d'Arce, Baron La Hontan (1666–1716), who was born in southwestern France in the Pyrénées-Atlantiques village of La Hontan, in the province of Béarn, between Pau and Bayonne. When Louis-Armand was eight years old, his father died, leaving debts, a multitude of enemies, including the local church authorities, bitterness, and court cases, one of which would go on for a century.[10] With few choices Louis-Armand opted for a military career, was admitted to the smart Bourbon Cavalerie regiment, which had been founded by the son of le Grand Condé, La Peyrère's patron and employer. However, believing he would have better chances for rapid promotion elsewhere, he grittily opted for the marine corps and embarked for Québec to fight the Iroquois.

Seeing in their lives the ideal of the "noble savage," he left a minutely described albeit problematic ethnography of native American life as well as a detailed description of the fauna and flora of North America. He started writing his travel accounts immediately. *Les Nouveaux Voyages de Mr. le Baron de La Hontan dans l'Amérique Septentrionale* (1703), a classic of eighteenth-century travel writing, was published in Amsterdam. It was not a commercial success, although it was translated into many languages, went through a dozen editions, and made its author famous.

Lehontan put forward a polygenist argument, similar to Bruno's, that it was impossible that Africans and native Americans could both derive from Adam as they were so different from each other: Africans were "black and pug-nosed with monstrous lips" while Indians "have neither body hair nor beards." However, like Vanini, he prudently distanced himself from this still dangerous view by attributing it to someone else—a no doubt fictitious "Portuguese doctor" who on his travels had become familiar with the Congo coast and South America.

Disingenuously, he declared that as far as he himself was concerned good sense dictated that "Adam was the lone father of all men." He wrote:

> I replied straightaway that when faith failed to persuade me that all men are generally descended from this first man, his reasoning would not be strong enough to prove the opposite, since the difference which exists between the peoples of America and those of Africa arise from no other cause, than the different quality of air and climate that they respectively enjoy. The *médecin* denied this, recalling that the offspring of a negro and a negress if they were born in temperate climes would be just as black as if they had been born in Guinea . . . and he added that descendants of the Portuguese who live in Angola, Cape Verde and so on more than a hundred years ago, were no less pale than the real Portuguese.

Faced with the differences between the peoples of the New and Old World the *médecin* suggests—against traditional Catholic teachings—that

> the peoples of the continents of America, Asia and Africa, were the product of three different fathers. This is how he proved it. The Americans are different from the Asiatics, as they have neither body hair nor beards; their facial features, their color and their customs are different . . . He thought it impossible that these two sorts of people could be descended from Adam. (Roy.1895; Ouellet, Beaulieu.1990; Sayre.2000)

Another contrarian spirit was John Atkins (1685–1757), a British naval surgeon and son of a swashbuckling and bad-tempered naval officer and traveler, Charles (who may have been one of the authors of the justly famous *General history of the Pyrates* [1724] and may also have been the model for Lemuel Gulliver, the hero of Swift's masterpiece). Charles had been disowned by his father, one-time governor of Barbados, perhaps because he once surrendered his sloop to Barbary pirates without firing a shot, thus provoking a small Mediterranean war of retaliation.

John Atkins is best known for his books, *Naval Surgeon* (1732) and *A Voyage to Guinea, Brasil and the West Indies* (1735). In his closely observed

Voyage to Guinea he noted the difficulty he had in accounting for the black skin of negroes in Guinea. He wrote:

> By Guinea here I mean all Negro-land, from about the River Senega North-ward, to within a few Degrees of Cape Bon Esperance because Ships bound to any part of this extent, are said to be bound to Guinea: and because the people, without these lines, alter to a dark color seen as the Moors at this, and the Hottentots at the other Extremity... The black color, and woolly Tegument of these Guineans, is what first obtrudes itself on our Observation, and distinguishes them from the rest of Mankind, who nowhere else, in the warmest Latitudes, are seen thus totally changed nor removing, will they ever alter, without mixing in Generation. I have taken notice in my *Navy-Surgeon* how difficulty the color is accounted for and tho' it be a little Heterodox, I am persuaded the black and white Race have, *ab origine,* sprung from different-colored first Parents. (Atkins.1737 p.38)

Atkins' thoughts about polygenism were part of a wider reflection about what he thought constituted race. Both his concept of racial constitution and his conviction that different races are subject to different diseases contributed to a more scientific or medical way of understanding racial difference[11] (Ernst, Harris.1999).

The French philosopher Voltaire (1694–1778) had something in common with a number of his polygenist predecessors in terms of how he viewed human difference.[12] In 1734 he wrote his *Traité de la Métaphysique* (1734), which remained discreetly unpublished until its appearance in 1785, seven years after his death. As the publisher correctly noted, its importance lay precisely in the fact that "its author was able to say exactly what was on his mind." It was in the *Traité* that his views on human difference were expressed most unambiguously. In the *Traité* Voltaire joined the polygenists by clearly stating his belief that white people, the yellow "races," and negroes were not descended from the same original parent. Cleverly presenting himself as an extraterrestrial visitor endeavoring to understand the planet

> and having no greater notion of man than man has of the inhabitants of Mars and Jupiter, I land on the coasts of the ocean, in the Land of the Kaffirs and to start with I set out to find a man. I see monkeys, elephants, negroes who all seem to have some glimmer of imperfect reason. . . . At Goa I met an even odder type than all the rest; it is a man dressed in a long black

cassock who claims to be there to instruct others. All these different men, he tells me, who you see, are all born of the same father; and then he told me a long story. But what this animal tells me is very suspect . . . It seems to me that there is every reason to believe that what goes for trees goes for men; that pear trees, fir trees, oaks and apricots, do not come from the same tree and that white people with beards, negroes with wool on their head, yellow folk with horsehair on their heads, and men without beards do not come from the same man. Indeed, I see men who seem superior to these negroes, as these negroes are to monkeys, and as the monkeys are to oysters. (Voltaire.1734 p.35)

Negroes apart, the other human group Voltaire singled out for special treatment was the Jews. Christians could be eventually cured of their errors and their innate European essence would be apparent once the filth of the Judaic excrescence that Christianity contained had been washed away. Jews were so different and so debased that they could never hope to be assimilated to European society (Hertzberg.1968). Underlying Voltaire's views on human difference was his contempt for Christian monogenism and the myth that God created every human in His own image. He could not see how the book of Genesis could possibly be taken seriously as the basis for any informed enquiry into human origins.

The sheer pointlessness of Genesis as a guide to the early history of life was a frequent topic in the *salons* of Europe. In the 1720s Benoît De Maillet (1656–1738), a well-travelled and studious French aristocrat who for ten years had been French consul-general in Cairo, wrote his major work, *Telliamed, ou entretiens d'un philosophe indien avec un missionnaire français* (Telliamed, or Conversations between an Indian philosopher and a French missionary). Telliamed (his own name written backwards) directly sought to undermine the overall credibility of Genesis by presenting the creation of the world, and its inhabitants, as the result of natural causes. To protect himself against accusations of heresy he followed the usual practice of disguising his work, thinly, as a kind of orientalist, literary fantasy.

In England, too, the credibility of Genesis was being questioned. One of Voltaire's closest English friends, Henry St. John, 1st Viscount Bolingbroke (1678–1751), the erudite and acerbic English politician and man of letters, knew Voltaire both before his exile in England and afterwards. Bolingbroke had a tumultuous career that included a period of exile of his own, in France, in the 1720s, at which time he acquired the magnificent estate of La Source, near Orléans. Voltaire was a regular visitor. It was in the gardens of La Source that Bolingbroke wrote his famous essay "The Study and Uses of History," in which he endeavored to show that the compilers of Genesis were only trying to write a limited history, one that set out to prove the Jews' title to the land, and explain something of its and their history, rather than write a universal chronicle of humankind.

Sarcastically, he joined the post–La Peyrère conversation, accusing those who wrote on the history of Adam and Eve of being themselves "pre-Adamites" as they spoke of Adam's great knowledge as if they had conversed with him, of his beauty as if they had been there and gazed upon it, of his great height as if they had measured it themselves. Genesis, Bolingbroke concluded, provided no material to help explain the origins of humankind (Delumeau, O'Connell.2000).

A year before Voltaire wrote the *Traité*, in 1733, the influential Jesuit *Journal de Trévoux* contributed to the debate over the origin of man with another prudently unsigned article entitled *Mémoire sur l'origine des Nègres et des Américains* (Note on the Origin of the Negroes and Americans). The author of this essay has been identified as Auguste Malfert, a priest of the Brothers of Charity order, who served in the Caribbean and had first-hand knowledge of African slaves. His purpose was to join the ranks of the many who had refuted the polygenist thesis of La Peyrère while at the same time accounting for what he saw as the radical differences between peoples.

Malfert, whose personal experience set him at odds with the majority of metropolitan commentators on blacks, followed many earlier exegetes by explaining the blackness of negroes not through polygenesis, but through the theologically more acceptable hypothesis that the black races were fathered by Cain. Malfert argued that Cain was the progenitor of negroes whose color represented the "mark of Cain," a view that would be repeated time and again over the following two centuries, and that at least had the effect of including Africans in Western sacred history, while also connecting them with the ancestors of the Jews. However, the invocation of Cain was not intended to have too many positives attached to it. Malfert's purpose was to validate the slavery he saw all around him in the Caribbean and to provide a way of framing the origin and status of blacks within the wider human family—but only just.

According to Malfert, man was originally white. It took miraculous, divine intervention to transform white into black. God "changed Cain from the white he originally was to black" in an instant, and from that moment on, wherever in the world they lived "from a negro and a negress only negroes and negresses would be born" and they would all wear their color as a badge of shame. A more substantial figure in the form of the great German naturalist

Johann Friedrich Blumenbach (1752–1840) fully agreed some decades later that white was the original color of man on the grounds that while white can easily degenerate into brown, it is well-nigh impossible for dark ever to be transformed into white. As we shall see, this would soon become a critical issue (Blumenbach.1865).

There were other attempts to explain the degeneration of white to black. In 1799, the committed abolitionist Benjamin Rush (1746–1813), one of the Founding Fathers of the United States, claimed that Africans' black skin was not natural and had been caused by a disease, something like leprosy, that had become hereditary but that could perhaps be "cured," and he suggested some ways in which this could be done. His 1799 article "Observations Intended to Favour a Supposition That the Black Color (As It Is Called) of the Negroes Is Derived from the Leprosy" was published in the *Transactions of the American Philosophical Society* (Volume 4) and echoed medieval and Renaissance convictions that the Jews' dark color was the product of a leprous condition. He argued that all blacks suffered from this form of leprosy and white women who lived with blacks would themselves become black and develop negroid features.

Malfert was also familiar with the color of native Americans. Their color he attributed to the relatively obscure biblical figure of Lamekh, son of Methushael, a descendant of Cain, whose sin (he killed someone and boasted about it) "was greater than that of Cain," so God exacted an even greater punishment by giving him, Lamekh, a new and vividly different color. Worse, he forced him to flee so far away from the known world that his descendants were deprived of the salvation of Christ until the arrival of the Conquistadors a few millennia later in the fifteenth century.

Before Lamekh's ancestors crossed the Atlantic, having now departed from the biblical narrative never to return, they had sexual relations with the descendants of Cain, thus forming another race—the "Caffres."[13] A few years later another French theologian, Jean-Baptiste Margat de Tilly (d.1747), responded to this in a testy article in *Mémoires de Trévoux* wanting to know why on earth people kept on attributing African blackness to diverse divine punishments and obscure biblical figures (Harvey.2012).

The great secularization of the late seventeenth and eighteenth centuries had an undoubted impact upon the way in which educated people viewed human origins, but it would take a long time before lip service to the Bible disappeared entirely. Moreover, tortured arguments trying to account for human diversity while respecting both religion and natural philosophy, sacred text and science, did not do much to turn ordinary people against the biblical account. Throughout Europe, superstition, an imagined world of ghosts, goblins, and fairies, was still the chief mode of explanation of disasters and misfortunes, and the demystification of religion and folk belief by European elites was still not part of the general discourse. Educated people in Western Europe, on the other hand, no doubt had misgivings about the Genesis account even before the Enlightenment. In *The Primitive Origination of Mankind* Sir Mathew Hale (1609–1676), the English Puritan jurist, observed gently:

> The generality of Christians, among whom I write, do generally believe this Truth of the Origination of the World and Mankind, as it is delivered in the Holy Scriptures. . . . Again, though the Creation of Man be generally acknowledged by Jews and Christians, yet we must likewise consider that many take it up only as a part of their Education, and not upon any serious, deep Conviction of the truth of it.

He himself tried to find natural ways of explaining diversity, and in particular he floated the idea, while ostensibly rejecting it, that some animals and black peoples "in some places, and at some times, especially between the Tropicks" might have been generated from the earth, in much the way that frogs were, according to Augustine, in a "pullulation of men and beasts" (Hale.1677 p.257).

A perplexed, but safely anonymous, Oxford graduate known only as L.P. (who would be fêted by nineteenth-century polygenists) took a more critical line in an essay published in London in 1695 as *Two Essays sent in a Letter from Oxford to a Nobleman in London. The First Concerning Some Errors about the Creation, General Flood, and the Peopling of the World. The Second Concerning the Rise, Progress and Destruction of Fables and Romances.*[14] L.P. set out a polygenist theory based largely on the irreconcilable difference between negroes and all the other races of humankind. He wrote:

> The origin of Negroes lies obscure; for time out of mind there hath been blacks, with a woolly substance on their bodies instead of hair, because they are mentioned in the most ancient records now extant in the world. 'Tis plain their colour and wool are innate, or seminal, from their first beginning, and seems to be a specifick character which neither the sun, nor any curse from Cham could imprint upon them. Not the first, because many

other nations living under the same climates and heats, are never black, as the Abyssines, the Siamites, the Brasílians, Peruvians, etc.; neither will any white ever become a black in Guinea, Congo, or Angola, though born there; neither will any Negroes produce whites in Virginia, or New England. The textures of their skins, and blood, differ from those of whites.

He argued, moreover, that there was no longer any possibility of accounting for human difference through "old Arguments fetch'd from Eastern rubbish, or Rabbinical Weeds" (L.P.1695 p.164).

Even though "old arguments" persisted for some time to come, the biblical explanation of the beginnings of humankind was not adequate for many thinkers, and all kinds of alternatives were starting to be offered up in its stead. However, liberation from the old dogmas brought with it new complexities. The Enlightenment's demolition of the myth of the Garden of Eden was destined to have a number of unintended consequences and to be replaced by a number of other myths, none of them helpful for the onward march of humankind.

The struggle to account for human difference in the early modern period formed unstable categories of peoples and races that remained essentially malleable. Nonetheless, from these shifting sands certain anthropological assumptions emerged around which the great naturalists of the time navigated. However, few of the naturalists devoted themselves exclusively to the study of man. They came at the problem of human origins from different perspectives. Carl Linnaeus (1707–1778) was essentially a botanist, Johann Friedrich Blumenbach (1752–1840) a naturalist, Immanuel Kant (1724–1804) a philosopher, Georges Cuvier (1769–1832) a paleontologist and comparative anatomist, Samuel Stanhope Smith (1751–1819) a moral philosopher. Warriors in the battle to demystify the understanding of the world and its peoples, what Max Weber called the "disenchantment (*Entzauberung*) of the world," boldly forced their way into the "iron cage" of rationalism with respect to human difference. The gentle vision of Adam and Eve as the progenitors of all humanity was increasingly challenged by a hard-edged scientific approach that sought to delineate the differences between peoples according to objective scientific principles and a variety of metrics.

Most natural scientists from the Enlightenment on, despite their different approaches, accepted that there was a fundamental distinction to be drawn between "varieties" and "species." "Species" were considered as more or less permanent, created perhaps by divine dispensation. On the other hand, "varieties" were a side effect of "sporting nature," as Linnaeus put it. As the study of anthropology unfolded, a good deal hung on whether particular human groups were separate "species" or simply "varieties." If they were different species, this could only be viewed by those still operating within a Christian framework as the result of original divine design. If, however, they were different "racial" varieties of *one* species, there were questions to be asked about what caused the differences between them, and this was to preoccupy naturalists and scientists from the Enlightenment to our own day (Greene.1954).

The first postclassical attempt to divide humanity into distinct "races" is thought to have been made by François Bernier (1620–1688), the French traveler and one-time physician at the court of the Mughal emperor. While being credited, rightly or wrongly, with the "invention" of race, he was in fact not particularly racist for his time and place. He was influenced by his friend and mentor Pierre Gassendi (1592–1655), the skeptical French empiricist and astronomer, who instructed him in physiology and prepared him for his medical examinations at the ancient University of Montpellier. There he followed a three-month accelerated course that qualified him to practice as a doctor anywhere in the world (except France). With this dubious medical license and an eagerness to see other countries, he set off for the East. Upon his return, Bernier, in a lighthearted way, attempted to establish a new foundation for the understanding of human variety that was based not on readings of sacred history but on his close observation of men and women—particularly of women.

His influential but brief *Nouvelle division de la terre par les différentes espèces ou races qui l'habitent* (New Division of the Earth by the Different Species that Inhabit it) was published anonymously in the *Journal des Scavans* (Europe's first academic journal) on Monday, April 24, 1684. Whereas the journal was undoubtedly forward looking, the extrication of scientific and anthropological issues from the biblical narrative was still a work in progress: One article in the same volume, dedicated to the history of shoes, was uncertain whether footwear formed part of Adam and Eve's wardrobe, even though it could be asserted that shoes were worn by the patriarch Abraham, if not by God.

As camouflage for Bernier's heretical analysis, *Nouvelle division* purported to have been sent to the *Abbé* of some unspecified ecclesiastical establishment "more or less along these lines" (*à peu près en ces termes*). Content to identify himself, for good reason, simply as "*un fameux voyageur*," the well-traveled Frenchman introduced his revolutionary thesis like this:

> Geographers up to this time have only divided the earth according to its different countries or regions. The remarks which I have made upon men during all my long and numerous travels, have given me the idea of dividing it in a different way. Although in the exterior form of their bodies, and especially in their faces, men are almost all different one from the other, according to the different districts of the earth which they inhabit, so that those who have been great travelers are never often mistaken in distinguishing each nation in that way; still I have remarked that there are four or five species or races of men in particular whose difference is so remarkable that it may be properly made use of as the foundation for a new division of the earth.

The first such division consisted of Europeans, North Africans, South Asians, Middle Easterners, and Native Americans. The second consisted of East Asians, Southeast Asians, and Central Asians. The third consisted of sub-Saharan Africans, and the fourth consisted solely of Lapps.

Bernier's short essay presented a taxonomic scheme that was based in part on color, like Bruno's, but also on the idea of the permanent racial imprint of physiognomy, which would become important toward the end of the eighteenth century and would remain a critical taxonomic tool until the time of the Third Reich. One example of this may be seen in his description of the people of Kashmir, whom he believed to be of Jewish origin. This belief was based on their Jewish "look"—"their countenance and manner and that indescribable peculiarity which enables a traveller to distinguish the inhabitants of different nations." However, a good part of the essay was devoted to the relative beauty of the women in the countries he had visited. We are told that the most beautiful of all were from Circassia, but that in the slave markets of Constantinople Jews and Christians were not allowed to buy them, as they were reserved for Turks. He admired the naked female slaves he saw being sold for three times the usual price at the market of Mocha. "There could be nothing in the world lovelier to see," he wrote. Further afield, in Lahore, he considered the women to be "the finest brunettes in all the Indies," while the faces of the women of Kashmir he deemed as handsome as any in Europe. His fourth great human category, as we have seen, consisted solely of Lapps. This category was arrived at on the fragile basis of seeing two Laplanders during a visit to Danzig. He considered them "wretched animals . . . very ugly and partaking much of the bear" (Bernier.1684; Stuurman.2000).

Bernier's essay was read by Gottfried Wilhelm Leibniz (1646–1716), the German mathematician and philosopher. It cannot have made a great impression on Leibniz, however, for when he mentioned the supposedly revolutionary text in a letter to the Swedish diplomat and lexicographer Johan Gabriel Sparwenfeld (1655–1727), he forgot the name of its author, where it was published, and much of the detail of its argument. His letter to Sparwenfeld indeed was arguing for the monogenist project of tracing back the various languages of the world to an original language, perhaps Hebrew, which would thus prove the unity of humankind (Eigen, Larrimore.2012 p.17).

However, the German physician, naturalist, and physiologist Johann Friedrich Blumenbach (1752–1840), who himself, while a monogenist, perceived significant differences between groups of populations, saw in Leibniz's brief, disapproving comment an endorsement of racial divisions. When he listed the twelve divisions of humankind that had been proposed, starting with Bernier in 1684 and finishing with his own proposal, he placed Leibniz in second place. In fact Leibniz, following Augustine, proposed the universality of "human nature," followed a traditional genealogical understanding of human groups as a "series of generations," and, overall, considered difference simply as part of the multiplicity of things that, while unconnected, rested on a firm bed of synchronicity, order, and unity (Smith.2013).

The kinds of divisions proposed by Bernier, with manifold modifications, would be reproduced for the next couple of hundred years. Carl Linnaeus (1707–1778) split humankind into five categories following the four major geographical divisions of the world: African, Asian, European and American, adding a further category of "wild." He argued that they were all one species, simply showing variations due to differences of geography and climate. He was followed by Blumenbach, who also opted for a fivefold division: Caucasian, Malay, Mongolian, Ethiopian, and American. Jean Léopold Nicolas Frédéric Cuvier (1769–1832), known as Georges Cuvier, the French zoologist and naturalist, enumerated three races, Caucasian, Mongolian, and Ethiopian (Cuvier believed Adam and Eve were Caucasian); James Cowles Prichard (1786–1848), the British ethnologist and physician, who will play an important part in this book, seven main "stocks";

Jean Louis Rodolphe Agassiz (1807–1873), the Swiss-American naturalist, twelve races; and Charles Pickering (1805–1878), the American naturalist, eleven. No consensus on the number of races was ever to be achieved.

As the 1858 issue of *The American Phrenological Journal* reported,

> "Buffon tells us man is made up of six varieties, Kant says four, Hunter seven, Blumenbach five; but Desmoulins says of sixteen species, and Jacquinot of three species—the Caucasian, Mongolian and Negro—a division in which Nott and Giddon apparently coincide; while Morton classes humanity in twenty-two families, and Luke Burke in sixty-three races, twenty-eight of which are intellectual; and thirty-five physical types or tribes.

This confusion was to continue until the time of the Third Reich (*The American Phrenological Journal*.1858).

Within fifty years of the publication of *Nouvelle division de la terre*, taxonomy became the spirit of the age. The Swedish naturalist Carl Linnaeus (1707–1778), taxonomy's so-called father and perhaps the most famous naturalist of all time, would also address the issue of human variety and taxonomies. The eldest son of a country parson of limited means, Linnaeus was driven by a burning ambition to be the world's leading botanist. After a protracted tenure battle, he was eventually appointed to a chair in medicine at the University of Uppsala. One of his tasks was to remodel the university's botanical gardens, in a corner of which stood the Botanical House, the professorial lodgings where he would spend most of his working life.

His most celebrated work, *Systema Naturae*, first appeared in 1735 as a slim volume, barely more than a pamphlet. Over his lifetime he brought out eleven further volumes, the total *oeuvre* constituting a compilation of the botanical and zoological knowledge of his day. In addition he threw himself into a variety of bizarre schemes: He dreamed of trying to turn Lapland into the local equivalent of the West Indies, with "plantations of nutmeg, mace, and cinnamon" or "teaching" tea or saffron to grow in the freezing Swedish tundra or introducing buffaloes, elks, or guinea pigs as domesticated Swedish farm animals.

In the 1758 edition of *Systema Naturae* he subdivided humankind into *Homo sapiens*, thus coining the term, and *Homo troglodytes*, which, on the basis of some travel reports, was a cave-dwelling wild man of the forest, somewhat akin to the more famous *pongo* of the West African rainforest. Man, overall, was in the class of mammal and in the order of primates. Humankind was classified into four varieties, depending on his physical and moral characteristics: American, European, Asiatic, and African. Linnaeus was what today would be called a spiritual man, and like Blumenbach, was unable to completely extract the Bible and God from his attempts to classify the world. As Marta Paterlini put it: "Linnaeus tried to describe all the things that had been 'put on Earth by God,' and therefore approached taxonomy with the tacit assumption that this task was finite. Whatever new species might have arisen from the original inhabitants of the Garden of Eden, he reasoned, they were still a part of God's design for creation, because they had always potentially been present." In a similar way, as far as human origins were concerned, he therefore stuck to the essential biblical proposition that humankind was derived from the same original source. Linnaeus, as we have seen, may have drawn a distinction between *Homo sapiens* and the anthropoid creatures that travelers in Loango in West Africa and Malaya had described, but as far as native Americans, Africans, Asiatics, and Europeans were concerned, Linnaeus did not doubt that they formed a single species (Blunt.2004; Paterlini.2007; Koerner.2009; Skott.2014).

Linnaeus boastfully said about himself, "God created, Linnaeus classified," but the life project of a contemporary Frenchman was even more ambitious. The encyclopedic *Histoire Naturelle, générale et particulière* of the famous polymath Comte Georges Louis Leclerc de Buffon (1707–1788) was intended to include everything that was known about every aspect of the natural world. Buffon derided his Swedish colleague as a dull classifier. Working as tirelessly in a tower of his half-ruined château in Montbard, Burgundy, as Linnaeus did in his garden house in Uppsala, Buffon completed thirty-six volumes of his *Natural History* before his death. Mathematician, comparative anatomist, biologist, and cosmologist, Buffon argued for the unity of the human race, not on biblical grounds, but because all known human types were capable of fertile interbreeding, which implied that they formed a single species.

He proposed that all the species of animals descended from a few spontaneously generated types. The ability to interbreed was one of the great differences between real humans and different species of animals, and "monsters," both human and nonhuman, who were generally considered to be incapable of reproduction. Buffon's ideas about the age of the world and specifically his contentions that seas created mountains, that the sun would eventually burn out, and that the planets were once part of the sun got him into trouble with the Catholic Church.

In January 1751, the deputies and syndics of the Faculty of Theology at the Sorbonne informed Buffon that various statements in the first three volumes of *Natural History*, which had already had a great publishing success, were at variance with Holy Scripture. He was forced to recant. He declared, perhaps truthfully, that he had no desire to deny Scripture and, as his printed recantation explained, he believed "most firmly" in everything the Bible had to say about the creation. However, in an unguarded moment, sitting in front of his fireplace in Montbard, he confessed to a young politician from Paris: "I have always written 'God,' but all that is to be done, is to substitute for this word, 'the power of nature.'" Iconoclast he undoubtedly was, but Buffon, like Linnaeus, attended church regularly. Outwardly he clung to the bare essentials of the Genesis account while claiming that man was not unique but formed part of the wider "animal kingdom" not far distant from the ape, from whom he could be distinguished by such slender criteria as speech and reason. But still, for him, too, *Homo sapiens* was but one all-inclusive species.

In 1783 *The European Magazine and London Review* quoted Buffon as having admitted that "the origin of black men has, at all times, been a subject of enquiry." However, he believed that

> Upon the whole every circumstance concurs in proving, that mankind is not composed of species essentially different from each other; that, on the contrary, there was originally but one species who after multiplying and spreading over the whole surface of the earth, have undergone various changes by the influence of climate, food, mode of living, epidemic diseases and the mixture of dissimilar individuals; that at first these changes were not so conspicuous, and produced only individual varieties ... transmitted from generation to generation, as deformities or diseases pass from parents to children. (*European Magazine and London Review*.1783 p.117)

In *Über die verschiedenen Rassen der Menschen* (Of the Different Races) (1775), Kant similarly said that blacks and whites "are not distinct types of people, for they belong to one tribe, and yet to two different races" and agreed with Buffon that the manifest success different races of men had in breeding with each other proved that humankind was one, although he also thought that the darker races were doomed to racial extinction through natural design. Kant initially believed that there was a rigid racial hierarchy, with negroes close to the bottom, although his insistence on this diminished toward the end of his life. He believed that all people belonged to "a single phylum, from which, notwithstanding their differences, they originated, or at least could have originated." Humankind was an undivided one but was nonetheless split into a number of distinct subcategories (Kant.2007).

Kant's elaborate armchair view of human divisions was mocked by the well-traveled German botanist, revolutionary, and outstanding travel writer Johann Georg Adam Forster (1754–1794), who had more experience than most of the different varieties of mankind and womankind, and who perceived the commonalities of different peoples more clearly than many of his contemporaries. Along with his cantankerous father, Johann Reinhold Forster, Georg went on a number of journeys, first to Russia and then with Captain James Cook (1728–1779) on the latter's second voyage to the Pacific (1772–1775). In 1789 he scornfully rejected earlier models of difference: "Most of the old divisions of the human species have long been rejected anyhow," he wrote. "Noah's sons, the four parts of the world, the four colours, white, black, yellow, copper red—who still thinks of these outdated fashions today?" (*Georg Forsters Werke*.1958 p.193). Well, of course, many people still did.

One such was Edward Long (1734–1813), the British planter, slaveowner, and colonial administrator, who was one of the leading champions of these "outdated fashions" and of the disunity of humanity. In 1774 he published his notorious *History of Jamaica*, which set out to prove that blacks were barely part of humankind and had as much in common, if not more, with orangutans—which, according to him, were capable of having sexual relations with women and of dressing like men and were able to eat, in a civilized manner, at a table with knives and forks.

We have seen how Linnaeus had drawn a distinction between *Homo sapiens* and certain anthropoid creatures in the jungles of Malaya, which travelers had also spotted in the West African kingdom of Loango, which for centuries had been the favored locus of Western speculation about monstrous races. Like his contemporary the polygenist German naturalist Christoph Meiners (1747–1810), Long was obsessed with African monstrosity and savagery. He was particularly obsessed by the thought of "amorous intercourse" between negro women and apes and devoted a good deal of his book to the subject. Indeed, in Western literature of the seventeenth and eighteenth century there was often a drooling interest in the idea of sex between primates and humans, which confirmed the lechery of African women as well as pointing to the allegedly slender dividing line separating negroes from animals.

The widespread interest in ape–human sex in Africa, and monstrous part-human brutes, was matched by a prurient interest in sex between whites and blacks. The product of such unions, known as mulattos (like the mule, from which the name mulatto is perhaps derived), were widely and critically deemed to be infertile. This singular thought, which was destined to have a long life, seemed to Edward Long to provide "an opinion, which several have entertained, that the White and the Negro had not one common origin. . . . For my own part, I think there are extremely potent reasons for believing, that the White and the Negroe are two distinct species" (Long.1774, ii p.336; Seth.2014).

A contemporary of Long's, Lord Kames (1696–1782), the son of an impecunious Scottish laird, had some difficulty in acquiring a formal education and was not able to attend a university. However, he was an avid reader and went on to study law. He became a judge in the Court of Session, Scotland's highest civil court, and a central figure of the Scottish Enlightenment. His wife Agatha inherited the estate of Blair Drummond, near Stirling (now home to a safari park), and for the last sixteen years of his long life he could take literary potshots from his Scottish castle at Buffon, who was nestled comfortably on the other side of the Channel in his feudal tower in Burgundy. Kames, like Buffon and Linnaeus, devoted his life to his main book: *Sketches on the History of Man* (1774). He labored on it for thirty years and was very optimistic of its chances of success.

Incapable of believing that climate or environment or any other natural cause could possibly account for what he saw to be the radical diversity of human varieties, his book constituted a spirited defense of the polygenist theory. As he explained:

> Thus, upon an extensive survey of the inhabited parts of our globe many nations are found differing so widely from each other, not only in complexion, features, shape, and other external circumstances, but in temper and disposition, particularly in two capital articles, courage, and behavior to strangers, that even the certainty of different races could not make one expect more striking varieties. Doth M. Buffon think it sufficient to say dryly, that such varieties may possibly be the effect of climate, or of other accidental causes? The presumption is, that the varieties subsisting at present have always subsisted; which ought to be held as true till positive evidence be brought of the contrary: instead of which we are put off with mere suppositions and possibilities.

A typical product of the autodidact, *Sketches*, in the words of Allegra de Laurentiis, consisted of "a peculiar mixture of venomous resentment against French and German science, a strong aptitude for non sequitur, and fearless appeals to common sense from a dog breeder's point of view... Unimpressed by conceptual distinctions among class, order, species, variety or race, Kames derides Linnaeus' common grouping of men and bats as mammals and concludes: 'What will a plain man think of a method of classing that denies a whale to be a fish?'" (Laurentiis.2014 p.624).

In a couple of instances, Kames did accept the basic argument of the monogenists, that the differences between peoples could be explained by recent natural causes and that climate could change physical characteristics. His belief was that a number of races of man had been created to settle in specific environments, and that in the event that such a race was moved to another kind of environment it could only be affected negatively. One of such "variations" Kames mentioned was an intriguing case along the coast of the Congo in West Africa, a critically important area rich in examples of perceived hybridity and difference that had fascinated European thinkers for centuries. According to Kames, "some Portuguese, who have been for ages settled on the sea-coast of Congo, retain scarce the appearance of men." His assumption was that as a result of the tropics these white Portuguese had reverted into some half-human animalistic figure, of which the travel reports were full.

Such mixture, it was thought, could only bring about racial degeneration. However, in general, in terms of the long-running debate between the claims of heredity or climate on the varieties of man, Kames was clear: He rejected the notion that climate would ever have much effect on racial types. If people were different, it was because they constituted different species. If all men had been of just one species, "there never could have existed, without a miracle, different kinds, such as exist at present."

For Kames, an important proof of the persistence of racial types over time was the existence in southern India of an ancient community of white Jews, who, according to him, had shown remarkable resilience to the effects of the hot climate of Kerala: "In the suburbs of Cochin," he wrote, "a town in Malabar, there is a colony of industrious Jews of the same complexion they have in Europe." As we shall see later, this community would be regularly invoked in the future as a proof of the fixity of human races, and perhaps Kames was the first to see Cochin's white Jews' usefulness for the polygenist argument[15] (Kames.1774; Kames.1807).

However, there were staunch and rational defenders of traditional monotheism. One such was the Reverend Samuel Stanhope Smith (1751–1819), a naturalist and the seventh president of the College of New Jersey in Princeton. In his *Essay on the causes of the variety of complexion and figure in the human species* etc. (New Brunswick, NJ.1810), which was, in part, an attack on polygenists and particularly Lord Kames, and the more scholarly Charles White (1728–1813), he judiciously summed up the situation. "The conclusion to be drawn from all this variety of opinions," he declared, "is, perhaps, that it is impossible to draw the line precisely between the various races of men, or even to enumerate them with certainty; and that it is in itself a useless labor to attempt it."

For some late eighteenth-century thinkers, even the most radical differences between peoples could be easily explained. John Walker (1731–1803), meteorologist, hydrologist, zoologist, economist, and geologist, as well as Regius Professor of Natural History at the University of Edinburgh (and one of Lord Kames's polymath friends), observed:

> I know not of any two varieties in the human race more widely different than the fair-haired European and the Angola Negro. But I am certain that, upon the principle of Hippocrates, I can account for all the peculiarities in the aspect of the African. That the difference in his hair proceeds from the climate; his splay-feet from the soil; and his color, his flat face and features, and prominent belly, from his manner of life. (Kames.1807 p.33)

But for many others, from Paracelsus to Kames, the African and Jew were the chief obstacle to the concept of the unity of humankind.

2
Blacks and Jews in the Western Imaginaire

Attempts to account for human difference almost always positioned blacks and Jews outside the normative human frame, as we have seen in the case of Bruno, Vanini, La Peyrère, Kames, Voltaire, and many others, and this fact forms part of the etiology of the sickness of anti-black racism and Jew hatred.

As far as blacks were concerned, color itself, the most obvious of human differences, played a major role. Since the time of Heraclitus (b.535 BC), and no doubt before, an associated set of black and white dualities existed between evil and good, death and life, night and day. The mind of man, explained Plato (428–328 BC), is a chariot pulled one way by the white horse of the gods and another way by the black horse of the underworld. Surprised by an African appearing unexpectedly atop Hadrian's wall, the emperor Septimius Severus (145–211 BC) took the soldier's black color as an evil portent of his own imminent death. Didymus the Blind (313–398), a Christian theologian in the Church of Alexandria, argued that Africans were black because of their allegiance with the devil, and in medieval representations the color black was an attribute not only of negroes but also of other evil entities, such as Jews and demons (Kaplan.2018 p.87).

Jerome considered that Africans had been blackened not by the sun but by the dark stain of sin, and frequently in medieval pictorial scenes black Africans would be present as symbols of evil, in one case hammering a nail into Christ's outstretched palm. Gratuitous black cruelty is suggested in the marginal depiction in the thirteenth-century Rutland Psalter of a hybrid with the body of a *blemmye* and set into its chest the black head of an African shooting an arrow into the backside of a harmless white monopod. On the beautifully embroidered fourteenth-century Marnhull Orphrey at the Victoria and Albert Museum in London there is, similarly, the image of a black African, or possibly a black Jew, beating Christ with a cudgel on the Via Dolorosa (Figure 1). In medieval scenes of the crucifixion or mocking of Christ, individuals in the crowd sometimes carry a banner with the head of a negro on it instead of the more usual Jew's hat.[1]

32 HYBRID HATE

Figure 1. The Marnhull Orphrey (1310–1325), made in England with silver-gilt and silver thread and colored silks on linen.
© Victoria and Albert Museum, London. Museum number: T.31&A-1936.

While white was usually virtuous and black was usually bad, black was not always indelible. Sin and cruelty created blackness, but it could be reversed. The English history of the world, *Cursor Mundi*, written around 1300, described how blue and black Moors could turn white simply as a result of physical contact with Christianity (Strickland.2003).[2]

In *Omnium gentium mores* (1520), translated in 1555 by William Waterman as *The Fardle of Facions*, the German Hebraist, ethnographer, and humanist Johann Boemus (c.1485–1535) made an early attempt at an ethnographic description of the varying populations of Africa. "There be in it," he wrote of Africa, "dyvers peoples of sondry phisonomy and shape, monstruous and of hugly shewe." And foreshadowing modern conceptions of human origins, he noted, "They are thought . . . to have bene the fyrst of all men, and those whiche of all other maye truelyest be called an homeborne people."³ But there were others who rejected the idea that all negroes were of ugly appearance, "of hugly shewe." In the seventeenth century in *Pseudodoxia Epidemica* (1646) Sir Thomas Browne argued that beauty was a question of form, and that black could be beautiful as well as white. Indeed, blacks were not to be considered "excluded from beauty . . . to make color essential unto Beauty, there will arise no slender difficulty." And poignantly, and in keeping with the Augustinian monogenist vision, Sir Thomas observed that too many people wasted their time trying to distinguish between black Africans and Europeans, or others, when in fact there was no substantive difference. Whatever Africans are, Europeans are too: "We are that bold and adventurous piece of nature," he wrote, "which he that studies wisely learns in a compendium what others labour at in a divided piece and endless volume" (Browne.1646). All the weird and wonderful things and creatures and men and hybrids are in us too. *Nous sommes tous Africains*.

By the end of the eighteenth century a race-based approach to difference had nonetheless started to fortify the religiously and ethnically inspired prejudices of the medieval and early modern periods. Biblically based explanations of blackness such as the curse of Ham gradually gave way to an understanding of blackness provided by anatomists.

Building on earlier models of anti-black prejudice, attempts were made to delineate and protect white boundaries by comparing white people favorably with non-white peoples from around the globe. As Europeans on the colonial frontiers strove to understand unknown peoples, they compared them unfavorably with white, Christian Europeans, but also compared them with minorities in Europe, or with other peoples, who were indifferently known, on the frontiers of Europe. In the complex web of analogies connecting blacks with other "others," they were compared to Jews as well as to the Irish, Gypsies, and the *crétins* of Switzerland. Such groups were intended to be reduced and debased by comparisons with blacks. At the same time blacks were denigrated and disempowered through analogies with Jews, Israelites, and other despised European minorities.

Fear of blacks and Jews was one of the factors that played into the new theories and that demoted them to a lower rank in the developing hierarchies. Blacks, it was imagined, were set to destroy Europe through their predatory sexual nature, innate violence, cruelty, and debasement. Fear of blacks' sexuality was nothing new. Wolfram von Eschenbach's thirteenth-century work *Parzifal* presents blacks as having uncontrollable sexual appetites. For centuries European travelers were busy bringing back accounts of impressively endowed African males, scantily clad or naked women, and unbridled African sexuality. There was an obsession with interracial sex (Walvin.1993).

African's primitive and animal-like sexuality was threatening on two counts: African women were so oversexed that they would prey on unwary white men, and worse, African men would violate any white woman they could get their hands on. As we shall see there are clear parallels between the general medieval fear of Jews and the fear of blacks. However, the troubled relationship between Jews and Christian Europe was almost two thousand years old. The close physical relationship between black Africans and Europe was more recent, and indeed only became critically important in the seventeenth century, as a result of the European conquest and exploitation of the Americas, and the perceived need for physically strong laborers less likely to succumb to tropical diseases in the colonial plantations. The seventeenth century was the historical moment when blacks became a truly significant element of European society and were to be found in increasing numbers in cities in Portugal, France, Spain, and Italy and to a lesser extent also in northern cities. There are some examples of ennobled blacks at European courts. In the early eighteenth century there was a vogue in Paris for black pageboys in the grand salons.

Since the beginning of the age of European exploration Europeans were challenged by the strange peoples who had now come within the European orbit. They were increasingly available not just for view by hardy explorers in distant lands but were brought back and displayed to the general public. At the beginning of the sixteenth century "Eskimos" were paraded in Bristol; a hundred years later native Americans were exhibited in their canoes on the River Thames. However, it was Africa that was the acclaimed fountainhead of the strange, hybrid, monstrous, and remarkable.[4]

As blacks became better known, from literary sources, from traveling to the colonies, or from meeting or seeing Africans in the European cities, contradictory discourses about them started to proliferate. Andrew Curran was right to observe that the Enlightenment image of the black was "more a shifting mosaic than a fixed portrait." Negative medieval conceptions were grafted onto a new set of pseudoscientific attitudes designed to give a technical explanation of blackness and also to justify, in an appropriately modern fashion, the institution of slavery. In the seventeenth century blacks were increasingly imagined as a kind of darkened mirror to European whiteness. From the eighteenth century an anti-black counterimage was generated, drawn in part from accounts of African life and realities, in part from greed and self-serving theological musings, and in part from the work of eighteenth- and nineteenth-century anatomists and racial theorists. As we have seen, blacks had already been excluded from the brotherhood of races in much of the early polygenist writing. Over the centuries the image worsened as the volume of trade in slaves increased. As it reached its peak toward the end of the eighteenth century it became even more imperative for white Europeans to exclude the negro from the human family. An overarching paradigm drawing on these discourses started to fashion the hierarchy of peoples. Whites, who were cleverer and more beautiful than blacks, were destined to dominate a debased and degenerate black race (Curran.2011).

Differing patterns of anti-black prejudice promoted legal and political changes. In eighteenth-century France, the small community of blacks was subjected to ever greater limitations on their freedom. An edict in 1716 and the Declaration of 15 December 1738 ruled that slave status could apply in metropolitan France, as in the slave colonies, and they curtailed the rights of blacks, including their right to marry in France. The Declaration of 9 August 1777, which denied blacks the right to enter France, made skin color a legal criterion for immigration purposes. These harsh measures, rooted in prejudice, magical thinking, and economic self-interest, struggled with Enlightenment principles. As anti-black prejudice grew, public commitment to notions of equality and liberty prevented most Enlightenment thinkers from supporting slavery too obviously, but in general they were muted in their condemnation of it. Bernadin de Saint Pierre, Jean-Jacques Rousseau's disciple, complained that "philosophers who combat abuses with so much courage, have hardly spoken of negro slavery except to joke about it." (Cook.1936 p.294)

This was true of many of the thinkers of France's "crusading eighteenth century," most of whom condemned slavery but "failed to arouse the impassioned and effective attacks which they had waged on other evils." But there were exceptions. Rousseau, the admirer of the "*bon sauvage*," had little direct experience of blacks but was well aware, like all his Enlightenment contemporaries, of African travel literature. Saint Preux, the hero of his novel *Julie, ou la nouvelle Héloïse* (1761), returning from a journey to Africa exclaimed: "I saw these vast and unfortunate countries which seemed destined only to cover the face of the globe with slaves. At their vile appearance, I turned away my eyes, out of disdain, horror and pity; and on beholding one-fourth of my fellow creatures transformed into beasts for the service of the rest, I grieved to think that I was a man" (*Julie, ou la nouvelle Héloïse*, p.343, quoted in Cook.1936 p.300).

Revolutionary France abolished slavery in the French colonies in 1794, although it was re-introduced in 1802, and granted political rights to Jews in 1791. Henri Jean-Baptiste Grégoire (1750–1831), the Catholic priest and revolutionary leader, usually known as abbé Grégoire, was a fervent believer both in the abolition of the slavery of blacks and in the conditional emancipation of the Jews. He wrote with passion about both issues. His influential tract *De La Littérature des Nègres* was published in Paris in 1808.[5] On the one hand the book took issue with the idea that blacks had never achieved anything in history. On the other, it made the same argument Grégoire had already made with respect to Jews: that in order for blacks to be compared with whites they should have been brought up, and lived, in the same kinds of conditions. He agreed with the general view that black slaves were prejudiced, violent, ignorant, and foolish but asked whether Frenchmen or Englishmen would not be equally prejudiced, violent, ignorant, and foolish in similar circumstances. He argued moreover that regeneration was possible for negroes and Jews and that the manifold vices of both these peoples were not innate.

Nonetheless, the conviction that blacks were innately inferior was winning the argument. David Hume (1711–1776), who, like other Emancipation philosophers, was only mildly against slavery, seems to have thought that blacks were naturally inferior. This at any rate is what he wrote in an infamous and much-quoted note to his essay "Of National Characters" in 1753. Unwittingly, I suppose, echoing Voltaire, he wrote:

> I am apt to suspect the negroes to be naturally inferior to the whites. There scarcely ever was a civilized nation of that complexion, nor even any individual eminent either in action or speculation. No ingenious manufactures amongst them, no arts, no sciences. On the other hand, the most rude and barbarous of the whites, such as the ancient Germans, the present Tartars,

have still something eminent about them, in their valor, form of government, or some other particular. Such a uniform and constant difference could not happen in so many countries and ages, if nature had not made an original distinction betwixt these breeds of men. (Garrett.2000)

For white Europeans who had some knowledge of blacks and lived alongside them in the West Indian colonies, terror of alleged black cruelty, suggesting a reawakening of medieval fear of monstrous black barbarity, played a significant role. The legalization, once again, of slavery and the slave trade in certain French colonies by Napoleon in 1802 led to the massacre of more than four thousand French colonists following the slave rebellion in the colony of St. Domingue in 1804. This provoked a more widespread fear of slaves and blacks in the French colonies, as well as in in France, and the victorious slaves' cry of "*Koupe tèt, brule kay*" ("Cut off their heads, and burn their houses") reverberated throughout the Caribbean and reached the shores of Europe. Among plantation owners and colonists attitudes toward blacks if anything hardened in the following decades (Dorigny.2003). In the aftermath of the ruthlessly suppressed 1811 Louisiana slave revolt led by Charles Deslondes, a mixed-race slave, there was intense fear and loathing on the part of whites. The black rebels were viewed more as animals than humans. Their mutilated corpses and heads stuck on pikes stretched for miles along the Mississippi (Rasmussen.2011). The idea that blacks in general had more in common with animals than humans gained ground as the century progressed. As Jason Darrow, a Kentucky theologian, put it in 1846: "The result of my investigations is this, that they are not human, or only partly so, a mixture, a mongrel tribe partly beast, partly human, a compound most enormous and revolting" (Darrow.1846). And if people of a more liberal temperament wondered if the excesses and rigors of slavery were justifiable, as Mark Twain put it, "the local papers said nothing against it; the local pulpit taught us that God approved it, that it was a holy thing, and that the doubter need only look in the Bible if he wished to settle his mind" (Twain.2010 p.212).

By the time Darrow was writing there had been centuries of encoding of one aspect of blacks' "physical constitution." *A New General Collection of Voyages and Travels* (1745), produced by the London publisher Thomas Astley (d.1759), summarized some of the increasingly rigid arguments about the origins of blackness that were flying around in his day, in the ports of West Africa as well as in the salons of Europe. He wrote:

As all the Inhabitants within this Division of Africa are black it may not be improper to inquire into the cause of this great change of Complexion: Which is the first Object that presents itself at landing amongst these People, as well as a Topic that has given Rise to numberless Conjectures and great Disputes among the Learned in Europe. This is the more extraordinary, according to Labat[6] as the Moors, who are their next neighbours, are white, or at most swarthy, with long black Hair; whereas that of the Negroes is short, and soft like wool, and they have nothing white but their Teeth and Eyes. Nor can this difference be ascribed to the climate, since Experience shows, that white Parents, however long Inhabitants here, will always have white Children; and that Negro Parents, though removed to the most Northerly Latitudes, will have theirs of their own color. If it be asserted, as it is generally believed, that the Human Race sprung from a pair of first Parents, the Question will be, Of What color they were? For if they were either white, brown, or reddish (as the Name of Adam signifies) it is impossible they could ever have a Negro Offspring. Mix white and brown in equal Proportions as often as you please and they will never produce a Black.

The author was dismissive of many of the earlier medieval explanations of the "riddle" of African blackness such as the connections with Cain mentioned above, calling them products of "the most Ridiculous Imagination."[7] Cain had been viewed as the progenitor of all the monstrous races (Strickland.2003) as well as the agent for blackness in the world. Auguste Malfert, a priest of the Brothers of Charity order, serving in the Caribbean in the 1730s, came up with a fusion of these ideas. He argued that negroes were descended from Cain but added that from the moment of Cain's curse they became a completely different species. He believed that Noah and his sons were all white, along with their descendants. The only way in which the blacks could have assumed their black color and type was if they had interbred with monsters "for it was impossible to engender a 'race of monsters' any other way" (Shelford.2013 p.74; Goldenberg.2017).

Another explanation of blackness had been that it was the result of the curse of Ham. Sir Thomas Browne (1605–1682), author of *Pseudodoxia Epidemica or Vulgar Errors*, noted that whereas "men affirm this color was a Curse, I cannot make out the propriety of that name, it neither seeming so to them, nor reasonably unto us; for they take so much content therein, that they esteem deformity by other colors, describing the Devil, and terrible objects, white" (Browne.1650 p.281). Similarly, in the 1770 edition of abbé Raynal's *Histoire philosophique et politique des établissemens & du commerce des européens dans les deux Indes* Denis Diderot (1713–1784) expressed his frustration and anger at the continued use of biblical explanations for blackness. He expostulated:

> Having made all men guilty and miserable through the fault of one man the theologians have now made a race of black men through the fratricide of that first man's son. From this Cain, the Negroes are descended. If their father was a murderer, we must acknowledge that his crime has been cruelly expiated by his children; and that the descendants of the peaceful Abel have well avenged their father's innocent blood. Great God, what wrath, what atrocities, what abominations, what extravagances are heaped upon your just, good, wise, and holy being! (Raynal.1770. book XI. p.119)

With the contempt for biblical stories so trenchantly expressed by Enlightenment figures, it became clear that the pre-Enlightenment near-consensus that negroes were black because of some ancient biblical curse or another was not good enough. The search for a more scientific explanation of the puzzle of African difference would continue apace (Goldenberg.2017).

Attempts to demonstrate an identifiable, explicable, and calculable physical difference between negroes and Europeans served the interests of colonialism and the slaving lobby and opened the way to dehumanize blacks even further (Hall.2012; Hondius.2017). Learned societies, such as the Royal Society, paved the way for the increased racialization of blacks by placing a remarkable emphasis on the puzzle of African color (Malcolmson.2016). In order to address this puzzle one English naturalist, John Woodward (1665–1728), fellow of the Royal Society, compiled *Brief Instructions for Making Observations in All Parts of the World*, which was authorized by the Royal Society in 1695. *Brief Instructions* was aimed at travelers to "all parts of the world" and urged them to gather information about the peculiarities of the color of "true Negroes." An appendix "relating to the Natives of Guinea, Monomotapa, and other the less known parts of Africa: of the East, and West Indies: Tartary, Greenland, or any other remote, and uncivilized, or Pagan Countries" asked for very specific information:

> As to their Bodies, observe the features, shapes, and proportions of them; but more particularly the features of their faces: their Eyes whether large, or

small: their noses whether flat and low, or sharp and raised: their Hair long, or short and curled or woolly: the colour of their Skin whether white, brown, tawny, olive, or black: the colour of their Infants when first born: whether white people removing into hot Countries become by degrees browner, &c. and Blacks removing into cold Countries, paler: whether People that inhabit the Countries which are hottest, be in Complexion of all the blackest: whether there be true Negroes, Natives of any parts of the world, besides Guinea, and the adjacent parts of Africa. Observe also the size or bigness of their Bodies: their strength, agility, &c: and to what age they commonly live. Observe likewise whether they paint their bodies: what parts of them they paint, what colours they lay on: what figures they paint: and how they do it. (Woodward.1696. *Appendix* p.9)

As travelers' observations on the phenomenon of blackness started to arrive in metropolitan centers, scientific explanations of blackness begun to proliferate. Antonie Philips van Leeuwenhoek (1632–1723), the Dutch scientist known as the father of microbiology, was convinced that blackness was brought about by microscopic scales on the skin. Thomas Astley (d.1759), the London publisher mentioned earlier in the chapter, set out further solutions to the problem. "Whatever Way this Contrariety happened," he wrote, "it must obviously be owing to some Difference in the Juices or Texture of the Teguments of the Body." Astley went on to note that some claimed that

the Blackness in Negros proceeds from the color of the Epidermis (Cuticle or Scarfskin) and not that of the skin itself. . . . On the contrary the Anatomists of the Royal Academy of Sciences, at Paris, who were at great pains to search into this Affair, have at last discovered, that this Blackness is neither in the Skin nor the Flesh, but a small Reticula, or Network (composed of extremely soft and delicate Fibres) placed between the Epidermis, and Skin; which reticula in Whites is white, and in the Negroes, black. It must be allowed that this Reticula does not appear in the Soles of the Feet of Negros, nor in the Palms of their Hands, which in all are white. But the Question is not so much in what Part the Blackness lies, but whence that Blackness proceeds? Not whether the *Reticula* of the Negros be black, but why is it black? Why it should in the Blacks be black, and in the Whites, white. (*A New General Collection of Voyages and Travels*.1745 p.270)

Pierre Barrère (1690–1755), an ornithologist and physician from Perpignan, was one of those savants who moved away from any kind of biblical exegesis in the direction of this sort of medical analysis. In *Dissertation sur la cause physique de la couleur des Nègres* (Dissertation on the physical cause of the color of Negroes), which appeared in 1742, he, too, attempted to solve the problem of African blackness. Barrère served as a doctor in the military hospital in Cayenne, where he personally carried out anatomical dissections on slaves. His experiments showed that the negro had an abundant dark bile, which while coursing through the body stained the epidermis and the blood (Curran.2011; Malcolmson.2016). A further notion was put about by the German anatomist Johann Friedrich Meckel the Elder (1724–1774) that in fact blackness was the result of the black color of negro brains. Not to be outdone, in 1784, the Göttingen anatomist and savant Samuel Thomas von Sömmering (1755–1830), who among other things discovered the macula in the retina of the human eye, declared that science had finally discovered the true explanation for the radical difference of negroes, and particularly their brute stupidity, in the coarse "strings" that connected the brain to the rest of the body (Curran.2011). There were continuing attempts to "enlist anatomy," in abbé Grégoire's phrase, in the attempt to account for the blackness of negroes. We have seen the English sailor George Best (d.1584) explain blackness in part from a sickness of the blood, while even Malfert reinforced his biblical argument by explaining blackness as the result of "germs" (*germes*). Grégoire was fully aware of the differing opinions of Meckel the Elder, Sömmering, and others. However, he was also aware of the fact that the majority of the scientists of his day still attributed the color of blacks and other non-white populations in the world to climate, style of life, and heat (Grégoire.1808).

The color black was also a frequent ingredient in the palette of tints associated with the construction of Jews. For centuries a sense had prevailed that Jews were radically different, that they were outside the usual framework of normative humanity, and that like black Africans they were excluded from white Christian European normalcy.

A part of their supposed difference was the conviction that they were of a dark color, perhaps black, perhaps brown, and had negroid traits. These suspicions coexisted with diametrically opposed fears that the color and look of Jews were indistinguishable from the color and look of Christians. Thus, the Fourth Lateran Council of 1215 complained that that Jews "cannot be distinguished by any difference" and called for some way of identifying them.

In 1218 the Jewish badge was introduced in England. Subsequently signifiers such as the Jewish hat and badges of different colors, sizes, and shapes were introduced all over Europe (Kaplan.2013). Sander Gilman, among others, has pointed to gentile perceptions that Jews were just as black as negroes. According to Gilman Jews "were quite literally seen as black" (Gilman.1994). As Melamed, following Gilman, put it, there was "a strong European tradition, dating back to the Middle Ages which maintained that Jews were 'black' or at least swarthy and finds sharp expression in modern anti-Semitic literature" (Melamed.2003 p.31).

HaCohen, in a revisionist article, shows that some, but not all, of the evidence used to support the notion of a long and continuing tradition of perceived Jewish blackness in fact does no such thing, but he also provides some new evidence of his own of perceptions of Jewish blackness (HaCohen.2018). Much of the evidence produced by Gilman and Melamed stands, and a good deal more evidence is provided throughout this book, but such evidence should be understood in the context of the overarching caveat that the general concept of Jewish color was chronically unstable.

Nonetheless, there clearly was a longstanding discourse, not only in religious and liturgical works but also in early naturalist writing, that constructed the color of Jews not simply as metaphorically black through their perceived relationship with, for instance, transgression, but also as somatically black. As early as the twelfth century "not only theology but medicine and natural science conspired to treat the Jews' black or dark complexion not only as an image of the soul but also as an empirical fact supported by scientific explanation" (Resnick.2012 p.295). The humoral theory which dates back to Hippocrates (c.460–370 BCE), understood the body as consisting of four humors or liquids, one of which, "black bile," was known as melancholy. M. Lindsay Kaplan, explained that melancholy was identified as "black bile" which carried associations with evil and with night. The Jews' dark, melancholy complexion was the result of a malign influence, as well as a punishment for their alleged murder of the son of God. The blood of Jews was "black and putrid," and they were associated with blackness in a variety of other ways (Kaplan.2013).

Jews' black, melancholy nature was expressed through their association with Saturn, as medieval astrology shows. Saturn, the planet of the Jews, exerted its special influence over Jews as well as over anything black. Alchabitius (d.967) (Al-Qabisi), the Arab astrologer from Aleppo, who became, through Latin translations, a standard authority on astrology in medieval Europe, argued that Saturn "had the faith of Judaism, black clothing . . . to him belong . . . everything whatsoever that is black" (Zafran.1979; Abrahams.1961).⁸

One Christian critic of the supposedly "Jewish" pope Anacletus II, elected in 1130, noted that the pope was "dark . . . more like a Jew or an Arab than a Christian." Similarly, the English Benedictine monk and chronicler Orderic Vitalis's (1075–c.1142) description of a descendant of converts from Judaism characterizes him as "*nigrum et pallidum . . ., magis Judaeo vel Agarena quam Christiano simile*" ("black and pallid, more like a Jew or Muslim than a Christian") (Kaplan.2013). Kaplan argues that the frequent conflation of blacks and Jews through the figures of black or dark Jews in English psalters from the twelfth to the fourteenth centuries, as well as other factors, suggests that in England there existed an immutable Jewish "racial identity" which corresponds to a contemporary sense of race (Kaplan.2007). The cognitive double vision that transforms white into black would be an important factor in the perception of Jews for centuries to come, and would achieve its malign flowering during the period of the Third Reich.

Kaplan later expanded the idea of the racialization of the Jews through a study of the Christian concept of permanent, immutable, hereditary Jewish inferiority, which racial characteristic was also applied to Moors and Africans (Kaplan.2018). According to Kaplan there was a regular conflation of the somatic essence of Moors, blacks, and Jews. Non-Christians are regularly portrayed as pallid, blue, or black, and these colors similarly portray death, illness, or melancholy. The color representation of Jews, while regularly portraying Jews as black or dark, was unstable as it also exploited the larger palette of colors associated with infidels (Kaplan.2007; Kaplan.2018 p.214). The color of Moors or Muslims was also unstable: there were white Moors as there were Blackamoors. The color problematic in English, as well as in European constructions of Jewish and black identity, in the medieval and early modern periods, was to some extent a function of the convergence and conflation of ideas about Jews and Moors, while ideas about Moors were similarly conflated with ideas about black Africans, who came to be known as Blackamoors, whether they were Muslim or not (Mackay.2008).

Among the Blackamoors, or perhaps beyond the Blackamoors, on the furthest horizons of the European imagination, there were supposed to be vast numbers of Jews, who potentially represented a mortal threat to Christendom. The well-known legends that flowed from the account provided by the mysterious ninth-century figure Eldad the Danite, referred to by Adolf Neubauer as "the Arabian Nights of the Jews," suggested that there were substantial, well-organized Jewish populations in Africa.

In 1523, a pamphlet printed in Augsburg warned that there were 600,000 "*schwartz und rodt juden*" (black and red Jews) who were poised to capture Jerusalem from the Moors. (Gow.1994 p.263).

In German-speaking areas of Europe the *Rote Juden* (red Jews), representing the supposedly lost Ten Tribes of Israel, were imagined to be allies of the Antichrist and were expected to invade Europe and destroy Christianity at the End of Days.[9] Germans were terrified of these horrific, pestilential people, who were out to destroy them. Red and black Jews from outside the European orbit were perceived for centuries as the elemental enemies of Christendom, and no doubt the idea that the enemies at the gate, like the enemies within, were of colors other than white played a significant role in denigrating Jews and promoting the idea that all Jews were inherently black or colored, as well as adding to social coherence among the gentile population in German-speaking lands (Hund.2011).[10]

One of the most widely quoted sources suggesting that Jews were considered to be somatically black is from the German Christian Hebraist and cosmographer Sebastian Münster (1488–1552). Published just a few years after the pamphlet about black and red Jews, *Messias Christianorum et Judaeorum* (Basel, 1539) (*The Messias of the Christians and the Jewes*. London, 1655) recorded a graphic dialogue between a Christian and a Jew, which was written in both Latin and Hebrew so that both Christians and Jews could read it. It starts with the Christian speaking to the Jew in Hebrew. Taken aback, the Jew asks the Christian how he knew he was a Jew. The Christian replies (in the language of the 1655 English translation): "You Jewes have a peculiar color of face, different from the form and figure of other men, which thing hath often fill'd me with admiration [astonishment] for you are black and uncomely, and not white as other men" (Münster.1655 p.2).

Rev. Robert Kirk (1644–1692), the Gaelic scholar and collector of legends about fairies, fauns, and other Good People (by whom he was widely thought to have been abducted as a punishment for revealing their secrets) considered Jews to be "black men" characterized by indistinct reasoning. His contemporary Sir William Brereton (1604–1661), the English Parliamentarian, soldier, and writer, who happened to visit a synagogue in Amsterdam, noted that the Jews there were very dark-skinned and lascivious. "They were most black," he wrote, ". . . and insatiably given unto women."

One of the arguments deployed to explain the darkness or blackness of Jews was the food they ate. In 1599 Henry Buttes (d.1632), one-time master of Corpus Christi College, Cambridge, produced an entertaining food guide called *Dyets Dry Dinner*. He noted, correctly, that the Jews were great lovers of goose, which creature, according to him, filled "the body with superfluous humours." This resulted in the Jews being "passing melancholious, their color swart [black] and their diseases very perilous." If they had eaten hare instead, he opined, they might possibly have become paler and more beautiful: Indeed, the Italians, he observed, had a saying "which speaketh thus of a fair man, 'He hath eaten an hare.'"

In *New Voyage to Italy* (1699) (which would be the standard guidebook to Italy for the next half century) François Maximilian Misson (c.1650–1722), the French Protestant writer and traveler, is quoted by Gilman and many others as suggesting that the Jews were black. In fact, he said something rather more interesting. He noted simply that Jews came in different colors and that it would be a mistake to suppose that they were all "*basané*," or swarthy, when many of them were actually white (Misson.1699; Gilman.1992; HaCohen.2018). The French naturalist Georges Louis Leclerc de Buffon read Misson correctly. Interrogating the new trope of multicolored Jews, Buffon wrote:

> It has been claimed that the Jews, who came originally from Syria and Palestine, have the same brown complexion they had formerly. As Misson, however, justly observes, the Jews of Portugal alone are tawny. As they always marry with their own tribe, the complexion of the parents is transmitted to the child, and thus with little diminution preserved, even in the northern countries. The German Jews, those of Prague, for example, are not more swarthy than the other Germans. (Buffon.1792 p.262; cf. Lipton.2014)

Some Jews accepted the argument that, as a kind of retribution for their sins, they had been gradually darkened, by the intervention of the Almighty, until they were black. This was the position of Isaac ben Judah Abrabanel (1437–1508), the Portuguese Jewish statesman, exegete, and financier, who observed that once long ago the Jews had been light-skinned, but that they had grown dark as part of the punishment of exile. The thirteenth-century polemical text of Rav Yosef b. Nathan Oficial tried to account for the Christian accusations that Jews were dark and unattractive. "Why," asked Rav Yosef, "are the majority of gentiles white and attractive, while the majority of

Jews are black and ugly?" The writer explained this through an analogy of ripening fruit. Plums and sloes, he argued, are white at the start and gradually become dark when they are ripe, whereas fruits like apples or apricots, which are red to start with, finish up white and shriveled. This analogy was intended to present the Jews in a better light: As Jews have no contact with the red of menstrual blood at the moment of their conception, because they refrain from sexual intercourse during the menstrual period, they finish up black, like plums. Christians, who are polluted by menstrual blood, start off red but finish up white, like apples. *Sefer Yosef ha-Mekanneh* thus boasts that "we Jews are from a clean and white seed; therefore, our faces are black, but you are from the red seed of menstruation, therefore your visages are pale and reddened" (Schorsch.2004 p.180; cf. Gilman.1992; Melamed.2003; Parfitt.2013).

Religion in general was thought to manifest itself physically in such a way that one's inner religious convictions were visible externally. Judaism, like other religions, was thought to manifest itself physically. The English play *A Christian Turn'd Turk* (1612), by the dramatist Robert Daborne, includes a dialogue in which one character asks another: "Doth religion move anything in the shapes of men?" The other replies, "Altogether! What's the reason else that the Turk and the Jew is troubled (for the most part) with gouty legs and fiery nose? To express their heart-burning. Whereas the Puritan is a man of upright calf and clean nostril."

Mutability of color, which would become a major theme of nineteenth- and twentieth-century racial discussions, was framed in the seventeenth century in terms of conviction. We have seen that blacks exposed to Christianity were capable of turning white. Similarly, in 1648, Thomas Calvert (1606–1679), a vicar of Trinity Church, York, published a translation of the testimony to the truth of the Christian faith of one Rabbi Samuel, a converted Jew from Fez. This anti-Jewish diatribe, which was first published in 1339, was called in Calvert's translation *The blessed Jew of Marocco: or, A Blackmoor made white*. It explained that through conversion to Christianity a Jew's naturally black color could be changed. Three hundred years later the French theologian Isaac La Peyrère, himself of Jewish ancestry, noted that a Jew's black color would turn as white as a dove's breast once he was baptized.

Conversion affected Jews in predictable ways, one of which was smell, one of the most powerful and obvious triggers of ethnic contempt. Jews were thought to give off a particularly unpleasant odor, known as the *foetor judaicus*. However, this would disappear once a Jew converted to Christianity.

Caesarius of Heisterbach (c.1180–c.1240), the popular author of miracle tales, wrote of a Jewish girl converted to Christianity who was able to pick up the scent of her unconverted, and therefore smelly, Jewish father from a great distance. However, in his famous *Pseudodoxia Epidemica or Vulgar Errors* (1646) Sir Thomas Browne dismissed this olfactory superstition impatiently, while recognizing that it was all too prevalent. "In the conceit of the evil odor of the Jews," he wrote, "Christians without a farther research into the verity of the thing, or inquiry into the cause, draw up a judgement upon them from the passion of their Saviour." According to this superstition Jews could immediately be identified by their odor, which was reminiscent of the smell of the male goat, "the Jew's beast." As soon as they were baptized, however, as Misson put it, "their noisome smell vanished" (Misson.1699; Resnick.2012).

From the beginning of the thirteenth century, Christian images of Jews, like those of negroes, were often aggressive and hostile and included demonic features, bristling beards, brutish expressions, and large or hooked noses. Routinely represented in every kind of visual representation from stained glass windows to manuscript illumination, Jews often appeared as freaks, demons, hybrids, or monsters. The intrepid aristocrat Ludovico di Varthema (c.1470–1517), author of *Itinerario de Ludovico de Varthema Bolognese* (Rome, 1510), noted for being perhaps the first non-Muslim European to visit Mecca, intriguingly described encountering some pygmy Jews, suggestive of the so-called "monstrous races," on a mountain near Medina. In the English translation provided in *Purchas His Pilgrimes* these "pigmei" Jews were

> of very little stature, as of the height of five or six spannes, and some much lesse. They have small voyces like women, and of blacke color, yet some blacker than others... They are circumcised, and deny not themselves to be Iewes... They wandered in that Mountayne, scattered like wilde Goates or Prickets. (Holmberg.2012 p.117)

The same association of Jewish pygmies, goats, and "monstrous races" appears in the margins of the thirteenth-century Rutland Psalter, where there is an image of a small male figure, no doubt a pygmy, looking quizzically at a flute-playing goat. As other "monstrous races" from the classical repertoire, quite apart from pygmies, figure in the marginalia of this psalter, it is reasonable to suppose that the Jew and goat motif is intended to conjure up an allusion to both the "monstrous races" and "the Jew's beast." As Strickland points out,

> the bright, orange pointed hat, long nose, and beard mark this Pygmy as a Jew.... in addition, the Jew is standing next to a goat, an animal associated with both the Devil and the Jews in medieval art and thought. Both the Jew and the goat in this image share certain physical characteristics: both stand on two legs, both wear beards, and according to contemporary belief, both are horned.

Trachtenberg similarly identified the goat both as a symbol of "Satanic lechery" and as an animal associated with Jews, who would often be portrayed riding a goat. Strickland cites a northern French manuscript from the same period where a hybrid Jew, again with an orange cap, is seen shooting an owl, suggesting that the Jews were not just monstrous but also "blind and despised": The owl was a common bestiary figure, often associated with Jews, that was thought to shun the light, in the same way that Jews shunned the light of Christ. Another thirteenth-century hybrid from Salisbury in England consists of a manticore, a creature with a lion's body and the poisonous tail of a scorpion, with a "grotesque Jewish profile" and a long beard. The monster is gnawing on a human leg. Notwithstanding that marginal hybrids were often playful or jocular, and intended to entertain, the overwhelming sense of portrayals of Jews is that they were in the same conceptual category as "monstrous races" (Trachtenberg.1983; Strickland.2003).

In the early modern period, the fear of Jews as dangerous and violent polluters also spread to learned elites, and particularly to humanist circles. This can be seen in the views of polygenists such as Bruno and Vanini and also in the way Renaissance humanists generally responded so enthusiastically to the blood libel, the medieval accusation that Jews use the blood of Christian children to make Passover wafers or for some other ritual. Such a case, in 1475, in Trento, a city on the Adige River in Trentino-Alto Adige in northern Italy, ended with all the male Jews of the town being judicially murdered, and the women and children forcibly converted to Catholicism. Kenneth Stow wrote:

> Members of what we might presume was an enlightened intelligentsia had come to perceive the Jewish presence as a danger; Jews were evil miscreants and polluters of social and religious purity. They were also seen as ever

ready to act out their hatreds ... Their humanist opponents fundamentally wanted [the Jews] 'to go away', sometimes attributing them with magical prowess and the darkest of desires ... That which principally animated the Humanists, therefore, was the desire to neutralize imagined Jewish aggression. (Stow.2017 p.17)

Humanist hatred of Jews' brutish untutored violence played into eighteenth-century thinking in a number of ways. Edward Long, as we have seen, maintained that Jews "antient and modern," just like the black Africans about whom he knew rather more, were aggressive and engaged in "vile Practices" and "rascally tricks." Indeed, throughout the century a number of negative motifs informed the construction of Jews, including references to the transgressive and transnational "wandering Jew" motif, which had the effect of putting Jews, as nomadic, stateless wanderers, outside the normative framework of the national body politic. Because of their perceived refusal to assimilate to European norms Immanuel Kant (1724–1804) considered that the Jews were outside the norms of civilized peoples, as they were noisome "social vampires" who were harmful to society. Baleful qualities of violence and exploitation were attributed to Jews and blacks alike. Blacks were regularly accused of stealing and lying, and "the same proverbial cunning" in business dealings, which was often associated with blacks, was also regularly attributed to Jews. Both Enlightenment theists like Voltaire (1694–1778) and atheists like Baron d'Holbach (1723–1789) and his followers promoted "a monster image" of Judaism and portrayed Jews as subversive anti-citizens in their debates over Jewish emancipation (Schechter.2003; Davison.2004; Kleingeld.2007).

Jews' dark ignorance of things was often stressed, as it was with respect to blacks. At the dawn of the eighteenth century a French Protestant, not badly disposed to Jews, could firmly state that "no Body can doubt that those of the *Jewish* nation are destitute of all authentick Tradition; and, that, as being Jews, they have not any particular Knowledge, either of the Laws and Customs of their Ancestors, or even of the *Hebrew* language" (Misson.1699). As long as they clung to their tired and wrong beliefs and rituals, they could not expect to play a full part in Western society. For many Enlightenment thinkers the Jews, like blacks, had nothing to offer.

In 1780, Gotthold Ephraim Lessing (1729–1781), the Enlightenment philosopher and dramatist, argued that while biblical Judaism could perhaps be viewed as "the childhood of mankind" and biblical Jews as archetypes of primitive innocence, with the arrival of Christianity, Jews along with Judaism stopped being relevant and left the stage of history. But if for some they lurked uselessly in the shadows, for others malign, black-faced Jews were still viewed, as they had been in medieval times, as an ignorant and misguided, terrifying and monstrous, dangerous and fearful menace to Christian European society. Eighteenth-century popes, as opposed to Jews as they were to the *philosophes* of the Enlightenment, re-enunciated the most restrictive anti-Jewish legislation in the face of what was generally regarded as monstrous Jewish cruelty to Christians (Stow.2017; Chisick.2016).

Blacks and Jews, along with Moors, were fundamental "others" for Christian Europeans, were often mentioned in the same breath for that reason, and were regularly imagined to have shared ancestry. Linkages of different sorts between blacks and Jews in medieval Europe were extremely widespread. Indeed, there was a general tendency on the part of medieval Christians to confuse or link Jews with all sorts of minorities, "with other Others," as Schorsch puts it. The linkage of Jew, and Moor or Turk or Blackamoor, as "others" is to be found throughout the texts, songs, and prayers of Christendom. In 1606 the Spanish Benedictine monk and historian Fray Prudencio de Sandoval (1553–1620), then Bishop of Pamplona in northwest Spain, made a clear connection between Jews and blacks through the indelible nature of their respective, essential characteristics. On the one hand Jews all suffered from the sad effect of failed beliefs and ingratitude, while blacks suffered from their indelible blackness, of which they and their progeny could never rid themselves, no matter how many times they slept with white women. In other words, there was never a chance of a male black producing anything but a dark child with a white woman, any more than there was a chance of a Jew producing offspring who would fail to demonstrate the arrogant wrongheadedness represented by their failed religion.

Writing polemically against new Jewish converts to Christianity in about 1541, Francisco Machado linked Jews and blacks through their innate undesirability. He tried to imagine Portugal "cleansed of heresies and of Jewish ceremonies, and of Moors and Blacks." On occasion, the darkness of the skin of Africans and Jews, as we have seen, was perceived as being not due to inheritance but to the effect of diseases such as syphilis, a trope that would persist until recent times. The "negritude" of the Jew was thus not only a mark of sin or racial inferiority, or of shared blood with Africans, but was a pathological taint.

The Bavarian writer Johann Pezzl (1756–1823), who visited Vienna in the 1780s, described the specifically negroid character of Polish Jews in Vienna. In his view, they were perceived in the same way that black Africans often were, as apelike and with woolly matted hair. He wrote:

> There are about five hundred Jews in Vienna ... excluding the Indian fakirs, there is no category of supposed human beings which come closer to the Orang-Utang than does a Polish Jew ... their necks exposed the color of a Black ... the hair turned and knotted as if they all suffered from the *plica polonica*.[11]

Although HaCohen, in his 2018 article, was correct to view this much-quoted passage as indicating that the necks of Jews were either dirty or sunburned rather than black like the rest of the body, and that this is no indication that Jews were seen as somatically black, the description of Jews' matted hair and the reference to apes urges the reader in the direction of negritude (HaCohen.2018).

The Jewish Enlightenment physician Elcan Isaac Wolf, author of *Von den Krankheiten der Juden* (On Jewish Illnesses) (1777), also saw Jews' yellowish-brown "tawny" skin color as a pathological mark of the sickly Jew that was ultimately due to endemic poverty, and in 1808, the enlightened (and Hebrew-speaking) English physician and ethnographer James Cowles Prichard (1786–1848), from Bristol, made the same kind of connection between the national character and psychology of Jews and their color as medieval Christians had made. He stressed that the "choleric and melancholic constitution of the Jews" was such that "they usually have a skin color somewhat darker than the English people" (Gilman.1992 p.5).

The long preoccupation with Jews' physical difference and their dark color flowed into a new or perhaps reawakened emphasis on the specific and technical racial makeup of Jews, as the most obvious not altogether white "other" in the European sphere, on the one hand, and black Africans, whose racial characteristics were usually thought to be the furthest removed from those of Europeans, and who thus constituted the most extreme external other, on the other hand.

What was there about the racial origins of Jews and blacks that made them so uniquely different, and so much discussed? How did Jews and blacks fit into the biological map of humankind? And how, in the Age of Enlightenment, were they expected to fit into Western, white Christian societies? While distinctions between the early modern period and the nineteenth and twentieth centuries should not be blurred, similarities between earlier and later discourses cannot be dismissed. Many of the questions that had perplexed men in the late medieval period become central to the Western academic study of race and racial categories in the modern period. Over many centuries vastly more attention was paid to understanding the physicality of Jews and blacks than all other human groups.

The linkages between Jews and blacks, embedded as they were in the cultural landscape of medieval Europe, became more pronounced during the period of the Enlightenment as both were scrutinized anew. The precise interrelationship of Jews, whether they were perceived as dark or pale, and blacks would preoccupy some of the finest minds among European and American thinkers for the following two centuries. Anthropology in the service of polygenesis would soon seek to provide evidence not only for the difference but also for the *irreducible* difference both of Jews and blacks, thus following a direction that medieval commentators had already signposted. It was the study of the physical and mental differences of Jews and blacks in the period of the High Enlightenment and later, drawing to an unacknowledged extent on medieval stereotypes and the earlier polygenist thinkers (described above), that conspired to produce modern racism.

Yet the Enlightenment brought with it the principle that all citizens of a state, unless there were very good reasons to forbid it, had the right to civic participation and equality before the law. How could it then be argued that blacks and Jews were excluded from such political emancipation? Some thought that Jews were potentially capable of gaining respect as citizens by shedding their alien religion and culture. After all, Jews and blacks had not always been debased. A discourse emerged that viewed Jews and blacks as ancient, unchanging people connected with the dawn of time. This trope too would persist throughout the nineteenth century and beyond. For others yet, Jews even had a redemptive role to play in Europe's and the world's future. The German philosopher Johann Gottfried Herder (1744–1803) constructed the noble Israelites of old as an alternative model to classical Greeks for Germans to follow. In the twenty-sixth chapter of his *Essai sur la régénération physique et morale des Juifs* (1789), abbé Grégoire understood that the physical and moral character of the Jews was such that it required complete reform. He wrote:

> The reform of the Jews is not, in truth, the work of a moment, for one knows that in general the onward march of reason, like that of the sea, is only noticeable after centuries; but although ordinarily moral revolutions are very slow, this one will be more rapid. If you listen to the likes of Mm Michaelis and Schwager, even in ten generations the Hebrews will still not be cut out for a military profession ... certain more tenacious vices, either through their very nature, or because habit will have reinforced them, such as the greed of gain, will only disappear, entirely, in a hundred years ... but still we would like to believe that two generations should be enough for this reform. (Grégoire.1789 p.189)

Throughout his book he remarked that the debased condition of the Jews, like the blacks, should be a source of compassion rather than blame, and that anyone looking at these alien people in their pitiful circumstances could only be moved. He was horrified by the persecution of the Jews, whose history was little more than a "*sanglante tragédie*" (bloody tragedy) that still cast a dark shadow over them, and whose lot in some respects was even worse than that of blacks (Grégoire.1789).[12]

As the nineteenth century progressed, the improvement in the lot of the Jews was at best patchy. Even the material improvement of Jews in western Europe had a downside. They gradually came to represent and personify the dangers of European modernization that allegedly had undercut the lower middle classes of Europe at a time when Jews appeared to be thriving. Indeed, in some discourses, but not all, from the late eighteenth century until the Second World War, venomous misrepresentations of Jews circulated. They were accused of poisoning European society and destroying it. They were typified as dangerous and monstrous, as goats, apes, insects, or rats.

For hundreds of years in Europe and later in the Americas, a binary opposition had been produced between sets of physical characteristics that were deemed white as opposed to characteristics that were supposed to be black. For many of the taxonomic systems that were developed, "black" and "white" became key criteria. The standards represented by "white" were almost always positive, while those evoked by "black" were usually negative. White was beautiful, black was ugly. The very term "negro," which had originally, as an adjective, suggested simply a darker skin tone, came to imply ugliness and barbarity. During the Romantic period in Germany and in many parts of Europe, from the latter part of the eighteenth century to the middle of the nineteenth, racial distinctions came to be seen in part as based on aesthetic principles. In this respect too there was an overlap between perceptions of Jews and blacks. The development of both anti-black racism and anti-Judaism or antisemitism had recourse to a vision of white, "Caucasian," and classical beauty as opposed to dark and/or Semitic ugliness. As Mosse put it: "Most racists consequently endowed inferior races whether black or Jew with several identical properties such as lack of beauty and charged them with the lack of those middle-class virtues, and finally with a lack of any metaphysical depth" (Mosse.1978 p.xxvi).

The study of *racism*—racially based prejudice—in modern times has concentrated on attitudes toward Jews and blacks, as expressed in Western anti-black prejudice and European antisemitism. The latter is sometimes represented as a particularly German pathology and the former mainly an American one, but in fact both are recognizable products of the wider Western Enlightenment and nineteenth-century race science, thought, and culture, and both have their roots in the relationship between Europeans and non-Europeans in the medieval and early modern world.

The words used to describe these pathologies changed somewhat over the period, but the intent remained much the same. There are different kinds of history. Some histories disappear forever; others remain. The parallels between Jews and blacks in the premodern European imaginaire with the current situation in Europe and the United States of America and with discourses embroidered around migration are so obvious as to barely require comment. Suffice it to say that many contemporary discourses reject the idea of Europeans "of color" and reflect attitudes that are centuries old and have barely changed over time (Tudor.2014).

The study of racial difference throughout Europe, from the time of the Enlightenment and throughout the nineteenth century and first half of the twentieth, was dominated by the problematic of Jews and blacks. Many different discourses were undoubtedly in play. Jews and blacks were admired and pitied, feared and loathed; they were both often considered to be monstrous and animalistic, different and radically apart, not to be considered part of the regular mass of humanity. In their different ways, they were often viewed as a threat to Europe. Jews were perceived as potentially or innately black or dark, and sometimes, disturbingly, as white as the whitest European. Jews, like Muslims, were capable of being both black and white. The much-discussed subject of white negroes, which will be considered in the next chapter, suggested that blacks, too, were also capable of being white as well as black, and in colonial societies often "one drop" of black blood from some remote African ancestor sufficed to transform a light-skinned person into a black one.

Connected, twinned, and unified, Jews and blacks were becoming an alien and mystifying hybrid abstraction with much in common with the hybrids that had once adorned the margins of medieval prayer books, and that continued to lurk in the darkest and rankest corners of the European imagination. Such fantastic and monstrous hybrids were still thought to exist in a variety of marvelous forms in the outer reaches of the world. But the place where they were thought to flourish more abundantly and luxuriantly than elsewhere was a small area of west Africa, barely known today, called Loango. And the perplexing hybrids of Loango would soon reveal themselves to a wondering world.

3
All Africa and Her Prodigies

The overused adage that there is always something new out of Africa in all probability started with Aristotle's observation that "Libya always produces something new." For the great philosopher, the novelties that Africa could be counted on producing were fearsome hybrids. Because of the lack of water in Africa, Aristotle surmised, animals met every evening at watering holes, and promiscuous coupling inevitably ensued, giving rise to all sorts of exotic crosses.

For hundreds of years the European imagination had been haunted by tales of African hybrids and "monstrous races." Johann Boemus (c.1485–1535), the German Hebraist and ethnographer, wrote that in Africa there were "dyvers peoples of sondry phisonomy and shape, monstruous." They were typically ugly to look at—of "hugly shewe." Similarly, the Italian poet Torquato Tasso (1544–1595) warned of "monsters which hot Africke forth doth send." Even the ever-reasonable Sir Thomas Browne (1605–1682) saw Africa as being exceptional and wrote of "all Africa and her prodigies" and described the continent as "that bold and adventurous piece of nature." The whole of chaotic sub-Saharan Africa was viewed as the antithesis of European order, but it was the African kingdom of Loango, well known to generations of European scholars from the fifteenth to the nineteenth century, that seems to have exerted the greatest fascination as a source of the monstrous and the hybrid. At first glance it is difficult to understand why this was so, as Loango was a relatively well-ordered little state.[1]

Loango's reputation was constructed from an exuberant wealth of sixteenth- and seventeenth-century sources.[2] Throughout the eighteenth century, too, the Loango state and its coastline continued to be the object of a particular interest to Western scholars and the subject of many published reports and accounts, in part because of the weird life forms thought to flourish within its borders, and an interest in the monsters of Loango was to continue until the dawn of the twentieth century. The reports that came back to Europe were eagerly awaited and contributed to eighteenth-century naturalists' attempts to decipher the world.[3]

The period of the Enlightenment may have been an era of demystification of religion and politics, but the fascination with unnatural phenomena and "monstrous" human deformation continued in publicistic writing as well as *belles lettres*. Diderot's "Jeux de la Nature et Monstres," which appeared in the 1777 supplement to the *Encyclopédie*, understood that monsters could and did occur. The problematic of hybridity and radical otherness that had troubled St. Augustine was still an irritant in the eighteenth century. How should monsters be classified? Were they simply freaks or wonderful creatures of nature? How could Siamese twins, dwarfs, or albinos, for instance, be considered? Were they abnormalities or did they constitute separate species of humankind? Were the reports of monstrous and exceptional births revealing of something, as earlier generations of thinkers had assumed, perhaps of impure thoughts on the part of their mothers? In Loango, it was known, for instance, that a pregnant African woman was so shocked at the unexpected appearance of a white person that she gave birth to a white child.[4]

Questions asked about monsters were similarly asked of hybrids. A cleric of the Dominican order on the Caribbean island of Saint-Domingue thought of hybrid mixed-race children, with a white and black parent, quite literally as monsters and a "third species of men." Beneficial or positive hybridity, cultural or biological, was impossible in this colonial context. Monstrosity was the only outcome of the mixing of races. Absorbing all that was bad, from blacks and whites, hybrids were a people apart, a monstrous race. In his controversial essay "Occasional Discourse on the Negro Question" (1849), reprinted as a pamphlet four years later as "Occasional Discourse on the Nigger Question," Thomas Carlyle (1795–1881), the indefatigable Scottish historian, philosopher, and social commentator, the great defender of existing order and structures, prophesied that liberal attitudes toward slavery and, among other things, the mingling of races, would lead to "progenies and prodigies; dark extensive moon-calves, unnameable abortions, wide-coiled monstrosities, such as the world has not seen hitherto!" (Young.1995 pp.5–6; Shelford.2013).

Loango had attracted attention as a locus of the exotic, monstrous, and unnatural long before Africans became stock entertainment in European cities. For centuries it had been the locus par excellence of terrifying creatures, which were minutely described by travelers who often incorporated earlier material from classical and medieval sources. The Dutchman Olfert Dapper described the fearsome pongos, which had a close resemblance to men but were thicker-set and taller. The pongo became a potent symbol of the many questions provoked on the colonial frontier in part through colonial desire and sexual fear. The belief in "the preference of the Oranootan for the black women," in Thomas Jefferson's infamous words, was widespread and was an effective way of controlling and dehumanizing black women. The trope of pongos dragging off black females and producing exotic hybrids lived on. Eighteenth-century cultural debates about amalgamation (the newer term "miscegenation" was not invented until 1864) and hybridity, which had been going on for centuries, were often directed at what was perceived as the gray area between humanity and the animal kingdom, and this continued late into the nineteenth century. In 1868 *The American Cyclopædia*, much of which had been compiled during the American Civil War, revealed that stories of pongos carting off negro women "long discredited as travelers' exaggerations, seem now to be authenticated, beyond the possibility of doubt." The hybrid products of these unions had always been culturally troublesome. A common way of imagining the product of these closely described encounters, full of latent sexual interest, was to revert to earlier paradigms of hybridic otherness. Christoph Girtanner (1760–1800), the Swiss writer and scientist, wrote of "negresses who consorted with ... monkeys and were impregnated by them and bore monsters." Jean-Jacques Rousseau (1712–1778), the French Swiss-born philosopher, believed that the pongo could be perfected and attain full humanity, which has been taken by some scholars as suggesting that Rousseau anticipated Darwinian models of human evolution (Moran.1995; Rousseau.2012; Hund.2015).[5]

Quite apart from the famous pongo there were other equally strange creatures in the monster-rich country of Loango, including the embamba, which had a deadly sting in its tail. Like the basilisk of the medieval bestiaries, the embamba could kill a man with a single look, even without using its fatal sting.[6] There was also a blue and green scaled creature the size of a ram with the wings of a dragon, a long tail, and in its snout several rows of razor-sharp teeth. Filippo Pigafetta (1533–1604), the Italian historian and explorer, recorded the existence of empachas, which had red skin and black horns and whose breath was as deadly to other creatures as it was to man. Not to be outdone, in his *Istorica descrizione de Tre Regni: Congo, Mantamba et Angola* (Bologna, 1637), Giovanni Antonio Cavazzi da Montecuccolo (1621–1678), the Italian Franciscan missionary, described creatures that roamed the Loangan forests with two heads, one at each end (Pigafetta.1591; Randles.2013; La Gamma.2015).

Perhaps the most startling revelation about the inland territories of Loango—what one French writer unsurprisingly called this "terrible region"—came from the abbé Liévin-Bonaventure Proyart (1743–1808), the prolific anti-revolutionary French writer and cleric.[7] In *Histoire de Loango, Kakongo et autres royaumes d'Afrique* (1776) (A History of Loango, Kakongo, and Other African Kingdoms), he wrote of French missionaries who had witnessed the tracks of an enormous creature, which for the next two hundred years would persuade some people of the existence in the unexplored hinterland of Loango of the last living dinosaurs on the face of the earth (Pinkerton.1814; La Gamma.2015).[8]

It was not only spectacular creatures, drawn in part from medieval bestiaries and in part from fertile imaginations, that made Loango such a complex space in the Western imaginaire. Its most disturbing feature was precisely the fact that in Loango the distinction between the human and animal world was so blurred.[9] Animal-like humans, such as the pongo, revealed the immanent fear of biological hybridity as well as the fear of African sexuality in early modern Europe. Guy de la Brosse (1586–1641), the French botanist and doctor, one-time physician to King Louis XIII, noted that Loango was the place par excellence for monsters because women there regularly had sexual relations with powerful, well-endowed apes. There was one Loango woman who allegedly had spent three whole years with such a creature. In the jungles of Loango, Pieter van den Broecke observed the issue of such unions, "*hommes sauvages*," complete with long tails. Even the normal inhabitants of Loango were marked by the unusual and by the hybrid: The sixteenth-century Portuguese explorer Duarte Lopez had seen the blackest of negroes with bright red hair in the area. A further oddity was noted in 1774 by the industrious Lord Kames. It was clear to him that there was something in the very air of Loango that transformed the normal and expected into the monstrous and exceptional. He observed that there were Europeans who had landed along the coast and that the "descendants of those polished Europeans have become, both in their persons and in their manners, more like beasts than like men." Loango clearly was capable of turning men into monsters. A place of endless taboos and fetishes, the very fabric of normal life in Loango seemed to be utterly different (Pigafetta.1591; Kames.1774).

One of the Loango hybrids that most fascinated Europeans was the "white negro." Barely any other African marvel had the same power to draw gaping crowds, and "white negroes" would be exhibited throughout Europe until way into the twentieth century. The first description of the Loango white negroes, known as dondos, was provided by an Englishman, Andrew Battell. "These are the king's witches, and are brought up in witchcraft, and always wait on the king. There is no man that dare meddle with these dondos. If they go to the market, they may take what they list, for all men stand in awe of them. The king of Longo has four of them" (Battell.1905 p.48). The armchair traveler Olfert Dapper (1636–1689) noted that in Loango there were "certain white men" who

> at a distance seem like our Europeans having not only gray eyes, but red or yellow Hair; yet coming nearer, the discovery grows easy; for they have not a lively colour, but white, like the Skin of a dead Corps, and their Eyes as it were fixed in their Heads, like people that lie a dying: the sight they have is but weak and dim, turning the Eye like such as look asquint, but at night they see strongly, especially by Moon-shine. (Curran.2011 p.88)

Dapper claimed that the dondos were in a state of constant war with the blacks. For this reason, blacks did not allow the white negroes to procreate, for fear that they would multiply and threaten the state, and that in order to avoid miscegenation they were hunted down like animals. In essence, as Curran puts it, the case of white negroes seemed "to confirm a long-standing belief that nature escaped its conventional boundaries in Africa" (Curran.2011 p.88). For this reason the excitement generated by the phenomenon of the white negro spread far beyond the confines of Africa. (See also *General Collection of Voyages and Travels*.1745; Dodounou.2011.)

In 1744, a white negro child was brought from somewhere in Africa to Paris. Pierre Louis Moreau de Maupertuis (1698–1759), the brilliant French mathematician and philosopher, at the time president of the *Académie des sciences* and a member of the *Académie française*, was naturally one of the first to see "this prodigy," for before being exhibited in the splendid Hôtel de Bretagne on the Rue de la Chaise, it was first shown in a private house. Maupertuis was immediately asked to write a book about this remarkable phenomenon. Published the same year, *Dissertation physique à l'occasion du nègre blanc* summed up what was known at the time of the mechanics of procreation and heredity. He argued that the hybridity of the white negroes did not actually violate any laws of nature. This hybrid was certainly human. Indeed, the white negro provided clear and exciting proof of the original color of man (Maupertuis.1744).

Voltaire (1694–1778) saw the child shortly afterward and disagreed. The monstrous little "white Moor" was certainly not fully human. He was intrigued by the "little white animal" he saw at the Hôtel de Bretagne, with its remarkable pink eyes, the iris covered in a yellow membrane, which would imply that the colors it saw would be different from the ones humans perceived. If such animals ever produced a Newton, he observed drily, he would produce optical principles "very different from ours." Intended to live in caves, like St. Augustine's troglodytes, these curious animals, whose "principal habitat" was Loango, had longer, straighter ears than humans. For Voltaire, whites, blacks, and these white negroes were "*races entièrement differentes*" (entirely different races) (Voltaire.1879). John Hunter (1728–1793), the eminent Scottish surgeon and fellow of the Royal Society, contributed to the excitement by claiming that the white negro's importance was that it provided proof of the original *black* color of man. This was, in part, because "many black animals will breed white ones accidentally, but no whites breed black ones" (White.1799 p.100).

The real fascination of the dondos for Enlightenment scholars was the simple question of their color and how they came by it. Andrew Battell had observed that dondos, while being born of black parents, were, for reasons unknown, as white as any white man. Almost two hundred years later this transformation from black to white was still a mystery. "Scholars," explained Diderot, "have been at a loss to understand from where the color of white negroes comes. Experiment has made it known that it could not be from the commerce of whites with negresses, since this only produces mulattos." Diderot noted that

> Some have thought that the white negroes came from monstrous commerce between the large monkeys of the country and negresses, but this belief seems unlikely, given that it is assured that these white negroes are capable of propagating themselves. Whatever it may be, it appears that we do not know of all the varieties and quirks of nature. Perhaps the interior of Africa, so little known to Europeans, contains numerous peoples of a kind entirely unknown to us.

For Diderot it was clear that in Loango and its immediate hinterland, almost anything was possible (*Encyclopédie of Diderot and d'Alembert*.1765 p.79).

The publication of the first volume of the German equivalent of the *Encyclopédie*—the 242-volume *Oekonomische Encyklpädie*—appeared in

1773. It was compiled by the German encyclopedist Johann Georg Krünitz (1728–1796), who died in Berlin while working on the seventy-third volume (the preface noted that he had reached the entry for "corpse"). It goes without saying that Loango was discussed in his magnum opus as it had been in so many other Enlightenment works. The thirty-first volume of the *Encyklopädie*, which was not published until 1800, dealt at some length with the royal town of Loango and particularly its mysterious and strangely pigmented dondos, which were part of the wondrous alternative reality of the Loango coast. They were considered to be a completely separate and monstrous race. They could not be the natural result of relations between white men and negresses, because such a union would only produce mulattos. They could not be the result of union between apes and black women, because the resulting hybrid offspring, like monsters in general, would be unfertile, while white negroes were understood to be capable of reproduction (Browne.1850).

This corner of Africa seemed to be a realm dominated by blackness. The abbé Grégoire observed in 1808 that Blumenbach, "the learned scholar of Göttingen," had argued that "in Guinea, not only men, but dogs, birds and above all the fowl are black." The abbé also turned for support in this to a recently published book—*An Analytical Inquiry Into the Principles of Taste* (1806)—by the English aesthete, writer, collector. and color theorist Richard Payne Knight (1750–1824). Knight claimed, following the Scottish surgeon and race theorist John Hunter, that original man was black and that the color black was the original color of the primitive race in all animals (Grégoire.1808).

And yet here, where everything was allegedly black, there was also a confusing profusion of color hybridity. Loango was a place where hybridity challenged expected norms and posed difficult questions. But it was outlandish for other reasons. In *The Principles of Sociology* (1898) Herbert Spencer (1820–1903), the English polymath and philosopher, who in the 1870s was perhaps the most authoritative intellectual figure in the Western world, deplored a country where a king was obliged to kill his son and have him quartered just because that son happened to see his father drink. Sigmund Freud, in *Totem and Taboo* (1919), complained that the more powerful a king of Loango became the more taboos surrounded him until the point came when he was suffocated by them.

These accounts of radical difference, grotesque barbarity, replete with a remarkable array of hybrids, monsters, and successors of the "monstrous races," created a new and awful world. Until the twentieth century wild men, apes, satyrs, and monstrous races were, in the Lévi-Straussian phrase, "good to think." They provided ready-made categories into which could be inserted all sorts of poorly understood "others." Loango with its long-eared, red-eyed, white Moors or dondos possibly the product of "monstrous commerce" between apes and women; pongos, Lord Kames's magically transformed Europeans, great apes with human consorts; dragons, ferocious serpents, dinosaurs; magic and warring nocturnal factions, was about to produce another extraordinary hybrid. This new hybrid, which would mystify the scholarly world for generations to come, as the pongos and dondos had done for so many centuries, was inserted into the elaboration of Loangan marvels, freaks, and wonders in Johann Georg Krünitz's great encyclopedia almost as an afterthought.

4
The Loango Turn

"There are black Jews here *too*, who are not part of nature's deviants, but constitute a distinct class of people" (Krünitz.1804 p.778). So read the entry right at the end of the seventy-ninth volume of *Oekonomische Encyklopädie* in a section dealing with Loangan marvels and freaks. In addition to white negroes, pongos, and all the other oddities and hybrids, there were also black Jews in this remarkable kingdom. Krünitz did not reveal the source of his startling information, but it was undoubtedly a book entitled *Geschichte der Mission der Evangelischen Brueder auf den Caraibischen Inseln St. Thomas, St. Croix, St. Jan* (A History of the Mission of the Evangelical Brethren on the Caribbean Islands of St. Thomas, St. Croix and St. John), which had been published a few years before, in 1777, in Barby, which at the time formed part of the Electorate of Saxony. The "Evangelical Brothers" of the title, otherwise known as the Moravian Brothers, were engaged in missionary work among African slaves in the Danish Caribbean colonies.

Its author, Christian Georg Andreas Oldendorp (1721–1787),[1] reported, on the evidence of a Loangan slave, that

> there are black Jews in Loango, who celebrate the Sabbath so stringently that they do not speak a word all day. They live scattered all over the place and engage in trade. Whether they are exactly the same in appearance as the others or not, they are certainly similar to the other negroes; they are so despised by them that they do not eat with them. They have their own burial place, which is far away from the homes of the negroes. Their graves are made of masonry and adorned with figures of serpents and lizards painted on by those who come to bury the corpse. This seems ridiculous to the negroes. As the latter custom is so unlike Jewish usage perhaps we can assume that it is not unlikely that the *lettering or letters* on the Jewish tombs appear to the negroes like serpents and lizards.[2] (Oldendorp.1777 p.287)

Africa was uniquely productive of hybrids and, as we have seen, for Europeans, Loango was one of the places where hybrids could most reasonably be expected to flourish. Oldendorp's hybrid, a new type of Jew, an actual black, negro Jew, was yet another Loangan marvel. It might have been a hybrid between blacks and white Jews, or perhaps an indigenous and novel breed of Jew, that had developed, as a result of climate or other factors, over a very long period. Whatever produced this new hybrid, its appearance caused quite a stir in scientific circles.[3]

For the hundred years following the publication of Oldendorp's book no new cultural or historical information about the cause of this stir—Loango's black Jews—entered the scholarly or general literature. Indeed, there were those who cast doubt on their very existence and on Oldendorp's reliability. In 1803 Theophil Friedrich Ehrmann (1762–1811), the German geographer and ethnographer, expressed extreme skepticism on the issue.[4] The scientists of the Enlightenment, as he well knew, were dependent on the accuracy of the reports of travelers and missionaries, such as Oldendorp. But information unfiltered and unchecked would hardly help the forward march of science. To stress this point, he wrote a savage indictment of Olendorp in *Allgemeine geographische Ephemeriden*:

> How on earth did the black Jews of Loango get into our geography? Oldendorp, who has never even *been* to Africa, reported in his West Indian Missionary History that among the negroes he interviewed about the state of their homeland, there was a Loango negro who told him that there was a people in Loango, who observed one day a week very strictly, who did not eat with others, who placed figures of snakes and lizards on their tombstones, and from this the missionary concluded, very prematurely, that these had to be black Jews ... Let us shine the torch of criticism on Oldendorp's statement ... how does it stand in all its nakedness?!— Consider: it is most likely, yes, in fact almost certain, that the negroes in Loango, who are distinguished by their customs, were not called Jews by the negro slave who reported the matter to Oldendorp (how would he have known anything about Jews?). Oldendorp hastily concluded from this unconfirmed statement that it was Jews the slave described, simply because the slave-narrator said that they observed their Sabbath day strictly, had no fellowship with others, drew strange characters upon their gravestones and so forth ... And what was the source for this important information? A single wretched negro slave with no culture or knowledge.

In a footnote he concluded sarcastically that "it is possible that black Jews live in south Africa; it is possible that Falashas of Habesch (as Mr. Bruns suspects, though it has not yet been proved that these Falashas are *real* negroes) also settled here; it is possible that these black Jews (as Sprengel presupposes) may be Jews from Portugal; *but geography cannot be built on possibilities!*" (*Allgemeine geographische Ephemeriden*.1803. xi p.435).

The doubts raised by Ehrmann seemed to be confirmed in 1849 by John Clarke, a Jamaican missionary with the Baptist Missionary Society. Clarke had been sent to set up a West Africa mission, although this enterprise failed. His subsequent book on the countries and customs of Africa mentioned that Oldendorp had claimed that there were Jews in Loango, but he noted that "no confirmation of this has been met with." There simply were, at the time, no real facts in support of the presence in Loango of Jews.

Even accepting the notorious delibility of facts, the absence of anything in this case was striking. In 1855, a report in *The Nautical Magazine and Naval Chronicle* noted that it was unlikely that the Jews of Loango were descended from Jews exiled to the island of São Tomé in the fifteenth century as was sometimes suggested. Such a descent was "unknown to the present inhabitants of the country, and it would have been somewhat singular if the Roman Catholic missionaries at Loango had not detected this circumstance instead of regarding them as a pure African family of Jews" (*The Nautical Magazine and Naval Chronicle for 1855*.2013 p.532).

However, in 1864, William Winwood Reade (1838–1875), the son of an Oxfordshire squire, failed novelist, and fairly intrepid explorer, who will come into our story again, visited West Africa and wrote about Jewish children who had been enslaved by the Portuguese and sent to colonize the island of São Tomé. The Portuguese had provided "all the unmarried males with a negress" and together they had created a "mixed race," some of whom had settled in Loango. Reade did not perceive anything specifically Jewish about this "mixed race." He must have given the matter some thought because he concluded that the disappearance of the Jewish element in this hybrid was something of a blessing, as far as western interests in Africa were concerned. A Jewish-negro hybrid—"a union of the Jew and the negro would be commercially speaking, dangerous to Christianity." What did he mean? One can only speculate. But perhaps he meant that an amalgamation of Jewish brain and negro brawn would produce a human type superior to Europeans, and thus a danger to Western business and enterprise.

Eventually, as we shall see, the existence of black Jews in Loango was conclusively proved. But long before this came about the rumored existence of Jews in Loango added to the existing millennium-old ambivalence about Jewish color and became a topic of enduring interest for ethnographers, geographers, naturalists, race scientists, and laymen, polygenists as well as monogenists. Oldendorp's revelation was timely. As we have seen, there was a deep interest in scientific Enlightenment circles in what made skin color, and under what circumstances skin color could change into another color. A striking illustration of this preoccupation may be seen in the title of a book by the French surgeon Claude-Nicolas Le Cat. *Traité de la couleur de la peau humaine en général, de celle des nègres en particulier et de la métamorphose d'une de ces couleurs en l'autre, soit de naissance, soit accidentellement* (Treatise on the color of human skin in general, on that of negroes in particular and of the transformation of one of these colors into another, either through birth or by accident) appeared in 1765 and summarized the various contemporary theories on the origins of racial difference, the reasons for the black skin of negroes, and the various hybrids, such as white negroes, that were then known to exist.

Initially, in a number of general works, such as Johann Christian Schedel's 1803 *Neues und vollständiges geographisches Lexikon für Kaufleute und Geschäftsmänner* (New and Complete Geographic Dictionary for Merchants and Businessmen), encyclopedias, and school geography textbooks, Loango's new and fascinating example of color transformation was listed alongside the equally mysterious tribe of Loangan white negroes. The *Handbuch der Geographie für die Jugend* (A Geography Manual for Young People) (1834) by the popular Catholic writer Joseph Annegarn (1794–1843), twinned Loango's white negroes and black Jews as striking examples of African hybrids. But it was not long before black Jews, the epistemological richness of whose existence would soon be evident, emerged, uncoupled, as a unique species of Jew, with its own significance and usefulness (Fabri.1784; Annegarn.1834).

The first reactions to Oldendorp's discovery came from orientalists, theologians, geographers, and Hebrew professors at the great German universities. One of the first was Anton Büsching (1724–1793), the author of the seven-volume *Neue Erdbeschreibung* (Earth Description) (Hamburg, 1754–1792). Büsching was a theologian as well as a geographer, and his first comments on the black Jews were from a mainly theological standpoint. Büsching admired the Hebrew Bible but was contemptuous of post-biblical Judaism. The Loango Jews stimulated some revolutionary theoretical thoughts about hybridity in the mind of Büsching. First, he suspected that the fact that they had degenerated all the way from white to black mirrored the radical racial degeneration of modern Jews, who had created such a debased form of Judaism from such a sublime prototype: A debased race brought forth a debased religion. It was also possible that these Jews had been turned black *because* they followed a degenerate religion: A debased religion brought forth a debased race. By some unexplained religious mechanism, white Jews had turned into black Jews. Nonetheless, as a practical geographer as well as a speculative race theorist cum theologian, he was puzzled. First of all, no previous author had ever, to his knowledge, reported the existence of Jews in Loango. In Oldendorp's brief account, as he pointed out, there was not enough information to be certain that this was really a question of degeneration. Yes, it was possible that "old or original" Jews somehow penetrated Africa and stayed there until such time as their original white color degenerated into black. But perhaps there was another explanation: Could it be that these "Jewish negroes, by means unknown, somehow acquired the Jewish religion?" This was a puzzle, as Büsching put it, which "still has to be solved."

It was not long before news of Loango's black Jews passed beyond the confines of the German-speaking world. In 1783, the British *Critical Review* attempted to provide a solution to Büsching's dilemma and suggested that the black Jews were in reality the descendants of Iberian Jews and "from these banished Jews, the black Portuguese, as they are called, and the Jews in Loango . . . are descended." In 1808, in France, the abbé Grégoire mentioned, probably in reference to the Loango Jews, that descendants of white Portuguese along this coastline had turned black. The existence of black Jews in Loango was perhaps to be expected, given the Jews' tendency to travel the world and, in addition, confirmed his belief that "black was the original color of mankind" (Grégoire.1808).

The controversy over the black Jews of Loango was addressed most comprehensively by the Danish-French pro-Revolutionary encyclopedist Conrad Malte-Brun (1775–1826),[5] who was one of the chief geographical authorities in post-Revolution France. Shortly after his arrival in Paris in 1803, he started work, along with the well-known French geographer Edme Mentelle (1730–1816), on the sixteen-volume *Géographie mathématique, physique et politique*, which was finished in 1807, and between 1808 and 1814 brought out the periodical *Nouvelles Annales des Voyages*. Much of his work on Africa was published, in English translation, in Edinburgh in 1823, and later in editions in the United States. Among other things, Malte-Brun gathered together a number of Enlightenment perspectives on the black Jews that had arisen since 1777. In his review, Malte-Brun observed first of all that the leading intellectuals of the day, including Büsching, had no problem believing in the existence of a race of black Jews in Loango. Johann David Michaelis (1717–1791), the famous Prussian orientalist and Hebrew scholar, and close collaborator of Büsching, was also open to the possibility. So was Eberhard August Wilhelm von Zimmermann (1743–1815), the well-traveled geographer, economist, and zoologist from the important intellectual center of Brunswick. Zimmermann thought that the negro characteristics of the Loango Jews had developed over a very long period, while Professor Kurt Sprengel (1766–1833), the German physician and botanist, considered these black Jews to be the descendants of Portuguese Jews whose skin had darkened over a matter of a few hundred years (Malte-Brun.1823).

As the century progressed, the Loango Jews were sometimes constructed as cultural hybrids as well as racial hybrids. Ernst Georg Ravenstein (1834–1913), the German geographer, was contemptuous of cultural claims made about the black Jews. In particular he described as "absurd" the claim that in "Makoya, near Chinchosho . . . one of the villages of the supposed Jews" they kept the Jewish Sabbath "when in reality they have fetishes and *casas da tinta* like their neighbors."[6] If they celebrated such barbaric rituals, so went Ravenstein's argument, the black Jews of Loango could hardly be considered Jewish in any way at all (Ravenstein.1900). Not long afterward, Richard Andree (1835–1912), the German ethnographer, geographer, and author of *Volkskunde Der Juden* (Folklore of the Jews) (1881), was also drawn into the discussion. By this time, the idea of racial mixing was considered to be productive of nothing but bad. Andree spoke of these Jewish hybrids as a "despised rabble" who slyly exploited the simple negroes of Loango through their sharp business practices. He proposed that Jewish personality and cultural traits had somehow been grafted onto the original stock of the Loango negro. However, at the same time he was convinced that degeneracy had eliminated all traces of their original Jewish "race." Inherited behavioral patterns had survived. Racial characteristics had been lost. He ridiculed the idea that Semitic features could be traced "in the physiognomy of these negroes." The idea that they looked or were Semitic, as some had claimed, was nonsense: 'There can be no question of a direct lineage, it is at most one which was initiated and nourished by continual degeneration."

In 1799, not long after the discovery of the existence of black Jews, the German theologian and orientalist Paul Jakob Bruns (1743–1814) of the University of Helmstadt brought another community of black Jews into this critical discussion. He suggested that the Loango Jews were in all probability "descendants of the Falashas of Habesch, or Abyssinia" (Bruns.1799).[7] Bruns was no doubt aware of the account of the Falasha that had been published just nine years before in *Travels to Discover the Source of the Nile* by the Scottish adventurer James Bruce, the laird of Kinnaird (1730–1794). In 1773, Bruce had returned to Europe after a dozen years of travel, first in North Africa and then in Ethiopia.[8] Many of Bruce's ideas seemed outlandish and were badly received. It was difficult to believe that he had eaten lion's meat, or that Abyssinian soldiers sliced off juicy steaks from the rumps of living cows, then stitched them back up again, or that there were black Jews who were ruled by black Jewish kings and queens in the Ethiopian highlands. A hostile review of the second edition of *Travels* complained about the unsettling cultural and racial hybridity of the people he described: "half Jews, half Christians; half savage, half-civilised; half black, half white, half cannibals."[9]

Bruce's account included one of the first mentions of the existence of black Jews in Africa, but initially, unlike the revelations about Loango, it had rather little impact, partly because few people believed the "Abyssinian liar,"[10] as he became known, and partly because Ethiopians were already perceived as "half black, half white" anyway, and the idea of Ethiopian Jews was not as unsettling as "negro" Jews (Thompson.2007; Moorefield.1975).

Connecting groups of negroid but "superior" sub-Saharan Africans with Ethiopia or with Egypt, with peoples who were considered to be closer to Europeans or Caucasians, to be "half black, half white" was a common trope throughout the increasingly racialized nineteenth century. By way of example, Thomas Edward Bowdich (1791–1824), a traveler in the service of the British African Company of Merchants, thought that the Ashanti were of Ethiopian origin, and there were similar theories for scores of other African ethnicities that were systematically constructed as being of Israelite or occasionally Egyptian origin (Parfitt.2002, 2013).

The notion, suggested by Brun, that the Loango negro Jews were connected to the Falasha of Ethiopia was revived a couple of decades later by the Jewish orientalist Ludwig Markus (1798–1843),[11] one of the founders of the German secular Jewish Studies movement, *Wissenschaft des Judentums*. Markus provided both the first considered Jewish reaction to the existence of the Falashas and the first Jewish reaction to Oldendorp's revelation about black Jews in Loango. By and large Jews had very little interest in black Jews in Africa. The struggle for political and social emancipation for Jews throughout the nineteenth century carried with it a struggle to be seen as European. To acknowledge kinship with black brothers living on the edge of the Congo rain forest or scratching out a frugal existence on the thin earth of the Ethiopian highlands did not serve Jewish political or social interests. Ludwig Markus, however, was the exception.[12]

Born in Berlin, Markus was active in early Jewish German Enlightenment circles. Once he moved to Paris in 1825, he became interested in the study of Ethiopia and particularly the Ethiopian Jews. For this reason the eccentric yet erudite Markus, who ended his life in the "lunatic hospital" at Chaillot, became known in the intellectual salons of Paris and its boulevards as the "king of Abyssinia."[13] In addition to reacting to Bruce's discovery of the Ethiopian Jews, he also provided a possible explanation of the origins of Loango's Jews. His article in the *Revue Asiatique* of 1829 was important because it was the first response on the part of world Jewry to the supposed existence of the black Jews of Loango.

The entirety of Markus's work on Ethiopia was never published, although a long extract from the *Revue* was printed in book form. Markus formed a general theory that Ethiopians had ventured south from their highlands and had created satellite colonies throughout sub-Saharan Africa. He claimed to have evidence proving that some of these colonies were Judaic, and that descendants of these ancient Ethiopian colonists were in his day to be found in the three black Jewish communities at the time thought to exist in Africa.

The research he was engaged in, as he put it, "has to do mainly with the Jews of Melli, Lameen and Loango, of which several Muslim, Jewish, Portuguese, German and English writers speak and on the links which exist between Ge'ez, Amharic and Agau of the Abyssinian peoples, and the idioms of the nations of Senegambia, Guinea and Congo, and the traces of the Coptic language which one encounters in the languages of the Sudan." Markus maintained that a "colony of Abyssinian Jews, mixed with other inhabitants of this country and of Sennar, established itself in days gone by in the countries situated to the south-east of the mountains of Senegambia and to the east of Haute Guinée."

He continued: "I even think that the Jews of Melli, Lameeen and Loango, about whom I have collected some valuable documents, came from Abyssinia and it is for this reason that one finds in the languages of the people of Senegambia, Guinea and Congo, so many Ge'ez, Amharic, Agau and

Hebrew words, which you do not find in Arabic" (Marcus.1829 p.16). It has not proved possible to trace Markus's "valuable documents." Perhaps they contained important historical information about Loango's Jews, perhaps not. It is a pity, of course, because we have little information about this community, which would become a point of reference in Western discussions of human origins, race, alterity, and color for the next hundred years.

The sparse information about this community provided by Oldendorp, Malte-Brun, Markus, and others constitutes little more than a footnote to Jewish history. However, metropolitan theorists were increasingly more interested not in *how* these Jews got there—or, indeed, *if* they got there at all—but rather in what, theoretically, their color had to say about some of the central issues of race. Many of the earlier controversial theories of human origins, as we have seen, had established Jews on the one hand and blacks on the other, as separate creations. What did this apparent hybrid have to say about that? Was this race a kind of monstrous race akin to the tribe of white negroes? This new hybrid was not like other easily explained hybrids for the good reason that it was universally acknowledged that Jews never intermarried with other groups. It might therefore shed some light on the mystery of human pigmentation. As the Jews of Loango would not have intermarried it followed that, unless they were converts to the Jewish religion, some other natural, external factor had led to their remarkable transformation from white to black.

There had been references in Western travel and other literature to black Jews even before Oldendorp's revelation. The existence of Jews in Cochin had been known among scholars in Europe since at least the sixteenth century, when Jesuit sources, such as the works of Alexander Valignano, referred to Cochin's Jews. The Dutch minister and traveler Father Philip Baldaeus (1632–1671) mentioned that there were Jews in Cochin who were "neither white nor brown but quite black" in his book of travels, which was published in 1671 (Cf.Fischel.1962; Efron.1994). And at around the same time the Portuguese rabbi Menasseh ben Israel (1604–1657), in a pamphlet addressed to Oliver Cromwell urging the readmission of the Jews to England, noted that in Cochin there was a Jewish community "one part of these Jews being there of a white colour, and three of a tawny; these being most favoured by the King" (Segal.1983 p.235). However, whereas there was some knowledge of the fact that some of India's Jews were black, this did not provoke any particular discussion among race theorists.

It was Anton Friedrich Büsching's *Geschichte der jüdischen Religion* (History of the Jewish Religion) (1779) and an article the following year in his *Magazin für die neue Historie und Geographie* (Magazine for the New History and Geography), as well the reviews of his book, that disseminated throughout the German-speaking world and beyond the idea that a color spectrum existed for the Jewish people and that there were white and black Jews in Cochin, black Jews in Bombay, and black Jews in Loango.[14] Georg-August von Breitenbauch (1731–1817), the German Enlightenment geographer, also helped circulate this information in *Vorstellung der vornehmsten Völkerschaften der Welt* (Presentation of the Most Distinguished Peoples of the World) (1786). In 1808, in *De la littérature des nègres*, abbé Grégoire made the point that there were good and bad types to be found among all peoples, including blacks and "Jews *of all colors,* as there were black Jews to be found in Cochin" (Grégoire.1808).[15]

Similarly, in 1812, Friedrich Carl Lang's (1766–1822) *Abriss der Sitten und Gebräuche aller Nazionen, oder kurze Darstellungen der merkwürdigsten menschlichen Wohnpläze, Beschäftigungen und Gewohnheiten in den fünf Theilen der Welt* (Outline of the Manners and Customs of all Nations, or Brief Representations of the Strangest Human Dwelling places, Occupations and Manners in the five Regions of the World) revealed that *"there are Jews of all colors, even very black ones* on the coast of Malabar, in the district of Rajapur [and] in Loango. They, too, call themselves children of Israel, circumcize their sons, and observe the Sabbath." Thus, following the widely disseminated discovery of black Jews in Loango in 1777, the news that Jews existed in many different hues rapidly became part of the store of contemporary knowledge, initially in Great Britain, France, and the German-speaking lands.

Breitenbauch's *Vorstellung* featured a list of all the Jewish communities throughout the world of which he was aware. The list included the recently discovered Jews of Loango, the black Jews of Cochin in southern India, and the Falashas of Ethiopia. In Loango, he wrote, "there are black Jews, who perhaps were originally negroes, who adopted the Jewish religion." He applied the same strictures to the black Jews of Cochin, whom he described as converts, descended from Indian slaves. However, the Abyssinian Jews he considered to be "authentic" Jews, who had come from "Saba" in Arabia and in his day were living under the name of "Falasha" in "Dembea und Samen" (Breitenbauch.1785 p.12).

A little later, in 1793, he went on to publish a map of the various populations of the world, which superimposed two partly overlapping systems, one containing seven or eight *Bildungen* (formations) on the basis of physique, and the other on the basis of seven colors. In this essentially polygenetic work Breitenbauch referred to Oldendorp's black Jews but was careful to stipulate that they were not necessarily anything to do with the Jewish "race." His conviction that the black Jews of Cochin and the black Jews of Loango were descended from converts and slaves prevented either community from having to be presented as hybrids, which would not fit into his polygenist conviction that all races were immutable.

A different perspective was produced in 1803 by Georg Friedrich Hildebrandt (1764–1816), the Enlightenment chemist, sleep expert, and naturalist from the University of Göttingen. In his school textbook *Lehrbuch der Anatomie des Menschen* (Textbook of Human Anatomy) he too introduced the topic of Jews "of color." We do not know if he had come across the black Jews of Loango. However, his theories about color and pigmentation required an endogamous group that (1) could be counted on never to mix with surrounding populations, (2) was to be found in different parts of the world, and (3) was white in one place yet black in another. As he put it: "The Jews prove the effect of climate more than any other . . . because they only marry among themselves, therefore mixing with other nations will have contributed nothing to their transformation." He observed: "The Jews scattered everywhere are whiter in northern areas, and darker in southern ones. In our areas, for instance, are to be found many Jews who are particularly white, as white as other Europeans. In Abyssinia the Jews are as black as negroes" (Hildebrandt.1803 p.325).[16]

Hildebrandt explained that the color changes that had occurred in the case of the Ethiopian Jews, from white to black, took a long time but nonetheless were entirely due to climate. "The Jews' case," he wrote, "shows that the changes in their progeny move very slowly and gradually." In the same way, African slaves taken to North America remained perfectly black for a number of generations, but then under the influence of climate they could be expected to turn white. In the case of admixture with other peoples, "black people with whites beget so-called mulattoes, in cold as in hot climates, who are yellow. Mulattoes with Mulattoes beget yellow children. Mulattoes with blacks beget children who are blacker, Mulattoes with whites beget children who are whiter and so forth" (Hildebrandt.1803 p.326).

An important 1813 work of medical classification, *Geographische Nosologie* (Geographical Nosology),[17] by the German Enlightenment epidemiologist and medical geographer Friedrich Schnurrer (1784–1833), expressed a similar conviction. He believed that the natural world had a great influence on the development of living organisms and that the transformation of the color of people was a prime example of this. Schnurrer observed that in West Africa Portuguese settlers had become black and that further south, in Loango, climate had brought about the blackening of Jews. These black Loango Jews, of a "negro formation" (*bildung*), who had achieved this feat of racial darkening, he described as following their religious rites with the same attention as in their homeland.

As discussions about color developed throughout the nineteenth century, evocations of Jewish hybrid communities, "the Jews of all colors"—Loango's black Jews, the white and black Jews of Cochin, the Falasha, or Jews of Ethiopia, plus other useful Jews of color, harvested from other parts of the world, whose numbers and sightings would grow throughout the century—became more and more important, for no less a reason than they helped to prove the unitary origins of humankind.

Unknown to themselves, the black Jews of Loango had a considerable impact on the intellectual world of the eighteenth and nineteenth centuries, in the long race wars around the origins of humankind and the various types of people. From 1777, and the first discovery of the black Jewish hybrid by the German missionary scholar Christian Georg Andreas Oldendorp, and the subsequent discovery of many more black Jewish communities, the idea of a Jewish racial and color spectrum, which had been proposed in medieval iconography, became firmly established. Loango's black Jews represented a fusion of negro and Jew, and the arrival of this hybrid was an important milestone on the path that led to a general conflation of blacks and Jews. They were largely responsible for an important "turn" in perceptions of Jews as racial objects, which started at the end of the eighteenth century and carried on, gaining force as it went, throughout the nineteenth and into the twentieth century.

5

"The Most Striking Circumstance"

Black Jews and Sustaining the Doctrine of the Unity of Mankind

The critical importance for race theorists of the black Jews of Loango, and growing numbers of black hybrid Jewish communities elsewhere, emerges clearly from a stray comment made in 1854 by Joseph Barnard Davis (1801–1881), a physician and fellow of the Royal Society. Davis was one of the polygenist British natural scientists who started thinking of racial difference not as a result of climate or other external agency, like the monogenists for whom climatic determinism was crucial, but as innate, unchanging, and biological. Polygenists increasingly looked for confirmation of racial hierarchies and signs of racial immutability in physiological aspects, one of which was the skull, interest in which started with the new discipline of phrenology, as postulated by the German physiologist Franz Joseph Gall (1758–1828) in the late eighteenth century. Measurable human features, including bones, head angles, and skulls, were fast becoming accepted criteria for measuring human difference and would remain so for well over a century.

Davis gathered 1,700 skulls from around the world—the biggest collection by far in Great Britain. Davis, who would eventually become one of the fiercest critics of the Darwinian model of organic development, believed that the study of the skull—"the palace of the soul," together with bones, would prove the immutable racial character of different peoples.[1]

For Davis, the polygenist, the anxieties provoked by the startling expression of hybridity represented by the black Jews of Loango were not very different from the anxieties provoked by such hybrids in pre-Enlightenment days. Hitherto, weird folk or bestial hybrids, who were neither one thing nor another, candidates for inclusion in the "monstrous races" of the past, provoked consternation because they challenged the expected norms of the world. For Davis and generations of race scientists, the same thing was true.

These Loango hybrids upset their cherished scientific views of how the world should be seen. Black Jews were a particular thorn in their flesh because of what they were taken to represent in terms of racial mutability. When Davis read *Researches into the Physical History of Mankind*, the most important English-language anthropological work of the pre-Darwin period, by James Cowles Prichard (1786–1848), he was struck most by one thing. In 1854 Davis wrote a letter to his polygenist colleague, the American physical anthropologist Josiah Clark Nott (1804–1873). "In the whole of Prichard's work," he wrote, "the most striking circumstance . . . was that of the change of the Jews to black" (Nott, Gliddon.1854 p.414). For him, as for others, a key point in Prichard's massively influential work was the issue of black Jews. For Davis the basic tenets of polygenism and the fixed, universal immutability and permanence of races was fatally undermined by the apparently magical transformation of white Jews into black Jews.

Prichard, a practicing doctor as well as an anthropologist, was of Anglo-Welsh origins. He grew up in Bristol, a port city that was a prosperous, bustling place, albeit somewhat in decline, that throughout the eighteenth century was the British end of the trans-Atlantic slave trade. Prichard's parents were Quakers and he shared their essential religious views. After studying medicine at Edinburgh University, where he came under the influence of the Scottish Enlightenment, he converted to evangelical Anglicanism in order to be able to pursue his studies at the University of Cambridge, which was closed to dissenters. However, his inner Quakerism remained an important part of him. His essentially anti-Enlightenment goal was quite straightforward: to prove that the Bible itself furnished a reliable description of the history of the origins of humankind. His concern, in particular, was to find definitive proof for the notion of the unitary origins of all the peoples of the world, as presented by the Hebrew Bible. He became the nineteenth century's most devoted defender of the Augustinian model of monogenism.

His *Researches into the Physical History of Mankind*, based on his Edinburgh doctoral thesis, was first published in 1813. It was subsequently published in a number of different editions, the last one appearing in 1837. In 1843 he wrote a more popular book: *Natural History of Man*. His defense of the biblical account of man's origins led him to trace back to a single source all of the races of men from their first appearance in the historical record. All kinds of evidence—linguistic, ethnological, literary, historical—demonstrating affinities between these human groups informed his work. He was a very considerable linguist. While a student at Edinburgh he learned Latin, Greek, and French. He went on to learn German, Arabic, Celtic languages, and Sanskrit.

A Bristol colleague of his once observed him speaking with hospital patients in Welsh. In addition, "It was said that he had talked Hebrew with a Jew."

His evidence took many forms and significantly relied, as did so many Enlightenment works, on the labor of travelers and adventurers who brought back useful philological, cultural, and historical information from the lesser-known regions of the earth. Expanded in its later editions to five volumes, Prichard's *Researches* was to remain the major compendium of ethnological knowledge in the English language until the second half of the nineteenth century. By the 1840s, however, there was growing opposition to his monogenist thesis. In a detailed and hostile review of Prichard's *Natural History of Man* in *Blackwood's Edinburgh Magazine*, the great monogenist's credo that "we are entitled to draw confidently the conclusion, that all human races are of one species and of one family" was torn to shreds (*Blackwood's Edinburgh Magazine*.1844, volume 56, p.314).

The origin of human pigmentation and the original color of man were issues of great concern for Prichard as they had been for Enlightenment thinkers. As we have seen, seventeenth-and eighteenth-century scholars had been fascinated by the unexpected color of the dondos of Loango, and Prichard, too, mentioned castes of white negroes who had been born of black parents. Throughout the nineteenth century the potential whitening of negroes continued to be a source of fascination.[2] Buffon, as we have seen, had argued that the natural and original color of man was white. He explained that it was between the 40th and 50th degree of latitude that the world's most temperate climate was to be found, and it was here that the most beautiful specimens of humanity were to be located. He argued that this was the area from which the original color of man must have come, on the grounds that the intemperate extremes were alien to the essential beauty and truth represented by the peoples of the temperate zone. However, he thought that skin color could change on the basis of environmental factors within a single lifetime (Harris.2001). This seemed to be a proof that the socially positive and advantageous development of turning from black to white could be achieved in the natural world.[3]

The existence of the black Jews of Loango was an evident proof of the opposite phenomenon—racial darkening—and so was the color of the other black Jews in Ethiopia and India. Was it indeed possible that black, not white, was the original color of humans? Richard Payne Knight (1751–1824), the aesthete and "man of taste," argued that "Adam in Paradise was an African

Black." And Prichard, along with the abbé Grégoire in France, also thought that the starting point in human pigmentation was probably black. He wrote:

> It must be concluded that the process of nature in the human species is the transmutation of the characters of the Negro into those of the European, or the evolution of white varieties, in black races of men. We have seen that there are causes existing which are capable of producing such an alteration, but we have no facts which induce us to suppose that the reverse of this change could in any circumstance be affected. This leads us to the inference that the primitive stock of men were Negroes, which has every appearance of truth. (Prichard.1813 p.233)

And elsewhere he thundered: "There are no authenticated instances either in Africa or elsewhere, of the transmutation of other varieties of mankind into Negroes" (Prichard.1851 p.343).

However, if Oldendorp was to be relied on, there was apparently an exception to this rule in the form of the black Jews of Loango, "whose physical characters have assimilated to those of the native inhabitants." Initially, Prichard was ready enough to rely on Oldendorp, on whom he lavished extravagant praise, even though Oldendorp's account got in the way of one aspect of his deeply held doctrine, and this "excellent missionary" was quoted frequently throughout the book as a reliable source on matters to do with African populations. In *Physical Ethnography of the African Races*, which appeared in the third edition of *Researches* (1837), he wrote:

> A remarkable fact in the history of Loango is that the country contains—according to a statement which was fully credited by Oldendorp, himself a writer of most correct judgment and of unimpeachable veracity—many Jews settled in the country, who retain their religious rites, and the distinct habits which keep them isolated from other nations. Though separate from the African population, they are black, and resemble the other Negroes in every respect as to physical character. (Prichard.1837 p.309)

Clearly this was problematic. If these Jews had not interbred with the negroes, which was a reasonable assumption as Jews were universally known to be endogamous, and assuming they had once been white, how could their blackness be accounted for?

Prichard's brief description of the Loango Jews was seized on by likeminded monogenists such as the Welshman Arthur James Johnes, county court judge, comparative philologist, and translator of the great Welsh poet Dafydd ap Gwilym. He noted in his book, which attempted to prove the unitary origins of humankind from a philological standpoint, that

> from the facts collected by Dr. Prichard, it appears to follow very distinctly, not only that Human Physiology is extremely mutable, but also that the transitions do not occupy a very long interval of time. Thus, Jews are resident in the African Kingdom of Kongo, whose complexions are as black as those of the native Negro population. (Johnes.1846 p.xxix)

In the sixty years between Oldendorp's discovery and the publication of the third edition of Prichard's *Researches* no traveler, missionary, or ethnographer had returned from west Africa with fresh information about the black Jews of Loango. No Jewish delegation had been sent to look into their condition. No merchant had recorded dealings with them. They had certainly been greatly discussed in German and French scientific writing particularly, but a question mark still hung over their authenticity.

As a result, Prichard, meticulous researcher that he was, started to doubt whether the Loango Jews were really a reliable proof of color change. In the 1851 edition of *Researches* he admitted:

> We are not sufficiently informed respecting the fact asserted by Oldendorp, on the authority of his black informant, that there are many Jews in Congo, whose physical characters have assimilated to those of the native inhabitants. We have, however, examples of very considerable deviation in the *opposite* direction. The descendants of genuine Negroes are no longer such: they have lost, in several instances, many of the peculiarities of the stock from which they sprang. (Prichard.1853 p.343)

Here Prichard is advancing his view that what he called "amalgamations" give rise not to hybrids, but rather to new races. One of his examples for this was the Barabra or Nubian people of the Nile, who, while originating from negro mountaineers of Kordufan, in today's central Sudan, and "exempt, as they are said to be, from intermixture with the Arabs, and other inhabitants of the Nile valley, have nevertheless, acquired and now display, physical characters of a very different description from those of the Negro" (Prichard.1853 p.343).

However, the Loango Jews were not the only Jews to suggest that color change from white to black was possible: There were also the black Jews of Abyssinia. Prichard claimed that this community, clustered around "Jews' Rock," formed part of an ancient movement of peoples, which included Egyptian Jews, into western Abyssinia, where they were now to be found. He wrote:

> It is very probable that Judaism was introduced into Abyssinia, particularly the western provinces, through the medium of Ethiopia and the kingdom of Meroë and Napata. . . . Egypt at that time contained a great number of Jews, and it is probable that both Judaism and the Egyptian idolatry were spread from thence by way of Ethiopia and the Nile into the different provinces of Abyssinia. (Prichard.1837 p.147)

His suggestion, then, was that there had been mixture between Egyptian Jews and other local peoples.

The other black Jewish community about which he had some information was the critically important community of black Jews in Cochin. Prichard noted:

> They hold communication with each other in their eastern colonies, which appear to be of one stock or migration; but at what era they reached these countries it is unknown. Their residence in Cochin appears to have been from ancient times; and they are now black, and so completely like the native inhabitants in their complexion, that Dr. Claudius Buchanan says he could not always distinguish them from the Hindoos. He has surmised that the blackness of the Jews spread through different parts of India is attributable to intermarriage with Hindoos; *but of this there is no evidence*: it is probable that the preservation of the Jews in these countries as a distinct people, is owing, as elsewhere, to their avoiding all intermixture with the native inhabitants.

Here Prichard clearly assumes that either the black Cochin Jews had always been black, or became black as a result of external factors, other than admixture with locals (Prichard.1855 p.132).

Few travelers had such impact as Prichard's source, Dr. Claudius Buchanan (1766–1815).[4] Under the influence of the evangelical Anglican churchman and former slave-ship master John Newton (1725–1807), Buchanan was ordained in the Church of England and in 1796 was appointed to a chaplaincy in Bengal. In 1806 and 1807, he traveled through south India and made the acquaintance of the Jewish communities in and around Cochin, alienating the Jews by obliging them to part with ancient Hebrew and Aramaic manuscripts. In 1811 he wrote his highly successful *Christian Researches in Asia*, which by 1813 had gone through nine editions.[5]

Like Oldendorp's earlier revelation about the existence of black Jews in Loango, Buchanan's description of black and white Jews of Cochin also did something to change the attitudes towards color and human origins in the English-speaking world. As the American historian John Efron noted, Buchanan made a contribution to modern anthropology by pointing out that there was more than one kind of "Jewish type" in the world. Of course, as we have seen, Buchanan was not the first to do this. In fact, by his time, the idea of "Jews of all colors" had been well established in scientific circles by Büsching, Grégoire, and others. Nonetheless, Buchanan's description of black Jews in India would be cited throughout the nineteenth century by geographers and historians, but particularly by naturalists, monogenist and polygenist alike (Efron.1994).

The regular invocation of the issue of black Jews in the last years of the eighteenth century and the first eighty years or so of the nineteenth had an unintended effect of emphasizing that the generality of Jews was *not* black. However, the intended consequence of such conclusions was to prove various racial points of exceptional contemporary importance.

The question of the impact of climate on skin color, as it was critical to the monogenist doctrine, was widely debated. Evidence for color change, as for many other phenomena, was assiduously collected from the writings of natural scientists but also from a very wide array of texts penned by travelers, explorers, and missionaries, like Buchanan, who had brought back information from little-known regions of the world.

The people who collated and analyzed this material were not always professional naturalists. Many were energetic amateurs. One such, with an interest in change wrought by climate, was the polygenist John Gideon Millingen (1782–1862). As a child he survived the Terror in Paris, where he met Robespierre. Later he became a British soldier serving at the Battle of Waterloo as principal surgeon of cavalry. When he was not engaged in medical matters, he wrote books about lunatic asylums and dueling, and in 1837 he wrote *Curiosities of Medical Experience*, where he commented at length on the polemic around the "external agency" of climate.

"Montaigne, Montesquieu, Buffon, and Zimmermann," he wrote, "have considered the modification of the individual and the degeneration of the offspring as the result of this external agency. Lord Kames, Hume, and many others have entertained a contrary opinion." As a convinced polygenist, he was interested particularly in the white Jews of Cochin because, despite the searing heat of southern India, their racial characteristics had not changed. Indeed, for Millingen they could not change: Their racial characteristics were pure and immutable. As for Cochin's black Jews, they should be considered fake Jews. He pointed to other groups throughout the world who, like the white Jews of Cochin, lived in hot, sunny places but who retained their original light color. These included "a race of fair people, near Mount Aurasius in Africa,[6] with red hair and blue eyes, . . . who are, according to tradition, descended from the Vandals. We find the red Peruvians, the brown Malay, and the white Abyssinian in the very zones peopled by jet-black races" (Millingen.1837).

It was difficult to navigate the puzzling testimony of all these black Jews who got in the way of the theory of racial immutability. In 1860 the Lutheran *Evangelical Review* noted that "a great number of witnesses testify that the black Jews in Cochin and Africa have become really black; others dispute this, we suppose that the truth lies between the extremes, viz. that they approach to black." However, Jews were not the only population to have undergone radical color change. "We can here give testimony," continued the *Review*, "upon the truth of which may be fully relied, which places it beyond all doubts, that Europeans in hot climes, become really as black as Caffirs" (*Evangelical Review*.1860).

How exactly did this transformation take place? Samuel Metcalfe (1798–1856), an American physician and scientific writer, proposed that the "Caloric theory" might have the answer. This was an eighteenth-century notion, which persisted at least until the middle of the nineteenth century, arguing for the importance not of climate, as such, but of heat. If you applied sufficient heat to an individual, even in a cold climate, over a period of time, the same color change would occur. Heat itself, it was argued, consists of a self-repellent fluid called "caloric" that flows from hotter to colder bodies. Thus, in his *Caloric: Its Mechanical, Chemical and Vital agencies in the*

Phenomena of Nature (1843), Metcalfe argued that any change in color was brought about not by the sun's burning rays but by heat.

A chief and critical proof of this theory was that if Jews, any Jews, were to finish up on the unbearably hot equator, their color would soon change entirely not because of the sun, which, in any case, they would do their best to avoid, but because of the heat. The fact that there were black Jews in equatorial Africa who categorically did not bask in the sun, or interbreed with the aboriginal population, was proof of this. He observed that

> Loango in tropical Africa, contains black Jews scattered throughout the country. It is therefore undeniable, that notwithstanding the rigid adherence of this remarkable nation to their original manners, customs and modes of living, their complexion is as various as the climates in which they have long resided.... There is also reason to believe, that in the course of two thousand years, and perhaps a much shorter time, the blackest negroes of central Africa would become perfectly white in such a climate as that of Great Britain and undergo a corresponding change in their whole organization. For it has been observed that, after the third generation, the descendants of negroes brought from Africa to the United States, are several shades lighter than their ancestors,—the hair longer, softer and less curly; the eyes more animated, the mouth smaller, the nose more elevated, and all the features more agreeable, with a corresponding improvement of the intellectual faculties, the change being much greater among domestic servants than field laborers who are exposed more to the sun ... I have also been informed by a highly intelligent gentleman of color from St. Domingo, that he has observed a considerable change of his own complexion, and that of his countrymen in general, after a few years residence in Paris or London. (Metcalfe.1843, ii, pp.66ff.)

Prichard's views on race and color, which were echoed by the likes of Metcalfe, were widely accepted. In 1845, two years after the publication of *The Natural History of Man*, a lengthy review appeared in *The Dublin Review*, an influential Irish Catholic periodical founded in 1836. The *Review* quoted an 1844 letter from the well-known Irish-French orientalist and traveler Antoine Thomson d'Abbadie d'Arrast (1810–1897). This letter was sent from Gondar, in northern Ethiopia, where d'Abbadie had encountered the Falashas, about whom he would write an influential and famous report.[7] He acknowledged Prichard's influence on him and explained the reasons for his hazardous journey to the Horn of Africa. He had been caught up in the great debate between polygenists and monogenists and had hoped to resolve some of the fundamental issues by going to see for himself whether the negro peoples really formed part of the human family.

He was particularly struck by some Ethiopian tribes that seemed to him to form a missing link proving there was a clear connection between "the straight-nosed Ethiopian and the groveling Negro" and therefore between the Caucasian race and black Africans, from whom, ultimately, they descended. He wrote:

> The learned Prichard had striven to prove the unity of origin between the Negroes and Caucasians. I did not feel myself satisfied with his reasons, and the desire of throwing more light on this obscure and interesting topic was one of the principal incentives which urged me into the heart of the African Continent. I have now come, on personal observation, to the same conclusion as Prichard; and if I am ever doomed to return to Europe, nothing will give me more pleasure than adding my slender stock of philosophical and physical observations to prove that community of origin *which revelation teaches, but which science has often doubted.*

Despite the view of scientists, d'Abbadie, now a confirmed monogenist, wrote that his recently embraced doctrine was based on the "modifying influence of climate on the physical system." The doctrine could best be proved "in the consequences which have resulted from the dispersion of the Jews."

For d'Abbadie, as for many others, Prichard's color argument, drawn from Jews worldwide, was critical. "The Jews have assimilated in physical characters to the nations among whom they have resided," wrote d'Abbadie, quoting Prichard, "though still to be recognized by some minute peculiarities of physiognomy. In the northern countries of Europe, they are fair or Xanthous. Blue eyes and flaxen hair are seen in English Jews, and in some parts of Germany the red beards of the Jews are very conspicuous. Those of Portugal are very dark... There are many of them in the towns of Cochin and the interior of Malabar." In addition, there were also the by-now-famous black Jews of Loango, whose complete authenticity d'Abbadie was more inclined to accept than Prichard. The Loango Jews

> retain still their religious rites and keep themselves distinct from other nations. Though separated in this manner from the African population, they

are quite black, and resemble the other Negroes in every respect as to physical characters ... It must be admitted that these variations in the Jewish people from the blue eyes and flaxen hair of Germany, to the dark complexion of Cochin and Loango, have a most important bearing upon the present question. (*The Dublin Review*.1845 pp.85–86)

Another British scholar who strove to understand race, color, and human origins from a more or less monogenist perspective was Sir William Lawrence (1783–1867), a craniologist and comparative anatomist. His *Lectures on Physiology, Zoology, and the Natural History of Man* (1819) were the means by which many of Blumenbach's ethnological concepts entered British and American race discourse.

Lawrence's brief defense of monogenism in his 1819 work was assured and confident. It would be some years before monogenists felt that they were on the back foot. A prominent surgeon—he became Serjeant Surgeon to Queen Victoria and President of the Royal College of Surgeons of London—Lawrence became a controversial figure when his book was denounced as atheistic and heretical. "The *odium theologicum*," he growled, "is the most concentrated essence of animosity and rancor. Let us not then open the fair garden of science to this ugly fiend; let not her sweet cup be tainted by the most distant approach of his venomous breath" (Lawrence.1819 p.7).

One of the sweet-smelling plants in the "fair garden of science" that was of great importance to Lawrence, despite his monogenist views, was the idea of the immutable purity of the Jewish race. In his famous 1819 lectures delivered to the Royal College of Surgeons he set forth his central question: "Is there one species of man only, or are there many distinct ones? ... How is man affected by the external influence of climate, food, way of life?" Lawrence certainly believed, like Prichard, in a single human species, but he differed from Prichard insofar as he placed a greater emphasis on racial, biologized difference. This Lawrence had culled from the French monogenist and comparative anatomist Georges Cuvier (1769–1832), who believed that Adam and Eve were Caucasian and that the Caucasians were the most advanced and beautiful race, while black Africans were the least developed on account of their *crâne comprimé* (compressed skull). Lawrence, like Cuvier and almost all of his contemporaries, believed in a biological hierarchy that placed the Hottentots of southern Africa at the bottom, closest to the apes, and Caucasians at the top. But although for Lawrence there were considerable differences between races, they were not sufficient for them to be regarded as separate species. But environment, all by itself, was never going to be able to create the degree of racial diversity there was in the world.

Consequently, he adopted one of the proofs that was customarily taken up by polygenists, namely that for thousands of years the Jews had remained "uncommonly pure" and this purity of race had not been compromised by "climate and situation." It followed that "the advocates of the power of climate have made very erroneous representations respecting these people; asserting that their *color* is everywhere modified by the situation they occupy."

How could there be black Jews as well as white Jews, if the characteristics of the Jews were immutable? Lawrence's solution to the quandary was simple. He wrote:

> The Jews, like all the native people adjoining their original seats, have naturally a white skin and the other attributes of the Caucasian race. In hot countries they become brown by *exposure*, as an European does; but they experience no other influence from climate. Their children are born fair; and the countenance and other characters are everywhere preserved in remarkable purity, because their religious faith forbids all intermixture with other races.

For him, like many others, one of the clearest living proofs of the Jews' "purity of race" and color, unaffected by climate, was again the white Jewish community of Cochin, whose ancestors "have preserved their native color and form amidst the black inhabitants of the country, excepting in instances, where they have intermarried with the Hindoos. Those of pure blood are called white Jews, in contradistinction from the others, who are termed black Jews." The black Jews of Cochin he dismissed as unimportant in this debate because they were "impure" and had mingled with other, lower races (Lawrence.1819 pp.352–353).

These issues were, of course, of great importance for believing Christians. Dr. John Charles Hall (1805–1878), the labor reformer, anatomist, and physician, who worked at the Sheffield Medical School in England, was an evangelical Christian whose faith compelled him to believe "that all the races of man are, as the Gospel clearly expresses it, 'of one blood.'" In his introduction to the monogenist Charles Pickering's *The Races of Man* (1853), which argued for the existence of eleven races, he declared that "the black man, red man, and the white man, are links in one great chain of relationship, and alike children which have descended from one common parent."

Hall argued that this "chain of relationship" in fact implied that *all* races could be absolutely any color at all.

In his introduction, titled "Analytical Synopsis of the Natural History of Man," he argued vehemently that the existence of white and black Jews was a fundamental issue, as it demonstrated the *flexibility* of races. All races were equally capable of change and mutability. Specifically, the racial and color spectrum of Jews showed that the Caucasian race, to which general category he believed the Jews belonged, demonstrates *"every variety of color, from pure white down to melanism nearly as deep as the genuine Negro"* (Pickering.1850 pp. ix, xlix).

Two years before Hall's "Analytical Synopsis," in 1848, Wilson Armistead (1819–1868), the erudite English Quaker who used much of his family fortune, derived from a successful mustard factory in Leeds, to fight the evils of slavery, joined the discussion about color and race. One of the main points of his book *A Tribute for the Negro*, much of it based on Prichard, argued that color, being skin-deep, had no particular racial significance, and that in any case all peoples, nations, and races were entirely capable of changing color, as a result of various external circumstances. For Armistead, Jews in general were the absolute proof of the mutability of races:

> Descended from one stock and prohibited by the most sacred institutions from intermarrying with the people of other nations, and yet dispersed, according to the divine prediction, into every country on the globe, this one people is marked by the colors of all: fair in Britain and Germany; brown in France and in Turkey; swarthy in Portugal and in Spain; olive in Syria and in Chaldea; tawny or copper colored in Arabia and in Egypt; whilst they are "black at Congo in Africa."

In general, too,

> the skin of Whites becomes, either wholly or in part, black. On the other hand, it is well known that the Black loses part of his original tint in a state of civilization . . . Other instances are recorded of Negroes, in different countries, without the action of any apparent disease, gradually losing their black color and becoming as white as Europeans. (Armistead.1848 p.64)

In defense of such transformations and against the notion of the immutability of race, Armistead cited the Enlightenment Czech anatomist Joseph

Thaddäus Klinkosch (1734–1778) and the Italian physiologist Leopoldo Marco Antonio Caldani (1725–1813). In his *Programma quo divisionem herniarum novumque hermiae ventralis speciem proponit* (Prague, 1764) Klinkosch had mentioned "the case of a Negro who lost his blackness and became yellow," and in *Institutiones anatomicae* (Venice, 1791) Caldani (who pioneered the use of electricity in the "physiology of the nerves") similarly described a black African shoemaker "who having been brought very young to Venice, had so far changed his color, as to be no darker than a European."

In addition to the shoemaker and yellow negro, Armistead noted that "there are throughout Africa several nations, unquestionably Negro originally, who have acquired handsome forms and faces, as well as lighter tint, in consequence of their living in mountainous regions, approaching to the temperate climate." Thus, movement from a state of ugliness and blackness to a state of whiteness and beauty was more likely than movement in the opposite direction. "Instances of white people who have become black, in consequence of migrating into tropical latitudes," he wrote, "are more rare, and not so distinctly made out." However, the scientific literature of his day had examples of such changes. He cited three further well-known and "accurately informed and scientific writers" who had given examples of transformations from white to black.

The first of these was Samuel Ferrand Waddington (1759–1829), an argumentative Kent hop merchant and polemicist whose claim to a modicum of scientific fame was based on his translation from the German of J. C. Goldbeck's *The Metaphysic of Man; or, the Pure Part of the Physiology of Man* (1806).[8] The second was Dr. Wilhelm Peter Eduard Simon Rüppell (1794–1884), a traveler in Arabia and Ethiopia as well as a naturalist (he claimed that giraffes had three horns). The third was the French soldier, explorer, and geologist Claude Antoine Rozet (1798–1858), who served as an engineer on the French general staff during the conquest of Algeria.

On the authority of this trio of experts he wrote that

> there are black races in Africa, among the genuine descendants of emigrants from Arabia. Detachments of the Arabian family emigrated, eleven or twelve hundred years ago, into northern Africa, where they have founded states of some importance, and, in some instances, they have passed into a perfectly black complexion; although improved in form and stature, and notwithstanding that they reside to the north of the Negro countries.

Indeed, in Fezzan "we have, with black skins, Negro faces, and woolly hair, a people descended from the white tribes of Arabia, and who still speak the language of that country."

The existence of black Jews in Loango was another example of this movement from white to black. "A remarkable fact," wrote Armistead, "in the history of Loango, in the empire of Congo, is that the country . . . contains many Jews settled in it . . . Though thus separate from the African population, they are black, and resemble the other Negroes in every respect." He added that he thought it likely that a black Jewish community in Africa, "the descendants of a colony of Jews, originally from Judea" (mentioned without any further detail by the well-known African-American writer and former slave Charles Pennington [1807–1870]), were also this community of Jews in Loango (Armistead.1848 p.65).

As the American Civil War approached, the issues of racial difference became ever more critical. Charles Loring Brace (1826–1890), founder of the Children's Aid Society, Congregational minister, and a pioneer in the development of the social services in New York City, was incensed by the "perverted argument for the oppression of the Negro." While not a professional scientist or scholar, he set out to redeem American scholarship in the eyes of European intellectuals by refuting, for once and for all, the polygenist doctrine of the separate origin of races that was being so warmly embraced in the American South and that will be discussed in the next chapter.

In *The Races of the Old World* (1863) Brace asked the rhetorical questions usually posed by polygenists:

> Who ever sees, they triumphantly inquire, a race-type changing? When has the Ethiopian changed his skin? When did a European ever become a negro? Where has man seen an American Indian pass into a white? Where, even, has a Jew, without crossing with other races, acquired a Greek or English form of features? Whoever hears of Englishmen or Frenchmen becoming black under the Tropics? Where does straight hair change into frizzled, or thin lips to negro-lips? Where is the process going on which shall convert one race to another? (Brace.1863 p.327)

These questions, the stock in trade of polygenists, he set about answering by using the example of the color spectrum of Jews. Toward the end of his book he wrote:

All races of men, so far as we know, are capable in time of becoming acclimated to any new country or climate; as witness the Jews living from the heats of tropical Asia and Africa to the cold of Russia . . . It is true that after centuries or ages of residence on a given soil or under a given climate a new physical type is formed, fitted for all its circumstances, which may not be easily and at once transplanted. . . . This Treatise has been full of instances of corresponding variations in recognized races. Thus what greater apparent contrast could there be than between the blonde Jew of Eastern Germany, and the black [Jewish] Arab of the banks of the Jordan—both now reckoned of one origin; or between the brown Jew of Abyssinia and the black Jew of Cochin China [sic] or the Great Desert? (Brace.1863 p.469)

Brace here introduced a new black Jewish community into the arsenal of colored Jews that could be deployed against the polygenists: the black Jews of the "Great Desert." He was no doubt referring to Jews from somewhere in today's Libya, who had been mentioned by James Richardson (1809–1851), a young English traveler from Boston, Lincolnshire, who in 1845 set off for Ghadames, the beautiful oasis desert town in what is today northwest Libya, and Ghat, further south, on the current border between Algeria and Libya.[9]

Richardson's journey was related in *Travels in the Great Desert: including a Description of the Oases and Cities of Ghet Ghadames and Mourzuk* (1848). One story that sprang from the page for monogenists like Brace, looking for fresh evidence, was that he had met a negro slave who had just returned from "Soudan" with his master. There in central Africa, said the slave, "the Black Jews keep the Sabbath and get drunk on that day. They drink *bouza* (or grain liquor). They also circumcise as we Mohammedans." Richardson was not sure how to account for "these corrupt, degenerate, black Jews, amongst the tribes of Central Africa" (Richardson.1848 p.293).

Discussions about the mutability and immutability of races and the proof-role of the black Jews of Loango, Cochin, the Great Desert, Ethiopia, and elsewhere continued throughout the century on both sides of the Atlantic. Sir Richard Owen (1804–1892), the renowned comparative anatomist and biologist, was another of the naturalists who followed Prichard's line of argument.[10] Owen studied briefly at Edinburgh University, without taking a degree, but this did not seem to get in his way, as he was elected a fellow of the Royal Society at the tender age of thirty. In 1842, he coined the taxon "dinosaur" and in 1862 was referred to by Gladstone in a speech at the House of Commons as "the great genius."

In May 1859 he delivered a lecture at the Senate House in Cambridge, "On the Classification and Geographical Distribution of the Mammalia," in which he emphasized the critical importance of the color of Jews for discussions of human racial differences. "With reference to the characteristics of color, which are extreme," he noted, "we have now opportunities of knowing how much that character is the result of the influence of climate. *We know it more particularly by that most valuable mode of testing such influences, which we derive from the peculiarity of the Jewish race.*" To prove his point that climate change brings color change, he produced yet another group of black Jews, this time in Palestine, who had been described by "trustworthy travellers" but had barely been mentioned in such discussions before.[11]

This group had degenerated from white to black. He wrote:

> There are some Jews still lingering in the valleys of the Jordan—a *low* race of people and described by trustworthy travellers as being as black as any of the Ethiopian races. Others of the Jewish people, participating in European civilization, and dwelling in the northern nations, shew instances of the light complexion, the blue eyes, and light hair of the Scandinavian families. The condition of the Hebrews, since their dispersion, has not been such as to admit of much admixture . . . We are thus led to account for the differences in color, by the influence of climate, without having to refer them to original or specific distinctions. (Owen.1859 pp.96–97)

The liberal German anthropologist Theodor Waitz (1821–1864) was one of the leading monogenist figures in the anthropological world of the mid-nineteenth century. A disciple of Johann Friedrich Herbart (1776–1841), Waitz collected ethnographic material from all over the world, hoping to prove, like Adolf Bastian, who will come into our story, the "psychic unity of mankind." Born in Gotha and educated at the universities of Leipzig and Jena, Waitz was appointed to a chair at the University of Marburg.[12] As an empirical anthropologist, Waitz labored to defend the unity of humankind against polygenism and racial determinism, which saw all of history through the lens of racial difference. However, like most if not all nineteenth-century monogenist theorists, Waitz believed in some kind of racial hierarchy, even if such a hierarchy was not immutable.

Thus, he argued that "the development of civilization is, with some few unimportant exceptions, limited chiefly to the Caucasian race" and that "all uncultured nations possess, in comparison with civilized nations, a large mouth and somewhat thick lips" (Waitz.1863 p.74). However, Waitz warned, prophetically, of the consequences of the polygenist doctrine. Eventually it would inevitably lead to wars of extermination. He wrote:

> *If* there be various species of mankind, there must be a natural aristocracy among them, a dominant white species as opposed to the lower races who by their origin are destined to serve the nobility of mankind, and may be tamed, trained, and used like domestic animals, or may, according to circumstances, be fattened or used for physiological or other experiments without any compunction. To endeavor to lead them to a higher morality and intellectual development would be as foolish as to expect that lime trees would, by cultivation, bear peaches, or the monkey would learn to speak by training. Wherever the lower races prove useless for the service of the white man, they must be abandoned to their savage state, it being their fate and natural destination. All wars of extermination, whenever the lower species are in the way of the white man, are not only excusable, but fully justifiable. (Waitz.1863 p.13)

For Waitz, as for other contemporary monogenist anthropologists, the change of color within a race was an absolutely critical issue. Waitz argued that "no matter what intermixing may have occurred, anyone who lived for a lengthy period in Guinea and is much exposed to the sun, becomes almost copper colored." Waitz did not have any personal experience of the matter but took it from the work of the French explorer Anne Raffenel (1809–1858), author of *Voyage dans L'Afrique Occidentale comprenant l'exploration du Sénégal etc.* (Journey in West Africa including the Exploration of Senegal) (1846). Raffenel, a naval officer and distinguished member of French geographical and ethnological societies, on a second journey of discovery in northwest Africa following his previous travels in 1843 and 1844, was captured and incarcerated by the king of the Bambara for eight months and was thus given ample time to write his second book, *Nouveau Voyage dans le Pays des Nègres* (New Journey in the Land of the Negroes) (1856). On the basis of his personal observation in Africa Raffenel stated unequivocally that "people of the Caucasian race who are for a considerable time exposed to tropical sun gradually assume the color of the negro" (Waitz.1863 p.86).

Waitz also quoted the German anthropologist and physician Franz Ignaz Pruner (1808–1882), usually referred to as Pruner Bey, another monogenist with some knowledge of distant lands.[13] Pruner, the author of *Krankheiten des Orients* (Diseases of the East) (1847), declared that after a while any European living in Egypt would automatically acquire "a tawny skin." In Abyssinia he would acquire "a bronzed skin," whereas "he becomes pallid on the coast of Arabia, cachet white in Syria, clear brown in the deserts of Arabia, and ruddy in the Syrian mountains; whilst the hair does not merely become darker, but acquires a softer texture, with a tendency to curl" (Waitz.1863 p.47). The closer Europeans were placed to the center of Africa, the more like negroes, in all respects, they became. The clinching proof of this theory was to be found among the Jews. Waitz wrote of the "interesting gradation of all shades" to be found among Jews "down to the negro-black." "West of Tomsk, in the Barabinsky Steppes," he explained, "they have a clear skin and light hair, which is uncommon in England and in Germany. In Spain, Portugal, Syria, the East Indies, and Congo, they exhibit different shades." There had been various ideas about the color of the Jews of Loango, including the theory that they were hybrids, descended from Sephardi exiles from the Iberian Peninsula. Reluctantly, Waitz acknowledged that perhaps they were "Jews, banished by John II, in 1492 . . . as Sprengel[14] asserts." But he insisted that the fact of having mixed with the "Negroes of St. Thomas . . . must not be considered as the *sole* cause of their altered complexion." In other words, climate had played a significant role in their transformation from white to black (Waitz.1863 p.47).

The question of the Indian Jews, black and white, from in and around Cochin, remained a thorny issue within the scientific world for years to come. They served polygenists and monogenists alike: Monogenists pointed at the Cochin black Jews and marveled how their color had changed as a result of climate; polygenists celebrated the white Cochin Jews and rejoiced that over something close to two thousand years, in the torrid climes of southern India, they had retained their original, pure white color. Even toward the end of the nineteenth century battles were still being fought over the complexion of this remote community, as may be seen in a heated and not unamusing debate that took place during a session of the Paris Anthropological Society in March 1863. The meeting was presided over by the monogenist ethnographer and biologist Jean Louis Armand de Quatrefages de Bréau (1810–1892).[15]

Quatrefages, while a staunch monogenist, nonetheless was hardly sympathetic to blacks and other non-European "inferior races." In 1843 he had labeled "the African negro" as an "intellectual monstrosity," although as the negroes' current condition was the result of climate, they were perhaps capable of change. One of the main subjects of discussion during the 1863 session was the "*coloration de la peau*" (coloration of the skin) (Staum.2003). The great debate included contributions by the German physician Pruner Bey and Louis Adolphe Bertillon (1821–1883), one of the founders of the French school of anthropology (whose son, Alphonse, an inventor of forensic anthropometry and a notorious antisemite, would play an important role as handwriting expert in the Dreyfus trial some years later).

In the course of the debate on skin color Bertillon noted sharply that the major issue of the black Jews of Cochin had by now, through the admirable efforts of the American polygenists and others, been put to rest, and that henceforth this tired and hackneyed case neither could nor should be cited in defense of the influence of climate, as it had been proven time and again that the famous Indian black Jews were nothing more than converts and were in fact racially Indians, whereas the white Jews were still the same beautiful, shining, pristine, white color they had been when they arrived in India from the Holy Land hundreds of years before.

There followed a heated discussion that finished with the chair, Quatrefages, coming back to the issue of the Jews of Cochin, but with a new argument. He ran through the case point by point, recalling that the famous American polygenist Dr. Josiah Nott, of Mobile, Alabama, had attempted to prove that in all latitudes the Jews had stayed the same, and that naturally he had had to confront the issue of black Jews. All the authors cited by Nott, he explained, were in agreement that the white Jews of Cochin had had nothing to do with the black Jews historically and that they did not intermarry. As far as the white Jews were concerned, he continued, no one was in any doubt about "the purity of their race." If his polygenist opponents felt any stirrings of elation at Quatrefages's acceptance of this stock polygenist argument, they were to be short-lived, for he was about to use the argument about the white Jews for his own monogenist ends.

"These Jews, who have remained so pure, have they really retained the skin color of their ancestors?" he asked slyly. "Do they really have the color that we see around us among our Jewish compatriots? Do they truly deserve the epithet 'white' in the sense we give the word in Europe? You will judge!" He then triumphantly produced the testimony of a well-connected New York rabbi, the Swedish-born Rabbi Morris Raphal (1798–1868) (his father had been banker to the king of Sweden). Raphal enjoyed a certain notoriety as he had published a sermon, *The Bible View of Slavery* (1861), arguing that slavery could be justified biblically; it had been predictably well received in the American South. But he had also expressed himself on the crucial subject of the white Jews of Cochin, and as a well-known rabbi, his testimony was worth something. We can well imagine the muffled cry of joy when Quatrefages first came across this critical passage.

"This," declaimed Quatrefages with a flourish, "is how he expresses himself. Allow me to quote the text. 'These Jews . . . still retain their Jewish cast of features, and though of dark complexion, are not black.' I shall translate this provisionally as: '*Des Juifs . . . conservent encore les traits de la race juive, et quoique dark ils ne sont pas black*.'" He continued:

> To be quite clear about this, the French reader has to be sure of the meaning of the words "dark" and "black." For the latter there is no doubt. It signifies *noir noir*. This is the expression applied by all the travelers to the blackest negroes of Africa; and many of them note that the blacks of Australia, the Melanesian negroes in general . . . are not black like the African negroes. The expression "dark" corresponds to our term *basané* and signifies the result of the undeniable action of the sun and the open air on white skin. . . . the term is often used to describe the Samoans or the people of New Guinea. These examples suffice to show that there is nothing in common between the color white, in the sense in which we use it in Europe, and the dark color of the "white" Jews.

Quatrefages had turned the usual polygenist argument on its head and presented the "white" Jews of Cochin as the latest monogenist proof-community and the best possible example of a people whose original white color had precisely been transformed by generations of external influence to something akin to black. Dr. Josiah Nott was simply wrong to refer to the skin color of these so-called white Jews as "white." They were only termed "white" "to recall their original color," even though "they do not merit today this description except by comparison with their co-religionists of more or less pure indigenous race."

> We may also note *en passant* that the correspondent of Nott makes exactly the same observations and in the same terms, on the subject of Jews of pure race in the Sahara and at Timbuctoo.[16] These too, he says, though of dark complexion, are not black. Thus, this expression, whose true value we can now appreciate, will apply for all those Jewish populations dispersed in distant regions with very hot climates. I have insisted on this story of the Jews of Cochin because it has given rise to contrary interpretations and it

seemed important to me to be very precise about the meaning of this community . . . not only the complexion but also almost "toutes les parties de l'organisme" are so striking that even Knox[17] was forced to recognize their existence . . . similarly the French race in the north of the United States has lost its (original) color, its hair type and the physiognomy which it brought from the mother country.

Quatrefages went on to cite M. Elisée Reclus (1830–1905), the distinguished geographer whose scientific work was primarily concerned with the interrelationship of man and his environment. Reclus, initiator of the antimarriage movement, as well as an anarchist and a nudist, had declared that in the Americas, "in the space of 150 years, Blacks as far as external appearance goes, have covered a good quarter of the distance which separates them from Whites." Struck by the distinct tendency of all the varied peoples who lived along the banks of the Mississippi to turn red, Reclus added that "if other influences do not balance those of climate, it is entirely possible that after the lapse of centuries the Americans will have the color of the indigenous Indians, whether their own ancestors came from Ireland, France or the Congo" (*Bulletin de la Société de géographie*.1863 pp.142–148).

The perplexing issue of color for which the black Jews of Loango and elsewhere were such a useful test case was still exercising minds toward the end of the century. African-Americans, having suffered the consequences of color more than most, were particularly intrigued by the issue. *The Afro-American Encyclopaedia* (1895) concluded, along with the century's monogenists, that color was the result of climate and nothing more. Again, the Jews seemed to be the best proof of this, and again the clincher in the argument were the Jews of Loango and southern India:

> Yet nothing is more easily accounted for than this difference of color among the same people, and even under the same circumstances. Climate and climate alone, is the sole cause . . . The Jews, however slightly their features may have assimilated to those of other nations among whom they are scattered, from the causes already stated, certainly form a very striking example as regards the uncertainty of perpetuity in color. Descended from one stock . . . this one people is marked with the color of all . . . tawny or copper-colored in Arabia and in Egypt; whilst they are black at Congo, in Africa . . . The Portuguese who planted themselves on the coast of Africa a few centuries ago, have been succeeded by descendants blacker than many

Africans. On the coast of Malabar there are two colonies of Jews, the old colony and the new, separated by color, and known as the "black Jews" and the "white Jews." (*The Afro-American Encyclopaedia.*1895 p.11)

Ever since the first known reference to the black Jews of Loango in 1777 and right up to the 1860s, black Jews, wherever in the world they might be and whose numbers and sightings grew year by year, were deployed in the first line of monogenist defense against the polygenists. By midcentury, polygenism, linked as it was with colonial fantasies of white supremacy, had become more politically expedient. A great deal suddenly depended on the ability of race scientists to defend polygenist dogma. In order to do this the monogenist arguments, substantially drawn from the existence of black Jews in the world, would have to be demolished once and for all.

6
Polygenists, Black Jews, and the Proofs for the Disunity of Man

The trend towards polygenesis seems to have started with Paracelsus. It continued by fits and starts through the works of Bruno, Vanini, La Peyrère, Kames, and many others and reached its zenith in the nineteenth century with increasingly specific accounts of the separate origins of peoples.

It was Charles White (1728–1813), the knowledgeable and scholarly polygenist, and a follower of Kames, who would set the scene for the insertion of Jews, blacks, and black Jews into the great origin debate from a polygenist perspective. Author of *An account of the regular gradation in man, and in different animals and vegetables and from the Former to the Latter* (1799), White was co-founder of the Manchester Royal Infirmary and an able and innovative surgeon.[1] He countered the monogenist argument of Buffon (that humankind consisted of one, and only one, species on the grounds that only members of the same species are able to interbreed) by arguing that different species, such as jackals and foxes, could in fact interbreed. Following Bruno and others, White argued that each race was a separate species specially designed for its own specific region.

Using a wide variety of physical metrics, from arm length to facial angle, he maintained that negroes were of a distinct origin and were descended from primates. According to White, humankind consisted of descending gradations. He observed that the most obvious difference between men was color. He wrote:

> Various are the opinions which have been entertained by the ablest naturalists, concerning the primitive cause of differences in the color of man; it has usually been attributed chiefly to climate: the extreme of heat, and likewise of cold, being supposed to produce the black color. But, this being found insufficient, some have added to it the state of society; comprehending under this head, the effects of diet, clothing, lodging, manners, habits &c. all which, it has been argued with much ingenuity, are

competent to produce the effect. Others have conjectured ... that diversity of color might be given to man and various tribes of animals, by the provident Creator, as a safeguard from their enemies.

He then set up the monogenist argument with the sole intention of dismantling it:

All those naturalists who contend that the color of the human species is caused by climate, advance that there cannot be a more striking instance of this than in the Jews. "These people," they say, "are scattered over the face of the whole earth. They have preserved themselves distinct from the rest of the world by their religion and as they never marry any but their own sect, so they have no mixture of blood in their veins, that they should differ from each other; yet nothing is more true than that the English Jew is white, the Portuguese swarthy, the American olive, the Arabian copper, and the African black; in short, that there appear to be as many *different species of Jews* as there are countries in which they reside."

White swiftly dismissed this argument by claiming that throughout the world the different colors of Jew could be explained not through climate but through interbreeding with the populations alongside whom they lived. But, in fact, it was not even necessary to use the interbreeding argument because no matter where they were, the Jews in fact had the identical color: They were "swarthy in every climate." The monogenist argument about the multicolored Jew was nonsense (White.1799 p.105).

Anticipating the argument of the monogenist ethnographer Jean Louis Armand de Quatrefages de Bréau (1810–1892) in 1863, White found support for this in the usual places. "In the suburbs of Cochin, a town in Malabar," he wrote, there was "a colony of industrious Jews" of a dark complexion, which was "the same complexion they have in Europe." Wherever they were, Jews were exactly the same color: brown. Climate had had no effect. The polygenist argument was thus saved (White.1799 p.104 note).

It was in the United States that the polygenist argument garnered the greatest support, particularly among the supporters of the Confederacy before and during the American Civil War (1861–1865), but it was popular elsewhere too.

In both scientific, literary and popular circles, in the first half of the nineteenth century, polygenism was becoming fashionable. In 1828 even Johann

Wolfgang von Goethe (1749–1832) had proclaimed that Jews, blacks, and Europeans had different founding fathers (Schutjer.2015). Prichard, the arch-monogenist, noted gloomily that polygenists were gaining followers among natural scientists in France and even among historians and antiquarians in Germany. In France polygenesis was supported by the naturalists Jean Baptiste Bory de Saint-Vincent (1778–1846) and Louis-Antoine Desmoulins (1796–1828), while the Franco-Danish geographer Conrad Malte-Brun (1755–1826) argued in favor of autochthony, suggesting that human diversity was both organic and primordial. In Sweden the anatomist and phrenologist Anders Retzius (1796–1860) concluded that different national skull shapes and sizes were proof enough of distinct acts of creation, while in Great Britain the controversial and embittered Scottish anatomist Robert Knox (1791–1862) and Richard Burton (1821–1890), among many others, were committed polygenists.

In the United States a group known as the American School was formed; it included major figures such as Josiah Clark Nott (1804–1873), Samuel George Morton (1799–1851), George R. Gliddon (1809–1857), and Louis Agassiz (1807–1873). It was encouraging for this group to note the progress their creed was making both in the United States and elsewhere in the Western world. "With optimism and a sense of accomplishment," Nott wrote to Morton in 1850, "it is gratifying to see what rapid progress Ethnology has made in the last few years—we have now daylight and fair play and the truth will soon be as fully acknowledged in this department, as it is in Geology and Astronomy" (Erickson.1986 p.111). During the antebellum years there was a sense that polygenism was cutting-edge science, that America was way beyond the old-fashioned constraints of Old World tradition and religion, and that therefore scientists were permitted whatever modern view they could scientifically justify.

Polygenist views contributed to the increasingly harsh views held by whites of African-Americans. Shortly after American independence ten of the thirteen states had permitted free blacks to vote. By the time of the Civil War, of the by now thirty states, only Rhode Island, New Hampshire, Maine, Vermont, and Massachusetts extended the franchise to blacks. Until the second year of the Civil War, Abraham Lincoln (1809–1865) himself was in favor of sending negroes back to Africa on the grounds that the physical difference between them and white Americans was so vast that they could never hope to enjoy equal rights. "What I would most desire," he declared, "would be the separation of the black and white races" (Reynolds.2008 p.28).

The American School achieved the apogee of its social influence in the United States just before the Civil War. But after the defeat of the Confederation, it withered and was "scathingly rebuked and accused of scientific casuistry in making the Negro a separate species to soothe a southern rationale" (Haller.1970 p.79). Moreover, the appearance in 1859 of Charles Darwin's *On the Origin of Species by Means of Natural Selection* also contributed to a reduction in the influence of polygenism in some quarters and to changing the nature of the debate on human origins. However, even after the theory of evolution was widely accepted, different forms of polygenism continued to thrive, even in the academy, for the simple reason that evolutionary scientists found it impossible to renounce an essentialist, racist perspective on humanity. Moreover, as we shall see, polygenism would have a rank efflorescence in the twentieth century, as it was adopted by many of the racial theorists of the Third Reich.

In the early years of the nineteenth century in Great Britain the strong commitment to equality of the antislavery movement fed into a deeply held, liberal, monogenist sense that all races derived from a common source and were capable of improvement and salvation. In 1866, the *Juvenile Missionary Magazine* informed its youthful readers: "You see that man, through all his varieties, has a common parentage" and therefore anyone of any race was capable of acquiring "the knowledge of reading and writing almost as speedily as Europeans." British Nonconformist churches adopted this view, though elements of the established Anglican church were not so sure (Evans.2016).

A major figure of Victorian Britain, the Anglican clergyman Frederic William Farrar (1831–1903), usually referred to as Dean Farrar, was attracted by the racist arguments of Richard Burton and other polygenists. He gave a sly and novel twist to the doctrine of polygenesis by arguing, in a typically Anglican way, that it was not necessary to believe in the genetic unity of man to accept the spiritual unity of humankind. In a paper entitled "Aptitudes of Races" read at the Ethnological Society of London in March 1866, he explained,

> I do not require the notion of a physical or genetic unity as a motive to philanthropy. Though but a single race should ultimately be proved to have descended from that great Protoplast of Eden, such a conviction will not shake the sense of universal charity in any mind which has only thereby been deepened in the belief that there is a far higher unity in the

fact that for every child of humanity there is one God and Father of us all. (Farrar.1867 p.126)

For Dean Farrar it was clear that the dark races of the world had different remote ancestors than Europeans. The same was true of the Jews, who for him, as for sixteenth-century polygenists, were the only issue of Adam and Eve.

Imperial setbacks, chief of which was the so-called Indian Mutiny of 1857, followed by the rapid expansion of British colonies in the "scramble for Africa" and elsewhere, contributed to a growing sense of British entitlement and racial superiority. The widespread feeling that the Anglo-Saxon race was superior to the dark races of the world promoted and justified empire, just as similar feelings in the United States justified slavery. In the human zoos that started to proliferate throughout Europe, Africans were displayed, often in the most humiliating way. Entire African villages were constructed to better show off Zulu warriors, who were shown in Great Britain from 1850 on. In 1855, John Conolly (1794–1866), the Quaker physician and reformer of the treatment of the insane, noted that "scarcely a year [passed] in which, among the miscellaneous attractions of a London season" one could not find "some exhibition illustrative of the varieties of mankind." This bounty resulted from the "commercial relations of England" with the entire world, which permitted all kinds of "opportunities of intercourse with all the races of men." In 1886, in Berlin, too, there were all kinds of people on display, from Sioux Indians to Bedouin to a family of African pygmies, the father of whom, at four feet six inches, according to the local newspapers, was "a giant in his own land." Dahomey's one-breasted female warriors or "Amazons" were exhibited in France, soon after their lands were taken by the French, in 1890. In 1893 over fifty Africans from different countries were exhibited at London's most popular entertainment center, the Crystal Palace.

The more exotic and unusual Africans were, the greater the desire to see them. There was a long-lived interest in African hunchbacks, giants, and pygmies, six of whom arrived in London from the Congo in 1906. They had been enticed from the Ituri rain forest, in the hinterland of Loango, by Colonel James Harrison of Brandesburton Hall, in East Yorkshire, a traveler, soldier, and big game hunter. They appeared at the Hippodrome in central London and a little later performed at Buckingham Palace. Colonel Harrison was onto a good thing: About a million people saw them before they were returned to the rain forest[2] (Green.1999; Friedman.2000; Qureshi.2011; Bruce.2017).

The way in which Africans were displayed did little to dispel the idea that they were innately inferior to Europeans. In 1895 Joseph Chamberlain, the British Secretary of State for the Colonies, refuted the idea of climatic determinism and pinned his flag to the mast of racial immutability by declaring that "this Anglo-Saxon race, so proud, tenacious, self-confident and determined, this race which neither climate nor change can degenerate... will infallibly be the predominant force of future history and universal civilization" (Eldridge.1996 p.108).

In this atmosphere, polygenism often became equated with a kind of obvious common sense, as a rhetorical and racially charged question from Robert Knox's biographer indicates:

> Looking upon the human family at large, were the Southern Islanders luxuriating upon their enemies' warm vitals or an occasional relish of "cold Missionary"—the Esquimaux peering out from beneath his bearskin coverings like a timid hedgehog, yet feeding with a forty-parson stomachic power, on whale blubber—the black-ebony African in his nude, chewing the sugar-cane—the countless families of deep olive, sooty, and ochre-red, grandly feathered and tattooed, some with noses rung like a Durham ox, others with lower lips fashioned like egg-cups, or seeking beauty in paint, mutilation, and deformity, fetish worshippers and other animalized anthropoids:—were all these sprung from the loves of Adam and Eve, and were they to be held of the same stock as Socrates, Galileo, and Newton? (Lonsdale.1870 p.286)

Politically, however, the doctrine of polygenesis was not without its problems. Clearly it served the pro-slavery lobby in the United States. But in Britain, and particularly before the 1870s, it was a potentially hazardous creed. In 1831, Prichard, the polygenists' greatest *bête noire*, explained that in Britain's multiracial empire the promotion of polygenism in the British press could hardly be allowed because of the "degree of odium that would be excited by it." Twenty-three years later, in 1854, Josiah Clark Nott, the slave-owning physician from Mobile, Alabama, claimed that on the issue of polygenism London newspapers were still "muzzled by government" and were not allowed to publish the truth. British *scientific* journals, he conceded, were starting to discuss the origins of humankind sensibly, to fly the banner of polygenism and "assume a bolder and more rational tone." But in the public arena the truth was being suppressed, although there was still some hope that "the stereotyped errors of Prichard . . . will soon pass at their true value," as they were beginning to do under the influence of American polygenist scientists in the United States (Nott, Gliddon.1854 p.52).

The most influential of the American polygenists, Samuel G. Morton, a Philadelphia man, was an important player in the vibrant scientific community that spanned the Atlantic Ocean in the first half of the nineteenth century. Morton, like his British opponent Prichard, was from a Quaker background. He studied at the University of Pennsylvania Medical School and became a member of the Academy of Natural Sciences of Philadelphia, which had been founded in 1812. Like many of his scientific contemporaries his interests were nothing if not varied: He wrote on medicine, paleontology, anatomy, geology, craniology, mineralogy, natural history, ethnology, anthropology, and Egyptology. Eager to prove fundamental and immutable racial difference between peoples, he made a collection of skulls from different parts of the world. Even larger than the collection of Joseph Barnard Davis in Great Britain, it was reputed to be the biggest collection in the world[3] and was known, by his colleagues, as "the American Golgotha."

Morton's belief was that he could determine the origin of a skull simply by pouring lead pellets into the cranial cavity and thus measure its volume. The bigger the skull, the more intelligent the particular race was. According to this measure, the part of the globe associated with the biggest skulls was England, China was second, and sub-Saharan Africa last. It is not surprising that on Morton's death in 1851, the *Charleston Medical Journal* could publish a much-quoted notice proclaiming that "we of the South should consider him as our benefactor, for aiding most materially in giving to the Negro his true position as an inferior race."

Morton's chief findings (refuted by the paleontologist Stephen Jay Gould in *The Mismeasure of Man* [1981]) were published in two books. The first—*Crania Americana; or, a Comparative View of the Skulls of Various Aboriginal Nations of North and South America: to which is Prefixed an Essay on the Varieties of the Human Species* (1839)—dealt with native American populations and set out his polygenist views. In the other—*Crania Aegyptiaca; or, Observations on Egyptian ethnography, derived from anatomy, history, and the monuments* (1844)—he argued that the ancient Egyptians were Caucasians and opened up a controversial field of comparative physical anthropology that would be of great importance for the rest of the century.

In Morton's racial hierarchy, the Jews were positioned below the English, Germans, and Anglo-Americans but somewhat above negroes, who occupied the lowest rung. As we have seen, in the pre-Enlightenment theories of Bruno, Vanini, and La Peyrère, Jews and negroes had been linked by their exceptionality, often on theological grounds but also on somatic and behavioral grounds. They were both outside the common run of humanity. For Morton, Jews were linked with negroes, as approximate neighbors in his racial hierarchy, and also because they both constituted what he imagined to be pure and immutable races. Much of Morton's evidence for the racial immutability of Jews and negroes came from Egyptian statues, reliefs, and images, which appeared to show that both groups were exactly the same as they had been three thousand years earlier.

After Morton's early death, two of his disciples—George Robbins Gliddon, the British-born American Egyptologist and diplomat, and Josiah Clark Nott, the slave-owning physician—spread his message far and wide. In the 1840s Nott had stirred controversy and, in the process, made a name for himself by lecturing on the ruinous outcomes provoked by racial hybridity, the mental and anatomical differences between races, and the irrefutable evidence for these providentially provided by Egyptian archeology. Indeed, Nott and Gliddon were responsible for developing this key piece of cultural evidence for racial theory, which would enjoy great popularity over the following decades. In the years leading up to the American Civil War, Nott and Gliddon produced a massive volume that was a monument to their mentor. *Types of Mankind: Or, Ethnological Researches: Based Upon the Ancient Monuments, Paintings, Sculptures, and Crania of Races, and Upon Their Natural, Geographical, Philological and Biblical History, Illustrated by Selections from the Inedited Papers of Samuel George Morton* (1857) was published six years after Morton's death and despite its size became an instant bestseller. The outspoken views of Nott and Gliddon on the inferiority of negroes were received with joy and jubilation in Alabama, and the South in general. Europeans, of course, took pride of place at the summit of their system of classification too. It was virtually self-evident that negroes were the most inferior of peoples, but how exactly to account for the Jews?

Gliddon suspected that Jews were not so pure in racial terms as others, including Morton, had suggested. According to him they had similarities to negroes, which arose from a certain proportion of negro blood. At the least, he thought, they had "not entirely escaped adulteration." Fully negro Jews like those of Loango, or the fully black Jews of the Malabar coast in India, reinforced the views of Morton and Gliddon that there was a significant commonality between Jews and negroes. Nott also harbored a suspicion that originally, long ago, Jewish blood had already been contaminated by negro blood. However, he believed that with the passage of time, Jews' racial characteristics had become fixed and immutable.

In 1844, Nott wrote:

> The difference to an Anatomist, between the Bushman or Negro and the Caucasian, is greater than the difference in the skeletons of the Wolf, Dog and Hyena, which are allowed to be distinct species; or the Tiger and Panther. Now can all these deep, radical and enduring differences be produced by climate and other causes assigned? It is incumbent on those who contend for such an opinion, to show that *such changes either have taken place, or that similar changes in the human race are now in progress.* (Nott.1844 p.25)

The monogenist argument that "Jews of all colors" provided the evidence for such changes was, of course, not acceptable. It was inconceivable that pure Jews could in recent centuries have turned into something else, and therefore the only way to account for fully black Jews, in Africa, India, or elsewhere, was that they had "intermixed with the natives of the country" and, as a result, had little "Semitic blood in their veins." Despite the negro admixture millennia before, there was no mechanism that could now, in modern times, turn the Jewish race into the negro race.

In his lectures and discussions of what he called "Niggerology," Nott's chief aim, as an apologist for slavery, was to prove the eternal inferiority of blacks. However, a secondary aim was to pinpoint Jewish racial specificity. It is worth recording that in the organization of *Types of Mankind* (whose importance as a racist textbook can hardly be exaggerated), Jews are given a prominence that has hitherto gone unremarked. The first chapter deals with the geographical distribution of animals and different human races, the second consists of "general remarks on types of mankind," the third of "specific types—Caucasians," and the fourth is "Physical History of the Jews." Blacks are not dealt with specifically until the sixth chapter, "African Types," and then in the eighth chapter, "Negro Types." The immutable, unchanging purity of the Jewish race was a main and defining feature of this book. However, Nott was fully aware that "it has ... been contended that Jews in certain climates have not only lost their own type but become transformed into other races" (Nott, Gliddon.1854 p.117).

As useful black allegedly "transformed" Jewish communities as well as white Jewish groups were discovered in different parts of the world by intrepid Victorian travelers attempting to satisfy the unquenchable thirst for knowledge of Enlightenment and post-Enlightenment Europe, they were swiftly dragooned into service on one side or other of the race war.[4] To counter this heresy of race mutation, it was the communities of Jews in Loango, Cochin, and Ethiopia, as we shall shortly see, that were Nott's principal proof-communities.

Nott's first Jewish example was the regularly cited community of light-skinned Jews of Cochin in southern India, which he deployed in defense of the purity of the Jewish race. Some years before he had written: "It is now 1,700 years since the Jews were banished from their native country, and soon after this event a colony of them settled on the coast of Malabar, amongst a people whose color was black" (Nott.1844 p.25). However, despite the lapse of time, the weather, and the proximity of people of a dark hue, "they still preserve the characteristics of the Jews of Europe." On the other hand, as Buchanan had indicated, their hybrid neighbors "the *black* Jews . . . are a mixed race, descended in great part from the natives of the country, whom they resemble in physical character" (Nott.1844 p.25). This exercise in comparative ethnography revealed a great truth. The white Jews, descendants of the Chosen People in the Land of Israel, had retained their innate purity. The hybrid black Jews who had interbred with inferior stock were dangerous degenerates, and as such a "violation of nature's laws."

Anthropological inquiry of any sort was often perceived as subversive of the idea of the divinely inspired truth of biblical revelation. In the ongoing battle between church and science in the United States, it has been suggested that the first victory of science was achieved by physical anthropology, and particularly with its theories of the polygenist origins of humanity. The American polygenists, who were warmly applauded in freethought publications such as the *Boston Investigator*, must have felt that they were on the right side of history. Many polygenists were scathing about the clergy: Nott was famous for castigating his opponents as "advocates of murky theology and benighted science" and loved to provoke men of the cloth (he called this pastime "parson skinning"). Like many Enlightenment and post-Enlightenment theorists they considered that religion was outdated and religious opposition to polygenism would have to give into reason. Insisting that "the diversity of races must be accepted by Science as a fact, independently of theology," Nott perceived himself as a latter-day Galileo fighting against the obscurantism of blind religious prejudice. His ambitions with respect to the Bible were the exact opposite of Prichard's: He wished to "cut loose the natural history of mankind from the Bible and to place each upon its own foundation."

His co-author, the English-born Egyptologist Gliddon, was equally outspoken. He referred to the clergy as "skunks" and was contemptuous of the idea that the book of Genesis contained any useful information about the creation of man. He noted that

> viewed as a narrative inspired by the Most High, its conceits would be pitiful and its revelations false, because telescopic astronomy has ruined its celestial structure, physics have negatived its cosmic organism, and geology has stultified the fabulous terrestrial mechanism upon which its assumptions are based. How, then, are its crude and juvenile hypotheses about human creation to be received? (Nott, Gliddon.1854 p.565)

Deriding the English version of the Bible as nothing more than a "fetiche," Gliddon lamented that "our brief span of life will have been measured long before a new English version may be authorized, because the developments of science will have rendered any new translation altogether supererogatory among the educated, who are creating new religions for themselves" (Nott, Gliddon.1854 p.594).

Nott believed, like many polygenists before him, that in any case the Genesis account was intended to describe not the whole spread of humanity, but only the limited world known to the Hebrews. The writers of the Bible were ignorant of other peoples, and so the text was only ever meant to apply to the biological origins of the Jews. The same was true of the fortunate few who survived the flood: They were all Jews. Negroes and others had a different founding event. "Negroes," wrote Nott, "existed in Africa before this date of the flood, and . . . there is reason to believe that they did not descend from Noah's family" (Nott.1844 p.9). Moreover, negroes, with their immutable characteristics, could not adapt to conditions outside of Africa. As Nott observed, "a cold climate so freezes their brains as to make them insane or idiotical" (Nott.1844 p.19). It was similarly impossible for the Jewish race to change in any way: The unmistakable type of the Jew was indelibly marked and had not changed in any way over eight thousand years. In Alabama, it was widely believed that the negroes too were marked: They were branded with the mark of Cain, which was understood to be their dark skin. For Nott, then, negroes and Jews were marked and unique, and separate from the family of humankind.

The heresy of the black Jew remained an obstacle, of course, for the Americans' argument. Nott missed few opportunities to aim potshots over the Atlantic at Prichard and what he had argued about black Jews. "In his laborious work," he sneered, "he slurs over all these facts with the simple remark that there is 'no evidence' to prove that black Cochin Jews were not of the Jewish race. This," he continued, "is but one of Dr. Prichard's many unfair modes of sustaining the doctrine of the unity of mankind." The black Jews of Cochin, Africa, and Ethiopia, on whom Prichard and his disciples had in considerable part based their monogenist convictions, were declared either converts or of spurious origins. "We think it is now shown satisfactorily," wrote Nott, "that the 'Black Jews' of India are not Jews by race" (Nott, Gliddon.1860 p.122).

He also decreed that the various black Jews of the Sahara and north Africa were not racially Jews but were of obscure and perhaps convert origin. There was another group of would-be Jews closer to home. In the nineteenth century there were many people in the United States and elsewhere who were convinced that indigenous Americans in both North and South America were descended from the supposedly lost Ten Tribes of Israel (Parfitt.2002).[5] If this was indeed the case, the ruddy-skinned American natives would surely constitute an example of Jewish racial metamorphosis from white to red. Nott dealt with this possibility too:

> There are authors living who insist that the aborigines of our American continent are lineal descendants of the lost ten tribes, which have run so wild in our woods as to be no longer recognizable! Other examples of Jewish physical transformation have been alleged, but they are even less worthy of credit than the preceding. (Nott.1854 p.122)

But it was in sub-Saharan Africa, the land of the negroes proper, where the most egregious examples of mutation had apparently occurred, and it was important for Nott to deal with them:

> In the interior of Africa many Negroes are found who profess to be Jews, practice circumcision, and keep the Sabbath. These are held to be the descendants of slaves who were converted by their Jewish masters, and then manumitted. All the Jews in the interior of Africa who are of really Jewish

descent, as, for instance, in Timbuctoo, the Desert of Sahara, &c., though of dark complexion, are *not* black, and retain the characteristic cast of features of their race. (Nott, Gliddon.1854 p.122)

Earlier, in March 1850, Nott had lectured on the topic of Jews at a meeting of the American Association for the Advancement of Science held in Charleston. His talk was subsequently published in the Association's journal as "An examination of the Physical History of the Jews in its bearing on the Question of the Unity of the Races." The Charleston meeting, which was keenly anticipated by local clergy and scientists, created quite a stir. Nott started his talk by stating that "from the time of the Patriarch Abraham to the present, the Jewish race has preserved its blood more pure than any of antiquity . . . and that consequently its original type ought to be the same, as its type of the present day." Second, he noted that "we have abundant evidence to prove that the original type brought by Abraham from Mesopotamia, 4000 years ago, has been substantially handed down to his descendants of the present day." He continued that "although the Jewish race has been subjected during this immense lapse of time, in the four quarters of the globe, to every possible variety of moral and physical influence, yet in *no instance* has it lost its own type, or approximated that of others." Finally, he said,

> this race having thus for 4000 years preserved its type unchanged, under all known influences which could change a race, it follows as a corollary that no physical cause exists, which can transform one race into another, *as the white man into the negro,* etc. . . . It is clear, therefore, from the history of the Jewish people from first to last, but more especially since the Babylonish Captivity . . . that the Israelites have preserved, in a remarkable degree, their purity of blood. (Nott.1850a p.98)

However, there were so many examples of black or dark Jews in the world that Nott was forced to make some slight concession, allowing that at least some limited color change could and did occur:

> It is true that all races of men are more or less influenced by the extreme of climate—the Jews, like other fair races, become more fair in cold, or more dark in hot latitudes, than in their native land; yet there is a limit to this change, and that limit is far short of other types—the complexion may be bleached or tanned in exposed parts of the body. (Nott.1850a p.101)

However, full mutation from white to black was not possible.

This position ran against monogenist doctrine, as he was quick to point out:

> Prichard (who is inconsistent with himself on this and numerous other points) contends that Jews *have,* in various parts of the world, been transformed into other types, and several examples have been brought forward by himself and other advocates of Unity of the Races. We have examined them all with care and have no hesitation in saying *that they have not the slightest foundations in truth*—nor is there a single instance of transformation of any race in PRICHARD'S book, which cannot be refuted from his own writings.

The proof-community used by Prichard he was quick to dismiss, in the most contemptuous way. "The most prominent example and hawked about by every periodical scribbler," he declared haughtily,

> is that of the *Black Jews* of India, respecting which MR. PRICHARD has dodged the difficulties opposed to him in a most extraordinary manner, for one professing to write the "Physical History of Mankind." Though the testimony is *certainly* strong, not to say *conclusive,* to prove that the so called *Black Jews* are in reality *not Jews,* he suppresses the facts entirely, and passes it over without assigning a reason for his assertion, and with the simple statement that there is "no evidence" to show that they are *not Jews.*

Nott's intemperate tirade against Prichard included a quotation from Buchanan ("than whom there can be no more competent or reliable authority") stating that the black Jews had entertained marriages with families "*not Israelitish*" and that the white Jews "look upon the Black Jews as an *inferior race* and as *not of pure caste, which plainly demonstrates that they do not spring from a common stock in India*" (Nott.1850a p.101).

Nott went to some trouble to demolish the idea of the pure black Jew. One of his lines of attack included evidence about the Falashas or black Jews of Ethiopia that he had found in the writings of Charles Tilstone Beke (1800–1874), the distinguished English traveler, orientalist, geographer, discoverer of the origins of the Blue Nile, and, in his own way, race theorist. Nott needed to prove that the Falashas were not racially Jews, but there was not much evidence for this at the time. Prichard, on the other hand, as we have seen, had suggested that they *were* in part racially Jews.

One of the obstacles to the latter conclusion was that the language of the Falashas was suspiciously similar to that of the large Ethiopian tribe the Agau, among whom they lived, and that therefore the Falashas were likely to be native to Ethiopia, not immigrants from the Holy Land. Prichard had doubted whether in reality the language of the Falashas and the language of the Agau were in fact all that close. His research into the proposed similarity between the two languages "leaves this assertion in some doubt." Specifically, he noted that the Falashas had "a distinct idiom of their own, unconnected with the Semitic languages, and they have always been a separate race from the Agaazi [Agau] or the people of the Axumite kingdom" (Nott.1850a p.103).

However, at a meeting of the Philological Society in London in 1845, as recorded in the *Proceedings of the Philological Society* for April 1845, Beke had actually declared (correctly) that the two languages were in fact closely related. Brandishing Beke's "pamphlet," Nott used the kind of philological/racial argument that was common at the time to show that the black Jews of Abyssinia, like the black Jews of Cochin, were not of "pure blood." He declared that James Bruce thought the black Jews of Abyssinia were "pure Jews" but that even Prichard had opposed this idea and had supported the "opinion of Beke" (Nott.1850a p.103). But Prichard in fact had done no such thing. It was not surprising that Nott played around with the evidence, as this recondite linguistic detail concerned the specific question of the impossibility of racial change in a pure race. This was part of a greater enterprise, which was to identify the Jews, like blacks, as a people distinct, different, immutable, and apart (Prichard.1837; Beke.1845).

At the end of Nott's 1850 lecture, Jean Louis Rodolphe Agassiz, the Swiss-American, Harvard zoologist, announced a change of heart with respect to the Jews: He now agreed with Nott. Jews, he declared, like negroes on whom the obvious mark of color had been placed, were a separate creation, apart from all other races, for "God has put a mark upon them, by which they may be always known, and for the mere purpose of distinguishing them from other races" (Erickson.1986 p.110).

By this time Agassiz, at the time one of the most famous scientists in the Western world, had a very considerable authority that he now put at the service of the notion, which had been mooted for centuries, that Jews and negroes were uniquely different from the rest of humankind.[6] Agassiz was not just famous in the United States—he was adulated. Occasionally reports on the state of his health would appear on the first page of the *New York Times*. A fierce opponent of Charles Darwin, his life's work, in the words of one of his many obituarists, was "an offering on the Altar of Religion" that would prove that true science inevitably must lead to true faith (Irmscher.2013 p.37). Although he professed to be an abolitionist, Agassiz never deviated from his view that the United States belonged to the white races, and the white races alone. He clearly did not like blacks. Indeed, his interest in racial issues came about when a visceral wave of disgust engulfed him when he first encountered negroes on his arrival in the United States. In a letter to his mother he wrote:

> It is impossible for me to repress the feeling that they are not of the same blood as us. In seeing their black faces with their thick lips and grimacing teeth, the wool on their head, their bent knees, their elongated hands, their large curved nails, and especially the livid color of the palm of their hands . . . and when this nauseating hand moved close to my plate to serve me, I wished that I could get away from here, in order to eat a piece of bread sitting away from them rather than eating with such attendants. (Perin.1990 p.152)

Throughout his academic career he maintained his convictions about the constancy of racial types: Indeed, his last article, published after his death, was titled "Evolution and Permanence of Type." Whereas Agassiz, like the other members of the American School, was most interested in African difference, he also, as we have seen, developed a parallel interest in the racial specificity of Jews. His polygenism was clearly stated in an article entitled "The Diversity of Origin of the Human Races," published in a Boston-based liberal journal. In it he argued, echoing pre-Enlightenment theorists such as Bruno, that the Jewish account of the creation of the world was not valid for most other races: It was only about them. "On that ground," he wrote, "we would particularly insist upon the propriety of considering Genesis as chiefly relating to the history of the white race, with special reference to the history of the Jews." As far as other races were concerned, he wondered if "we are not entitled to conclude that these races must have originated where they occur, as well as the animals and plants inhabiting the same countries" (*The Christian Examiner*. July.1850 p.19).

Despite his aversion to blacks, Agassiz displayed a more liberal spirit than other American polygenists, and one partially embedded in the Christian teaching he had imbibed as a youth, when he stated, after Nott's Charleston lecture, that

> he regarded all the races of men as one in the possession in common, of all the attributes of humanity; as one in the possession of moral and intellectual powers, that raise them above the brutes, and by which they are allied to the Deity... but these races did not originate from a common center, nor from a single pair, but according to the laws which still at present regulate their existence. (Nott.1850a p.107)

On the other side of the Atlantic, a major contributor to the polygenesis argument was Lieutenant-Colonel Charles Hamilton Smith (1776–1859). A contemporary and close friend and disciple of the French naturalist Georges Cuvier (1769–1832), Smith wrote *The Natural History of The Human Species: Its Typical Forms, Primeval Distribution, Filiations, and Migrations* (1848), which was one of the main British works to support polygenist theories. Smith was not a professional scientist but rather an indefatigable amateur and enthusiast in a number of disparate fields. He was a well-known artist, illustrator, and antiquary. In addition, he had served with the British army in the West Indies, West Africa, Europe, and the Americas. Smith, drawing heavily on Cuvier, argued for the existence in the world of three immutable, distinct, and pure human types: the Caucasian, the Mongolian, and the negro.

The dilution or mixture of types and the creation of hybrids, he believed, were disasters that led to "decreasing vitality" and finally the extinction of peoples. However, like all polygenists he had to face up to the apparent impediment to the concept of racial immutability provided by the complicating issue of diverse Jewish types. This he did by ignoring the existence of different Jewish types. He asserted that the Jews "are a remarkable proof that climate and mode of living do not change human races to any great extent; wanderers in every land, they are now as distinct as they were two thousand years ago; the unmixed Jew is recognized at a glance." As confirmation of this—and as evidence for the great truth that no separate race had ever been produced by change of climate—he produced "proof-communities" from the same pool as his monogenist opponents—in this case, once again, the white Jews of south India and the black Jews of Loango. Of the black Jews of Loango he wrote,

> A Portuguese colony which settled on the coast of Congo, has now become lost by amalgamation with the black races; but by a suppression of a part of the facts, the impression has been given that they were changed into Negroes by the effect of the climate, while the true cause of their extinction was the intermarriage of a few whites for fifteen generation, among a larger body of blacks. Yet this, and such as this, has been adduced as a proof that climate changes races.

In a footnote he conceded that there were black Jews also in Malabar, "probably a mixed race, of proselytes of low caste" who had mixed with the native population. "This fact," he observed tartly, "is carefully kept out of sight by those who wish to use the 'Black Jews of Malabar' as the other side of the question" (Smith.1848 p.86).

Another stalwart champion of the notion of the immutability of Jews and blacks was the social reformer and labor union supporter John Campbell (1810–1874), who was born in Armagh, Ireland. A fervent Chartist, he was a political refugee from Great Britain[7] and emigrated to the United States in 1843, where he founded a bookselling and publishing firm in Philadelphia. He threw himself into radical racial politics and the union movement with the same enthusiasm he had previously devoted to the Chartist cause. His progression from Chartist to racist was nourished by the idea that blacks, like capitalists, were the unproductive enemies of the (white) working man. His defense of radical racial views, *Negromania: Being an Examination of the Falsely Assumed Equality of the Various Races of Men*, was issued by his own publishing house in 1851 and drew largely on earlier writers whose views on racial immutability had been widely expounded in the previous years. The opening words of *Negromania* set the scene for what would follow:

> That there are various races of men now upon our globe none will deny. These are composed of black, white, brown, yellow, fair, Caucasian, Mongolian, Malay, Indian, Negro, Saxon, Celtic, Sclavonic, Australian, Tasmanian, Gipsey, Jew, Arab, Copt, Nubian, with an endless variety. The most arbitrary distinctions have been made to endeavor to classify the races of man: one asserts that all are descended from one pair, another entirely dissents from this view, all are equal says the ignorant fanatic, negroes and red men as well as whites. It seems to me, therefore, a work not only of necessity but of justice, to place this matter in a compact method before the people of America. (Campbell.1851 p.3)

Although the book was chiefly about blacks, Jews, too, were important, indeed critical, for Campbell's argument, as Jews "exhibit one of the most striking instances of national formation" and proved that groups who did not intermarry would maintain their racial distinctiveness and their color unchanged for millennia, no matter what climatic conditions pertained. Like other polygenists he understood that the universal, immutable, pale, natural color of Jews, could it be proved, was critical to his doctrine. In the case of Jews, as of blacks, climate by itself could have nothing to do with turning one racial color into another. Black Jews, of course, had to be eliminated, if this theory were to hold. The black Jews seized on by Campbell were the Falashas or Beta Israel of Ethiopia. The Falashas, he conceded, were black and were derived from Jews, but there were very considerable differences between them and genuine negroes.

His authority for this was the German naturalist and explorer Wilhelm Peter Eduard Simon Rüppell (1794–1884), who had traveled widely in Ethiopia. Campbell wrote:

> There are two physical types prevalent among the Abyssinians. The greater number ... are a finely formed people of the European type, having a countenance and features precisely resembling those of the Bedouins of Arabia. The characteristic of their exterior consists principally in an oval shape of the face, a finely pointed nose, a well-proportioned mouth, with lips of moderate thickness, not in the least turned out; lively eyes; well-placed teeth; somewhat curled or smooth hair; and a middle stature. The greater number of the inhabitants of the high mountains of Samen,[8] and of the plains round Lake Tzana,[9] as well as the Falasha or Jews, the heathen Gamant,[10] and the Agows,[11] notwithstanding the variety of their dialects, belong to this class.

His argument, then, was that these Jews were black but not negroid. They looked European. They *looked*, in fact, like European Jews. There in Africa, surrounded by negro peoples, they had maintained their specific racial purity. The origin of the negro race was an altogether separate event: They were outside the usual human framework. The old arguments that blacks had descended from Ham and were therefore necessarily a part of the humankind that peoples Western sacred history were similarly dismissed out of hand. For Campbell, the sons of Ham were white Caucasians, and the ancestors of the Egyptians. Negroes had a separate genesis (Campbell.1851 p.60).

One of the most influential opponents of the notion of the single origin of humankind was Joseph Arthur, "Comte" de Gobineau (1816–1882) (he was born with the noble *particule*—"de"—but arbitrarily decided to bequeath himself the title of count).[12] Like other polygenist race theorists he was able to ignore the spoke in the polygenist wheel provided by a Jewish color spectrum. He was as convinced as any of the immutability of race and color but, returning to an earlier racial paradigm, he believed that European Jews were *not* white and consequently were not, in fact, significantly different from Jews in Africa or Asia. Having scrutinized the face of a Polish Jew whose eyes he found "unforgettable," he set forth his argument, calculated to undermine the doctrine of the "Unitaires." "This denizen of the north," he declared, "whose immediate ancestors had lived, for many generations, in the snow, seemed to have been just tanned by the rays of the Syrian sun." The Jew was still "bruni ... par les rayons du soleil syrien." Despite centuries in the frozen north, Jews were still marked by the brown complexion that the climate of Palestine had originally bequeathed them (Gobineau.1853 p.207).

However, Gobineau's argument was not yet the predominant view. On the whole, European Jews were still taken to be white, and therefore the change of color from white to black among the black Jews of the Jordan Valley, along with their putative cousins in Loango, Waregla, Timbuctoo, the Great Desert, the Jordan Valley, Bombay, Cochin, and Ethiopia, still had to be accounted for. In 1861, the English physician and great authority on pigmentation John Beddoe (1826–1911) embarked on a further line of attack. One of the most important English ethnologists, and future president of the Royal Anthropological Institute of Great Britain and Ireland, Beddoe studied medicine, first at University College, London, and later at Edinburgh. He served with distinction in the Crimean War in the British field hospital made famous by Florence Nightingale, and while he was there did a physical anthropological study of the multinational population incarcerated in the hospitals of the Dardanelles.

Beddoe's main body of work consisted of a description of the eye and hair colors mainly of the peoples of the British Isles, but also of the countries of Europe. He started his work in 1846 and for the rest of his life helped lay the foundations of the pigmentation surveys that would be carried out in Germany and elsewhere in Europe. In 1861 he added to the work he had already done with a lengthy and closely argued paper entitled "On the Physical Characteristics of the Jews." One of his achievements was to create a meticulously annotated "index of nigrescence" of the population of Great

Britain (Jews scored fully 100 percent). Beddoe fully understood the contemporary significance of the "varieties of complexion and color among the Jews" for the defense of the doctrine of the unitary origins of mankind, and also that the various "ethnological writers, and . . . many observant travelers" had held widely different views on the subject. The aims of "On the Physical Characteristics of the Jews" were first to determine "what peculiarities of form and feature" constituted the type "which most of us believe to distinguish the Hebrews from every other people."

Beddoe, like many others, perceived the Jews as a separate and unique racial entity. As the great expert on pigmentation, he wanted to present the Society with all the information he had at his disposal on the critically important question of the color of Jews. His aim was to draw the veil on "the varieties of complexion among the Jews, and to make a few remarks on their probable origin." He went on to observe that

> Dr. Prichard seems to have believed that the Jews, without having sullied the purity of their blood to an extent capable of producing notable effects on their physique, had been, by the influence of climate and modes of living, almost assimilated to the nations among whom they dwelt. "Among the Jews of Northern Europe," he says, "the xanthous variety becomes general," and he instances particularly those settled in North Germany as being conspicuous for their bushy red beards. These views and this illustration have been frequently quoted and made much of. I suspect them to be doubly erroneous. I doubt whether red beards are more common among German than other Jews; and I doubt whether any evidence can be adduced to show that climatic influence, without crossing of blood, has produced any change in the Jewish physiognomy. (Beddoe.1861 p.223)

Having dealt with Prichard, he took on the towering figure of Sir Richard Owen:

> It is true that Professor Owen has lately expressed himself very positively in the same sense with the illustrious ethnologist just quoted. He professes, indeed, to derive, from the variations of the Jewish race, a proof of the unity of origin of mankind. "For 1800 years," says he, "that race has been dispersed in different latitudes and climates, and they have preserved themselves distinct from intermixture with other races of mankind. There are some Jews still lingering in the valleys of the Jordan, having been oppressed

by the successive conquerors of Syria for ages, a low race of people, and described by trustworthy travelers as being as black as any of the Ethiopian races. Others of the Jewish people, participating in European civilization, and dwelling among the northern nations, show instances of the light complexion, the blue eyes and light hair of the Scandinavian families. The condition of the Hebrews, since their dispersion, has not been such as to admit of much admixture by the proselytism of household slaves. We are thus led to account for the differences in color by the influence of climate, without having to refer them to original or specific distinctions." (Beddoe.1861 pp.223–224)

Beddoe accepted that if, in fact, these "negroid Jews" existed, they would, as Owen argued, inevitably undermine his own position. But did they exist? In the usual manner adopted by anthropologists, he looked for his counter-proof in the published works of travelers and missionaries:

I have examined many books of travels and interrogated many travelers but have not been able to get any confirmation of the existence of these negroid Jews. I am informed by Mr. Hodges of Bristol, who was long a missionary among the Jews in different countries, that there are no Jews in the Ghor, or lower valley of the Jordan. There is a populous settlement, of ancient date, at Tiberias, on the low hot shore of the Lake of Gennesareth; but the Jews there present no striking peculiarities, certainly not black skins or crisp hair. Some of them are quite fair.

Beddoe's source, Edward Richmond Hodges (1826–1881), was the accomplished Hebraist and orientalist who had been sent first to Palestine and then Algeria by the Society for Promoting Christianity Among the Jews and was therefore an excellent authority.[13]

Carrying on with his reading, Beddoe came across *The Great Sahara—Wanderings South of the Atlas Mountains* (1860) by Canon Henry Baker Tristram (1822–1906), which had only just been published. The widely traveled and justly famous canon was a Bible scholar and ornithologist. He was traveling in the Sahara, partly for medical reasons, with the Rev. James Peed "also in quest of health." According to the *Spectator*'s review of *The Great Sahara*, Peed "was the archaeologist and draughtsman of the party." Both of them, according to the *Spectator*, were "hardy, good-humoured and sensible, as English gentlemen should be." "Thus qualified," their travels brought some interesting information about black Jews in Ouargla in southern Algeria, a very dark-skinned Jewish community in the desert town of Ghardaia, and a community of lighter-skinned Jews who had converted to Islam, called Mahadjeriah, in the neighboring former oasis sultanate of Touggourt. What Tristram and Peed discovered, Beddoe pointed out, in the remote oasis of "Waregla" (Ouargla) was a community of Jews "deeply stained with negro blood." According to Tristram, these Jews afforded

> an interesting example of the effect of climate, which, in the course of generations, seems to have produced the dark coloring pigment. They were almost as black as negroes, much darker than their brethren of the M'zab and Wed R'hir; yet there was not the slightest trace of the negro features: all the lineaments were as distinctively Jewish as in any clothes-dealer in Houndsditch. They were as dark as the black Jews of Abyssinia, whom I have seen in Jerusalem . . . The Jews of Ghardaia, in the Wed M'zab, are also stated to be very dark, dark as Hindoos, but "with features intensely Jewish."

On the other hand, wrote Beddoe,

> Mr. Tristram found in and near Tuggurt a sect of Mussulmans, who never intermarry with the others, and who are very fair, with strongly marked Jewish features. They are called Mahadjeriah, and are said to be of the earliest date of settlement, who submitted to the Koran several centuries ago. Mr. Ginsberg[14] . . . who also met with these Hebrew Moslems, says that the characteristic signs of the Jewish face are very recognizable; and that, in spite of the influence of climate, the Jew retains his white complexion, and forms a striking contrast to the native Arabs, and even Moors. Mr. Ginsberg did not visit Waregla; but his remark is probably meant to extend to the Jews of the M'zab and other oases, which he did visit. These last facts seem to neutralize that stated respecting the Jews of Waregla. At all events, one can hardly attribute the wide difference between the Mahadjeriah and the Waregla Jews, who are separated by little more than a degree of latitude, counterbalanced by a considerable difference in elevation, to the effects of climate alone. It would be at least as legitimate a conjecture if we supposed the Wareglan Jews to be hybrids, deriving their color from the negro, and their features from the Jewish parent . . . As for the black Jews of Cochin,

> I believe it is now generally acknowledged that they are not Jews at all, except in religion. (Beddoe.1861 p.230)

Beddoe's ethnography, underpinned by pious evangelical sentiment, attempted to depict the physical characteristics of the Jews throughout the world, largely on the basis of the reports of travelers and theorists. The centrality of this issue and other issues of human difference and origins, and the passions such subjects unleashed in Victorian Britain, can barely be exaggerated. The importance of these issues may be gauged from the proliferation of ethnological societies. The Ethnological Society of London, one of whose founders was Beddoe, was established in 1843 as a separate body from the more humanitarian Aborigines Protection Society, which had broadly Quaker and abolitionist origins and had been founded in 1837. The Ethnological Society had less of a welfare and more of a theoretical agenda and more or less took for granted the monogenist teaching of Blumenbach and Prichard. In general it stood for the doctrine that social factors and climate adequately explained the diversity of humankind. However, in around 1860 the presidency of the Ethnological Society was taken up by the Scottish doctor and colonial administrator John Crawfurd (1783–1868). According to Charles Darwin in the *Descent of Man*, Crawfurd, a passionate polygenist, believed in sixty discrete races. According to the diplomat and traveler Sir John Bowring, Crawfurd was known "in the clubs by the name of 'the inventor of forty Adams,' a title he obtained for repudiating the doctrine that the various races of mankind are descended from one single ancestor" (Bowring.1877 p.214).

Crawfurd's outspoken and extreme views, along with the disruptive activities of his outspoken colleague James Hunt (1833–1869), undermined the society. In 1863 Richard Burton, about whom we shall hear more, and Hunt founded an even less liberal breakaway organization called the Anthropological Society of London, of which Hunt and later Beddoe were presidents, that was intended as a haven for polygenists. In 1871, it merged with the Ethnological Society and became the Royal Anthropological Institute of Great Britain and Ireland, but in 1873 some members of the original society, including Burton, set up the breakaway London Anthropological Society.

Hunt was undoubtedly one of the most devious players in this maelstrom of Victorian intellectual activity. Ethnographer, speech therapist (he numbered Lewis Carroll and Charles Kingsley among his patients), and, like his father before him, an expert on stammering, his life, according to the obituary in the *British Medical Journal* of September 1869, "was spent in hot water, but it seemed to agree with him." Argumentative, unpleasant, and opinionated, there are ample grounds for believing that Hunt was not merely sympathetic to Southern American apologists for slavery, as the comparative anatomist Thomas Huxley (1825–1895) famously claimed at a heated meeting in London's Jermyn Street, but was actually a paid agent of the Confederate States, controlled by the smooth-talking Swiss-American Henry Hotze (1833–1887), a Confederate propagandist stationed in London.

Hotze had emigrated from his native Zug, on the Zugersee lake, to Mobile, Alabama. He had served with Confederate forces, had translated Joseph Arthur de Gobineau into English, and had started working as a journalist for the *Mobile Register*. Between 1862 and 1865 Hotze edited *The Index, A Weekly Journal of Politics, Literature, and News; Devoted to the Exposition of Mutual Interests, Political and Commercial, of Great Britain and the Confederate States of America* and made every effort to persuade the British of the rightness of the South's cause. Hunt was taken in by him and took the Confederacy's shilling.

In 1863, at the height of the American Civil War, Hunt read a paper at a British Association for the Advancement of Science meeting in Newcastle. In an apparent reference to Huxley's recently published pro-Darwinist *Man's Place in Nature* (1863) Hunt delivered an anti-Darwinist paper, "The Negro's Place in Nature," which argued that firstly there was

> as good reason for classifying the Negro as a distinct species from the European as there is for making the ass a species distinct from the zebra; and if we take into consideration its classification, there is a far greater difference between the Negro and European than between the gorilla and chimpanzee. 2. That the analogies are far more numerous between the Negro and apes than between the European and apes. 3. That the Negro is inferior intellectually to the European

and so on. His extreme views did not go down well in Newcastle (or among the scientific community in general), and according to his own testimony his speech was "received with such loud hisses that you would have thought the room had nearly been filled with a quantity of Eve's tempters instead of her amiable descendants" (Hunt.1864 p.23).

Significantly, Hunt dedicated his offensive Newcastle paper to his friend and collaborator, Richard Burton. In September 1869, at another fractious meeting of the British Association, this time in Exeter, Hunt collapsed and soon after died. *The Western Mercury* gave the cause of death of the unfortunate race theorist as "brain fever" brought about by over-excitement, but according to the improbable testimony of J. F. Collingwood, his friend and colleague and the secretary of London Anthropological Society, his demise in Exeter was brought about by "sunstroke." The *British Medical Journal*, while distancing itself from his views, ironically hailed him as one of the "martyrs of science" and concluded that these days apparently "the pursuit of science is more exciting than that of theology."

Hunt, a disciple of the embittered Scot Robert Knox, saw "race" as the most important motor of life and history and saw it as his mission in life to undermine the older British comparative ethnographic traditions represented by Prichard and the Ethnological Society of London. Hunt's view of the black, by which he meant "the dark, woolly-headed African found in the neighborhood of the Congo river," was that they were only just human, and that they should remain in eternal subservience to whites. Knox, for his part, also thought that Jews, as a dark and partially negroid race, were inferior to lighter races, such as the tall, strong, fair-haired Anglo-Saxon race. But here Hunt broke with his mentor. In February 1862, he read a rambling paper on what was becoming a topic of burning interest—"The Acclimatization of Man"—at a meeting of the British Association, chaired by John Crawfurd. The main point he wanted to get across was that "it is as difficult to plant a race out of its own center, as it is to extinguish any race without driving it from its natural center."

The worldwide Jewish diaspora presented a significant obstacle to his thesis. It was true, he argued, that there were millions of Jews in Europe. However, the idea that they had come from Asia and adapted to the new circumstances was simply wrong. Jews were not in fact dark Asiatics, as was generally supposed, but the remnant of some ancient *European* conquests of the Near East. "The modern Jews," he wrote, "are vastly superior to any purely Asiatic race. Never was the Jew more calumniated than by saying that he is an Asiatic! We all know the distinctive characteristics of the various Asiatic races, and nowhere do we find a people at all resembling the Jews." Not being Asiatics, Jews could not naturally survive in the one place in the world that could be considered their original homeland—Palestine—and he cited the high mortality of Jews in Palestine at the time as proof (Hunt.1863 p.30).

On ideological grounds Hunt could not accept the arguments about the adaptability of Jews. As a polygenist, he was naturally opposed to all the theories centering on black and brown Jews, which suggested that Jews were in some sense "cosmopolitan" and could "live and thrive all over the world," could change and adapt according to circumstances and climates, and were "subject to different physiological laws." Indeed, Hunt insisted that even though people made the claim that, along with the Chinese, the Jews were the most cosmopolitan of races, in fact the parts of the Jewish population that seemed to have assimilated fully into the local racial environment should be scrutinized more fully as "many of the people reputed to be Jews have no claim whatever to that questionable honour; such, for instance, as the many reputed cases of black Jews" (Hunt.1863 p.75).

Always a contrarian, Hunt argued that the reason for Jewish success in adapting so well in Europe was, as we have seen, that they were actually Europeans. It was not the adaptability of Jews that made them superior to some other races but "the fact that they are a pure race. All pure races support the influence of change better than mixed races." If people came from an inferior center they might flourish, as the Jews had done in Europe: "Any race coming from an inferior center to a higher center is thereby improved, other conditions being equal, and provided of course that the change be not too violent . . . the Jew has not degenerated in Europe but has greatly improved in spite of all disadvantages" (Hunt.1863 p.77). On the other hand, of course, "no one will contend that the climate of Palestine will suit an Englishman as that of England suits a Jew." However, the magic of the "superior center" did not work for negroes. "The farther they go north," sneered Hunt, "the higher becomes the rate of mortality: they seem to die of consumption, just like the monkeys . . . in the Zoological Gardens" (Hunt.1863 p.75).

Alfred Russell Wallace (1823–1913), co-creator with Darwin of the concept of natural selection, was one of the most talented of the British race theorists. His research in the Amazon and "the Malay Archipelago," the title of his celebrated book of travels, would radically change the way the origins of life were viewed. Although his work was mainly concerned with the animal world, and particularly with insects and beetles, he also considered the development of the various branches of humanity and questions of racial difference. Wallace contributed somewhat to the polygenist argument by arguing that natural selection stopped having any effect on humanity long ago and that such divergences as are to be found between races of humans occurred in prehistoric times. This view, to some extent, prepared the way for a modified kind of scientific polygenism.

In 1864, he delivered his revolutionary paper "The Origin of Human Races and the Antiquity of Man deduced from the theory of 'Natural Selection'" at a meeting of the Anthropological Society of London, which was published later in the year in the Society's *Journal*. Here Wallace attempted to calm the passions of polygenists and monogenists alike by applying his own version of the laws of natural selection. He noted:

> The advocates of the original diversity of man ... have much to say for themselves. They argue that proofs of change in man have never been brought forward except to the most trifling amount, while evidence of his permanence meets us everywhere. The Portuguese and Spaniards, settled for two or three centuries in South America, retain their chief physical, mental, and moral characteristics; the Dutch Boers at the Cape, and the descendants of the early Dutch settlers in the Moluccas, have not lost the features or the color of the Germanic races.

However, if all races retained their characteristics, in an unchanging way, for thousands of years, how could the diversity represented by the presence of those troublesome black Jews be accounted for? As the great Wallace put it, quite uncontroversially: "It was thought at one time, by Prichard and the older ethnologists, that it was a strong argument for the unity of the race that the Jews were white, black, and brown" (Wallace.1864 p.clxxxv).

But the idea of the "multi-racial Jew" as a paradigm for the unity of humanity, as Wallace was well aware, had its flaws. Wallace argued that in fact, in all known cases, black Jews were not really Jews as they were no more than converts to Judaism. They could not be *real* Jews if they were black, and converts, for him, were not real Jews. "It is known," he wrote, "that in every case in which the Jews have changed color apparently, it has been the Jewish converts who have been treated as Jews, simply because they have embraced that religion." Thus, for Wallace, the widespread argument about mutability, created by the presence of black Jews, in various places in the world, failed to counter the more important truth of the relative immutability of race. According to Wallace, in all cases, the black Jews were simply converts to the Jewish religion, and not racial descendants of the ancient people of Israel (Wallace.1864 p.clxxxv).

No one embraced this view more fervently than the Victorian adventurer Richard Francis Burton. Burton, as we have seen, was the collaborator of James Hunt in founding the Anthropological Society of London. A towering but controversial, even scandalous, figure, Burton was a prodigious traveler, "the most exotic explorer in the world," a gifted orientalist and writer. His clandestine visit to Mecca, in 1852, disguised as a Muslim, and his discovery of the great lakes in central Africa elevated him, at least in the eyes of the general public, to the giddy heights of a Livingstone or a Stanley. Utterly convinced, like most Europeans of his generation, of the absolute preeminence of the West, he was driven by an all-consuming curiosity. His obituary in *Nature* proclaimed: "He was one of the few survivors of the old type of adventurer of whom our country has been so prolific—men who have been the makers of our Empire and the founders of modern knowledge. Science is bound to remember him as one of the pioneers into the great unknown" (*Nature*.October 30, 1890 p.646). He was certainly noteworthy; however, in the words of the British journalist Jeremy Paxman, "like many noteworthy men, he was slightly nuts" (*Financial Times*. May 1, 2015).

Burton's attitude towards Jews was complex. There is reason to believe that until 1870 he was, if anything, philo-Semitic and at least in some ways admired the Jewish people. In any event, in 1869 he wrote that if he could choose his "race," it would be the Jewish race. During his consulship in Damascus (1868–1871), however, he became virulently antisemitic, and stayed so until the end of his life (Vincent.1985).

For Burton, Jews played an important role in his understanding of the nature and evolution of humanity. The Jews were racially pure but, at the same time, capable of racial change. They were the product of both blood and climate. They were thus unique racial specimens, a race of their own.

Among the works Burton relied on for this understanding of the Jewish race were Josiah Nott's *The Physical History of the Jewish Race* (Charleston, 1850), which we have discussed, and *Le Juif, le Judaïsm et la Judaïsation des peoples chrétiens* (The Jew, Judaism and the Judaisation of the Christian peoples) (Paris, 1869), a notorious work (which the British historian Norman Cohn called "the Bible of modern antisemitism") by Gougenot des Mousseaux (1805–1876), a writer who was otherwise preoccupied by the study of magic and the supernatural. *Le Juif* had little immediate impact—its day would come later in the century, when it became a classic of political antisemitism. The two books pored over by Burton in fact have very little in common: The one thing they did have in common, however, was that the Jews were a people apart, and Burton absorbed this central idea.

Burton was knowledgeable about medieval attitudes toward Jews. His infamous antisemitic book *The Jew, the Gypsy and El Islam*, published in 1898, started with the ominous sentence: "The history of the Jew as well as his physiological aspect are subjects which still remain to be considered and carefully to be worked out from an Aryan point of view." In his work in general we see a fusion of the most poisonous and embittered medieval concepts of the Jew as the paradigmatic, loathsome "other" and the racial, polygenist views of his day, which would later be embraced by the Nazis, in which Jews start to be expelled from the accepted hierarchies of race, indeed expelled from the collective of humanity.

Burton fully understood the implications of Jewish racial purity or Jewish mutability in the discussions around polygenesis, and attempted a synthesis of what previously had been incompatible categories: that the Jews were a racially pure people who nonetheless were capable of considerable change as a result of climate. He invited

> the ethnologist and the student of general history . . . to consider the annals and the physical and intellectual aspects of the children of Israel, perhaps the most interesting subject that can occupy their attention. The Jew, like the Gypsy, stands alone . . . Traditionally, or rather according to its own tradition, the oldest family on earth, it is at the same time that which possesses the most abundant vitality. Its indestructible and irrepressible life-power enables this nation without a country to maintain an undying nationality and to nourish a sentiment of caste with a strength and a pertinacity unparalleled in the annals of patriotism . . . The people that drove the Jews from Judæa, the empires which effaced the kingdoms of Israel and Judah from the map of the world, have utterly perished. The descendants of the conquering Romans are *undistinguishable* from the rest of mankind. But eighteen hundred years after the Fall of Jerusalem, the dispersed Jewish people have a distinct existence, are a power in every European capital, conduct the financial operations of nations and governments, and are to be found wherever civilization has extended and commerce has penetrated; in fact, it has made all the world its home. One obstacle to a matured and detailed ethnological study of the Jew is the difficulty of becoming familiar with a people scattered over the two hemispheres. *Though the race is one, the two great factors, blood and climate, have shown it to be*

anything but immutable, either in physique or in character. Compare, for instance, the two extremes—the Tatar-faced Karaïte of the Crimea with the Semitic features of Morocco, the blond lovelocks of Aden and the fiery ringlets of Germany with the greasy, black hair of Houndsditch. And as bodily form differs greatly, there is perhaps a still greater distinction in mental characteristics: we can hardly believe the peaceful and industrious Dutch Jew a brother of the fanatic and ferocious Hebrew who haunts the rugged Highlands of Safed in the Holy Land. Yet though these differences constitute almost a series of sub-races, there is one essentially great quality which cements and combines the whole house of Israel. The vigour, the vital force, and the mental capacity of other peoples are found to improve by intermixture; the more composite their character, the greater their strength and energy. But for generation after generation the Jews have preserved, in marriage at least, the purity of their blood . . . Physically and mentally the Jewish man and woman are equal in all respects to their Gentile neighbours, and in some particulars are superior to them . . . a keen thirst for blood engendered by defeat and subjection, combined to make him the deadly enemy of all mankind, whilst his unsocial and iniquitous Oral Law contributed to inflame his wild lust of self, and to justify the crimes suggested by spite and superstition. (Burton.1898 p.23)

The crimes he had in mind were the blood libel and other medieval accusations. His views on blacks were not dissimilar. The idea that blacks could really be compared to whites was anathema to him. "God's image in ebony," a phrase describing a negro that was used as the title for H. G. Adam's pro-black book of 1854,[15] was one that "lashed" Burton to "fury." Similarly, he could not stand Cowper's view that "affection dwells in white and black the same," as Burton was convinced that blacks, like Jews, had no affection and were innately cruel. "No humane Englishman," he noted, "would sell his dog to a Negro." As his biographer, Thomas Wright, put it:

He says that the negro is an inferior race, and that neither education nor anything else can raise it to the level of the white. After witnessing, at the Grand Bonny River, a horrid exhibition called a Juju or sacrifice house, he wrote, "There is apparently in this people [the negroes] a physical delight in cruelty to beast as well as to man. The sight of suffering seems to bring them an enjoyment without which the world is tame."

Similarly, according to Wright, when he was writing about Jews

> he seems in its pages to be constantly running up and down with a whip and saying: "I'll teach you to be 'an Ebrew Jew,' I will." His credulity and prejudice are beyond belief. He accepts every malicious and rancorous tale told against the Jews, and records as historical facts even such problematical stories as the murder of Hugh of Lincoln. Thus, he managed to exasperate representatives of almost every class. (Wright.1906 p.219)

He may well have nursed the same ambivalence about the color of Jews as did many of the antisemites of his own day, and of previous centuries, an ambivalence that would also mark the attitude of Nazi polygenists during the Third Reich. Perhaps subconsciously echoing the medieval fear of the vengeful black and red Jews expressed in the Germanic legend of the "*schwartz und rodt juden*," he noted that "we still find both amongst the Ashkenazím and the Sephardím red Jews and black Jews" (Burton.1898 p.53).

As we have seen, in 1863 Theodor Waitz had defended the principle of "Jews of many colors" (Waitz.1863 p.47). The following year, as a confirmed polygenist, Burton rebutted Waitz's views on black Jews and their importance for the origins-of-mankind debate. In *The Anthropological Review* he penned an article entitled "Notes on Waitz's Anthropology." Burton naturally knew all too well the importance of black Jews for the monogenist argument and was therefore obliged to categorically deny their existence: "I do not believe in a pure black Jew" (Burton.1864 p.235).

For similar reasons, he was, like other polygenists, equally eager to establish the idea of a Jewish race, which might have developed certain physical characteristics in different parts of the world, but which had usually maintained its original light color since biblical times. As proof of this he cited the Jewish community of Aden Province (which had been seized by forces of the East India Company in 1839). In Aden, Burton claimed, one of the hottest places in the world, and "surrounded by a swarthy population, the very old Hebrew colony is light haired and fair skinned." Even on the edge of the deserts of Arabia, Jews maintained their original color. (He added for good measure that the Arabs of the area, unlike the Jews, were often black because "they have mixed for centuries with Africans, preferring black women as cooler, in summer, and yellow women in winter") (Burton.1864 p.235).

Burton was one of the few writers on racial matters who had actually traveled to a number of the places where black or dark Jews were said to reside.

When he was in Loango he made no reference to the black Jews, and when he had reason to write about the Falashas in Ethiopia, he did not refer to their "blackness" in the context of the theories for which their color had often been employed. The reason for this, following the line of most polygenists, was that he considered the Ethiopian Jews, like the black Jews of Cochin, to be converts. "The other families in Africa," he wrote, "are the Falashas, or Black Jews of Abyssinia, mere proselytes like those of Malabar." And elsewhere he wrote:

> Jerusalem is sometimes visited by some of the "Black Jews" of Malabar and Western India, concerning whom *so much absurdity has been written*. The "White Jews" of India have a tradition according to which their ancestors, numbering ten thousand souls, emigrated Eastward about A.D. 70, and settled about Cranganore on the Malabar coast. Here they remained till A.D. 1565, when they were driven into the interior by the Portuguese. As no synagogue can be founded without a minimum congregation of ten free and adult males, the white Jews when necessary, simply bought back their nine Hindu slaves, manumitted them, circumcised and bathed them, and thus obtained their wishes. (Burton.1898 p.58)

By midcentury honors were perhaps evenly divided between monogenists, for whom the "change of the Jews to black" was the "most striking circumstance," and the polygenists, for whom such change was invented and amounted to "so much absurdity." However, a sea change was about to occur. In *The Descent of Man* (1871) Charles Darwin pointed out that once the theory of evolution was accepted, the controversy between monogenists and polygenists would no longer be relevant or necessary and the longstanding dispute would disappear, along with the squabbles over terminology. He wrote:

> It is almost a matter of indifference whether the so-called races of man are thus designated or are ranked as species or sub-species; but the latter term appears the more appropriate. Finally, we may conclude that when the principle of evolution is generally accepted, as it surely will be before long, the dispute between the monogenists and the polygenists will die a silent and unobserved death. (Darwin.1871 p.180)

Darwin's prophecy did not come to pass. As the British postcolonial theorist Robert Young wrote,

> As so often with racial issues, instead of being abandoned altogether, the scientific arguments in support of racial prejudice moved elsewhere, to the theory of "types," to questions of psychological, intellectual and "moral" differences, to the terrifying ideas of social Darwinism and eugenics, and the adaptation of evolutionary theory to ideas of racial supremacy and the extinction of races (Young.1995 p.12)

Moreover, as we shall see, with the advent of Nazi anthropology, polygenism would have a dramatic resurgence. The updated polygenist theories also depended on Jews and blacks, and the links between them, and found reasons aplenty to refer to hybrid black Jews. Indeed, these groups, if anything, became more important as issues of types, the purity of race, and the importance of physiognomy moved center stage.

7
The Racial Face

In 1844 Bartholomew Eliot George Warburton (1810–1852) described the "Jewish face" with its "fierce dark eye, and noble brow, that medallic profile." This face, he opined, "had been transmitted unimpaired through a thousand generations and a thousand climates" and thus the very face of the Jew formed part of "nature's own illustrations". The unchanging physiognomy of the Jew could, moreover, be expected to "vindicate old history" (Warburton.1844 p.300).

The eighteenth-and nineteenth-century passion for physiognomy—judging or assessing character, and in this particular case proving history, through facial forms and expressions—seems somewhat at odds with Enlightenment or post-Enlightenment rationalism. It was, after all, difficult to argue that there was anything objective about the reading or judging of facial expression. Even Johann Kaspar Lavater (1741–1801), the Swiss Protestant poet and pastor from Zurich who made physiognomy a universally accessible and popular discipline, which would go on from strength to strength, did not hesitate to affirm that the links between individual traits of character and facial features were subjective and metaphysical. Lavater's ideas about the face were published between 1775 and 1778 in his influential four-volume *Physiognomische Fragmente zur Beförderung der Menschenkenntnis und Menschenliebe* and, in English, *Essays on Physiognomy designed to Promote the Knowledge and Love of Man* (1789–1798). In its day the techniques and practical tips contained in *Physiognomische Fragmente* were used in a wide variety of ways. At the more ethereal end of the spectrum, William Blake (1757–1827), who contributed engravings to the English translation of *Physiognomische Fragmente*, studied physiognomy intently in his search for the "divine likeness." It had more down-to-earth applications too and was deployed in the selection of servants and even wives or husbands. Moreover, as we shall see, Lavater's book and physiognomy in general had a significant bearing on the natural sciences as they related to the study of man.[1] But Lavater, aware that physiognomy was not *only* a science, explicitly framed his work in terms of art. "Is painting," he inquired, "not the mother and daughter of physiognomy?" (Lavater.1866 p.2).

Lavater had a poor opinion of the negro face and the negro head. "Could the mind of Newton," he asked, "have invented the theory of light, residing in the head of a Negro?" In the last volume of the French translation of *Fragmente—Sur les Lignes d'Animalité* (Paris, 1803)—Lavater included prints, slightly modified, that were based on diagrammatic charts by the celebrated Enlightenment figure Pieter Camper (1722–1789), the Dutch anatomist, physician, naturalist, midwife, and amateur painter.

Camper had taken Buffon's ideas about animals and applied them to humankind, arguing that the original man was an ancient Greek. As man moved from this Grecian starting point, he degenerated as a result of climate and other variables. Camper's drawings demonstrate a hierarchy of skulls from the ape to Apollo, with the negro skull next to the ape and the European skull next to Apollo.

He accepted that some negroes were more or less human, but Africans south of the Congo region were probably not. Indeed, throughout the nineteenth century there was a consensus that the features of the negro of the area just north and south of the Congo were the most debased. "The protuberant jaws, the flat nose, the thick lips, and black color," wrote John Crawfurd (1783–1868), the Scottish physician, "appear in their most exaggerated form in the Negro of the Guinea coast but in a greatly mitigated one in the Kaffirs of the eastern" (Crawfurd.1866 p.213).

The Jewish head, features, and dark-colored face were also a source of great interest to Lavater. They, too, seemed to include special signs or identifiers. He enthused:

> It appears to me remarkable that the Jews should have carried with them the marks of their country and race to all parts of the world; I mean their short, black, curly hair, and brown complexion. Their quickness of speech, haste and abruptness in all their actions, appear to proceed from the same causes. I imagine the Jews have more gall than other men. (I add, as characteristics of the national Jewish countenance, the pointed chin, pouting lips, and well-defined middle line of the mouth). (Lavater.1853 p.579)

However, to really decipher what the Jewish face was all about, art was necessary. Lavater noted that even Camper had confessed that he failed to "delineate the distinguishing traits" of Jews and that he had "not yet been able accurately to draw the countenance of a Jew, although they are so very remarkable in their features" (Lavater.1827 p.129). If Camper had difficulties in determining the precise nature of the elusive Jewish face, others did not, and the application of the study of the Jewish face to the study of racial difference was not slow in coming.

Over the next century and more, the Jewish face, in different parts of the world, would provide testimony to the immutability of racial phenotype. In the early stages of this development race scientists recognized that in order to distinguish the subtle differences between faces they would have to accept guidance from the experienced eye of an artist. To this end, Johann Friedrich Blumenbach discussed the issue of the "Jewish face" with Benjamin West (1738–1820), the painter, designer to George III, Surveyor of the King's Pictures, and president of the Royal Academy of Arts. West suggested, perhaps unwittingly evoking the medieval conflation of Jews and goats, that the Jewish face had something particularly hircine about it, which "he was of opinion lay not so much in the hooked nose, as in the transit and conflux of the septum which separates the nostrils from the middle of the upper lip" (Blumenbach.1865 p.234).

The description of the face and profile of the Jew as goat-like would continue and would eventually become a standard slur in the antisemitic literature of the late nineteenth century, as we can see in the work of the pseudonymous "Docteur Celticus" who maintained that Jews shared both the instincts and foul smell of the goat (Celticus.1903). The medieval construction of Jews riding goats, the Jew's beast, had already emerged in the eighteenth century. Voltaire famously criticized the fact that the Jews, uniquely, had laws forbidding them to bugger goats,[2] which suggested to him that the practice was so widespread that the law was deemed necessary. At about the same time in England male "buggering Jews" were imagined to have relations with goats and men, as well as with women (Webster.2006). In *Les Races humaines* Abel Hovelacque (1843–1896), the French linguist, radical political figure, and from 1890 president of the *École d'anthropologie*, argued that the chief characteristic of Jews was the "accentuated profile of the goat," while negroes looked like apes (Hovelacque.1882 p.139).

One aspect of the racial face that was regularly commented on was the eyes. The eyes of Jews were often considered to be their most characteristic feature. Poring over images in a book by the French engraver Bernard Picart, the naturalist Blumenbach found a number of examples of "typical" faces "of which the Jewish race presents the most notorious and least deceptive, which can easily be recognized everywhere by their eyes alone, which breathe of the East." The work, he went on, "represented an immense number of Jews" and that "as far as the lineaments of the face go, each differing from one another, yet all bearing the racial character, and most clearly distinguished from the men, intermingled with them, of other nations."[3] In *Eastern Life* (1875), Harriet Martineau (1802–1876), the British journalist and sociologist, wrote of the Jews' "eyes which seem to distinguish them from the rest of mankind—large, soft and of the deepest expression." Bayard Taylor (1825–1878), the American poet and travel writer, described seeing Jews in Palestine in 1852:

> On the evening of my arrival in the city, as I set out to walk through the bazaars, I encountered a native Jew, whose face will haunt me for the rest of my life . . . but the eyes—shall I never look into such orbs again! Large, dark, unfathomable, they beamed with an expression of divine love and divine sorrow, such as I never before saw in human face. (Lavater.1866; Taylor.1863; Blumenbach.1865)

The eyes of negroes were also discussed as a particular sign of difference (Blumenbach.1865 p.234). Enlightenment thinkers, such as the French man of letters Guillaume Thomas Raynal (1713–1796), were exercised by the extreme whiteness of Africans' eyes. One apologist for slavery from Mississippi claimed that the body of the negro had been specially adapted by kindly providence to support the rigors of the slave's life. In particular, the eye of negroes, "like the eye of fowls," had a specially designed membrane, which "serves as a protection to the Negro against the effects of hardships, necessarily incident to the conditions of slavery" (Estes.1846 p.65). The physician Charles Kollock of Charleston, South Carolina, in 1892 penned an article entitled "The Eye of the Negro" and suggested that the low incidence of trachoma and myopia among blacks were indicators of their low level of civilization.

With the development of racial science, the preservation, in paint, of human faces and "types" became a tool of physical anthropology and a weapon in the great nineteenth-century race wars. Charles Henri Joseph Cordier (1827–1905), a French sculptor and traveler with interests in ethnography, devoted himself to creating busts of subjects from around the world. Attached to the ethnographic gallery of the *Muséum d'Histoire Naturelle*, he was also was a member of the Anthropological Society of Paris and gave a lecture on the lifelike busts of what he called "types" in 1862.[4]

A few years later the *British Medical Journal* (September 1869) lamented that "the study of anthropology as a special department of science clearly enjoys more favour in France than with us." The journal drew particular attention to a Paris museum "for the reception of all objects bearing on the natural history of man" that had just been "enriched by a collection of types, life-size, of the natives of the Valley of the Nile." These "types" of "different races" had been painted in oil by the French traveler and "historical painter" Gabriel Lefébure, who had just returned from "a mission to the East" where he had studied the anthropology of Egypt, whose living people, as well as those of its remote past, were critical to the polygenist argument.

For the monogenists, too, the face afforded a wonderful example of the mutability of physiognomy. Blumenbach was convinced that climate, and climate alone, was the basis of facial difference. He wrote:

> I am persuaded, myself, that climate is the principal cause of the racial face, on three grounds especially; 1st, we see the racial face so universal in some populations under a particular climate, and always exactly the same in men of different classes and modes of life, that it can scarcely be referred to in any other cause. 2nd, Unless I am mistaken there are instances of peoples who after they have changed their localities and have migrated elsewhere, in process of time have changed also the original form of countenance for a new one, peculiar to the new climate . . . 3rd, We see nations which are reputed to be but colonies of one and the same stock have contracted in different climates different racial faces. (Blumenbach.1865 p.234)

For polygenists, on the other hand, neither the Jewish nor negro face had ever changed. It seemed identical, over time and over space, wherever it was to be found. In his *Historical Display of the Effects of Physical and Moral Causes on the Character and Circumstances of Nations* (1816), the industrious English schoolmaster John Bigland (1750–1832) was highly impressed by the fact that even in "Cashmere," far away on the other side of the world, the inhabitants, whom he imagined to be Jews, had preserved not only their pale skin but also their "Jewish physiognomy" (Bigland.1820 p.307). The monogenist and proto-evolutionist Sir William Lawrence (1783–1867), following Blumenbach, similarly asserted that the Jews' "peculiar and distinctive countenances" were "preserved in every climate" (Lawrence.1822 p.366).

The clever but embittered surgeon and amateur anthropologist Robert Knox (1791–1862), as we shall shortly see, took this story back to the beginnings of recorded history with more zeal than was usual even at the time. Born and bred in Edinburgh, Knox began his medical studies at Edinburgh University and later studied in Italy and France. A prize-winning student, after graduating he joined the British army as assistant surgeon, gaining experience operating on the wounded after the bloody battle of Waterloo. In 1825 he was appointed conservator of a new museum at the Royal College of Surgeons in Edinburgh and started giving well-attended lectures in the university. To this end he needed corpses for public dissection. Unwittingly he would purchase dead bodies from two notorious murderers, William Burke and William Hare, and the impression was given that killings had been carried out for the sole purpose of providing the industrious Knox with cadavers. When the scandal broke, students stopped attending his lectures. He applied for a couple of university chairs but was turned down, and finally, discouraged, he moved to London.

He was now free to express his views about race without wondering how they would be received by his employers. He supported himself with provincial lecture tours, which brought a new racial kind of antisemitism, as well as the creeds of polygenism and the preeminence of race, to the wider British public. For Knox there was no time to lose: "Race," he wrote, "is everything: literature, science, art—in a word, civilization, depend on it" (Knox.1850 p.7). In 1850, he published his lectures, in book form, as *The Races of Men—a Fragment*, and the work was well received, particularly in freethought and atheistic circles. He subsequently tried to get work at the British Museum and failed. He was not accepted for military service during the Crimean War either but did eventually get some work at the Free Cancer Hospital in Brompton, now known as the Royal Marsden.

His reputation had been ruined, his medical career had more or less failed, but he still had his ethnological interests, and he sought comfort in the company of like-minded people. In 1862, a little surprisingly given his extreme views, he became Honorary Fellow of the Ethnological Society of London and Honorary Curator of its museum (Alexander.2018).[5]

For Knox, the unchanging, immanent face of Jews was a critical factor in his overall argument, and he linked it with the remote past. The year before his book came out, Sir Austen Henry Layard (1817–1894), the English diplomat, archaeologist, and excavator of Nimrud and of Nineveh, published *Nineveh and its Remains. A narrative of an expedition to Assyria* (1849). "A great section of the Jewish race was probably Chaldean," wrote Knox, "for on the Nimrod monuments the Jewish cast of features is quite discernible"

(Knox.1850 p.317). But what particularly fascinated him was the colossal granite head from Thebes of the Nineteenth Dynasty pharaoh Rameses, which had been acquired by the British Museum in 1821 and had become known in London as "the young Memnon." Knox wrote:

> Willing to embrace every opportunity of looking at those glorious specimens of art in the British Museum . . . I repaired to the Museum, where, again contemplating the bust of the young Memnon, new light broke at once on my view. It seemed to me that I had, at one time or other, and that even lately, seen persons who might have sat to a sculptor for a likeness of the head of the Coptic prince; that the precise features and form, even to the most perfect resemblance of look, were to be found to this day unaltered in Britain, that the Coptic blood, or at least a race analogous, remained unaltered and strongly affiliated even to this day here in Britain; this fact, for such I felt convinced it was, excited in my mind the deepest reflections. (Knox.1850 p.136)

Knox really did not like Jews. His observation that "Jews seem to have been trafficking in cast-off garments since Rome itself was founded" (Knox.1850 p.138) achieved a certain notoriety. Knox had already decided that at some point soon he should visit Amsterdam, where there was a large Jewish community:

> So soon as I began to suspect that I had seen persons in the streets of London from whose face the sculptor might have modelled the bust of the Memnon . . . I became more anxious to visit the Jew-quarter of Amsterdam, where I was told I should meet with ten thousand Israelites, male and female, walking about, or in collected groups, apart, to a certain extent, from the other race; that other race, the Saxon, strongly contrasted with the Jew . . . Having repaired to the quarter of the city occupied by this race in Amsterdam, I found the synagogue open and crowded; divine worship was going on, the people standing in crowds around the high altar; it was not proper to take off the hat. Near me, almost within reach, stood a youth about sixteen, and not far from him others, the perfect likeness of the young Memnon. I borrowed from him a Hebrew book he held in his hand, that I might the better observe his face . . . The women, seated in the gallery, were not visible; but in the streets they could not be mistaken: unveiled and upright, a forward look, and eyes fixed on you as you passed: nor did the eyes

quit their glance until you had fairly passed them. No one turned the head but gazed at you until you and they passed each other. In that fixed look nothing could be seen more than in the statue. (Knox.1850 p.137)

The "fixed look" of the Jewish women in the streets of Amsterdam proved to him that the Jews were essentially of African origin. "Thus, I learned," he wrote, "that originally the ancient Copt and a large section of the Jewish people were one and the same race, with slight differences, however, which the Egyptian sculptor knew how to caricature" (Knox.1850 p.137).

In addition, whatever physiological laws were known to exist for Europeans, they were not applicable to Jews. The Jews were different and apart and were associated with the dark races of men. With the rediscovery of ancient Egyptian and other Near Eastern sites and artifacts in the first half of the nineteenth century, the idea was born that the perceived reflection of Jewish and negro faces in ancient figures provided a valuable key to the mysteries of human origins. For many sober as well as intemperate people, the face of the Jew, and the face of the negro, were reflected, mirror-like, in the ancient monuments.

Dr. Knox was one of the believers. He was admittedly discouraged, unhappy, and bitter, but he was also well trained and knowledgeable. For a while, midcentury, as his story indicates, polygenesis and associated doctrines were not just the marginal obsession of subversive and contrarian cranks but became the thinking man's creed. Indeed, in its opposition to the Bible-based monogenism of Prichard and his disciples, polygenism became an intrinsic part of the freethought movement both of Victorian Britain and the United States. The *Truth Seeker*, the leading freethinking periodical in the United States, produced a cartoon with caricatures of racial types, a noble Anglo-Saxon in the center, surrounded by lesser breeds including a negro, a Jew, a native American, and others, which posed an ironic question to the "theological ethnologist": God made man in his own image. But what was the image? (Knox.1850; Mosse.1978; Alexander.2018).

For radical polygenists such as the Anglo-Irish race theorist and anti-black campaigner John Campbell (1810–1874), the unchanging quality of the Jewish face in every climate buttressed the polygenic argument just as well as did the unchanging nature of Jewish color. Wherever they were, he wrote, Jews afford examples of peculiar and distinctive casts of countenance being preserved in every climate. These well-known facts are quite sufficient to overturn the hypothesis which refers the difference of features to climate; and a short examination of the races in any part of the world will soon supply numerous additional ones. Indeed, I do not know a single well-established fact or sound argument in its favor. (Campbell.1851 p.120)

This argument spread throughout the Western world.

One of its more zealous proponents was Frederic William Farrar (1831–1903). An establishment figure, *avant la lettre*, he was at various times fellow of Trinity College, Cambridge; author of one of the most popular Victorian books for boys, the moralistic *Eric or Little by Little*; successively master in and headmaster of Marlborough School; important educationist; honorary chaplain to Queen Victoria; widely read author of bestselling theological works; Archdeacon of Westminster; chaplain to the speaker of the House of Commons; and finally Dean of Canterbury. Like others before him, Dean Farrar found testimony to the unchanging nature of a number of races in the monuments of ancient Egypt. "On the oldest Egyptian monuments," he wrote, "as, for instance, on the tomb of Ramses-Meiamoun and the hypogeum discovered by Belzoni near the ancient Thebes" were to be found negroes and Jews, as well as others, "depicted with a fidelity as to color and feature hardly to be surpassed by a modern artist" (Farrar.1865 p.395).

For Farrar it was the overlapping categories of blacks, Jews, and gypsies that provided the best proof of the immutability of racial types. He wrote:

> The negroes are known to have existed some twenty-four centuries before Christ; some would assert that we have historic evidence of their existence even thirty or forty centuries before Christ . . . Under whatever climate they are placed, there is material variation in the apparently indelible characteristics of their race, and no known set of conditions is capable of producing their color, much less their conformation, in any historical period of years. How, then, is it possible to account for the appearance of well-defined negroes by the side of equally well-marked European, Asiatic, and African nations, only a few generations after the period of Noah? And if, in the space of four thousand years, we see in these races not the slightest tendency to change, what right have we to assume that, by natural causes a change ever took place in them at all? Neither heat, nor cold nor moisture, nor scarcity of food, nor an arid soil, nor degraded habits, nor any known

physical agent, is adequate to produce in any given term of years the characteristics of this race. (Farrar.1865 p.398)

The indelibility of African blackness and the indelibility of physical Jewishness were common themes that linked Jews and blacks from medieval times to the twentieth century. By the nineteenth century the immutability of racial types had become for many a source of wonder. Dean Farrar saw the indestructible Jewish essence as a remarkable thing. After all, for "little short of two thousand years they have been a... roving community, in every region from heat to almost arctic cold, and yet in spite of frequent marriages with people of other blood, the race continues unalterably true to its well-known type" (Farrar.1865 p.399). The dean was perfectly aware of the impediment posed by the black Jews to this argument and gave it short shrift:

> The supposed black Jews of whom so much has been made, are, in point of fact, as fabulous as white Indians. On close examination, and on unimpeachable testimony, they turn out to be either non-existent in the localities mentioned, or people with but a slight admixture of Jewish blood, or else the descendants of proselytes, half-converted Arabs or Africans, not Jews at all. The Jews, though they have adopted the costume, language manners of every people among whom they have dwelt, resemble each other all over the world, not only in lineaments, but also in conformation, temperament and moral character... What he was in Egypt, perhaps three thousand years before Christ, that he is in Sweden and Poland nearly two thousand years after Christ. The vigorous caricatures which the Egyptians drew of him in the hypogeum of Thebes, have lost none of their comic force, and might be reproduced at this day, with perfect fidelity from many living members of the race. (Farrar.1865 p.399)[6]

Underlying these discussions lurked the elemental question of the origin of peoples and the reasons for their differences. The Welsh-born explorer, geographer, biologist, and anthropologist Alfred Russell Wallace (1823–1913), co-creator with Darwin of the concept of natural selection, was a kind of polygenist insofar as he saw the divisions of humankind to have predated the emergence of modern man. Wallace was convinced that the ancient immutable face in general was a much better guide to racial type than color and that the Jewish face, above all, was the most marvelous anthropological tool. "A better proof than color," he wrote, "is physiognomy, which you see maintained in the Jews all over the world. Physiognomy maintains itself much longer than color; and it seems as if the physiognomy of the superior race maintained itself much longer than the inferior; whereas the color of the inferior race is often most lasting." In his famous and paradigm-shifting 1864 paper "The Origin of Human Races and the Antiquity of Man deduced from the theory of 'Natural Selection,'" he observed that "the Jews, scattered over the world in the most diverse climates, retain the same characteristic lineament everywhere" (Wallace.1864 p.clix).

The year before, William Winwood Reade (1838–1875), the eldest son of an Oxfordshire squire, explorer, Oxford dropout, failed novelist, and influential social Darwinist historian, wrote extensively of the physiognomy of the negro in an odd book devoted in part to proving the existence of unicorns and "tailed men" in west Africa. For Reade, the typical negro could most easily be identified by his eyes and specifically by the "flatness of his cornea" and also by "the muzzle-like extension of the jaws . . . his flattened nose, elongated cranium, simplicity of cerebral convolution, rounded larynx." Scientific measurements "by microscopes, by analyses" showed that the "typical negro is something between a child, a dotard and a beast." Moreover, this type was as old as human history and could readily be perceived in the Egyptians'

> old stone books as early as the 20th dynasty, 1300 B.C. . . . faithful pictures of negroes dancing, clapping their hands, and beating their drums, precisely as they may be seen in Africa at the present day . . . To those who follow the Mosaic chronology, this will be sufficient to establish the special creation of the negro . . . Their historical antiquity, however, does much toward explaining the persistence of the type transplanted. During at least three thousand years, the negroes have been influenced by certain climatic conditions, the results of which have been defined and strengthened by hereditary transmission. (Reade.1863 p.400)

The other type as old as human history was of course the Jews, images of whom were to be found throughout the Near and Middle East. The Cambridge anthropologist Alfred Cort Haddon (1855–1940) considered that the Assyrian depictions of Jews were the most reliable, as far as Jewish faces were concerned. For this insight he was indebted to the orientalist George Bertin, author of *The Races of the Babylonian Empire* (1888), who considered that the Assyrian reliefs were better representations of the Jewish face than Egyptian depictions. Haddon was convinced of the unchanging, persistent nature of the Jewish "look" and, quoting Goethe, proclaimed: "*Es ist das beharrlichste Volk der Erde. Es ist, es war, es wird sein*" ("It is the most tenacious people on earth. It is, it was, it will be") (Haddon.1898 p.18).

Wallace, the Welshman, made the critical linkage between Jews and blacks that had underlined much racial speculation for the previous five hundred years and that would continue long after his death, particularly with respect to their unchanging, ancient pedigree and appearance. As he pointed out, it was "the Egyptian sculptures and paintings" that offered irrefutable proof that "for at least 4000 or 5000 years, the strongly contrasted features of the Negro and Semitic races have remained altogether unchanged" (Wallace.1864 p. clix). Even though the features of Jews and negroes, according to Wallace, were "strongly contrasted," the two were connected in the very fact of being eternally immutable. Both Jews and negroes were *irreducible* others, both peoples apart.

The obsession with Jewish and negro faces was not only British and American. In the 1880s Richard Andree (1835–1912), the German scholar and pioneer in the field of Jewish ethnography, entered the fray. Andree was principally a geographer (like his father before him) and cartographer—his best-known work was the comprehensive *Allgemeiner Handatlas* (Leipzig, 1881), on which the *Times Atlas of the World* (1895–1900) was based. However, like many nineteenth-century intellectuals, he was not afraid of forming multiple disciplinary affiliations, and threw himself into ethnographic and folklore studies. Perhaps his most important ethnographic work was his widely cited *Ethnographische Parallelen und Vergleiche* (Ethnographic Parallels and Comparisons) (1878). Andree shared the belief of the German philosopher Johann Gottfried Herder (1744–1803) and the ethnographer Adolf Bastian (1826–1905) that all primitive peoples, wherever they happen to be, had a similar outlook and a common mental and spiritual framework, which belief ran counter to the discipline, developed in the 1860s, of *Völkerpsychologie* (psychology of peoples). Herder, like many Enlightenment thinkers, thought of the Jews as an Asiatic race that was only relatively resistant to change, but Andree believed in the out-and-out unchanging and unchangeable purity of the Jewish physical type. Jews, while being part of the Caucasian group, were nonetheless a distinct and absolute racial category all of their own.

In his *Volkskunde Der Juden* (1881) (Folklore of the Jews), Andree found the usual pictorial evidence of the immutability of the Jewish race in the distant past and insisted, like many others, that the various racial types depicted on Assyrian and Egyptian monuments proved conclusively the unchanging nature of the Jewish type. You only had to look at the representations of Semites in the ruins of Egypt to see an actual, unchanged, contemporary Jew. In this the Jew was unique, as no other race had preserved its purity in the same way. However, Andree thought that Jews had certain chameleon characteristics. They can show signs of adaptation, but the adaptation is superficial; underneath, they never change.

Although Andree believed that Jews everywhere looked and acted and spoke the same now as they always had, the black Jews of Loango, and other black Jews, for him were an important exception, almost *l'exception qui confirme la règle*. They certainly did not look like other Jews, as some claimed. Indeed, they were no more than a hybrid "rabble" who had racially degenerated by mixing with the lowest group of all—negroes. The Jewish face had been erased from the facial map of Africa. Black Jews, whether they were Ethiopian Falasha or Loango Jews, were now of no importance because as degenerate hybrids they could be expected to disappear from the face of the earth (Andree.1881 pp.90–91; Hart.1995 p.163).

However, this was not everyone's opinion. The monogenist argument continued to maintain that the Hebrew face could be seen even along the African coasts. In 1855, the *Biblical Repertory and Princeton Review* was at pains to distinguish the phenotypes of the various ethnicities to be found in the area around Loango, one of which was

> the Jewish type, where the profile is strikingly Jewish, the complexion either a pale or reddish brown, the head well formed, figure slender, but well formed, and the hair nearly as woolly as that of the pure Negro . . . It is probable that the Jewish type of character above mentioned forms a larger element of population here, than it does on the Pongo coast; and this doubtless, was what led the Roman Catholic missionaries who labored here during the sixteenth and seventeenth centuries, to the conclusion that they had found *black Jews* in Loango." (*Biblical Repertory and Princeton Review*.1855, vol. 27, p.212)

After the first reliable descriptions of the faces of the black Jews during the German scientific expedition to Loango in the 1870s, the African Jewish face was confirmed, but there was still the question of determining of what the black Jewish face consisted. As luck would have it, art, "the mother and daughter of physiognomy," was able to lend a hand. On one of his trips to the village of Chinchosho, on the Loango coast, Bastian, the leader of the German expedition, met up by chance with a fellow German, a painter and, as Bastian stressed, an expert in physiognomy, who happened to be wandering around Loango in search of inspiration. A crowd of Loango Jews, now referred to as "Mavumbu," appeared and the German painter immediately commented to Bastian on their looks, which included, as he thought, many Semitic characteristics. The painter exclaimed moreover that they had about them the decided air of some "haggling Jew" (*Schacher-jude*). The painter was quite stunned when Bastian told him that indeed they were known as "Judeos" and were reckoned by some to be black Jews. Bastian was stunned that the painter had made his remark without knowing anything of their history, as he had never before had any dealings with the community whose story and background, in any case, for the most part were unknown to the foreigners and traders to be found along the Loango coast (Bastian.1874.i. p.43).

After the German expedition, references to the black Jews of Loango multiplied in literature dealing with racial questions, and they became an important proof-community for the persistence over generations of the Jewish "look." In 1898 the *Encyclopaedia Britannica* stressed their "strikingly Semitic features." The other remote Jewish proof-communities also made a contribution to the notion of the worldwide persistence of the Jewish face. During the cunning demolition by the monogenist ethnographer Jean Louis Armand de Quatrefages de Bréau of the polygenist argument centered on the Jews of Cochin in 1863, he triumphantly quoted the pro-slavery rabbi, Morris Raphal (1798–1868). Raphal had observed that the so-called white Jews of Cochin were not in fact white and that therefore their color had changed as a result of climate from white to brown. However, what was true of color was not true of physiognomy. In the case of the Cochin Jews, Raphal, like many others, maintained that despite the ravages of climate and the passage of time these "white" Jews of Cochin retained "their Jewish cast of features" (*Bulletin de la Société de géographie*.1863 pp.142–148).

In the early 1860s the liberal German psychologist and anthropologist Theodor Waitz (1821–1864) discussed the paramount and essential importance of Jews and blacks in the project of proving racial immutability, to which he was essentially opposed:

> Let us subject that assertion of an absolute immutability of race-types to a closer investigation. *The chief, if not the only proofs are derived from the old Egyptian monuments and the Jews.* Blumenthal recognized upon the

first [monuments] three different human types: that of the Negro, a second, which he calls the Indian type; and a third said to be produced by the influence of the Egyptian climate . . . At a later period Morton distinguished Pelasgic, Semitic and Negro skulls among those of the old Egyptians."

Waitz also referenced the famous American poet, journalist, and travel writer Bayard Taylor, mentioned earlier in the chapter, who had traveled in Egypt and written a vivid account of his journey. Taylor, whose expert views both as traveler and poet were valuable, was even more certain than others that the faces of contemporary Jews and negroes were reflected in the images along the Nile Valley. Taylor, according to Waitz, "still more decidedly points out upon the old Egyptian monuments the distinguishable form of Negroes, Persians and Jews." Many, Waitz pointed out, had argued that the Jews were the clinching proof of the importance of climate in changing color on the one hand and also of the "permanence of type" on the other. And indeed, he asserted that the Jews' unmistakable "national physiognomy" was everywhere to be found "depicted upon the ancient monuments of Egypt." However, Waitz pointed out, this was hardly surprising, as "in every region of the world" their "domestic economy and degree of civilization" had always been a function of the state of oppression in which they lived, and which forced them "to a closer connexion between themselves." In such a case, "no wonder if their cranial type as well as their character remained unchanged" (Waitz.1863 pp.223–224).

However, even accepting the special circumstances surrounding Jews, the unchanging look of the Jewish people took some explaining. For Lieutenant-Colonel Charles Hamilton Smith (1776–1859), the soldier, spy, illustrator, and naturalist, it was an open question:

> It is difficult to decide whether their own obstinacy of character, or the unceasing injustice of mankind, have been other than agents, mutually acting upon each other, to produce that permanent manifestation in their forms and opinions which separates them from human society, as it were, by a lasting miracle; still the persecuted Jew bears on his front the tokens of mental power, in his make the attributes of physical strength. (Smith.1848 p.878)

If anyone had doubted the objectivity of the Jews' alleged "look," there was, if you were ready to accept it, the ready-made, clearly objective, and recently discovered mass of proof in the reliefs and statues of Egypt and Assyria over which scientists pored in their determination to understand, among other things, the origins of humankind. As Josiah Nott, the slave-owning physician from Alabama, put it: "We have no reason to believe that the Hebrew race sprang from, or ever originated, any other type of man." Jews were everywhere discernible as Jews and were physically branded as such for "God has put a mark upon them, by which they may be always known, and for the mere purpose of distinguishing them from other races" (Nott, Gliddon.1857 p.118). As Nott declared,

> a well-marked Jewish face is never seen out of the Abrahamic race; and this fact alone should almost suffice to prove that the features of the Patriarch, and through him that of the ten generations before him, have been faithfully perpetuated . . . Even the dead, who have been sleeping in their tombs for 3 or 4000 years, have risen up to testify to the fact!

The witness that Nott now introduced was no less than the "mummified head of an Israelite" that he had seen in Samuel George Morton's skull collection known as "Golgotha." This head came from an ancient

> Memphitic tomb, in which the national type is so perfect that it would be pronounced in our day, a characteristic specimen of the race . . . The identical features presented by the Jews all over Europe and America, are still found in Mesopotamia, their original abode . . . and yet no one ever looks to climate, or any other cause but the blood of Abraham, to account for the Jewish features. It is true that all races of men are more or less influenced by the extreme of climate . . . but the pure-blooded Jew has never changed his lineaments.

But there were living examples of Jewish immutability even closer to hand than Morton's "Golgotha."

The conclusions drawn by Robert Knox as he scrutinized Jewish faces in an Amsterdam synagogue were similar to those drawn by Nott, at about the same time, as he wandered through the streets of Mobile, in the slave state of Alabama, where there was a small but active Jewish community. The "well-marked" face of the Jew was clearly observable, and fortunately, thanks to the scholarship of archeologists who had provided such useful templates, this well-marked face could now be compared with Jewish faces millennia before.

Layard, the excavator of Nimrud and Nineveh, had recently published his discovery of a number of massive heads in Kuyunjik. One of the heads, an illustration of which was included in Nott's text, struck him as being quintessentially Jewish. "Every resident of Mobile," he wrote, "will recognize in this Chaldean effigy the facsimile portrait of one of their city's most prominent [Jewish] citizens." The citizen in question was almost certainly Philip Phillips (1807–1884), the leading Jew in Mobile and the U.S. representative for Alabama's First Congressional District from 1853 to 1855 (Nott, Gliddon.1854).

Many people were excited by this new anthropological tool and perceived in the reliefs and monolithic statuary more or less what they wanted to see. Charles Darwin, however, was not so easily persuaded. He rejected some of the proposed similarities and took the opportunity to attack the polygenists who had set such store by them, observing that the French naturalist Félix-Archimède Pouchet (1800–1872), who had studied figures in the Nubian remains of Abu Simbel, had said that "he was far from finding recognizable representations of the dozen or more nations which some authors believe that they can recognize. Even some of the most strongly-marked races cannot be identified with that degree of unanimity which might have been expected from what has been written on the subject." Darwin was aware of the importance of the British Museum's "young Memnon" that Nott and Gliddon had claimed had European features but that Robert Knox had insisted resembled the Jews of Antwerp. As he noted,

> Thus Messrs. Nott and Gliddon ("Types of Mankind," p. 148) state that Rameses II., or the Great, has features superbly European; whereas Knox, another firm believer in the specific distinction of the races of man ("Races of Man," 1850, p. 201), speaking of young Memnon (the same person with Rameses II., as I am informed by Mr. Birch) insists in the strongest manner that he is identical in character with the Jews of Antwerp. Again, whilst looking in the British Museum with two competent judges, officers of the establishment, at the statue of Amunoph III., we agreed that he had a strongly negro cast of features. (Darwin.1871 p.218)

Toward the end of the nineteenth century ways of quantifying the racial significance of faces and "expressions" benefited from an improvement in the available technology. One of the proponents of Jewish physiognomy was the Australian-born Jewish anthropologist and prolific folklorist Joseph Jacobs

(1854–1916). Jacobs had studied anthropology at the Statistical Laboratory at University College, London, under the guidance of the polymath Francis Galton (1822–1911), half-cousin of Charles Darwin, and went on to write *Studies in Jewish Statistics: Social, Vital and Anthropometric* (1891), which established him as one of the first Jewish experts in Jewish race science. Jacobs had little doubt that there was such a thing as a "Jewish face." Like many others, he, too, was convinced that the faces of the Jews of his time were faithfully represented by the standard proof-texts of the ancient Egyptian and Assyrian paintings, reliefs, and other plastic arts. He thought that Jewish features could "be traced throughout the history of Art . . . to one of the earliest representations of Jews in Art, the Assyrian bas relief of the captive Jews of Lachish . . . being taken before Sennacherib. The subject is undoubted and well known, and the persistency of the Jewish type for the last 2,600 years is conclusively proved by it." According to him, any Jew could say of another Jew: "That is a Jewish face." In fact, even "the negroes of Surinam, when they see a European and a Jew approach, do not say, 'Here are two whites,' but 'Here is a white and a Jew.'"

Jacobs believed that Jews "even after many generations spent in a foreign climate . . . can still be recognized." However, a clear distinction had to be drawn between face and expression. Jacobs admitted that if one were to turn "from the separate features of the Jewish face to that combination of them which we term expression, it might seem impossible to give anything more than subjective impressions." However, he had discovered a scientific way of approaching this issue through the work of his respected mentor Galton, who had been successful in "compounding" photographs taken of Jewish boys at the Jews' Free School, which confirmed his belief in the immutability and eternal, unchanging purity of the Jewish face[7] (Jacobs.1886; Haddon.1898; Langton.2014).

The same argument was used by Joseph Arthur Gobineau (1816–1882), perhaps the most influential of the race theorists, in his *Essai sur l'inégalité des races humaines* (1853), which was translated into English, in abridged form, by the pro-slavery apologists and polygenists Josiah Nott and Henry Hotze in 1856 as *The Moral and Intellectual Diversity of Races*. Gobineau's overall objective was to combat the monogenism of Prichard and his allies—the "Unitaires," as he called them—who believed in a single creation. He argued that there were significant differences between races that were inherent and unchanging, and that the white race was superior to all others. In opposition to the *Unitaires*' argument about climate, he argued that wherever the Jews had settled, they still looked exactly the same. He wrote:

> They have settled in lands with very different climates from that of Palestine and have given up their ancient mode of life. The Jewish type has, however, remained much the same; the modifications it has undergone are of no importance and have never been enough, in any country or latitude, to change the general character of the race. The warlike Rechabites of the Arabian desert, the peaceful Portuguese, French, German, and Polish Jews—they all look alike. I have had the opportunity of examining closely one of the last kind. His features and profile clearly betrayed his origin. His eyes especially were unforgettable . . . The Semitic face looks exactly the same, in its main characteristics, as it appears on the Egyptian paintings of three or four thousand years ago, and more; and we find it also, in an equally striking and recognizable form, under the most varied and disparate conditions of climate. The identity of descendant and ancestor does not stop at the features; it continues also in the shape of the limbs and the temperament. (Gobineau.1915 p.122)[8]

In his "On the Physical Characteristics of the Jews" (1861), the polygenist John Beddoe (1826–1911), one of the founders of the Ethnological Society of London, was taken by Jews' unique eyes, unlike any others, and their expression, recognizable anywhere, which expressed "a degree of cunning." The pseudonymous Dr. Celticus, while allowing that Jews' eyes were marked predominantly by low cunning, also perceived a crinkling of laugh lines around the eye that he called "toad's eye, all the more so as the Jew has something of the toad. I do not wish to insult this pustular little creature which renders many services to agriculture and gardening." Like Blumenbach, Beddoe, Harriet Martineau, and the poet Bayard Taylor, Gobineau too was struck by the "unforgettable" eyes of his Polish Jew. The Jewish face, with its specific expressions and features, unchanging, in every climate, was the same face that appeared on "Egyptian paintings" (Gobineau.1915 p.122).

The acclimatization of Jews to different physical circumstances was, of course, noteworthy. The Welsh biologist and anthropologist Alfred Russel Wallace noted that the Jews were

> a good example of acclimatization because they have been established for many centuries in climates very different from that of their native land;

they keep themselves almost wholly free from intermixture with the people around them . . . This peculiarity of the Jews has been considered a racial trait . . . This ethnic trait of the Jews is said to have been slowly acquired by their constant migrations, even their temporary stay in Egypt. (quoted by Fishberg.1911 p.17 and taken from the entry "acclimatization" in Volume 1 of the ninth edition of the *Encyclopædia Britannica* 1875)

However, for the polygenist John Beddoe, there was something rather sinister about the Jews' alleged power of adaptability: "The Jews grow not only in number, living longer and dying less readily than the Gentiles among whom they dwell, but they are gradually attracting to themselves the whole wealth of the earth; and wealth is power, and the world must move or halt as wealth bids it" (Beddoe.1893). Finally, citing the French anthropologist, medical geographer, and army physician Jean-Christian Boudin (1806–1867), James Hunt (1833–1869), the excitable London ethnographer and speech therapist, explained that in Algeria, where the French habitually fell prey to the slightest disease, the Jews miraculously survived. The Jews were exceptional in this respect and were truly a race apart—but so were the blacks. Hunt wrote:

The negros offer the strongest proof of the fallacy of saying that all races of men are cosmopolitan. We have ample and positive evidence that they cannot perpetuate themselves beyond about the fortieth degree of north or south latitude. Indeed, in their own region the ascent of a high mountain will kill them, sometimes nearly instantly.

As far as the Jew was concerned, wrote Hunt, published statistics seemed to prove that "the Jew is subject to different physiological laws to those of the people by whom he may be surrounded" (Hunt.1863 p.74).[9]

***

The color spectrum among Jews, supposed by some to be a proof of their adaptability, was not a topic that interested Western Jewish historians, writers, and journalists, not to mention rabbis. They showed little if any interest in the world's black and brown Jewish communities throughout the nineteenth century. However, this was not true of *fin de siècle* Jewish race scientists, who knew of their importance in the great race wars. In his 1902 work *Die Juden als Rasse* (The Jews as a race), J. M. Judt, the Polish Jewish physical anthropologist, carried out a comprehensive study of Jewish racial identity, arguing somewhat like the German scholar Andree in favor of the unadulterated purity of the Jewish race. A keen supporter of Andree's position, Judt mentioned the Loango Jews but, like Andree, with little enthusiasm, as they did not support the idea of the unchanging purity of Jews. Whereas others, a little earlier, had written that the negroes of Loango had a Jewish "look" and "Semitic features," Judt vehemently denied this and stressed that the black Jews' "countenance and skin color" were simply negroid. Judt's overall understanding of Jewish "racial types" was expressed as a table that was split into three sections: "Jews both by religion and birth," "Jews by religion, but not by birth," and "Jews by birth but not by religion." The black Jews of Loango occupy a note referring to the second section, in which they were described as the "Mavumbu or Negro-Jews of the Loango Coast." Judt concluded that *racially* these Jews have stopped being Jews. They could not be considered Jews as their pigmentation was black; all that could be said was that they practiced the Jewish religion.

Judt's arguments about Jewish racial purity were to some extent influenced by the rise of different sorts of Jewish nationalism in central and eastern Europe over the previous twenty or thirty years. His theories constituted a kind of justification for the need for a Jewish homeland, discussions of which filled the Jewish and non-Jewish press by the turn of the century.

Arthur Ruppin (1876–1943), the celebrated Zionist leader and founder of Jewish sociology, who was well aware of the race discussions of his day, contributed to this debate in his 1904 *Die Juden der Gegenwart* (The Jews of Today) by arguing that there was a "racial unity," rather than purity, in Jewish racial makeup no matter where, almost, in the world Jews were to be found, and that there were certain commonalities between Jews and the peoples of the Middle East. This served the Zionist argument: Whereas the differences between Jewish racial characteristics and northern European ones were an impediment to Jews' integration in Europe, this would not be the case in the Middle East when the Jews would be reunited with their racial brethren. For Ruppin, the "Jewish type" was consistent over hundreds of years despite being geographically dispersed throughout the world. The Ethiopian Jews, the Bene Israel of western India, and the black Jews of Cochin, according to Ruppin, did not form part of this racial unity (Morris-Reich.2006).

Judt maintained that intermarriage between races, as apparently practiced by the black Jews of Loango and other Jews "of color," was wrong biologically, as well as it was socially or religiously, as it would lead to infertile unions. He maintained that the hybrid product of such unions, mulattos, like mules, would fail to reproduce and would eventually die out. Although by this time many naturalists had agreed that such amalgamations were fertile, Judt insisted that deviant mixed groups, such as the black Jews of Loango and other Jewish groups of color, would eventually disappear and would not therefore prejudice the purity of the Jewish race.

Other scholars, however, were reaching opposite conclusions about the alleged purity of the Jewish people. Within a few years the intense physical anthropological work involving tens of thousands of subjects worldwide started to give unexpected results. Indeed, they appeared to show that, using the available metrics, there was no such thing as Jewish racial purity and that the idea of a Jewish racial physiognomy, color, or "type" was unfounded. One of the leading figures to reach these conclusions was Maurice Fishberg. On the basis of a wide range of the "modern methods" of scientific racism such as craniometry and physiognomy, he argued that, on the contrary, Jews were universally similar, in physical respects, to the people among whom they lived (Fishberg.1911).

On the eve of the First World War, in one of the first ever concerted efforts to combat racism and understand racial and color difference, a conference was organized. The First Universal Races Congress met over four sweltering summer days in 1911 at the University of London. The conference had been largely organized by the Hungarian-born Jew Gustav Spiller (1864–1940), who was a naturalized British subject.[10] The objective of the conference was to improve the world of race relations. Two thousand one hundred delegates from fifty nations attended the conference, including the African-American sociologist and race activist W. E. B. Du Bois and the American anthropologist Franz Boas. The proceedings were published shortly afterward in a volume edited by Spiller.

Israel Zangwill (1864–1926), the Anglo-Jewish novelist, playwright, and public intellectual, was present at the conference. Three years before, his play *The Melting Plot* had been staged in New York. The play conceived of a utopian America in which all the races of the world would mingle, heralding a new era of world peace. "What is the glory of Rome and Jerusalem," asks the play's hero, "where all nations and races come to worship and look back, compared with the glory of America, where all races and nations come to labour and look forward!"

During the conference Zangwill argued that Jews were already far from being a pure race. Jews and gentiles had mingled for so long that there were evident differences among Jews from different parts of the world, which undermined the idea that they could constitute a "race" at all:

> Gentile blood and the blood of Israel have mingled pretty freely. And if the Jew, with that strange polarity which his historian Graetz remarked in him, displays simultaneously with the most tenacious preservation of his past the swiftest surrender of it that the planet has ever witnessed, if we find him entering with such passionate patriotism into almost every life on earth but his own, may not even the Jewish patriot draw the compensating conclusion that the Jew therein demonstrates the comparative superficiality of all these human differences? Could Jews so readily assimilate to all these types, were these types fundamentally different? The primitive notion of the abysmal separateness of races can scarcely survive under Darwinism. Every race is really akin to every other. Not only is every race akin to every other, but every people is a hotch-potch of races. The Jews, though mainly a white people, are not even devoid of a colored fringe, black, brown, or yellow. There are the Beni-Israel of India, the Falashas of Abyssinia, the disappearing Chinese colony of Kai-Fung-Foo, the Judeos of Loango.

Zangwill and others at the conference concluded that color itself was not a powerful motor of difference. Moreover, blacks, despite all theories to the contrary, were really part of the human race, and Jews in different parts of the world tended to look like their neighbors. Now it was clear that through a study of the color spectrum of Jews, finally some clarity about race was being achieved. As Zangwill put it: "[The Jew] is the pioneer by which the true race theory has been experimentally demonstrated . . . And even the color is not an unbridgeable and elemental distinction" (Spiller.1911 p.276).

For a few hot days, then, on the eve of the Great War, there was a lull in the race polemics in which Jews, black Jews, and blacks had figured so prominently for centuries. But it was just a lull before the storm.

8

The Black/Jew

Sander Gilman, the leading scholar of gentile attitudes toward "the Jew's body"—the title of one of his best-known books, published in 1991, perhaps overstated it when he wrote that the "general consensus of the ethnological literature was that the Jews were 'black' or, at least, 'swarthy.'" The perceived color of Jews in the eighteenth and nineteenth centuries, as it had been in the medieval period, was, in fact, controversial and unstable, and there really was no widely held consensus. Jewish color was entirely in the eye of the beholder. The Zionist leader and sociologist Arthur Ruppin, writing in 1904, like many race experts, did not see a dark color as a racial feature of Jews or a racial issue at all. "The one really important race distinction, skin-colour," he wrote, "a distinction which often calls up a deep-seated instinctive antipathy, does not enter into the question between Jews and Europeans" (Ruppin.1913 p.171).

Indeed, as we have seen, for a whole range of anthropological and racial theories, it was essential that Jews be regarded as white. Polygenists needed to prove the immutability of the Jewish race, and this they did by often pointing to the famously white Jews of Cochin. Similarly, for many of the monogenists, it was equally vital that European Jews be perceived as white, in order that the effects of climate determinism be perceived in the black Jews of Loango, India, the Jordan Valley, Ethiopia, the Sahara, and elsewhere. If the Jew was in fact white, at least in Europe, and if this white Jew could be changed into a black Indian, Middle-Eastern or African Jew, the monogenist argument about the importance of climate determinism was confirmed and the doctrine of the unitary origin of humankind was preserved.

This, as we have repeatedly seen, put an obstacle in the path of the polygenist theory. Some, like the knowledgeable and scholarly polygenist English surgeon Charles White (1728–1813) or the French anthropologist Jean Louis Armand de Quatrefages de Bréau (1810–1892), got around the racial immutability theory, often supported by the fact that the white Jews of Cochin had managed to stay the same color for millennia, by arguing that Jews were not actually white anywhere. As White wrote:

"These people," they said, "are scattered over the face of the earth . . . have preserved themselves distinct from the rest of the world by their religion and as they never marry any but their own sect, so they have no mixture of blood in their veins, that they should differ from each other; yet nothing is more true than that the English Jew is white, the Portuguese swarthy, the American olive, the Arabian copper, and the African black: in short, that there appears to be as many species of Jews as there are countries in which they reside." Now granting them the fact as to color, the premises are by no means just; for the Jews have gained proselytes in every part of the world where they have resided, and they are at liberty to marry those proselytes. But the truth is, that the Jews are generally swarthy in every clime. (White.1799 p.104)

White was not alone. There was a persistent line of reasoning, which grew in strength during the nineteenth century, particularly in polygenist anthropology, that, in order to get out of the snare set by the existence of a color spectrum among Jews, argued that all Jews were the same color: brown. In addition, following a much older template, which we have already discussed, there was a parallel line of thought that argued that Jews everywhere were black, were derived from black Africans, had "black blood," and displayed a negroid "look."

This perspective was to burgeon in importance in the second half of the nineteenth century and on into the twentieth, when, during the period of the Third Reich, it flowered into a conflation of black and Jew in which not only were Jews accorded many of the supposed physical attributes of blacks but were also perceived as manipulating them in the Jews' remorseless war against Aryan racial purity. The perceived typologies of Jews and negroes within this discourse ranged from close to identical, and they constantly fed into each other.

The increasing racialization of blacks, particularly during the periods of the American Civil War, and the European "scramble for Africa," was mirrored by an increasing racialization of Jews, in black terms. As Gilman put it: "In the eyes of the non-Jew who defined them in Western society the Jews became the blacks" (Gilman.1986 p.8). This metaphorical but not necessarily somatic leap involved, as Bruns accurately put it, "taking the Jew at once as the ambivalent inner and outer, black and white, Other" (Bruns.2011 p.112). In other words the Jew, as the archetypal European internal other, became by this process the archetypal external other, which since medieval times had always been a dark figure from the Global South—a Moor, a negro, a blackamoor.

The ambivalence in this construct, as we shall see, arose in part from the fact that doubts persisted about the actual, somatic color of Jews. However, the construction of Jews as black clearly involved a lot more than color. Neil MacMaster explained the construction of the "Africanization" of Jews from the simple "logic of associating Jews with the racial category that immediately and 'instinctively' aroused the most negative and powerful feeling of revulsion in European society ... In searching for an 'interactive' metaphor which would most readily convey the eternal fixity of Jewish racial Otherness, anti-Semites turned to the black" (MacMaster.2000 p.19). What he meant by this is that in trying to convey the unchanging otherness of Jews, European society selected an equally immutable figure to typify Jews: the African black. This process was interactive because it also influenced, markedly, the way in which people of color, throughout the world, were constructed. This interactive process involved Jews being constructed as blacks, and at the same time and for similar reasons blacks being constructed as Jews.

The conflation of Jew and negro was constructed on the earlier foundations of centuries of writing and thought detailing the inseparable links between Jews and negroes and their unique position in the world as peoples apart from the generality of humankind. It was constructed on the occasional medieval conviction that Jews were black and on the more recent obsession with the notion of Jews of color throughout the world. This conflation was thus the culmination of an ancient historical and racial theory and produced the fusion of two ancient streams of hate: the hatred of Jews and the hatred of blacks. The fusion of these hatreds did much to radicalize feelings about Jews and blacks over the following years.

The antisemite Robert Knox was one of the first nineteenth-century physical anthropologists to argue, unambiguously, that Jews were of negro origin. His thinking, as set out in *Races of Men*, has to be viewed against the backdrop of the fight for political emancipation of British Jews, which Knox opposed but which, when he was writing his book, was well on the way to being won. Knox's disappointment with this turn of events drips off the page. Anticipating the arguments of the German anti-Semite Wilhelm Marr (1819–1904) a few years later, he argued that the Jews had no right to emancipation. They were categorically not part of the Caucasian race; indeed, they belonged to the dark races of men. They were African and Asiatic, not European . . . the purest of the Jewish race is a dark tawny, yellow-colored person, with jet-black hair and eyes seemingly colored: there is no mistaking the race when pure: it is Egyptian—that is, African . . . A series of incorrect observations, commencing with Blumenbach, but not terminating with Prichard, led to errors which no doubt will hold their ground for centuries. (Knox.1850 p.300)

Knox's conviction that Jews had black blood was shared by Gobineau, whose *Essai sur l'inegalité des races humaines* appeared in 1853. According to Gobineau, a distant alliance, millennia ago, between the Semites and Hamites had led to an infusion of black blood into the Jewish people. This black blood had remained and was largely responsible for the Jews' lack of true culture. Jews were no more than hybrid mulattos with a negro core. This ancient black core was the remnant of a very primitive people who lived in caves and was feared by travelers. The idea that Jewish cultural specificity was closely linked with African primitivism would linger until after the Second World War, as we will show.

Different countries had distinct purposes to which the exciting new science of physical anthropology could be put. In Germany, after 1870, it was used to demonstrate the links between the various populations of the new German Reich. In France, after the humiliation of the Franco-German War, physical anthropology was employed to restore national dignity through attempts to identify the ancestors of the modern French as a warrior people. In Great Britain, ethnologists in general, including Prichard and the monogenist Robert Gordon Latham (1812–1888), had a particular interest in analyzing the variety of the peoples who made up Britain's fast-expanding overseas empire and how they related to each other. This involved comparisons of a whole range of black and brown peoples throughout the world with their British masters. Latham was the author of *The Natural History of the Varieties of Man* (1850) and *The Ethnology of the British Colonies and Dependencies* (1851).[1] Like Knox, Gobineau, and a number of his contemporaries, Latham helped build the growing consensus that negroes were significantly different from Europeans and that Jews, while not necessarily sharing an identical color with negroes, were nonetheless very similar to them: "points of similarity," he wrote, "with the Semitic nations is the rule rather than the exception with the African tribes, Negro and *non*-Negro: a fact which makes the Jews, Arabs and Syrians, *African*, rather than the Africans Semitic" (Latham.1850 p.477).

The idea that Jews and negroes had common origins was expressed more and more frequently from midcentury. As was made clear in this discourse, signs of negroid characteristics and descent were more obvious in some Jews than others. In fact, there were sometimes assumed to be two distinct types of Jews: one mainly Semitic, and the other mainly negroid.

In *Les Races humaines* Abel Hovelacque (1843–1896) the lawyer, radical political figure, and, from 1890, president of the *École d'anthropologie*,[2] argued, following a medieval template, that while Africans resembled apes, the chief characteristic of the Jew was the "accentuated profile of the goat." But side by side with this finer type of goat-like Jew was a coarser negroid and simian Jewish type, "with wavy or frizzy hair, rather fat lips and a much wider nose." Hovelacque saw in this proof of "an ancient cross with a less advanced race," by which he meant that at some time in the more or less remote past Jews had mingled and crossed with black Africans (Hovelacque.1882 p.139).

The Cambridge anthropologist Alfred Cort Haddon (1855–1940) made a similar contribution to the question of Jewish origins. In *The Study of Man* (1898) he argued that there were in fact two quite different, fundamental types of Jews. One section of the Jewish people, the superior type, had an "intelligent and dignified appearance." The other type, seemingly negroid, descended from the lower elements. Like blacks everywhere these low types had a round head, "the forehead low and retreating, but the nose is rarely much developed; in many cases the lips are thick, the hair frizzly" (Haddon.1898 p.18).

Subsequently, in 1903, the ferociously, almost parodically antisemitic French pamphleteer, the pseudonymous Dr. Celticus, also perceived two distinct strands of Jews. He was initially led to this conclusion by the existence of two kinds of noses among the Jews: the typical "hooked nose" representing the "true Jew" and the "horrible" degenerate, round snub nose, which was considered to be typically African (Celticus.1903; Gilman.1998).

This African form of nose came about as a result of the crossing of Jews and negroes. Conflating two of the seminal symbols of Jews and blacks, goats and apes, he argued that as a result of this mixing of blood, while the Jews more often than not looked (and smelled) like goats, some of the younger ones, like negroes, also looked like apes, and in general the jutting jaw of the Jew, like that of the negro, was reminiscent both of goats and gorillas. The gorilla trope, introduced by Celticus, was not uncommon in constructions of Jews, and indeed was a way of associating them with negroes.

Ears were often viewed as potent carriers of somatic difference: Sir Arthur Keith (1866–1955), the conservator of the Hunterian Museum of the Royal College of Surgeons in London, was convinced that it was the human ear's external configuration that was the most visible racial label. Jews' ears, in particular, were often pounced on as being giveaway somatic indicators and were frequently compared, like those of negroes, to the ears of gorillas and monkeys (Taguieff.2008; Sagaert.2013).

Of the many shared characteristics of Jews and negroes, a foul smell was one of the most frequently evoked, as we have noted in an earlier age, and the olfactory slur against Jews and negroes was persistent over centuries. John Crawfurd (1783–1868), the Scottish polygenist, nicknamed because of his outspoken polygenism "the inventor of forty Adams," noted that Africans had "a peculiar odor of the skin, offensive to, and unknown in, the other races of man," and this was a universal motif in the anti-black rhetoric of the American slave states (Estes.1846 p.63). Wilhelm Marr (1819–1904), the self-styled "Patriarch of antisemitism," visited the United States and was initially well disposed to the blacks, but nonetheless was appalled by the smell of a group of blacks he encountered in a railway carriage. He complained that they stank "of ten muskrats" (Bruns.2014 p.127). "The Negro aroma," wrote Richard Burton, "can be distinguished, I believe, amongst all the pure tribes . . . Exertion of body brings it out, and mental emotion, as among ferrets; during coition it is painfully developed" (Burton.1864 p.237).

Burton found little to like in the Jewish body either, from the eyes—"the small fat-lidded organ of the Jew" (Burton.1898 p.140)—to the "Jew smell," which "went by the name bui shimit in Persia" (Burton.1864 p.237). Some years later Dr. Celticus developed this medieval Jew-odor trope as he sought to define precisely what the smell of Jews actually was. This, he admitted, was a difficult task, but according to the pseudonymous doctor, even the most costly French soaps of the time such as the "Congo" or the "*Trèfle incarnat*" (crimson clover) scent, introduced in 1898 by the Paris firm L. T. Piver, would do nothing whatsoever to help the wealthy Jewess get rid of her smell, no matter how hard she tried (Celticus.1903). George-Alexis Montandon (1879–1944) was a French-Swiss anthropologist and author of *Comment Reconnaître et Expliquer le Juif*? (How to recognize and explain the Jew) whose anthropological writing on Jews vied with that of Dr. Celticus for sheer viciousness. Montandon combined the trope of Jewish and negro odor by arguing that the bad smell of Jews was something inherited directly from their negro ancestors. In fact, the smell of a Jew was the smell of a negro (Montadon.1940).

The French historian Léon Poliakov argued that whereas Jews and blacks represented fundamental racial categories, there were nonetheless such great differences in the specificity of the hatred of Jews and the hatred of blacks that they could hardly be viewed in the same light. Poliakov pointed out that in the case of Johann Wolfgang von Goethe (1749–1832), the great writer's fundamental objections to Jews arose from their arrogant claim to be the chosen people and from their financial astuteness (Poliakov.1971 p.259). This, argued Poliakov, was akin to the hatred of the oppressive master or father figure, whereas hatred of blacks was based on their lustfulness (*lubricité*) and their animalistic qualities. Expressed in Freudian terms, the Jews embodied a "'*surmoi*' *répressif*" and the blacks a "'*ça*' *déchainé et menaçant*." The different expressions of the id and the superego thus explain why, according to Poliakov, criticisms made respectively of Jews and blacks in general have little or nothing to do with each (Poliakov.1971 p.259). However, the hybridic conflation of Jews and blacks, the alleged animalistic features they had in common, their disturbing color, smell, racial immutability, exceptionalism, the sexual fear and desire they both provoked, and the close-to-identical construction of Jews and blacks during the Third Reich and in Fascist Italy and earlier weigh very heavily against this analysis. Moreover, in 1828, even Goethe had no hesitation in proclaiming his polygenist convictions, which were becoming fashionable at the time, which included his belief that Jews and Blacks had different founding events from Europeans (Schutjer.2015 pp.5–6).

Powerful links between anti-black racism and the racial hatred of Jews may be seen in various European contexts. It has been argued, for instance, not least by the German Jewish political philosopher Hannah Arendt (1906–1975), that the seeds of the persecution and final destruction of Jews in Germany and other parts of Europe were propagated by colonial persecution of blacks and particularly by the racism and genocide perpetrated by the Germans in their colonies, especially in German South-West Africa (today's Namibia) and the genocide of the Herero and Namaqua peoples that occurred between 1904 and 1907. The idea of genocide, the model for genocide, had been produced as a template that could later be copied. However, there is a complicating aspect to this analysis.

Of all black Africans, it was the Khoikhoi or Khoi, the indigenous pastoralists of southwestern Africa, termed Hottentots by the Dutch and subsequently by other Europeans, who became the paradigm of the radically extreme "other" and the "ugly race" par excellence—a monstrous race that perhaps formed a missing link between true humanity and the orangutan. In 1497, right at the beginning of Western exploration of southern Africa, the Portuguese explorer Vasco da Gama referred to them as "small in stature, ugly of face," and this trope would continue. In a journal entry in 1657 Jan van Riebeeck (1619–1677), the Dutch colonial administrator who founded Cape Town, said that they were "very ugly and stinking people," while in 1684 François Bernier (1620–1688), the French physician and traveler discussed earlier, noted that they "seem to constitute a different type from those of the rest of Africa . . . usually smaller, thinner, with uglier faces . . . passionately fond of carrion-meat, which they eat raw, and they wind bits of the guts around their arms and necks." The French philosopher and mathematician Pierre-Louis Moreau de Maupertuis (1698–1759) concluded that while all black Africans constituted a new type of mankind, he had observed that on the southernmost tip of the African continent were to be found the most hideous people in the world—the Hottentots. The prurient interest shown in the ugliness of the Hottentots is exemplified by the regular exploitation of Khoikhoi in fairs, private homes, and circuses. One Khoikhoi woman, the famous so-called Hottentot Venus, Sara Baartman (1770s–1815), was exhibited as a freak in Great Britain and France. Another Khoikhoi girl was shown in the United States by P. T. Barnum as representing "the missing link" between apes and humankind. The French naturalist Georges Cuvier (1769–1832), who, as we have seen, believed that black Africans were the least developed human group on earth on account of their *crâne comprimé* (compressed skull), danced with Baartman at a voyeuristic Paris gathering. He was so intrigued that on her death he made a plaster cast of her body and preserved her skeleton, genitals, and brain, which were subsequently displayed in the *Museum d'histoire naturelle* in Paris. The museum's director, Geoffroy Saint-Hilaire (1772–1844), a specialist in teratology (the study of monsters or abnormalities), was even more obsessed by Baartman than Cuvier.

    The taxonomic racial tradition represented so tragically by Baartman intersected the taxonomic tradition that concerned Jews. Jews, black, or dark, and hideous to behold, were regularly inserted into the category of Hottentots. From the seventeenth century on Hottentots were regarded by many scholars and travelers as having Jewish biological roots—to be literally descendants of Jews.

One of these scholars was Peter Kolben (variously referred to as Kolb, Kolben, Kolbe, and Colbe) (1675–1725), an astronomer from Neustadt an der Aisch in Bavaria, who was sent by the Dutch to the Cape to explore southern Africa and make astronomical and meteorological observations. His book, *Caput Bonae Spei Hodiernum Das ist vollstandige Beschreibung des Africanischen Vorgeburges der Guten Hofnung* (Nuremberg, 1719) came out in Dutch in 1727, in French in 1743, and in English in 1731 as *The Present State of the Cape of Good-Hope, or, A Particular Account of Several Nations of the Hottentots: Their Religion, Government, Laws, Customs, Ceremonies, and Opinions; Their Art of War, Professions, Language, Genius*. It had considerable success (although it did not help Kolben, as he died in extreme poverty) and for the next fifty years at least was the definitive account of the Hottentots. He claimed not only that the customs and traditions of the Hottentots were similar to those of the Jews, but that biologically they should be counted among the children of Abraham and that they were of Jewish blood. Other scholars followed this same line of reasoning. In this radical conflation of Jews and blacks, the African people, widely considered to be the ugliest in the world, were in fact descended from Europe's ugliest people, the Jews (Kestling.1998; Parfitt.2013).

On the African colonial frontier there was a longstanding conflation of Jews and Hottentots: indeed, the biological origins of countless African tribes were explicated in Jewish terms, just as their religions and languages were found to derive respectively from biblical Judaism and Hebrew. Viewed from this perspective it may not be fanciful to draw a connection between the genocide of the Hottentots by the Germans and the later genocide of their supposed kinsmen. Arendt did not mention that the "Hottentots" had been constructed as Jews and as Africa's "ugly people" par excellence for hundreds of years in the work of European travelers and scholars.Nonetheless, this conflation of Jews and the ugliest of all black Africans was widely known and had long been inserted into the mental cartography of the West. The genocide of so-called Hottentots, and allied peoples, was also, in a sense, a genocide of Jews.

A number of political theorists have failed to find the continuities suggested by Arendt and have argued that the most potent seeds of the Holocaust are to be found in aspects of nineteenth-century German antisemitism or in excesses perpetrated by German troops during the First World War, or in Poland or France during the early stages of the Second World War (Kundrus.2005). But it could, perhaps, be argued that German racially inspired anti-black hatred (shown in German South-West Africa and elsewhere in German colonies, and consistently during the period of the Third Reich), the growing hatred of Jews (understood increasingly in racial terms), and the eventual conflation of these two seminal hatreds of the West were, among other powerful factors, responsible for the virulent form of Jew hatred that developed in Germany after the First World War and that culminated in the Holocaust.

European racism was undoubtedly affected by currents in other parts of the world. American anti-black prejudice and legislation, for instance, influenced German colonial and metropolitan treatment of blacks. The American legislative and social model of anti-black discrimination also had considerable bearing on the development of racial attitudes toward Jews, and would continue to do so, as we shall see, throughout the period of the Third Reich. A telling example of American influence may be perceived in the works of the important political agitator Wilhelm Marr (1819–1904), the self-styled "Patriarch of antisemitism," who is often termed the founder of modern antisemitism. Born in Magdeburg, the son of a flamboyant theatrical personality who was often assumed to be a Jew, Marr had three Jewish wives, was fond of their families, loved one of them to distraction, and recanted his odious views, rather pathetically, on his deathbed, which was attended by poverty and obscurity.

Marr started his political career in Switzerland as an out-and-out radical with anarchist leanings.[3] After the failure of the 1848 revolution and the reinstatement of the *ancien régime*, Marr decided to head off to Costa Rica to seek his fortune. Observing with growing approval the slavery of black Africans in Central America and also in the United States, he developed fiercely racist views (Bruns.2014 p.128). In Nicaragua he referred to indigenous people as "one third tiger, one third monkey, and the last third pig" and declared that "it would really be a pity . . . if it were true that all human beings are brothers." He was accused of having stated that "negroes were closer to animals than human beings" and was even charged with slave trading by the Berlin Central Colonization Society (Bruns.2014 p.128).

Back in Germany he wrote provocatively in defense of the American enslavement of blacks and, having turned his back on the progressive causes he had once supported, and through a process that involved the conflation of Jews and blacks, he become what he called an Antisemite. He is often credited with the invention of this term, although it now seems that he simply played a role in the process of the coinage (Bruns.2014 p.125).[4] In a polemical pamphlet called *Der Judenspiegel* (1862) (A Mirror to the Jews), following Knox, Gobineau, and many other contemporary naturalists, he argued that the despised blood of the negro flowed freely in the veins of Jews. He went on to write a bestselling tract, *Der Weg zum Siege des Germanenthums über das Judenthum* (1879) (The Victory of Jewry over Germandom). It had great success, and the last of the twelve editions was exploited to drum up support for his new political party, the *Antisemiten-Liga* (Antisemites' League), which, despite its failure, can be seen as launching modern political, racial antisemitism (Zimmermann.1986).

Marr became a racist in America. In this respect he may be compared with the Irishman John Campbell (1810–1874), the onetime progressive Chartist who transformed himself, in the United States, into a fervent anti-black racist with strong views about the radical difference of the Jew, or William Cobbett (1763–1835), the revered English radical political activist who went to the United States and became a reactionary pro-slavery bigot (as well as antisemite). He may also be compared with Alfred Ploetz (1860–1940), the coiner of the term *Rassenhygiene* (race hygiene), who learned to admire American racism during a sojourn in the United States and gradually became a leading racial theorist with respect to Jews. Indeed, as we shall see, German anti-Semites would continue to be nourished and inspired by the model of American anti-black racism for many decades to come. The message was clear: What America was doing to its negroes, Europe could do to its own negroes, the Jews. [5] As far as these figures are concerned—and figures much closer to our own time as well—there is a straight line connecting anti-black racism with antisemitism (Bruns.2014).

As Marr's career shows, at precisely the moment when European Jews were officially being perceived as citizens, and no longer as outsiders or pariahs, new ways of expressing hatred of Jews were being devised. It was no longer adequate to argue that Judaism as a religion or other social features of the Jews were at the root of Jews' difference and inferiority, as the Enlightenment had argued. Something more fundamental was now required.

Marr argued that all differences between Jews and others had to do with race and blood; nothing else mattered. Marr wrote of innate, ugly, inferior Jewish physical qualities, just as previously he had written of negroes' ugliness, bestiality, physical inadequacy, and incompetence. But for Marr the Jew had become more than just the racially different, inferior, and unchanging equivalent of the negro. The conflation of Jew and negro had created a hybrid: part Jew, part black (Zimmermann.1986; Scherr.2003).

Jews and negroes, as we have seen in the case of the so-called Hottentots, were often hybridized through their ugliness. Ugliness obviously acts as a powerful tool of identity demarcation and as an agent of devalorization, provoking contempt and hatred. Ugliness was the chief taxonomic tool of Christoph Meiners (1747–1810), the polygenist German historian, philosopher, and Göttingen professor who is considered one of the founders of scientific racism. Meiners had a great influence on Gobineau, Georges Vacher de Lapouge (1854–1936), and the embittered Scot Robert Knox. His views would later be greatly admired by the Nazis.[6] Meiners' *Grundriss der Geschichte der Menschheit* (Outline of the History of Mankind) (Frankfurt and Leipzig, 1785) argued that every race in the world had a separate founding event. He argued, moreover, that a principal characteristic of race was the extent to which it was ugly or beautiful, and he posited an overarching division of humankind into the "beautiful White race" and the animalistic and monstrous "ugly black race." A colleague called Meiners "the beloved philosopher of our Fatherland," but he showed little love to much of humanity. Blacks he demonized as cannibals and as monstrous: they had "a frightful, tiger-like, hardly human look." Their teeth "lock together like the bite of a fox." They so loved human flesh that "they bite huge chunks of flesh from the arms or legs of their neighbors, and fellow slaves, and swallow them down" (Figal.2010 p.76).

Jews were included in the ugly category: They were often understood to be both ugly and permanently degenerate.[7] Jews and negroes, linked in this widely articulated vision through their physical and spiritual ugliness, were two groups incapable, as we have seen, of being absorbed into Western society. The physical and moral ugliness, monstrosity, and blackness that had so often been attributed to Jews in medieval Europe inserted them automatically into the same category as negroes, the other archetypally primitive, ugly, monstrous race. Marked by these internal and external markers, Meiners insisted neither blacks nor Jews could demand the same rights as whites and Christians. Self-evidently monstrous Jews could not become Christians any more than monstrous negroes could become white (Sagaert.2013; Bruns.2011).

In the American slave states the absolute ugliness of negroes was regularly emphasized. "There is less beauty in the general form and outline of the Negro," opined Mathew Estes, of Columbus, Mississippi, in 1846, "than in that of the white man. He has a flat, ugly foot ... evidently designed, like the foot of a camel, to tread upon the sands of the great tropical deserts ... The

Negro has . . . a large mouth; ugly features" (Estes.1846 p.63). Of the nineteen principal defects found among Jews and elaborated in the racialized vision of the hate-filled Dr. Celticus, ugliness was paramount (Celticus.1903).

MacMaster has argued that the

> association between "black" and Jew can be interpreted as one particular example of this wider process of racialization: however . . . while the Jew was invariably racialized as a "Negro," the relationship rarely flowed in the opposite direction such that black people were denigrated as "Jews." This unidirectional linkage derives from the fact that blacks constituted, from an early stage, the basic model of the inferior racial Other, which was deployed to "blacken" and racialize the Jews. (MacMaster, Neil.2000 p.8)

In reality the linkage was not 'unidirectional'. Nineteenth-century race theorists linked Jews with negroes and also linked negroes with Jews. The odium attached to Jews long before the Enlightenment was at least as great as that attached to blacks. The articulation of the similarity in the skin tone and other features of blacks and Jews may be seen, on the one hand, as part of a project to denigrate Jews, but it must also be seen as part of the larger narrative of the inferiorization of black, colored, and other colonized people throughout the world.

Since the European voyages of discovery began in the fifteenth century, Europeans had systematically constructed little-known peoples from the Aztecs to the New Zealand Maori as Jews or Israelites. This is such a widespread phenomenon that it is strange that it has not been investigated more thoroughly by postcolonial theorists. The Judaizing hybridization of the colonial world had the perhaps unintended effect of inserting such colonized or soon-to-be-colonized peoples into a category of known and understood otherness, as well as a category of inferiority and subjugation.

With the exploration and colonization of Africa, black people with their various cultures came into view as they never had before, and had to be explained and understood. African blacks, from the "ugly people" (the so-termed Hottentots) to the Masai, the Yoruba, Igbo, Tutsi, Zulu, Xhosa, Bassa, Ibibio, Fula, Banyankole, Baluba, Khoikhoi, Shona, Makalanga, Esan, Efik, Baluba, Fon, Fulani, Meru, Nga, Soninke, Tiv, Yibir, among others, were regularly constructed, racialized, explained, perceived, and described, precisely as Jews, as people with biological, Jewish roots, in whose lives, ideas, and practices remnants of an ancient Judaism could still allegedly be made out, in whose languages traces of Hebrew could still allegedly be identified and in whose veins Jewish blood assuredly flowed. Unfortunately, space will not permit me to further describe this element of the conflation of Jews and blacks in the Western imaginary. In any event, these conflations have been exhaustively considered elsewhere. I first explored the construction of Africans as Jews in my *Lost Tribes of Israel* (2002) and subsequently in a book I co-wrote with Yulia Egorova, *Genetics, Mass Media, and Identity* (2005), and in my *Black Jews in Africa and the Americas* (2013). A number of scholars have contributed to this field, notably Edith Bruder, who completed her doctorate at the School of Oriental and African Studies, University of London, under my supervision, and went on to publish her work (Bruder.2008), and more recently Nathan Devir, William Miles, Marla Brettschneider, John Jackson, and a number of others. The projections that have been described in this growing body of scholarship were often internalized by Africans themselves, and in many cases developed into imagined ethnicities and new religious movements. Similarly, blacks toiling in the slave farms of the Americas perceived themselves as Israelites toiling in Egypt's bondage, and this metaphorical association fed into the development of new black-Jewish ethnicities in the United States and new religious movements more or less associated with the religions of Jews. Such conflations of the Jewish and negro experience had the effect of demeaning Jews by association with "primitive" black peoples and demeaning blacks by association with Jews (Parfitt.2013).

While colonized blacks in Africa and slaves in the United States were being constructed or were constructing themselves as Jews, Jews were being inserted into the category of colonized blacks. During the Enlightenment, particularly in Germany but elsewhere as well, Jews were repeatedly imagined into a classification of enslaved and subjugated peoples, particularly blacks. Johann David Michaelis (1717–1791), the distinguished Hebraist, was a member of the Göttingen school of history, which played a decisive role in the development of racial thought, principally through the work of Blumenbach and Meiners. In 1782, Michaelis proposed that Jews, who could not, a priori, be assimilated into the Prussian state, should, like black African slaves, be settled in overseas slave plantations. In discussions about the extent to which Jews could or could not be incorporated into European political structures, the expulsion and resettlement of the Jews became a popular option. Between 1774 and 1819 there were no less than forty proposals for settling European Jews in colonies in remote parts of the world such as the

Caribbean or Australia, where the first British penal settlements for convicts were established in 1788.

Michaelis argued that in Prussia there was no use for the Jews: they could not readily be made productive or beneficial, but they could be transformed into rather more useful negroes. If only Prussia owned "sugar islands," he lamented, Jews could be put to work in the Caribbean, where their non-European origins as a "southern race of Asiatic refugees" would enable them to engage in hard labor alongside their black brothers in the "unhealthy climate" of the slave colonies. Often constructed in this discourse as black, negro, and servile, Jews once again began to resemble representations of their medieval forbears (Hess.2000 p.59).

At the same time as Jews in Europe and the United States were being understood as having "black blood" and the model of American treatment of blacks was inspiring attitudes toward Europe's Jews, black ethnic groups throughout Africa, indeed people of color throughout the world, were being understood and explicated in every remote corner of the colonized world as having "Jewish blood." Suffice it to say here that an endemic feature of the colonial project was the universal construction of imagined Jewish and Israelite histories for a vast number of the world's peoples. This phenomenon is one of the most revealing of linkages between Jews and blacks (Parfitt.2002; 2013).

One of the most influential of all nineteenth-century race theorists, Houston Stewart Chamberlain (1855–1927), the influential Germanophile, British racialist writer, set himself the task of explaining both the written work and music of his father-in-law-to-be, Richard Wagner, in a systematic racial narrative. In 1899 he published *Die Grundlagen des neunzehnten Jahrhunderts* (The Foundations of the Nineteenth Century.1911), which expounded his belief in the greatness, beauty, and creativity of the Aryan peoples. Much influenced by Gobineau, Chamberlain, too, believed that the blood of blacks flowed in the veins of Jews.

This was not much emphasized by Chamberlain, and he did not waste time over it. As he put it:

> All historically great races and nations have been produced by mixing; but wherever the difference of type is too great to be bridged over, then we have mongrels . . . As a matter of fact, the current opinion is that the Semite and even that purest Bedouin type are the most absolute mongrels imaginable, the product of a cross between negro and white man! (Chamberlain.1911 p.389)

Racial mixing, according to him, was a normal phenomenon, but in the case of the Jews it involved a cross between two incompatible races, thus creating something monstrous. Chamberlain proclaimed that

> Gobineau preached this doctrine fifty years ago, and was laughed at: today his opinion is the orthodox one: Ranke [he meant Friedrich Ratzel] defines it thus in his *Völkerkunde* (ii.399): "The Semites belong to the mulatto class, a transition stage between black and white." (Chamberlain.1911 p.368)

The Friedrich Ratzel to whom Chamberlain intended to refer was a geographer and ethnographer, best known for inventing the word *Lebensraum*, in the Nazi sense of racial, nationalist expansion. Ratzel agreed that the Jews had indeed mingled with surrounding nations, which would explain the physical differences between, for instance, German Jews and their Portuguese co-religionists. But no matter with whom they mixed, the effect of negro blood was always present, even among the Jews of northern Europe. "Something of a mulatto strain" remained, even among "the blonde Jews" (Ratzel.1898 iii p.584).

The conflation of Jews' and negroes' racial characteristics, very much along the lines that they were imagined by midcentury racial theorists, was exploited by the revolutionary socialist, philosopher, and economist (and Jew) Karl Marx (1818–1883) in an attack in 1863 on the Jewish socialist leader Ferdinand Lassalle (1825–1864). Marx invoked the ancient antisemitic trope claiming that Jews descend from a rabble of negroes, lepers and Hebrews who had joined together in the exodus from Egypt. (British historian Paul Johnson called this allegation the "fundamental matrix of antisemitism, the Ur-libel, embroidered and repeated through the centuries with extraordinary persistence" Johnson, Paul.1988 p.29). Marx prefigured later conflations of anti-black racism and antisemitism by calling Lassalle a "Jewish nigger." He explained that

> as both the shape of his head and his hair texture shows, he descends from the Negroes who joined Moses' flight from Egypt (unless his mother or grandmother on the paternal side hybridized with a nigger). Now, this combination of German-ness and Jewishness with a primarily Negro substance creates a strange product. The pushiness of the fellow is also nigger-like. (Lindemann. 1997 p.164)

We can also briefly consider the well-known and much-quoted statement the following year, 1863, of the antisemitic German philosopher Bruno Bauer (1809–1882) in *Das Judenthum in der Fremde* (1863) that "the Jew is a white negro, but the robust nature and the capacity for physical work of the negro are missing and are replaced by a brain which by size and activity bring the Jew close to the Caucasian peoples." On one level, this indicates a nonsomatic connection between Jews and negroes, but at the same time, for the atheist materialist Bauer, the ugly and alien religion of the Jews was created in the first place by the Jews' physical and physiological nature (Stern. 1979. p.498).

Like African slaves, Jews could theoretically be shipped off to a distant land—Bauer proposed the Land of Canaan. Beyond their shared physical traits, they also shared a tendency to the primitive, and to barbarism. In the previous century, for the German Enlightenment, the Jews enjoyed a special status as "primitives" in terms of aesthetic sensibilities and the nature of their beliefs, and it was this primitive nature that formed one of the basic links between Jews and blacks.

The usual perception of anti-black prejudice and hatred on the one hand, and antisemitism on the other, is that they were practiced by different people, in different places, for different reasons, and at different times. However, we have seen that hatred of blacks was more likely than not to accompany hatred of Jews, and that in the construct of the "black/Jew" the two hatreds were intertwined.

By way of example, one would not automatically think that the viscerally anti-black theologian, polygenist, and polemicist Jason Darrow would have had much room in his wizened heart for much antisemitism. He lived in the virtually Jew-free slave state of Kentucky, where 25 percent of the population at the time was African-American. In his 1846 work *The New Light, Or, Discourses on the Christian Church, on the Evils of Sectarianism and on the True Manner of Becoming Christians*, Darrow devoted himself to the vilification of blacks. He proposed repellent views about African monstrosity and the coupling of negroes with pongos and other primates. Countering the monogenist idea that blackness was the result of climate determinism, Darrow wrote:

> There is another cause for the black skin, the wooly head, the flat nose, the thick lip, the inverted shin, and the diagreeable [sic] fetor. I can think of no reasonable cause but . . . the degeneracy of blood by bestiality. It is not for me to say with positive certainty, with what species of animal this unnatural

intercourse first existed. I will not indeed affirm that it was only with one species; for it may have been with several. But I will affirm my conviction that it was with some animal that approached very near in form and size to the human race, of which there are several varieties in the very countries whence the negroes come and where they are indigenous [sic]. Is it therefore unreasonable to suppose that in former times, in that warm country where passions are known to be strong and uncontrollable, the human race in some instances mingled with Ourang Outangs, baboons, or other similar African animals approximating very nearly to the size and figure of man? This, I believe is the source of the depravation of human blood in the negro tribe, of that fearful dissimilarity in form and color, which obtains between purely human persons and those degraded Africans who have been imported into our midst . . . Those almost semi-human African animals, as I am compelled to suppose, the "wild men of the woods" or Ourang Outangs, in relation to the human race . . . have formed a weak inferior kingdom, but there is no mutual cleaving together of the two different natures. What two things are further apart than a white man and a negro! (Darrow.1846 p.452)

Darrow finished his diatribe with a frank acknowledgment of the sexual relations between masters and slaves, which were an important part of the life of the slave states. The colonial desire for black women, and the colonial fear of black men, formed two of the most obvious pillars of the white experience of blacks in America. "What a gulf or chasm between them," Darrow lamented, "and yet strange to say, what an attraction is, by the vices of men, established between them! Forever repelling, yet for ever mingling; forever two, yet striving to be one!"

A couple of pages later, Darrow turned his venom on the Jews, whom he firmly inserted into the same bestial and monstrous category as negroes:

M. Voltaire, the witty French philosopher . . . spoke of the Jews as anciently guilty of bestiality, and, indeed, as the only people who had laws against this unnatural crime . . . "It is still uncertain," wrote Voltaire, "whether any monsters were produced by this unnatural copulation, and whether there is any foundation in the ancient stories of fauns, satyrs, centaurs, and minotaurs: history says there were, but natural philosophy has not yet cleared up this monstrous account." (Darrow.1846 p.453)

The colonial desire and fear that was attached to blacks was also attached to Jews. Darrow thought that some of the "more depraved" of the Jews in ancient times had practiced buggery with goats and other animals. This clearly "could not fail to confuse and corrupt human blood," and as a result of these practices among Jews and blacks, "monsters certainly often resulted." The Jew, carrying in his blood traces of the libidinous goat, was as much to be feared as the negro. Jews and negroes both had monstrous origins following distant coupling with animals and could not be considered fully human (Darrow.1846 p.454ff).

Dr. Arthur Talmage Abernethy (1872–1956) of Rutherford College, North Carolina, another formerly slave state, thought along the same lines. Abernethy was a well-educated man, a Methodist pastor, journalist, poet, and theologian, author of some fifty books and pamphlets. In 1938 he was nominated by U.S. president Franklin D. Roosevelt an "American Ambassador of Sunshine" and was elected to the American Association for the Advancement of Science. Abernethy, too, argued that Jews were of negro origin. His 1910 "ethnographic" work, proclaimed by *The Literary Digest* as "the most startling book of the year," was entitled *The Jew a Negro: Being a Study of the Jewish Ancestry from an Impartial Standpoint*. Abernethy argued that "the Jew of today, as well as his ancestors in other times is the kinsman and descendant of the Negro."

Abernethy admitted that it would be

> difficult for the Jews of to-day to recognize their less cultured African brother, whose skin, in his racial dependency and long years of uninterrupted repose under the degenerating climatic conditions of Africa has retained its ebon hue, and whose mind has not yielded so readily to the enlivening processes of the sharp practices of trade. (Abernethy.1910 p.105)

Nonetheless, he continued,

> the gradations of ethical culture, intermarriage, migration, and intimacies with Caucasian races have elevated the Jewish people to a condition where they control vast commercial enterprises, possess some social prominence, and but for their retained brunetteness, in many respects resemble the Caucasians. Yet thousands of years of effort to throw off their nigrescence have failed to eradicate those race characteristics, and the Jew of to-day is essentially Negro in habits, physical peculiarities and tendencies. The Jews

who have migrated in modern times into African and other Negro countries, have quickly drifted back into the habits and conduct of the uncivilized Negro races surrounding them. (Abernethy.1910 pp.105–106)

In other words, Abernethy argued that the Jews were both a mongrel race, which had been molded by centuries of intermarriage with Europeans, and also purely African. They were annoyingly white, but at the same time they were black. Their nigrescence was fundamental. Their attempts to throw off their negro characteristics were bound to fail. Once they moved back to Africa, they were revealed for what they were: a purely African race. We do not know the identity of those Jews who had "migrated in modern times into Africa and other Negro countries," but it is likely that the much-discussed black Jews of Loango were in his mind. For Abernethy, Jews were, moreover, full of bestial and monstrous traits, including sexual depravity, which were derived from their negro ancestors in the jungles of Africa. Negroid interracial sexual transgression and exuberance were also attributed to Jews. "Their pitiable disregard—especially among the men—for the finer conventionalities of social life, as well as for the regularities restricting sexual indulgencies, has become a by-word. The Jews, like the negroes, whom this mania often drives to crimes against womanhood, are equally abnormally full-blooded" (Abernethy.1910 p.110).

The construction of a depraved, monster image of the black/Jew in the race factories of the nineteenth century foreshadowed the years of racial lunacy that would soon engulf Europe. The historian Claudia Bruns perceived the racialization of the Jew particularly in Germany in the second half of the nineteenth century almost as a byproduct of Germany's growing involvement in its African colonies. European Jews became, so to speak, analogous to African colonial subjects. There is no doubt something to this argument, and as we have seen elsewhere this vision of Jews had something of a history in German-speaking lands (Hess.2000 p.59). However, the development of the black/Jew has a long history both in the United States and various European countries, was a major product of anthropological writing of the eighteenth and nineteenth century, and started to gather force in the middle of the nineteenth century, some decades before Germany's African adventures began. Nonetheless, Bruns expressed the result of the development of the black/Jew as symbolic of the system of racial hierarchy very clearly: "The complex shift toward racial antisemitism was condensed in the figure of the 'black' Jew, which also stood for the system of racial hierarchy itself" (Bruns.2011 p.112).

The racial confusion embodied in this figure straddled the Atlantic and would soon be applied as legislation in much of Europe. Identical views about monstrous and sexually predatory Jews and monstrous and sexually predatory blacks, implicit in the figure of the black/Jew, would now be expressed in ever more murderous form in Nazi ravings as Europe descended into what refugees from the European cauldron called *Rassenwahn*—race madness (Whitman.2017).

9
The Black/Jew in the Racial State

The *Rassenwahn* (race madness) that engulfed a great deal of Europe in the twentieth century was the grand culmination of the polygenist project. One of the many architects of *Rassenwahn* was Theodor Fritsch (1852–1933), the well-known antisemitic writer and publisher. His *Handbuch der Judenfrage die wichtigsten Tatsachen zur Beurteilung des jüdischen Volkes* (Handbook of the Jewish Question—the Most Important Facts for the Evaluation of the Jewish People) was first published in 1893 but was reprinted repeatedly until the end of the Second World War. Sometimes referred to as the antisemites' "catechism," this book would be read by millions of Germans. Fritsch never tired of asserting that the Jews were a mongrel race (*Mischlingsrasse*) with strong negro elements. Fritsch specifically articulated the view that had been in the mainstream of European thought for centuries, that neither negroes nor Jews could ever be transformed into Europeans: A negro could not change his color, and a Jew could get baptized every Sunday of the year, but it would not help him achieve the impossible (Figure 2) (Fritsch.1931 [1893]).

In 1914, Fritsch's *völkisch* magazine *Hammer* stressed that the Jews' chief characteristics could best be explained by their sub-Saharan African ancestry. This dogma would continue as a subtext in Nazi and Fascist discourses for decades to come. Indeed, the idea of Jews as a negroid cross, as a loathsome hybrid, persisted, crude and unchanged, throughout the Second World War and beyond. The acclaimed French novelist and Holocaust denier Louis-Ferdinand Céline (1894–1961) considered the Jew the most disgusting mix of Asiatic and negro blood. In his antisemitic pamphlet *L'école de Cadavres* (School of Corpses), first published in 1938, Céline dismissed the Jew as that "Juif négroïde bousilleur" (the negroid bungling Jew) (Céline.1942 p.84), and elsewhere he quite categorically noted that "le Juif est un nègre—la race sémite n'existe pas" (the Jew is a negro—the Semitic race does not exist) (Miller.1985 p.202). What was equally unsettling for the canons of racial hierarchy was the curious invisibility of the Jew. Jews, as a people, were apparently able to achieve a kind of invisibility by changing color through what the polygenist and pigmentation expert John Beddoe (1826–1911) had called

Figure 2. "Die Taufe hat aus ihm keinen Nichtjuden gemacht" ("Baptism hasn't turned him into a gentile"). From *Der Giftpilz* (The Poisonous Mushroom/Toadstool). Illustration by Fips (pseudonym for Philipp Rupprecht [1900–1975]). Nuremberg: Der Stürmer Verlag, c.1938, p.21. 10-5/8 × 8-1/4 inches (27 × 21 centimeters).

Image courtesy of the Wolfsonian–Florida International University, Miami Beach, Florida. Gift of Eric Feiler. XB1989.123. Photo: Lynton Gardiner.

their "double physical type." According to Beddoe in England, and Abernethy in the American South, the outward appearance of Jews did not reveal their nigrescence even though Jews had scored 100 percent on Beddoe's "index of nigrescence."[1] We have seen that certain theorists had maintained that the dark color of Jews derived from the mixture of two distinct racial groups, the superior group and the negroid group. But Beddoe argued, in addition, that extreme racial divergence was to be found in each and every individual Jew. "In their own body," Jews represent "the two extreme types of the Caucasian family" (Beddoe.1861 p.236). Jews enjoyed a chameleon-like characteristic that enabled them to achieve a kind of racial invisibility by changing color along a spectrum from "xanthous" (marked by light complexion and yellowish hair) or "rufous" (reddish hair) to "melanous" (dark brown or black hair and blackish skin) and thus to look exactly and disturbingly the same as the people among whom they lived (Beddoe.1861 p.236). The insistence by race scientists and physical anthropologists over so many decades that Jews *individually* embodied a color spectrum that led from dazzling white to black had become a discourse of habit, part of the regular stock-in-trade of race discourses in nineteenth-century Europe.

A study conducted in the 1870s in Germany by Rudolf Virchow (1821–1902) on behalf of the German Anthropological Society and published in the *Archiv für Anthropologie* had the perhaps unintended effect of taking this discourse around the intriguing somatic color difference of Jews, and their chameleon characteristics, out of the textbooks and learned articles of anthropologists and race theorists, such as Beddoe, and into the homes of millions of Germans. Virchow, a world-famous medical scientist and anti-Darwinist, polygenist anthropologist, was also a liberal politician, deeply opposed to antisemitism. For Virchow and many of his German contemporaries, racial difference was not something that could easily be judged by an uninformed amateur; the discernment of race required a specific set of skills and expertise.

In a compelling article Andrew Zimmerman argued that many of the techniques used in the nineteenth century to determine race interrogated *invisible* characteristics and in particular peculiarities and measurements of the skull. To acquire these measurements, special instruments were required, but the areas to be measured were not easily accessible. In some cases, indeed, the measurements could only be carried out on an empty skull. However, even the measures taken on a living person that could, among other things, determine the relationship of a given head to the so-called cephalic index required careful measurements with special equipment. This index was the ratio of the head's breadth to its length. People with longer heads were known as dolichocephalic and those with wider heads were referred to as brachycephalic. Monogenists had maintained that race could be situated, at least in part, in skin color and other characteristics that had been brought about by external factors. However, reliance on skeletons and bones often seemed to support the polygenist view that difference was innate and resistant to such external factors.

With the unification of Germany and the creation of the German Reich in 1871, the racial composition of its people needed to be assessed. The problem was that getting a statistically meaningful number of subjects to support a national racial study required an excessive amount of expert time. To get around this, Virchow and his colleagues decided to ask schoolteachers to perform this important national task. Rather than the difficult-to-measure, invisible-to-the-naked-eye head and bone metrics, they opted to use clearly visible hair and eye color characteristics. The study, which involved nearly seven million German schoolchildren, designated Jewish children and German children as racially different. The teachers were provided with a set of detailed instructions that required the children to stand in line with the blondest-haired children at one end and the darkest-haired at the other, in a continuum of hair color. The children thus learned that there was a hierarchy of color. Jewish children were required to identify themselves as Jews and constituted a separate category on the form that had to be filled in. Children who had originated from other countries, such as France, were not eligible to take part in the study.

Importantly, skin color was shown in the questionnaire to be a function not only of what was visible, but also of the relationship between skin color and hair and eye color. *Visible* skin color was in fact of no importance for the study. Children were asked to roll up their sleeves to reveal the pristine color of their arm, beneath their clothes, which would be unaffected by the effect of the sun. However, the form made clear that this secret, unrevealed color could be determined by an astute comparison of other factors, namely the color of the hair and eyes. If a subject had blond hair and blue eyes, that subject was automatically, without further investigation, deemed to be white. However, if the subject had blue eyes and brown hair, the skin color remained a mystery and would have to be determined by examining the forearm. If the subject had a number of hair–eye combinations, such as green eyes and black hair, or brown eyes and brown hair, the skin color was automatically deemed to be brown. In other words, the skin color that you perceived with your naked eye was not necessarily the real skin color of the individual (for that you would have to partially undress him or her), and there were "scientific" ways of determining what that skin color really was by a comparison of eye and hair variables.

The millions of children and teachers who took part in this national survey may have responded to the test as a ludic activity, but consciously or not, they learned two things: that determining people's color was not a self-evident matter, and that the Jews were a race apart. Whereas the violent persecution and destruction of the Jews was far away in an unknowable future, the survey helped construct what the Welsh social theorist Raymond Williams called the "structure of feeling" that would encourage the growth of hatred and suspicion of Jews in the decades to come (Zimmerman.1999).

Part of this hatred, as we have seen, was triggered by the widespread conflation of Jews and negroes. After the First World War, even before the rise of Nazism, many sources of different sorts point to a perception that Jews in German-speaking areas and beyond were negroid, somatically black, or dark-colored. Even the Jewish American physical anthropologist, Maurice Fishberg (1872–1934), an expert on the physical anthropology of the Jews, bound by the power of stereotype, could proclaim that "the type of the Jew is dark," when all the evidence he himself had assiduously amassed over half a century actually proved the contrary. What was true of Fishberg was true of many others.

In 1920, Franz Kafka wrote to Milena Jesenska, the Czech writer, that "for your father there's no difference between your [Jewish] husband and myself; there's no doubt about it, to the European we both have the same negro face" (Gilman.1993 p.20; HaCohen.2018). In the same year T. S. Eliot's poem *Burbank with a Baedeker: Bleistein with a Cigar* imagines the Jew Bleistein as an ape, "a saggy bending of the knees and elbows, with the palms turned out," the usual shorthand at the time, as we have seen, for a negro, while his portrayals of sex-mad blacks and Jews have much in common.

A hybrid Jew/negro similarly features in the postwar paintings of the German (gentile) painter George Grosz.[2] The features of a much-repeated Jewish figure in *Selbstmörder* (Suicide) (1916) and in *Grossstadt* (Metropolis) (1917) and another bigger painting with the same name and from the same year have black, cunning faces and hands. That this figure is indeed a Jew is made clear in a later lithograph, including this same figure, which also demonstrates the widely held, visual understanding that there were two essential kinds of Jew in the evolving racial structures of the time: the simian, negro type and the pinched, more refined, hircine type, who in Grosz's work was also black. Was the black Jew in Grosz's work a subconscious instinct reflecting the social attitudes of the time or was it a deliberate painterly act in which the Jew was given symbolic characteristics of the oppressed negro? In a poem *Mondnacht* (Moonlit Night) published in *Neue Jugend* in 1916, Grosz fantasizes quite explicitly about the mysterious "creaking shoe of the eternal Jew" and concludes his poem with the affirmation that in his very unusual mind the Jew and the negro were an inseparable irritation: "*Und der Schuh des ewigen Juden vollführt an meinen Nerven einen Negertanz*" (And the shoe of the eternal Jew performs a negro dance on my nerves), which sentiment could have been taken from the Nazi playbook. Grosz, who was stridently anti-Nazi, would have been shipped off to a concentration camp by the Nazis had he not wisely emigrated to the United States before Hitler came to power (White.2007).

Twenty years later, but for different reasons, in the antisemitic pamphlet *Bagatelles pour un massacre* (Trifles for a Massacre) (1937), Louis-Ferdinand Céline, mentioned earlier in the chapter, depicted a world in which all good Aryan emotion, thanks to the Jews, had been replaced by the "Nigger's tom-tom." The soul of the Jew, like his access to culture, was negroid in every way. For Céline the conflated image of the decadent, primitive culture of Jews and negroes presented an existential threat to European civilization.

An admirer of Céline was George-Alexis Montandon (1879–1944), the French-Swiss polygenist race theorist, fêted by the Nazis, who constructed a theory to account for Jewish nigrescence (Knobel.1988 p.107). In 1932 he wrote the first volume in a projected series for the *Nouvelles Éditions françaises* entitled *Comment Reconnaître et Expliquer le Juif?* (How to Recognize and Explain the Jew?). This work, like previous works of his, accepted that at the skeletal level there was nothing much to identify Jews. In lectures he would sneer that the Jews do not even "own their skeletons." It was only the soft parts of Jews' bodies that they really owned and that revealed their true ethnic and racial identity and their essentially negroid character—the thick noses, bulbous lips, sunken eyes, and frizzy hair (Staum.2011 p.202). The phenotype of negro/Jew was easily accounted for as a function of the topography of Palestine, perched as it was between Africa and Asia (Bach.1999; Staum.2011). *Le Juif et la France au Palais Berlitz* (The Jew and France at the Palais Berlitz), a pamphlet published in Paris in 1941, stressed the Jew's essentially negroid character. The Jew was a "negroid figure with thick lips, and vulture's nose" (*ce negroïde aux lévres charnues, au nez de vautour*).

Following an old line of racial speculation, there was a broad consensus among Nazi and Italian Fascist theorists that the Jews were a "bastard" or mongrel race. There were negroid elements in Jewish blood, which were sometimes but not always visible. Blacks were visible and needed no other signifier. Jews were not always visibly negroid, but they invariably did have internal, invisible, negro blood.

This joint construct of negrophobia and antisemitism, the collision of the Western world's two major racisms, was built from hundreds of years of polygenist speculation, sexual panic, and the repulsive shared otherness that had been a perceived characteristic of Jews and blacks since the sixteenth century. It implied that subversive, predatory, pornographic character traits were somehow inscribed in the physiological fact of the negro/Jew.

Nazis were convinced of the need to rid Germany both of negroid Jews and the even more inferior negroes themselves. As illogical, frenzied, and neurotic streams of Judeophobia and negrophobia clashed or ran together or in parallel to create this *Rassenwahn*, it emerged that negroes and Jews, as an indivisible entity, presented the greatest threat to white, Aryan civilization not only in Germany but throughout the world and to the racial hierarchy Nazis had constructed (Cook.1922; Whitman.2017).

The conflated black/Jew hybrid symbolized the wider fear of cross-breeding. The consequences of such cross-breeding had occupied science for a number of decades, and by the time racial hysteria and fear of pollution had reached their peak, some light was being shed on the issue. What might be called polygenic inheritance was suggested by the work of Gregor Johann Mendel (1822–1884), the founder of the modern science of genetics and abbot of St. Thomas's Abbey in Brno, Moravia. Polygenic inheritance had also been postulated in the early years of eugenics. This area of study was founded by Sir Francis Galton (1822–1911), who in 1883 coined the term "eugenics" to describe his project for the biological improvement of the human race. Galton's ideas were given a boost by the rediscovery of Mendel's laws of inheritance, which soon fed into the scientific world generally. Mendel's ideas were taken up by William Bateson (1861–1926), among others, the Cambridge biologist who coined the term "genetics."

In 1908, the German anthropologist Eugen Fischer (1874–1967) went to the colony of German South-West Africa, founded in 1884, to better understand cross-breeding. He was interested in the inheritable traits of mixed-race people, the product of "Boers and Hottentots," and his findings were published in 1913 as *Die Rehobother Bastards und das Bastardisierungsproblem beim Menschen* (The Bastards of Rehoboth and the Problem of Miscegenation in Man).

He concluded, on more or less genetic grounds, that such mixtures, and miscegenation in general, did not lead to any kind of racial degeneration, as was commonly thought at the time. Fischer's study demonstrated that the crossing of European and African groups produced no ill effects. This went against the eugenicist argument most famously expressed in Madison Grant's (1865–1937) popular *The Passing of the Great Race* (1916), which warned Americans that the mixture of higher racial types with lower racial types was a "social and racial crime" that could only lead to the destruction of the higher group. Fischer, however, concluded his book, entirely against its main argument that the crossing of whites and blacks caused no ill effect, by stating that "every European people ... which has assimilated the blood of inferior races-and only dreamers can deny that Negroes, Hottentots, and many others are inferior—had paid for this assimilation of inferior elements with intellectual and cultural decline" (Weingart.1989).

Fischer's actual scientific findings were echoed in contemporary work done on Jews by the German scholars Max Markuse (1877–1967), a sexologist, and Felix Theilhaber (1884–1956), a statistician. Nonetheless, for years to come, mixed-race people, mixed-race Jews and others, not to mention the morbid fear of miscegenation in general, were viewed as a dangerous and immediate existential threat.

The famous "Rhineland Bastards," Afro-Germans fathered by French colonial troops of African descent during the occupation of the Rhineland after World War I, were considered to be a particular source of racial danger, as well as national humiliation. Germany, formerly a colonial power, in an act of reverse colonization, was now being colonized itself by black colonized people. In *Mein Kampf* Hitler railed against "the black disgrace" that wreaks "havoc on the Rhine. Women, girls, and children pay for the bestial negroes' lust with their death. An uninterrupted stream of poison and disease flows into the blood of our people. Moroccan syphilis drives thousands of victims towards a cruel death."

Hitler's rant was a clear example of how classical anti-Jewish canards, which had barely changed over centuries, were effortlessly directed at blacks and how anti-black racism was effortlessly channeled at Jews. Clearly, Jews, who themselves, like their medieval forebears, had "black putrid blood," were responsible for this *Vernegerung*—the vicious introduction of racial hybridity. Hitler wrote:

> For the contamination caused by the influx of Negroid blood on the Rhine, in the heart of Europe, is in accord with the sadistic and perverse lust for vengeance on the part of the hereditary enemy of our people, just as it suits the purposes of the cool calculating Jew who would use this means of introducing a process of bastardization in the center of the European continent, and by infecting the white race with the blood of an inferior stock, would destroy the foundations of its independent existence.[3]

After the First World War Germany lost its African colonies, and the issue of what to do with the mixed-race "Bastards of Rehoboth" and Africans in general eventually would become somewhat less pressing. With the establishment of the Third Reich, however, it was decided that as soon as the colonies were regained, and as soon as Germany was able to reassert itself on the African continent, blacks would be enslaved. In Europe itself, as a straightforward public health issue, blacks in general would be prevented from polluting Aryan blood. In 1933 existing mixed marriages between blacks and whites were annulled and future marriages forbidden. Laws were passed forbidding miscegenation and socialization. In 1937 the decision was taken to sterilize hundreds of Afro-German adolescents throughout the Reich to prevent any further degeneration of Aryan stock by the injection of black blood. Blacks, like Jews, were increasingly segregated. Membership in the Nazi Party was forbidden to people with Jewish or "colored blood." The 1935 Nuremberg racial laws, which were designed as a *cordon sanitaire* to defend the blood purity of the Aryan population, were to apply to blacks as well as to Jews, and by 1939, more than four hundred additional regulations and decrees expelled Jews, blacks, and others to the margins of society.

Hitler argued that Germany had been deliberately "negrified" by the Jews, whose intent was to weaken and destroy German society through racial contamination. In the same way, he maintained that France, too, had been "negrified," so much so that it was possible to speak of "an African state on European soil." Such arguments were presented in the SS newspaper *Das Schwarze Korps*, which portrayed a French racial feebleness that could only be sustained through regular injections of African blood. Jews, according to Nazi ideologues, were responsible for this *Vernegerung* of France. A main culprit was the Jew Georges Mandel (1885–1944), who as Minister of the Colonies from 1938 to 1940 was held responsible for bringing negro troops into France to do the dirty work of the Jews.

The commonalities of Jews and French negroes were frequently stressed through the vital element of shared blood. As the German historian Raffael Scheck has shown in a meticulous study, during the German attack on France in 1940 thousands of west African soldiers, mainly *Tirailleurs Sénégalais* from French West and Equatorial Africa (the precise number is impossible to gauge), were summarily executed or treated so badly that they soon died. One factor that led to these massacres was the perception that these black troops were savages and racially inferior. This argument had been a constant factor in racial thinking in Germany and elsewhere for hundreds of years. Moreover, these negro savages had been introduced into the arena of conflict at the behest of negrified Jewish puppet masters (Scheck.2006).

Although blacks in Germany were sometimes used in medical experiments, and some disappeared without trace or explanation, there was never a Final Solution proposed for the blacks of the world or even for all blacks on German soil. The intention was simply to segregate blacks with the ultimate goal of either eliminating them through compulsory sterilization or expelling them from the Reich. Thus, in 1942, Robert Wagner, the *Gauleiter* of Alsace, introduced a policy of deportations that included all negroes and "colored hybrids." Jews from the area had been deported to France, two years earlier (Müller-Hill.1988; Grill, Jenkins.1992; Kestling.1998; Berenbaum and Peck.2002).

Nazi periodicals such as *Der Stürmer*, not to mention children's books like the one by Elvira Bauer, an eighteen-year-old art student, regularly portrayed Jews as black or dark. Elvira Bauer's book, published in 1936, was entitled *Trau keinem Fuchs auf grüner Heid und keinem Jud auf seinem Eid* (Trust No Fox on His Green Heath and No Jew on His Oath). This product of the Stürmer publishing house contributed to the ongoing construction of the negro/Jew. On the cover, an inset shows a dark-faced Jew raising a hand in a worthless oath (Figure 3). The cover image of Julius Streicher's 1935 pamphlet *Ohne Lösung der Judenfrage keine Erloesung des deutschen Volkes* (Without a Solution to the Jewish Question There Will Be No Redemption for the German People) shows a diabolical dark-to-black negroid face inside a Star of David, an image that was widely used elsewhere (Figure 4). Similarly, in 1941, a Nazi poster in the *Parole der Woche* (Slogan of the Week) series called *Das Jüdische Komplott* (The Jewish Plot) featured a dark-faced Jew, centrally

Figure 3. Image from the cover of the antisemitic German children's book *Trau keinem Fuchs auf grüner Heid, und keinem Jud bei seinem Eid* (Trust No Fox in the Green Meadow and No Jew on His Oath) by Elvira Bauer. Nuremberg: Stürmer Verlag, 1936.
Courtesy of U.S. Holocaust Memorial Museum. Museum Photo Archives CD#0105.

positioned, with short, frizzy negroid hair and the alleged links between the Jew and Stalin, Churchill, and Roosevelt (Figure 5). In order to emphasize the superiority of Aryans, Nazi propaganda would often set beautiful, young, white, blonde Aryan women or handsome, well-built Aryan men against ugly, black, old, Jewish-negroid *rassischen Gegner* ("racial adversaries"). Kurt Plischke's illustrated book *Der Jude als Rasseschänder: eine Anklage gegen Juda und eine Mahnung an die deutschen Frauen und Mädchen* (The Jew as Race Defiler: An Indictment of Judah and a Reminder to German Women and Girls), published in 1934, contained a striking image of a German woman's comely white face. Her youthful profile is ringed by dark, old, ugly menacing Jews, but she is wearing a talisman against the race defilers—a swastika (Figure 12). The dark color of the Jew is thus associated with age,

Figure 4. Cover from the antisemitic pamphlet *Ohne Lösung der Judenfrage keine Erlösung des deutschen Volkes*. Nuremberg: Stürmer Verlag, 1935. Courtesy of U.S. Holocaust Memorial Museum. Museum Photo Archives 40042.

ugliness, immorality, and danger. The white, moral, youthful future belongs to the National Socialists alone.

More thoughtful people might have wondered if Jews, on an individual basis, were really somatically black or dark given that so many of them in fact had light-colored hair and skin. There was, they may have suspected, a disturbing chameleon-like character about Jews. There was obviously a

Figure 5. Broadside, *Parole der Woche*, no. 50. Munich: Zentralverlag der NSDAP, 1941. 3-1/8 × 3-7/8 inches (8 × 10 centimeters).
Image courtesy of the Wolfsonian–Florida International University, Miami Beach, Florida. Gift of Steven Heller, XC2008.07.17.186.5 Photo: Lynton Gardiner.

blackness about Jewish blood and the Jewish essence, even if it was not immediately visible. Indeed, Jewish skin, if you were to look closer, under the sleeve, as Virchow's project had proposed, was not necessarily the color you might at first imagine. Jews were an unstable chameleon entity, slippery, difficult to pin down.

As Céline put it: "First of all, they are all camouflaged, cross-dressed, chameleon-like, the Jews changing their names as often as they change countries." At the same time, they were instantly recognizable. This was part of a wider paradox in which, as Gilman remarked, "Jews are inherently visible in the European Diaspora, for they look so different from everyone else; Jews are inherently invisible, for they look like everyone else" (Gilman.1993). Spraying the constructed Jewish body with a metaphorical black dye was one way to make the slippery chameleon Jew less elusive, more visible, and more consistent.

Juden Stellen Sich Vor (Jews Introduce Themselves) was a book of caricatures by Fips, the pseudonym for Philipp Rupprecht (1900–1975), which was published by Julius Streicher (1885–1946), the antisemitic propagandist and politician. The cover of the booklet shows a white, stereotypical profile of an elderly balding Jew. This is how the Jew wishes to present himself, but behind this profile lurks a black silhouette, indicating what the Jew was really like (Figure 6). Very neatly, but unconsciously, this embodies

Figure 6. Cover of *Juden Stellen Sich Vor* (Jews Introduce Themselves). Illustration by Fips (pseudonym for Philipp Rupprecht [1900–1975]). Nuremberg: Stürmer-Verlag, 1934. 9 × 6 ¼ inches (23 × 16 centimeters).

Image courtesy of the Wolfsonian–Florida International University, Miami Beach, Florida. The Mitchell Wolfson, Jr. Collection, XC1991.1024. Photo: Lynton Gardiner.

Claudia Bruns's acute definition of the Jew as "the ambivalent inner and outer, black and white, Other" (Bruns.2011 p.112).

For the legal enactment of the oppression and exclusion of the Jews, the Nazis had a useful model in American anti-black legislation. As James Q. Whitman, professor of comparative and foreign law at Yale University, put it, the United States was seen "as the innovative world leader in the creation of racist law" and America's "easygoing, open-ended, know-it-when-I-see-it way with the law" could be usefully applied to the German situation. Given the difficulties of identifying chameleon Jews, the American system of implied rather than explicit racism, in which American lawyers were able to apply racial law despite "its fuzzy concepts," had some attraction. "The beauty of the American example," wrote Whitman, "was that it demonstrated, as American law so often does, that it was possible to manage a functioning legal system without the sorts of clear concepts German lawyers cherished" (Whitman.2017 p.107). German legal theorists had been interested in the American system for a while. The German lawyer Heinrich Krieger, for instance, made a close study of American race law while he was a student in the United States. This fed into his 1936 book *Das Rassenrecht in den Vereinigten Staaten* (Race Law in the United States), which had a direct impact on Nazi legislation. The American "one drop" rule, which had the force of law in some American states after 1910, was a principle of racial classification that declared that anyone with even one remote sub-Saharan African ancestor, and who, therefore, had "one drop" of black blood, was considered "legally black," with all that this implied in the era of the "Jim Crow" laws, enacted to exclude African-Americans from many areas of life. Such an individual might have fair hair and a pale complexion but still would be deemed to have black blood. Even if the internal blackness was not obvious or visible, it was nonetheless, mysteriously, there.

The main problem with overall American racial legislation, from a Nazi perspective, was that officially it excluded Jews from the category of "coloreds." In 1934, at a meeting of Nazi Germany's leading lawyers to establish the legality of the proposed racial measures against Jews, Roland Freisler, later the presiding judge of the Nazi *Volksgerichthof* (People's Court), observed: "This jurisprudence would suit us perfectly, with a single exception. Over there they have in mind, practically speaking, only coloreds (*farbige*) and half-coloreds, which includes mestizos and mulattoes; but the Jews, who are also of interest to us, are not reckoned among the coloreds" (Whitman.2017 p.108). He went on to wonder if there was really any point singling out Jews in the particular context of German racial legislation. After all, defining what a Jew was or was not presented all kinds of obvious difficulties. Perhaps, he suggested, the term "colored," used along American lines, would serve just as well.

And then Freisler revealed something of great relevance to the argument of this book. If you spoke of "coloreds," he reflected, any German would understand this to include Jews without any further addition or comment. What he meant was that there was a generally accepted *Rassebild* (race image) reflecting a register of truth that implicitly understood that Jews, despite their outward appearance, were actually colored or black. By the alchemy of perception, the whiteness of Jews, in Matthew Frye Jacobson's phrase, was a "whiteness of a different color."[4] "It seems to me doubtful," explained Freisler, "that there would be any need to expressly mention the Jews alongside the coloreds. I believe that every judge would reckon the Jews among the coloreds, even though they look outwardly white" (Whitman.2017 p.49).[5]

In Germany, somatic Jewishness was no more evident than somatic blackness was in many "one drop" people in the United States who could have been blonde and fair-skinned. American law got around this by the application of a "know-it-when-I-see-it" approach. Similarly, in Nazi Germany, drawing on a long European conviction that the eternal physiognomy of the Jew was readily discernible, there was the certainty that a Jew could be instinctively sensed. There was above all the "racial face": According to some Nazi race experts, the most cursory glance at an old, faded photograph was enough to tell if the subject were a Jew or not. By a long process of othering, Jews had been discolored by the alchemy of prejudice. Their facial features had also been defaced, de-faced. And their defaced image and color had burrowed deep in the European imagination.

Hitler identified Jews as somatically "negroid parasites." In *Mein Kampf* he wrote: "This pestilential adulteration of the blood, of which hundreds of thousands of our people take no account is being systematically practiced by the Jew today. Systematically these negroid parasites in our national body corrupt our innocent fair-haired girls and thus destroy something that can no longer be replaced in the world." This contamination was an existential threat to the Aryan people: "Look at the ravages from which are people are suffering daily as a result of being contaminated with Jewish blood. Bear in mind the fact that this poisonous contamination can be eliminated from the national body only after centuries or perhaps never" (Hitler.1939 p.310). The fear of *Rassenschande* (race defilement) had been a German pathology for decades.

Eugen Dühring's 1881 work *Die Judenfrage als Racen-, Sitten- und Culturfrage* (The Jewish Question as a Racial, Moral, and Cultural Question) argued that injections of Jewish blood into Aryans would not only corrupt but also destroy Aryan blood. Just as the former slave states of the United States were terrified of even "one drop" of negro blood, so many German theorists were terrified of the effects of Jewish blood. In 1906, *Hammer* had warned of the high rate of "illegitimate" sex between Jews and gentiles, which was leading to the transformation of Germany through the medium of Jewish blood. Two years later it warned that Germany's racial purity was under threat of an inevitable *Vernegerung* (negrification) that would be brought about by negroes and Jews. In 1914 *Hammer* carried an anonymous article bitterly lamenting the attraction German women allegedly felt both for Jews and negroes and warned that Germany was facing inevitable *Vernegerung*. Hammer's editor, Theodor Fritsch, was convinced that the Jews were partially negroid and potentially could contribute to the wider *Vernegerung* of Germany, as German women were incapable of refusing the advances of either Jews or negroes. As violators of blonde Aryan girls negro-Jews were as bad as negroes themselves, and negroes were as bad as negro-Jews (Davis.2012 p.122).

A remarkable poster advertising an issue of Julius Streicher's *Der Stürmer* explicitly shows the stark image of the negro/Jew, a black face with stereotypically Jewish features set against a white, rather submissive, easily duped, female "Aryan" face, with blonde hair, while the text itself attacks the Jews for the large-scale and persistent defilement of Aryan women (Figure 7). The poster stresses that since 1933 race defilement had been a crime punishable by imprisonment, and yet somehow the Jews "systematically and in massive numbers" continued to defile German women.

The fact that race defilement was in fact a joint negro and Jewish enterprise was made clear by many other images showing Jews and negroes dancing and flirting with Aryan women, or raping and violating them. Linking Jews and negroes in the joint enterprise of racial defilement, Nazis continued the project of fusing and conflating antisemitism and anti-black racism. In particular, the fear of predatory Jewish and negro sexual appetites, which had been expressed in the American South, was also emerging in Germany, where there was a growing fear of Jewish-negro sexuality and interracial transgression.

From the 1920s on Nazi antisemitic propaganda was matched by an equally intense and almost identical anti-black campaign, warning against *Vernegerung*. However, in the 1920s there were few actual negroes in

Figure 7. Nazi propaganda poster advertising a special issue of *Der Stürmer* on *Rassenschande* (race pollution), c.1935. The text reads: "Race Pollution. Since 1923, Julius Streicher has enlightened the public about race pollution. In 1933, the Führer declared race pollution a crime, punishable by imprisonment. Nevertheless, thousands of race crimes continue to be committed in Germany by Jews. What is Race Pollution? Why did the Führer proclaim the Nuremberg Laws? Why do Jews, systematically and in massive numbers, commit racial crimes against the German woman? What are the consequences of race pollution for the German maiden? What are the consequences of race pollution for the German *Volk*? The new *Stürmer* special issue."

Image courtesy of U.S. Holocaust Memorial Museum, courtesy of *Deutsches Historisches Museum*. Photo archive: 32615.

Germany to provide the front-line troops in this much feared onslaught on German womanhood—no more than a few thousand out of a total population of around sixty-two million.

Despite the small number of blacks in Germany, the fear of black sexuality was as immanent and powerful as the fear of Jewish sexuality. The antisemitic press pointed out that the sex threat of Jews was not a uniquely German problem, for in America, too, Jews were plotting to mobilize blacks to overthrow white American civilization, which would be brought about in part by white women being forcibly given to negroes. In 1921, *The Searchlight*, a short-lived but official organ of the Ku Klux Klan, which was as antisemitic as it was anti-black, reported investigations allegedly proving that Jewish plotters were stirring up the negroes "so that the government will be destroyed." American anti-black racism was greatly admired and applauded by the Nazis. Indeed, the legal structures elaborated against blacks in the United States, the culmination of a long race war, provided a model for the Nazis to follow in their own race war against the Jews (Cook.1922 p.37).

If Germany had few blacks to worry about[6] (although that did not stop them from worrying), the same was not true of Fascist Italy with its East African possession—*Africa Orientale Italiana*, a large colony formed in 1936 through the merger of Italian Eritrea, Italian Somaliland, and the recently annexed Ethiopian Empire, whose combined African population was around twelve million. The Fascist project in Italy, like the Nazi project in Germany, had race at its heart. Fascist racial policies that included antisemitism and anti-black racism were swiftly applied to the Horn of Africa. The indigenous population was denied access to public transport used by Italians or to restaurants and bars frequented by Italians. In 1937 any form of conjugal union between Africans and Italians was banned. The following year the ban was extended to members of any "other race," including Jews. In 1940 mixed-race children were deemed to be "native" rather than Italian.

Italian racists had the wealth of literature produced in Europe in the nineteenth and early twentieth century to draw on. They also had produced some racial scholarship of their own, such as the tortured work of Cesare Lombroso (1835–1909), a Jew whose views on blacks and Jews were equally unenthusiastic. In Fascist Italy, academics and writers joined together to express hatred of the negro/Jew in propaganda literature, some of which was presented in a superficially "scientific" way through the newly formed discipline of "anthropology of race," which set out to justify imperial racial policies and rank bourgeois prejudice. In 1938 the *Manifesto della Razza*

(Race Manifesto), signed by a number of leading academics, succinctly summed up the basics of Italian racial ideology, which included the belief that blacks in general, and Italy's colonial subjects in particular, were mentally inferior and that it would be hazardous in the extreme for the Italian people to allow itself to be infected by this dangerous pollution. The *salute della razza* (health of the race) was paramount.

Moreover, it was argued that Jews were equally hazardous to the *salute della razza*. Chapter Eight of the *Manifesto* stressed the fundamental distinction that, as a matter of great national importance, had to be drawn between on the one hand Indo-Europeans and Aryans, and on the other hand Hamites and Semites (Sòrgoni.2002). This formulation yoked Jews and blacks in the same undesirable racial category. However, this formulation also revealed something of the incoherence of 1930s racial politics, which will be discussed more thoroughly in the next chapter. There was an extent to which Fascist racial ideology sought to align itself with Nazi racial policies, at least by the late 1930s. However, there was one obvious problem: The Italians, for the most part, did not correspond, and were not perceived as corresponding, to the "Nordic type." In *Mein Kampf* Hitler had warned that if negroid Jews continued with their contamination of the Aryan people, Germany itself would become as bad as southern Italy, which had already been negrified. Subsequently, there were frequent German taunts that the blood of central and southern Italians was contaminated by negro blood.

Italian race theorists could easily have argued, as had some physical anthropologists in the past, that the Italians were simply the southern Mediterranean branch of the Aryan or Caucasian people. However, annoyingly, Hamites, including the denizens of *Africa Orientale Italiana*, and Semites had both frequently been deemed to belong to this very same Mediterranean group. As a result, there was an effort to "invent an Italian race that was at the same time Aryan, but distinct from the German, and also Mediterranean, but separate from the Hamitic and Semitic peoples" (Sòrgoni.2002 p.6).

In December 1938, a young Italian anthropologist, Guido Landra (1913–1980), the first director of the *Ufficio Studi sulla Razza* under the aegis of the *Ministro della Cultura Popolare* (Racial Office of the Ministry of Popular Culture) and assistant in the Department of Anthropology in the University of Rome, met with Nazi race officials in Germany at a secret meeting of the Italo-German Committee on Racial Questions to iron out some of these issues. During the visit the Italian delegation visited the Sachsenhausen concentration camp and the group was awarded the German red cross for scientific merit by Hitler (Bernhard.2017).[7]

As Landra explained, there was a danger that, according to the current system of classification employed by the Nazi theorists, the Hamitic and Semitic populations of Africa, such as Arabs and Ethiopians, would have been included in the very same group as the Italians themselves. As the boundaries were so blurred in much racial discourse between Italians and Hamites (not to mention Semites), they would clearly have to be framed in a much more robust theoretical framework; otherwise, any Italian attempt at racial segregation in their African empire would be doomed to failure (Sòrgoni.2002 p.2). Constructing Semites as well as Hamites as black was one way of doing this.

In Italy as elsewhere, both Jews and blacks instilled the fear of racial pollution. The racial law of November 17, 1938, which banned miscegenation, contained thirty articles: Twenty referred to the Jewish racial threat, ten to the negro threat. The Fascist journal *La Difesa della Razza* (The Defense of the Race), founded by the antisemitic propagandist Telesio Interlandi (1894–1965), was edited by mainstream academics including Landra and first appeared in 1938. The second issue had a cover illustration collating in a striking manner the perceived joint Jewish–negro racial threat (Figure 8). On the left of the image lies the white, noble head of a Roman statue; in the middle is a dark-skinned, hook-nosed portrayal of a Jew, taken from a third century AD caricature; and to the right is a photograph of a negro girl, with beads around her neck. The Roman is protected from the Jew and the girl by a Roman sword held in a white hand. This image became the official emblem of the periodical and reappeared in most later issues as an inset on the cover (Pankhurst.2005). The sequence from a remote past (represented by the ancient Roman statue) to the present (represented by the photo of the African girl) suggests an eternal, unchanging predicament. No better illustration exists of the polygenist conviction that Jews and negroes, linked together through notions of racial immutability, color, and inferiority, were peoples apart from the rest of humanity, to whom they represented a mortal threat.

The fusion of antisemitism and anti-black racism is evident in another cover illustration from *La Difesa della Razza* showing a half-naked Italian maiden being seduced by a cunning Jew and a muscular negro (Figure 9). The two figures, negro and Jew, are allies, in league in a joint enterprise to deflower Italian racial purity. Yet in addition to this alliance of convenience, the somatic fusion of Jew and negro, chief players in the evolving construct

Figure 8. Cover of the Italian periodical *La Difesa Della Razza (Scienza, Documentazione, Polemica, Questionario)*, Year 1, No. 2, August 20, 1938. Rome: Società Anonima Istituto Romano di Arti Grafiche di Tumminelli & Co. 12-1/4 × 9-3/4 inches (31 × 25 centimeters).

Image courtesy of the Wolfsonian–Florida International University, Miami Beach, Florida. The Mitchell Wolfson, Jr. Collection. 83.3.79.3. Photo: Lynton Gardiner.

Figure 9. Cover of the Italian periodical *La Difesa Della Razza (Scienza, Documentazione, Polemica, Questionario)*, Year 2, No. 11, April 5, 1939. Rome: Società Anonima Istituto Romano di Arti Grafiche di Tumminelli & Co. 12-1/4 × 9-3/4 inches (31 × 25 centimeters).

Image courtesy of the Wolfsonian–Florida International University, Miami Beach, Florida. The Mitchell Wolfson, Jr. Collection. 83.3.79.17. Photo: Lynton Gardiner.

of race, may be seen in the fact that the muscular negro, with his hand on the girl's shoulder, has horns sprouting from his forehead—an undoubted allusion to the thousand-year-old antisemitic trope that portrayed diabolical Jews with horns or cloven hoofs.[8]

Yet another cover of *La Difesa della Razza* shows that the contamination threatened by the seduction from either source, is the same. A classical Roman statue, symbolizing the immutability and purity of the Italian race according to the time-honored polygenist paradigm of race purity, is defaced by a black stain with a Star of David at its center (Figure 10). A part of the construct of the negro/Jew, as we have seen, was the idea that behind every negro attack on the racial well-being of Aryan Europe there were Jews pulling the strings. Another cover of *La Defesa della Razza* shows an Italian baby, whose racial defense is the objective of the journal, behind which stands a negro woman and the wily, self-pitying, race-threatening Jew. Jews were part of the negro menace, as negroes were intrinsically part of the Jewish menace.

In Hitler's so-called *Zweites Buch* (Second Book), which was written in 1928 but only published after his death, Hitler emphasized that the threat posed by the eternally different and separate Jews and negroes was in effect the same threat. He blamed some of his foreign policy critics for ignoring the "syphilitization by Jews and negroes" of the *Vaterland* and the persecution of those brave Germans who had resisted and were continuing to resist the "de-Germanization, niggerization, and Judaization of our people" (Weinberg.2003 p.208).

One of the many phobias that plagued German society concerned African-American and Jewish culture, and particularly so-called *Entartete Musik* (degenerate music) such as swing and jazz, which Goebbels characterized as "jungle music." In 1933 the *Reichsmusikkammer* was established with the aim of bringing Nazi-style order to the musical life of Germany. Initially Jewish composers and musicians such as Giacomo Meyerbeer, Felix Mendelssohn, Bruno Walter, and Arnold Schoenberg were banned but the idea of decadent Jewish music soon expanded to include jazz. A number of 1920s American critics, too, saw jazz as a musical tradition that had started with negro syncopation but had been developed by Jews into its modern form. One such critic declared that "jazz is Negro music seen through the eyes of the Jews" (Oja, Tick.2018 p.315). Others were more extreme.

American antisemitism and prominent American anti-Semites such as the Detroit industrialist Henry Ford (1863–1947) were well known in Germany thanks to the publicity they received in the *völkisch Hammer* magazine and

Figure 10. Cover of the Italian periodical *La Difesa Della Razza (Scienza, Documentazione, Polemica, Questionario)*, Year 1, No. 4, September 20, 1938. Rome: Società Anonima Istituto Romano di Arti Grafiche di Tumminelli & Co 12-1/4 × 9-3/4 inches (31 × 25 centimeters).

Image courtesy of the Wolfsonian–Florida International University, Miami Beach, Florida. The Mitchell Wolfson, Jr. Collection. 83.3.79.5. Photo: Lynton Gardiner.

elsewhere.[9] Some Americans, it was clear, were just as alarmed by the corrosive danger of Jewish/negro culture as were Nazis. An article in the *Dearborn Independent* (August 6, 1921), a mass-circulation weekly newspaper[10] published by Ford from 1919 to 1927, noted that

> in view of the organized eagerness of the Jew to make an alliance with the Negro . . . it was Jewish "jazz" that rode in upon the wave of Negro "rag-time" popularity, and eventually displaced the "rag-time" . . . Popular Music is a Jewish monopoly. Jazz is a Jewish creation. The mush, the slush, the sly suggestion, the abandoned sensuousness of sliding notes, are of Jewish origin.[11]

Such views were eagerly pounced on by Nazis, who saw jazz and swing as no less than the subversive, political weapons of Jews in their war against the German people. In the same way as Jews were blamed for introducing negro blood into the Rhineland, Jews, as producers, performers, impresarios, and distributors, were blamed for diffusing this culturally hybrid Jewish/negro music. *Der Stürmer*, like the *Dearborn Independent*, argued that jazz was entirely a Jewish business. What did negroes in the African rain forest know about jazz? The Jews' underlying purpose was to subvert and corrupt German blood, culture, and morals through this decadent music, which was served up by negroes in their pay. Jews and negroes were perceived by the German antisemitic press as being similar in other social and cultural respects: They liked each other's company, they enjoyed going out together, and they liked the same kind of music and art.

"Degenerate" music was strictly supervised during the Third Reich and even before. In 1930, in Thuringia, when the Nazis had taken over the state government, an ordinance was passed banning "jazz band and drum music, negro dances, negro songs, negro plays" (Lusane.2003 p.184). The infamous *Entartete Musik* exhibition, which ran for a month in 1938, was created by the Nazi Party official Hans Severus Ziegler (1893–1978).[12] The exhibition's intent was to discredit "degenerate" music in general, which by now in practice meant Jewish and negro music. The cover of the exhibition catalogue featured a caricature of the black/Jew in the form of a black musician playing a saxophone (Figure 11). This culturally and ethnically hybrid figure was wearing a top hat, tuxedo, and white gloves, garb typical of representations of Jews and capitalists in Nazi propaganda cartoons (as well, perhaps, of minstrelsy performers in the United States) and a large earring, suggestive of

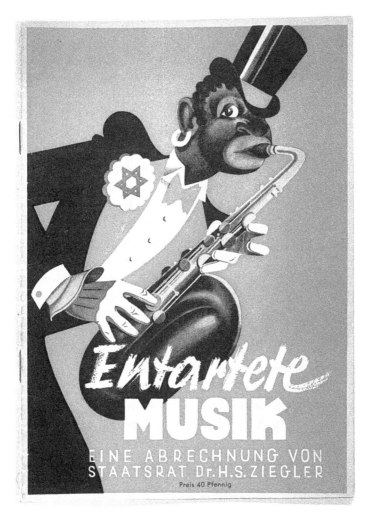

Figure 11. Pamphlet, *Entartete Musik: Eine Abrechnung*, by Hans Severus Ziegler (1893–1978). Illustrator: Ludwig Tersch. Düsseldorf: Völkischer Verlag, 1939. 8-1/4 × 5-7/8 inches (21 × 15 centimeters).

Image courtesy of the Wolfsonian–Florida International University, Miami Beach, Florida. The Mitchell Wolfson, Jr. Collection. XB1989.189. Photo: Lynton Gardiner.

some primitive African tribesman. The jazzman sported a Star of David on his jacket lapel.[13]

In the introduction to his haunting 1978 novel *The Bass Saxophone*, the Czech writer Josef Škvorecký (1924–2012) listed some of the clauses in the ban imposed on jazz and swing by a *gauleiter* in Bohemia during the

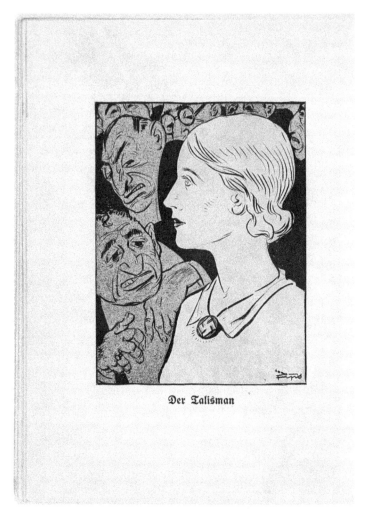

Figure 12. "Der Talisman," illustration by Karel Relink (1880–1945) from Kurt Plischke's *Der Jude als Rassenschänder* (The Jew as Race Defiler). Berlin-Schöneberg: NS Druck und Verlag, 1934, p.58. 8-1/4 × 5-7/8 inches (21 × 15 centimeters).

Image courtesy of the Wolfsonian–Florida International University, Miami Beach, Florida. The Mitchell Wolfson, Jr. Collection. TD1988.37.13. Photo: Lynton Gardiner.

war. "Jewishly gloomy lyrics" were to be avoided, while negro excesses in tempo, termed "hot jazz," or solos would not be tolerated. In the occupied Netherlands in 1942, *Joden, gesteriliseerde Joden, half-Joden en Negers* (Jews, sterilized Jews, half-Jews, and negroes) were banned from playing in clubs (Hondius.2017 p.261). In 1943 the Nazis banned a performance of *Porgy and Bess*, the "negro-Jewish" opera by the American Jewish composer George Jacob Gershwin (1898–1937), at the Royal Danish Opera in occupied Copenhagen, even though the cast was "Aryan," playing in blackface. The Nazis threatened to blow up the theater if the show continued. Negro/Jews, similarly, for years had been held responsible for the "decadent" theater and literature of the day. Jewish-negro–inspired music, literature, art and theater would conspire to bring about the cultural hybridization and *Vernegerung* of Germany and Europe (Lusane.2003; Dash.2012).

This same process of social, racial, and cultural *Vernegerung* was thought to be taking place in America. Theodor Fritsch, as we have seen, believed that the Jews, with the help of the blacks, who would act as their agents, were destined to wrest America from the grip of the Anglo-Saxon race (Fritsch.1927; Fritsch.1931). Indeed, when Hitler reflected on the United States, he constructed the emerging trans-Atlantic superpower in terms of a fusion of black and Jew, as a black Jewish hybrid, a black/Jew. As *Hitler's Table Talk 1941–1944: Secret Conversations* revealed, Hitler believed that the United States, like France, was already "half Judaised . . . half negrified" (Hitler.2013 p.145). In 1991, in a shrewd sentence, the historians Michael Burleigh and Wolfgang Wippermann noted correctly, although with no further elaboration, that "Hitler both fused and developed the ideologies of antisemitism and racism" (Burleigh, Wippermann.1991 p.42).

10
Rassenwahn

German science in the first few decades of the twentieth century was remarkably sophisticated. Between 1904 and 1937 no less than thirty-eight Nobel prizes were awarded to German scientists, some of whom, like Einstein, were Jews. The Nazis paid lip service to the world of science even in the field of persecution of the Jews. In 1919 Hitler himself had argued that there should be an "antisemitism of reason" (Steinweis.2008 p.7) Once the Nazis came to power and started to institute their racial legislation, they went to some lengths to give the impression that its various measures were based on scientifically valid research and experimentation. But as far as racial studies went this was not easy. Among scientists throughout the world, there was by now a growing conviction that race as a general concept was questionable. Even in Nazi Germany there was a persistent fuzziness about the way the term was understood and explained. The Nazis believed that there were immutably different human races, but there was never any consensus about how many there were, how they were constituted, or what relationship they had with each other.

During the first turbulent couple of decades of the twentieth century the unstable and slippery notion of race had been challenged in a variety of ways by anthropologists. Whereas most scholars of the time believed in racial difference, it was not clear how important such differences were in determining behavior. The old German tradition, exemplified by Virchow, had been non-determinist. There was also the question of racial immutability. In the United States the anthropologist Franz Uri Boas (1858–1942) and his followers argued that physical differences between populations, such as the shape of the head, were not fixed but could change in a single generation. Such differences, moreover, were less important than social and cultural differences. British functionalist anthropology was increasingly more interested in questions of social organization. While supporters of eugenics, and the younger generation of German determinist anthropologists, for whom race was all-important, were enjoying their heyday, for other theorists race was suspected to be of minimal importance or entirely illusory.

Over time the deep and ancient reservoirs of antisemitism and anti-black racism had flowed into the vacuities of polygenism and racial determinism. Efforts to stem this tide were made by people who were often opposed to racial determinism and were more likely than not to be monogenists. In this long-running race war, Jews and blacks were thus thrust even deeper into the maelstrom of conflicting ideas about race and difference.

The issue could be reduced to the simple matter of blood. The Prussian politician and jurist Hermann Wagener (1815–1889) wrote in 1862 "The Jewish tribe has indeed a different blood from the Christian peoples of Europe, a different body, a different constitution, other affects and passions, and with his physical constitution is connected his alienness (*Fremdschaft*)" (Stern.1979 p.498). In this spirit the 1920 program of the *Nationalsozialistische Deutsche Arbeiterpartei* (NSDAP) declared that German citizenship should be restricted to people who were *Volksgenosse*—part of the *Volksgemeinschaft* (people's community), which community was defined through the metaphor of blood. Jews did not have German blood and could not therefore be *Volksgenosse* (Ehrenreich.2007 p.69). After 1933, and the beginning of the criminalization of Jews and blacks on "race" or "blood" grounds, there was an urgent legal need to elucidate what the terms "black," "Jew," "blood," and "race" actually meant.

Perhaps it was more or less clear, but not entirely clear, what a black was, but it was not clear what counted as a racial Jew. Blood was seen to be at the root of racial difference. The term "blood" could be used, and was used, both literally and metaphorically, and this will be discussed later in the chapter. The "race" of Jews and blacks similarly was seen to be critical. Race was a term that was endlessly discussed but never adequately defined. Moreover, the various parts of the racial bureaucracy failed to work together and failed to reach agreement on the most basic theoretical definitions. According to Bernhard Lösener (1890–1952), an expert on Jews and an influential lawyer in the *Reichs Ministerium des Innern* (Reich Ministry of the Interior), there was "total chaos" on the Jewish question from a racial standpoint (Schleunes.2001 p.13).

As Lösener argued at a meeting of jurists in 1934, German law depended on clear and unambiguous concepts, and the concept of "Jew" was neither. As he put it: "An effective means of determining whether a given human being has an element of Jewishness on the basis of his behavior or outward appearance (*Habitus*) or blood or the like does not exist, or at least at present has not yet been found" (Whitman.2017 p.47). Lösener argued that it would be entirely against all the principles of German law to let an individual judge make decisions based simply on *Gefühlsantisemitismus* (a vague antisemitic sentiment). Quite apart from what constituted the racial Jew, there were discussions as to what percentage of this elusive category qualified someone to participate in it: Was a complete set of grandparents necessary to qualify, or one grandparent, or perhaps one great-grandparent? The July 1933 Law on the Revocation of Naturalization and the Withdrawal of German Citizenship declared that any person with just one Jewish grandparent should be considered a Jew. It was finally decided to make a fuzzy distinction between those who were actual Jews "having at least three Jewish grandparents, and those who 'counted' as Jews, having two Jewish grandparents while also practicing the Jewish religion, or having chosen to marry a Jewish spouse" (Whitman.2017 p.35). The inclusion of religious and social practice into what was supposedly a racial definition was typical of the essential incoherence of Nazi racial policy.

It was not difficult to determine Jewish descent for the majority of German Jews, through public and synagogue records. But there were many people of some degree of Jewish descent, or indeed of full Jewish descent, who fell below the radar. How could such people be determined? German Jews had undergone a century of thorough social and religious assimilation that included extensive intermarriage. According to the Nazi *Sippenforscher* (genealogical researcher) Heinrich Banniza von Bazan (1904–1950), there were 2.5 million people with some Jewish blood in Germany alone. This had already been established by an acknowledged authority on the physical anthropology of the Jews, the Russian-Jewish physician Samuel Weissenberg (1867–1928), who stressed the considerable and very recent mixing of Jews with other European populations. Weissenberg also argued that Jews overall did not have any particular "look" and that, to the extent that there were any discernible differences, they were the product of nutrition, lifestyle, and other variables (Efron.1994; Steinweis.2008; Hayes, Roth.2010).

It is not my purpose here, needless to say, to try to define any Jewish or black characteristics. The way people are perceived is to a very large extent subjective. As Sander Gilman put it so well, any attempt to draw a line between "the 'real' and 'fabled' aspects of the Jew" would founder on the sad fact "that all aspects of the Jew, whether real or invented, are the locus of difference" (Gilman.1990 p.588). The same would follow for people of African descent and other dark-skinned people. In any event, by strictly physical criteria, Jews and part-Jews were indeed hard to distinguish from gentiles.

Rudolf Virchow had shown that Germans and Jews did not look very different. In his 1886 study of close to seven million German schoolchildren, Virchow found that Jewish children were not readily distinguishable in terms of external characteristics from gentile German children, even if Jewish children were described as a separate "race" in that study. Similarly, the American physical anthropologist Maurice Fishberg (1872–1934) observed that a large number of Jews had "Aryan" physical characteristics, while a significant proportion of "Aryans" had "typically Jewish" features such as dark skin and a so-called Jewish nose. Moreover, even one of the most prominent Nazi racial theorists, Hans F. K. Günther (1891–1968), known as *Rassengünther* (Race Günther or the "Race Pope"), pointed out that there were "very many Germans, men belonging, that is, to a people speaking a Germanic tongue, who have no Germanic appearance whatever."

In an article in *American Anthropologist* in 1903 and subsequently in his 1911 magnum opus *The Jews: A Study of Race and Environment*, Maurice Fishberg concluded that all the long years of physical anthropological race scholarship throughout the world, which included large group studies of pigmentation; eye and hair color; and metrical analysis of crania, feet, ears, forehead angle, length of forearms and lower legs, and distance between the eyes (often such examinations included over thirty different metrics), had failed to find any specific external marker for Jews. Shortly before his death, at a 1934 meeting at Temple Emanu-El in New York, where Franz Boas was guest of honor, Fishberg reiterated his belief based on his lifetime study of physical anthropology that

> there is no such thing as a Jewish "race." The Jews resemble the type of people among whom they live. Over twenty, and in some countries thirty, per cent of the Jews are blonds. There is no more justification for speaking of a Jewish race than there is for speaking of a Christian or Mohammedan race. (JTA Bulletin, March 5, 1934)

Other Western anthropologists went even farther. Boas denied the existence of Jewish cultural as well as physical "particularism," and his student, the American anthropologist Melville J. Herskovits (1895–1963), also denied that the Jews were either a people or in possession of a distinctive culture. Other theorists whose work was available to Nazi theorists, from the American physical anthropologist Earnest Albert Hooton (1887–1954) to the British biologist Sir Julian Sorell Huxley (1887–1975) or the Cambridge anthropologist Alfred Cort Haddon (1855–1940), rejected the idea of a Jewish "race" on various grounds. This was a lot of science for the Nazis to contend with (Fishberg.1903, 1911; Gilman.1991,1994,1995; Siegel.1996).

In a characteristically perceptive essay, the American historian Mitchell Hart pointed out that it was not science that found the key to the problem Nazis had with Jewish physical identity; it was politics, Nazi politics. Nazi politics did this by following hate and ignoring reason and science. Nazi legal enactments against the Jews were also obliged to ignore reason and science. Legal measures against the Jews, as noted, were modeled to some extent on American measures against blacks. One of the things that the Nazis most admired in the legalization of anti-black prejudice in the United States was precisely that American law found a way to circumvent science and reason (Hart.2007; Whitman.2017).

Much of the science available to Nazi theorists undermined their racial argument. Whereas Nazi dogma insisted that Germans were racially superior to Jews, even German anthropologists had concluded that while Jews and Germans were perhaps somewhat different, Germans were not more racially "advanced." One such was the revered German polygenist biologist and naturalist Ernst Haeckel (1834–1919). Haeckel understood the difference between peoples largely in terms of how far advanced they were on a map of human progress. His scales of progress, explicated through the new graphic device of the stem-tree and copious diagrams, contradicted in very clear terms the idea of the absolute superiority of the Aryan race. In the early editions of his *Natürliche Schöpfungsgeschichte* (Berlin, 1868) (translated into English as *The History of Creation* [New York, 1876]), he argued that whereas blacks had not achieved the same degrees of progress as other races, Jews (and Berbers) were actually at the same level as Aryans. Even in much later editions of his work, when racial antisemitism had taken a firmer hold, Jews were placed only slightly below Germans in terms of development or human progress. Moreover, along with his coworker Josef Kollmann, Virchow showed that craniological studies indicated that all European races were "a mixture of various races." At the 1885 Anthropology Congress in Karlsruhe, Kollmann admitted that the results of years of craniological studies, including their own, "had failed to support any theory arguing for the superiority of any given European race" (Lozny.2011).

In order to maintain a gossamer-thin veneer of academic respectability Nazi anthropologists and scientists had at least to acknowledge research of this kind as they sought scientific legitimacy for their ideas of Aryan superiority. In some cases, they attempted to introduce scientific figures from the past into the Nazi pantheon by the simple expedient of ignoring or concealing what they had actually written. The botanist Heinz Brücher (1915–1991), a member of the SS think tank *Ahnenerbe*, argued that Heickel was a Nordic supremacist and Nazi forerunner, while Alfred Ernst Rosenberg (1893–1946), one of the most blinkered Nazi racial theorists, even tried to claim for National Socialism the great Prussian humanist Alexander von Humboldt (1769–1859).

As Nazi theorists looked over their shoulder at a century of scientific racial research, in some respects they were not much helped. Nineteenth-century race theorists had failed to arrive at any consensus with respect to human divisions and basic concepts. Haeckel's use of terms such as "tribe," "group," "nation," and "race" was loose and inexact, and the same may be said of Darwin and the Welshman Wallace, among others. Boas wrote about "races" without really believing that they existed. Such terminological inexactitude contributed to the confusion Nazis had about such categories. Günther (the "Race Pope"), for instance, knew that there was a consensus that the Jews were a *Volk*, not a race. However, he thought that in popular discourse it was permissible to use the term "race" in the narrower sense of *Volk*. Moreover, Hitler used the terms "race," "group," and "people" interchangeably.

A number of the important Nazi race theorists had little grounding in the disciplines that might have allowed them to speak with authority on biological difference. Günther, for instance, had been trained in comparative linguistics in Freiburg, and briefly at the Sorbonne, in which field he was awarded his doctorate in 1914. It was only later that he turned to race studies. In 1922, he published his influential *Rassenkunde des deutschen Volkes* (Racial Science of the German People), which showed signs of wide general reading and went on to sell half a million copies. This was followed by his equally influential and widely cited work *Rassenkunde des jüdischen Volkes* (1930) (Racial Science of the Jewish People), which went through sixteen editions within four years of its publication. *Rassenkunde des jüdischen Volkes* was a recapitulation of nineteenth-century polygenist and racially determinist theories about Jews, which accepted a fixed and recognizable hierarchy of races. A central element of the book was that the Jews were not in fact a "pure race" but a *Volk* (people) consisting of a specific, ancient, and noxious blend of Near Eastern, Asian, negro, and other elements and that this particular blend manifested an unmistakable racial difference with non-Jews. His overall theory was suffused with a kind of metaphysical antisemitism. But Günther's work was not one of a professional physical anthropologist (Morris-Reich.2006b).

An even less informed and more overtly antisemitic work was published the same year by Alfred Rosenberg, one of the most influential race ideologues of the Nazi Party. *Der Mythus des zwanzigsten Jahrhunderts* (The Myth of the Twentieth Century) (1930) combined standard nineteenth-century polygenist anthropology with a more extreme stratum of poisonous antisemitism, culled in part from Gougenot des Mousseaux's work *Le Juif, le Judaïsm et la Judaïsation des peuples chrétiens* (The Jew, Judaism, and the Judaization of the Christian Peoples) (Paris, 1869), the so-called Bible of modern antisemitism, which Rosenberg had translated into German in 1921. Jews and blacks were placed on the bottom rung of Rosenberg's ladder of human progress, on top of which perched the proud white Aryan. Disliked by Hitler and many of the leading Nazis, nonetheless *Der Mythus*, too, went on to sell over a million copies. Like Günther and other race theorists, Rosenberg had no grounding in any of the relevant disciplines. His education consisted of a period studying architecture and later a doctoral program in engineering in Moscow. He was a man of limited intellectual capacity: According to Ian Kershaw, Hitler's biographer, he had "a genius for misunderstanding," while William Shirer, the American journalist and author of *The Rise and Fall of the Third Reich*, called him a "dimwitted dolt."

While Rosenberg's book was never taken quite seriously by the Nazi leadership, Günther's was. It was studied by a number of the high-ranking Nazi civil servants who would have the responsibility for introducing anti-Jewish racial legislation, including Wilhelm Stuckart (1902–1953), co-author of the Nuremberg Laws, and Hans Globke (1898–1973). These anti-Jewish laws, as we have seen, had much in common with the anti-black "Jim Crow" laws of some American states and indeed were in part modeled on them. They excluded Jews from German public life just as surely as the Jim Crow laws excluded blacks from much of American life. Globke helped draft the critical 1935 *Gesetz zum Schutze des deutschen Blutes und der deutschen Ehre* (Law for the Defense of German Blood and German Honor) as well as legislation making it more difficult for Jews to change their names. Subsequently, Globke was involved in the legislation making it mandatory for Jews to have the Jewish identifier names Israel or Sarah appended to their public record. Forcing Jews to maintain Jewish-sounding names or adding identifier names to their official documents was an implicit admission that it was not possible to recognize Jews through somatic characteristics.

Nazi racial ideology, like twentieth-century American anti-black racism, was a continuation of the polygenist doctrines that had been present in European thinking since the time of Paracelsus and that had started to dominate American and European race-study circles from around the middle of the nineteenth century. Nazi ideologues accepted "micro evolution," the process of natural selection within a race, but they rejected the mutability of races and, like their nineteenth-century polygenist predecessors, emphasized racial purity and the stark separation of human races. Like the thinkers of the sixteenth and seventeenth centuries, Nazis, while noting the separate origins of all peoples or races, deemed the Jews to be a race mixture, unlike all others. An undated pamphlet of the German High Command entitled *Die Judenfrage und Ihre Bedeutung für das Deutsche Volk* (The Jewish Question and Its Significance for the German People) maintained this standard view that "Jewry represents not a uniform race but a race mixture. It consists of Near-Eastern and Oriental race ingredients, intermingled with Negro strains" (Weinreich.1999 p.209).

Racial "look" was itself controversial in the wider scientific world. Darwin had written that "the distinctive characters of every race of man were highly variable.... It may be doubted whether any character can be named which is distinctive of a race and is constant" (Darwin.1871 p.174). Yet, theorists such as Günther and Rosenberg were clear that Jews looked like Jews, and nothing at all like Germans. The very basis of Nazi racial thinking was that there was a visible biological basis for human diversity and that this was obvious on an individual basis. In *Mein Kampf* Hitler split humanity into categories that were largely the function of observable physical appearance. Günther insisted that there was a clear *Rassebild* (race picture) of Jews that distinguished them from Germans. This included dark brown skin, fat necks, rounded backs, small breasts, their famous noses, short limbs, fleshy lips, and a tendency to double chins. However, even for the Nazis, looks were not everything.

The Nazis asserted that all culture and mentality, not just appearance, were determined by biological "race." This was difficult to prove by any even superficially scientific method. There was, in any event, no real attempt to prove it. Even though the Nazis showed great zeal and efficiency in identifying and destroying Europe's Jews, paradoxically it could be said that there was a structural laziness in the Nazi racial state about everything to do with theories of "race" (Steinweis.2008; Ehrenreich.2007).

In the 1930s, as the need to be able to identify Jews was becoming more urgent, German scientists and anthropologists were enlisted to help out in a practical way by contributing their professional expertise to the task of determining how Jewishness could be discerned. In 1937, Ottmar von Verschuer (1896–1969), the director of the Institute for Genetic Biology and Racial Hygiene at the University of Frankfurt,[1] wrote to Eugen Fischer, by this time rector of the Frederick Wilhelm University of Berlin, now Humboldt University, urging that anthropological methods be used as well as historical evidence such as birth and death certificates and synagogue records, which were normally used by the *Reichsstelle für Sippenforschung* (the Reich Office for Genealogical Research), along with denunciations, to help identify persons of possible Jewish ancestry. Subsequently, race academics, first in Germany and later in Italy, in France, and throughout occupied Europe, were regularly called as expert witnesses to testify in court in cases of doubtful ancestry.[2]

One such was George-Alexis Montandon (1879–1944), the Swiss-born, naturalized French physician and polygenist anthropologist. In 1933 he took up the chair in ethnography at the *École d'anthropologie de Paris*, founded in 1875 by Paul Broca, Louis-Adolphe Bertillon, and Jean Louis Armand de Quatrefages de Bréau. His early work in African anthropology concentrated more on culture than race. Later, influenced by Eugen Fischer, Otmar von Verschuer, and other German anthropologists, and following a long line of polygenist scholars, including Chamberlain, Gobineau, Vacher de Lapouge, Ratzel, and others, he created a taxonomic system of humankind that posited four "great races" and around twenty races and sub-races.

Montandon developed his own kind of post-Darwinian polygenism, forming a general theory from the idea that the four "great races" were derived from different species of monkeys. The fictive claim that an anthropomorphic pongo-like ape had been discovered near the Tarra River in Columbia, called *Ameranthropoides loysi* after its alleged discoverer, François de Loys, fed into his scheme. Montandon suggested that the Jews may have derived from their very own ape, one specific to them (Lackerstein.2012 pp.213ff).

During the 1930s Montandon's work on race was applauded by German theorists, including Günther, and after the defeat of France, Montandon was enthusiastically promoted by the German high command in Paris. As a result glittering prizes awaited him. Within months, with German support, he became the leading authority on race and Jews in France. However, as a matter of national pride, Montandon and other collaborationist theorists went to some lengths to point out that the German racial policies, which they were enthusiastically implementing, actually originated in France with the polygenist works of the racial pioneers Gobineau, Gougenot des Mousseaux and Vacher de Lapouge.

As an acknowledged expert on Jews, Montandon was asked to help identify people of possible Jewish ancestry. If they were shown to be of Jewish origin they would be issued with a *certificat d'appartenance à la race juive* (a certificate of belonging to the Jewish race). Using crude and discredited methods, including craniometry and the cephalic index, Montandon examined some four thousand people and pocketed millions of francs in illicit payments and bribes. In 1943 he further helped the German cause by translating Otmar von Verschuer's manual on eugenics and heredity into French.

In the same year, 1943, not long before being assassinated by the Resistance, he interviewed a certain Mme. Karsenty in the Drancy internment camp in a northeastern suburb of Paris. He described her as having a

> rather elongated face, normally pronounced cheekbones, narrow ocular openings, finely shaped nose, a bit prominent . . . normal naso-labial gap, a bit fleshy. Average-size mouth; average-size upper lip; lower lip a bit fuller than the upper one. Average-size ears . . . General appearance of the features, more-or-less Judaic . . . since her morphology, despite the gracefulness of its expression, is rather strongly Judaic, the examined woman is to be considered Jewish.

For Mme. Karsenty, this patently approximate, "anthropological" decision was enough for her to be deported to Auschwitz. In other cases, too, the mere hint of "something Judaic" (*quelque chose de judaïque*) sufficed to condemn a victim of Montandon's "anthropology" to death (Bach.1999 pp.71–72; Staum.2011).

In 1940 Montandon contributed the first volume in a projected series for the *Nouvelles Editions françaises* entitled *Comment Reconnaître et Expliquer le Juif?* (How to Recognize and Explain the Jew?). But it was not enough for trained experts like Montandon to be able to distinguish the physical characteristics of Jews; French gentiles, as a whole, had to be equipped with this skill, in order to defend themselves. To this end an "ethnographic" exhibition was mounted by the *Institut d'Etudes des Questions Juives* (Institute for the Study of Jewish Questions), which had been created by the Germans early in 1941. Called *Le Juif et la France* (The Jew and France), the exhibition was housed in the Palais Berlitz on the Avenue de l'Opéra and ran from September 1941 to January 1942. It was seen by 200,000 people.

One hall was devoted to a "morphological study," which set out to delineate the specific somatic characteristics of the Jew. The real problem, as the official press release made clear, was that the Jews were difficult to spot. However, there were subtle telltale signs, which the exhibition promised to reveal. The morphological section displayed large, grossly stereotypical plaster casts of "Jewish" noses, ears, and eyes that had been assembled by Montandon. The plaster casts represented the most obvious stereotypical images, versions of which could be found everywhere in the antisemitic gutter press. Knowledge of such gross caricatures could hardly be expected to help track down the difficult-to-spot Jew in defense of the racial health of France. In September 1941 the *Institut d'Etudes des Questions Juives* put on a special commemorative event that made full reference to the morphological sections of the exhibition. The main speaker noted:

> Out of 10 Frenchmen of old French stock, at least 90% are true whites, pure of any racial mixing. It is not the same for the Jews. They are the result of interbreeding between Aryans, Mongols, and Negroes which occurred several thousand years ago. As a consequence, the Jew's face, body, bearing and gestures are peculiar to him.

The speaker took some comfort from the fact that the exhibition had been well attended and that as a result Frenchmen now would be better placed to defend themselves against the machinations of the Jews (Bach.1999 p.69).

A pamphlet, *Le Juif et la France au Palais Berlitz* (The Jew and France at the Palais Berlitz), published to promote the *Le Juif et la France* exhibition, stressed the need for French citizens to be able to protect their racial hygiene against the black/Jew by being able to identify "*ce negroïde aux lèvres charnues, au nez de vautour*" ("this negroid with thick lips, and vulture's nose") (Paris, 1869) (Figure 13).

In Germany, of course, defending the racial hygiene of the state was of the greatest possible importance, and new research was required to finally pin down the elusive characteristics of the racial enemy. In fact, neither the racial enemy nor his victim, the Aryan, was ever really defined. In order to shine more light on the question of race, the Nazi regime established eighteen university chairs, thirty-three research centers, and four research divisions within the Reich Health Office that were dedicated to racial hygiene and

Figure 13. Exhibition catalogue, *Le Juif et la France*. Cover illustration by René Peron (1904–1972). Paris: *Institut d'Étude des Questions Juives*, 1941. 9-3/4 × 8-1/4 inches (25 × 21 centimeters).

Image courtesy of the Wolfsonian–Florida International University, Miami Beach, Florida. The Mitchell Wolfson, Jr. Collection. XC1994.4289 (#2). Photo: Lynton Gardiner.

research. Eugen Fischer inserted twenty-five courses on *Rassenkunde*, racial science, into his Berlin curriculum. Moreover, from 1933 racial studies were made compulsory in German schools. There was no consensus on any of the basic terms, there was frequent disagreement among race theorists, and there were not even any school textbooks in this critical area of public policy to guide the teachers. They simply copied extracts from books by the likes of race amateurs Günther and Rosenberg and resorted to giving instruction in the correct use of head-measuring devices (Burleigh, Wippermann.1991 p.213).

Given the painfully obvious contradictions between basic Nazi ideology and scientific investigation elsewhere, the conclusions of much pre-Nazi science and physical anthropology in Germany, including those reached by scholars admired by Nazis (such as Ernst Haeckel and even Eugen Fischer), and the difficulties Nazi scholars and the Nazi leadership had defining "race" and especially the racial particularity of Jews, a kind of intellectual impasse was reached. Many German theorists, like Günther, or in France Montandon, still professed to believe that they could identify Jews by skull measurements or other metrics, even though they must have known that such methods did not work.

There was therefore a zealous desperation to unearth the holy grail of Nazi race science: one absolutely clear, unambiguous, and uncontroversial indicator of Jewish identity. Hans Günther was drawn to the promising issue of the peculiar and vile smell of Jews, which, as we have seen, had been a supposed marker of Jews in medieval times as it was among anti-Semites in the modern period: anti-Semites from Dr. Celticus to Hitler alluded to it. As a topic of scientific research, the supposedly idiosyncratic smell of Jews had been taken up by the important German biologist Gustav Jäger (1832–1917). Like Jäger, Günther was convinced that eventually the telltale odor of Jews would be scientifically identified through chemical analysis and would then provide a reliable way of immediately identifying Jews (Oisteanu.2009). Similarly, Otto Carl Reche (1879–1966), the German anthropologist and high-ranking academic, got very excited in 1940 when he thought he had finally stumbled on a physical peculiarity of Jews that no one had spotted before. In the way of scholars, he was reluctant to discuss his novel insight too widely. His hope was that he would obtain generous research funds, and there was always the fear that other scientists might steal his great idea. There had been, he eventually explained, countless studies of Jewish noses and bulbous Jewish lips, but there was a potential and "previously unexplored" racial trait that had not been adequately investigated and that would be ideal for identification purposes: Jews' ears (Boaz.2012).

Other scientists engaged in projects, with state research funding, that continued to pay lip service to the discredited techniques of old, thereby hoping to legitimize racial policies. Throughout the war such scholars made efforts to obtain, often in the most cruel, inhumane, and barbaric manner, skulls and bones of Jews, which could potentially be used to further research into Jewish difference, even though by then it was known perfectly well that skull size and shape and bone structure would not help to identify Jews.

In 1939, 440 male Jews were arrested in Vienna and were subsequently deported to the Buchenwald concentration camp, where they were murdered. However, before leaving Vienna they were subjected to a detailed anthropological examination by a team led by the Nazi anthropologist (and Olympic swimmer) Dr. Josef Wastl (1892–1968). During this examination measurements were taken and hair samples collected, but for some unknown reason the work was never finished or published. What studies were finished did not help (Ehrenreich.2007 p.74; Steinweis.2008 p.59).

Rare wartime anthropological research was conducted on behalf of the Anthropological Institute of the University of Vienna on the Jews of Tarnów by a mixed German-Austrian team, and authored by the Austrian anthropologist Dr. Elfriede Fliethmann (1915–1987), an assistant in the Race and Ethnic Science Section of the Institute for German Eastern Work in Kraków. She concluded that overall her large sample of 578 Jews did not look "typically Jewish" at all and their looks alone were not enough for them to be identified as Jews. Nor was there anything specific about them either demographically or anthropologically. She concluded, using the "know-it-when-I-see-it" approach, that nonetheless they gave an *Artfremd* (non-Aryan or alien) impression (Ehrenreich.2007 p.7).

Throughout occupied Europe SS units continued to engage in what were euphemistically referred to as "anthropological studies." Even so, there was significantly less physical racial research on Jews during the period of the Third Reich than there had been in Germany before. As Ehrenreich puts it: "The reason for the paucity of research on Jews seems clear: such studies would have undermined the asserted 'scientific' basis for the racial laws" (Ehrenreich.2007 p.7).

Before his dalliance with the old canard of Jews' ears, Otto Reche had been at the forefront of what seemed to be a promising new approach. In the 1920s, as Rachel Boaz's book *In Search of "Aryan Blood"* shows, it looked like serological research might be capable of distinguishing an individual's "race." During the Nazi period a number of German scientists, including Reche, continued with serological studies of Jews and other populations to try to distinguish the peculiarity of Jewish "blood" through the medium of blood.

Initially Reche was convinced that Jews could be readily identified by the presence of blood group B, but this was soon shown not to be so. The metaphorical and rhetorical use of the term "blood" confused background discussions of the issue, as Nazi science was convinced that everything about man and woman was to be found, metaphorically or somatically, in their blood.

But when it came down to it, non-metaphorically, Jewish blood and Aryan blood were indistinguishable, and the German courts were forced to acknowledge that there was no obvious link between blood type and racial identity. Subsequently, they did not accept sero-anthropological methods in cases of disputed racial identity. Indeed, for the most part, Nazi science relinquished the idea that the answer to the identification of Jews lay in properties of blood (Boaz.2012).

Some of the more practical Nazi officials realized that no conventional anthropological or medical investigation was likely to provide solutions in doubtful and undocumented cases of Jewish identity. Faced with the absence of physical anthropological evidence to underpin racial policies, it seemed worthwhile to find another way of constructing Jewish difference. One way, which a number of nineteenth-century race theorists had already proposed, was that the *real* racial characteristics of Jews were not obviously somatic but were rather spiritual or involved unseen properties that produced some barely discernible impression.

Eugen Fischer had unwittingly paved the way for a modern version of this approach with his work (supposedly read by Hitler) on the mixed populations of German South-West Africa in which he had pioneered a shift from the anthropometric models of craniometry and other measuring techniques to research on mental (*seelisch*) and physical characteristics from the genetic perspective of selection and heredity. By 1938, Fischer freely admitted that whatever physical and mental differences did exist between German and Jew were, in fact, subjective. There were no giveaway physical signs; however, the differences could be "instinctively" felt. Nonetheless, this was not a helpful aid to the easy identification of Jews by the racial bureaucracy.

The attempts to define Jewish difference included compromise formulas. One such was undertaken by a controversial figure in the German race studies hierarchy, Ludwig Ferdinand Clauss (1892–1974). Like Montandon, Clauss was not initially fueled by Jew hatred. During a four-year stay in the Middle East, principally in Palestine, in the 1920s, Clauss formed close relationships with Jews in the *Yishuv*. In Jerusalem, where he lived with his

Jewish mistress Margarete Landé,³ he was befriended by S. Y. Agnon, the great Hebrew writer and Nobel Prize winner, and his wife. Clauss and Landé then converted to Islam in order, perhaps, to get closer to the Arab population they were studying. This appears to be the point at which he started disliking Jews. Clauss developed a dualistic conception of Semitic peoples, common enough in Mandate Palestine, in which the noble Bedouin was set against the problematic, troublesome, pushy Jew (Wiedemann.2009; Weissblei.2016).

Clauss understood perfectly well that the basic system of biological, racial hierarchy that underpinned the Nazi racial state was unfounded. "Maybe," he wrote, "God knows the hierarchy of races, but we do not." A student of Edmund Husserl (1859–1938), the German-Jewish philosopher, Clauss attempted to exploit Husserl's theory of phenomenology to provide an ontological definition of racial difference. To this end he developed a field of racial psychology that proposed that each race had its own psychological *Rassenseele* (race soul) that coexisted with its biological makeup but was only partially dependent on it.

Adapting his work to suit the political climate, Clauss became one of the most prominent race theorists in Nazi Germany, even though his work was more popular with the public than it was with Nazi theorists, most of whom were fettered to the purely biological dogmas of race. His views, however, resonated with the part of Nazi theory that included the antimaterialist conviction that man was not just another animal, but a creature with a racial characteristic, which, in *Mein Kampf*, Hitler called *die ursprüngliche Seele* (original soul). Clauss's writing included a novel, compromise perception of "pure blood," which he defined as being a harmonious coexistence of body, understood as the field of expression of the soul, and the soul itself. However, his theoretical ideas did little or nothing to support the ideology of the racial state (Voegelin.1997).⁴

Nazi propaganda insisted on the clearly observable somatic difference of Jews. A hint of despair may therefore be perceived in the efforts to impose signifiers such as the mandatory use by Jews of the names Israel or Sarah on official documents or the mandatory J (designed by Hans Globke) on Jews' passports. If such measures suggested despair, the belated decree of September 1, 1941, suggested capitulation. This decree required Jews throughout the Reich and occupied areas to self-identify by wearing a signifier: a yellow Star of David with the word *Jude* ("Jew") inscribed on it in an ugly script intended to suggest something Hebraic. This followed the medieval practice of using mock Hebrew script to identify Jews and their homes.

In truth, in Nazi Germany, as in medieval Europe, the problem was that without such signifiers there was no other obvious way to tell Jews apart from gentiles. Jews looked like the people among whom they lived. As a collaborationist character in François Truffaut's film *Le Dernier Métro* observed: "*Si les Juifs avaient la peau bleue, ce serait beaucoup plus pratique*" ("This problem wouldn't arise if Jews had blue skin") (Bach.1999 p.75).

The American historian Alan Steinweis recounted the well-known anecdote contained in the satirical 1960 novel *Mendelssohn Is on the Roof* by the Czech Jewish writer Jirí Weil (1900–1959) in which an aspiring SS officer is ordered to remove and destroy the stone statue of the Jewish-born Felix Mendelssohn from a group of statues of composers that adorned the roof of the chief Prague concert hall. The statues were not labeled and no one had any idea what the Jew, Mendelssohn, looked like. In deft allusion to the most common of all stereotypical tropes, the officer ordered the workmen to select the statue with the biggest nose. This turned out to be Hitler's favorite composer, Richard Wagner (Steinweis.2006 p.23).

The absurdity of Nazi racial legislation is further illustrated by a 1935 photograph taken by a well-known Berlin photographer, Hans Ballin, of a German Jewish baby named Hessy Taft. This image was unwittingly used in Nazi publications as the perfect example of the authentic Aryan child and featured as such on the cover of a Nazi family magazine called *Sonne ins Haus* (Sun in the Home).

Shortly before his death, Hitler allegedly dictated his "political testament" to Martin Bormann (1900–1945), the head of the Nazi Party Chancellery. Hitler had spent much of his life thinking obsessively about Jews. Did he finally, in his last desperate days, realize that his ideas concerning polygenism, racial immutability, and the radical somatic difference of Jews were confused and absurd? At the end he allegedly observed that "the Jewish race is more than anything a community of the spirit." Moreover, like German Enlightenment figures such as Siegmund Baumgarten, Johann Salomon Semler, and others, he pondered the relationship between Jews and fate: "They have a sort of relationship with destiny ... and it is precisely this trait ... which defines the race and must reluctantly be accepted as a proof of the superiority of the spirit over the flesh" (Müller-Hill.1988 p.86).

As the Final Solution was being implemented, Jews were revealed in their true inner color, the color that had not been altogether visible before. I was struck, on a visit to the Auschwitz concentration camp, by the sophisticated, modern facilities that had been available for the daily ablutions of the SS and other German personnel, and by the total absence of such facilities, or of soap or clean water, for Jews and other victims. Jews, barely able to wash, were rendered black and filthy in comparison to the gleaming cleanliness of their persecutors. The contrasting visions in *Der Stürmer* and elsewhere of black or dark Jews and spotless white Aryans had been made flesh. German propaganda insisted that the filthy appearance of Jews, in such circumstances, was just a reversion to type. A Nazi pamphlet, *Der Jude als Weltparasit* (The Jew as World Parasite), explained that now the Jew "reveals once more the original appearance of his race: the stooped, little, filthy and greasy Jew." Many understood, like Roland Freisler, the murderous presiding judge of the Nazi People's Court, that Jews, while being "internally" black, were "outwardly white." But Jews were not only rendered somatically black through dirt. If, following Virchow's method, an Auschwitz victim's sleeve had been pushed up to reveal her true color, an eloquent black number, tattooed on the grimy skin of the outer or inner left upper forearm, would have been a reminder of the real color of the Jew.

Given the lack of progress in defining Jews biologically, Nazi scientific explorations of Jews through the old techniques of physical anthropology were, as we have seen, muted. However, considerable effort was devoted to understanding Jews by other means. Hitler had argued that Nazi antisemitism should be grounded in objective, evidence-based scholarship. This led to the development of *Judenforschung*—the antisemitic project of Nazi Jewish Studies. Jewish Studies academics, some of whom were serious scholars, produced a corpus of material in various academic disciplines, including theology, history, geography, sociology, and social anthropology, that attempted to reevaluate the history and sociology of the Jews from a Nazi perspective.

The antisemitic news agency *Welt Dienst* (World Service), which from 1939 was housed in the same building as the *Institut zur Erforschung der Judenfrage* (Institute for the Study of the Jewish Question) in Frankfurt am Main, was one of the Nazi organs that promoted and disseminated Jewish Studies research among scholars and others throughout occupied Europe. Montandon, for instance, subscribed to its newsletter, which was issued in nineteen languages. *Welt Dienst* was able to draw on the archival and published material of the *Einsatzstab Reichsleiter Rosenberg* (Rosenberg Taskforce), which was charged with the wholesale theft of cultural property, including Jewish books, during the Second World War. In 1943, *Welt Dienst* produced the pamphlet, *Der Jude als Weltparasit*, by Emil Reiffer and Erich Schwarzburg, which drew on these resources, if only superficially. The main purpose of the handbook was to justify the wholesale murder of Jews, which was then under way, by demonstrating that the Jewish "world parasite" was the deadliest disease to have infected Europe in thousands of years (Weinreich.1999; Steinweis.2008).

Succinctly recapitulating Nazi polygenist racial theory, which placed Jews outside the normal human framework, *Der Jude als Weltparasit* explained:

> If we thoroughly study the racial nature of the Jew, we conclude that Jewry is not a race in the ordinary sense of the word. Instead, as Houston Stewart Chamberlain wrote, it must be seen as a counter-race, although the term "counter-race" cannot be understood in a biological sense. From a biological standpoint, Jewry is a stable, inbred mixture of extreme races and racial rubbish.

In the bulk of Nazi Jewish Studies material, different Jewish communities, as racial objects, were often undifferentiated. However, there were fierce and ongoing debates, still not resolved in some cases by 1945, on the racial identity of some outlying Jewish groups. The ancient Karaite communities, for instance, which followed a form of Judaism and were to be found in various parts of occupied Europe, were initially deemed non-Jewish, in religious terms, by a 1938 decree issued by the *Reichsstelle für Sippenforschung*, the organ of state responsible for researching individual and group racial status. In the Lwów (now Lviv) Ghetto, established by the Germans in 1941, it was reported that the Karaites were given the paradoxical name of "Nazi Semites." Already in 1932 Michał Reicher-Sosnowski (1888–1973), a Polish anthropologist of Jewish origin, had argued that those who were racially Karaites were closer to Tartars than Jews. Others argued that they were racially Jewish. Serious doubts persisted about the Karaites from a racial perspective, and further academic studies were commissioned to clarify the position. Until the end of the war the debate continued, but suspicion lingered that they were at the very least *Artfremd* (non-Aryan, alien) (Green.1984; Trevisan Semi.1989).

Similarly, Persian Jews, a number of whom found themselves in wartime Europe, were represented, in part through the good offices of the Persian consul in Paris, Abdol Hossein Sardari (1914–1981), as racial Aryans who had accepted some elements of the Mosaic faith and were known as "Jugutis." In 1942, Adolf Eichmann (1906–1962) dismissed these arguments as the "usual Jewish tricks and attempts at camouflage," but some Nazi Jewish experts accepted the theory, and there was sufficient doubt in the matter for the majority to avoid deportation to death camps (Mokhtari.2012).

And again, during the German occupation of the northern Caucasus in 1942, there were lengthy discussions about whether the so-called Mountain Jews of the area were racially Jewish or not. The Nazis' hesitation in this case allowed the bulk of the community to escape destruction (Feferman.2007).

And what of those Jews whose dark color had contributed to the nineteenth century race wars and the growing conflation of Jews and blacks from the eighteenth century on? On the one hand Nazi and Fascist propaganda and rhetoric firmly maintained that all Jews were negroid or "colored," with black blood and black origins. However, Nazis, like other twentieth-century race theorists and like nineteenth-century polygenists, did not consider actual black or dark Jews part of the Jewish people from a racial perspective. Like Richard Burton, they did not "believe in the pure black Jew." A detailed German demographic work by Friedrich Zander (*Die Verbreitung der Juden in der Welt—Statistische Beiträge zu den Fragen der Zeit* [The Distribution of Jews in the World—Statistical Contributions to the Questions of the Time]), published in 1937, argued, for instance, that the Jewishness of the Ethiopian Jews was "controversial." Similarly, and predictably, the Italian Fascists during their occupation of Ethiopia maintained the polygenist view that the Falasha were not Jews, they should not be allowed to mingle with Jews, and to so describe them would fly in the face of "the prestige of race" (Trevisan Semi.1987).

Overall, given that basic Nazi theory, as expounded by Günther (the "Race Pope") and many other theorists, proposed that the Jews were in any case a "mixed people" and that part of this mixture was negroid, Nazi ideas about historical black Jewish groups were perhaps surprising. Taking the same line that had been established by generations of polygenist race theorists since the discovery of negro Jews in Loango in 1777, *Der Jude als Weltparasit* decreed that the Ethiopian Jews were not racially Jews and were the product of some ancient conversion. *Der Jude als Weltparasit* also decreed that the dark-skinned Yemenite Jews and black Bene Israel community of western India were not "racially" Jewish because of their external appearance.

Nazi and Fascist theorists could have argued that the wide color spectrum of Jewish communities worldwide was a wonderful proof of the mixed nature of Jewry and more specifically of the negroid stratum in the makeup of Jews. However, it was more important to preserve the Nazis' radical polygenist project, against which the existence of Jews of color had always been such a stout bulwark, and which had been such a persistent feature in the literature that had nourished the race theories of the Nazi project.

Der Jude als Weltparasit also mentioned the black Jews of Loango, whose discovery in 1777 had precipitated what I have called the Loango Turn. They were included in the list of groups who could be considered Jews by religion, perhaps, but not by race. The German Loango expedition and the work of Adolf Bastian, Paul Güssfeldt, Julius Falkenstein, and Eduard Pechuël-Loesche as well as the descriptions of the community by the German scholars Friedrich Ratzel and Richard Andree, had provided Nazi theorists with a mass of material on the black Jews of Loango. They extracted from this material that they were converts and therefore, supposedly, had some potentially Jewish *seelig* characteristics but no discernible Jewish racial characteristics. If they had any Jewish blood, it had been so diluted by negro blood that it was barely, if at all, obvious.[5]

The following year, 1944, *Der Jude als Weltparasit* was issued to the *Wehrmacht*. In the event, therefore, that German soldiers looking for Jews to murder in the towns, forests, or villages of Poland or the Baltic states encountered any Falasha, Bene Israel, or black Jews of Loango, they were to be left alone.

Of course, as it happened, with perhaps a couple of exceptions, there *were* no black Jews in Europe (assuming that Camilla, a delightful "African Jewess" who had enchanted audiences at the human exhibition at the Berlin Zoo in 1927 had made good her escape).[6] One exception was a black Jew called Joseph Nassy (1904–1976). Nassy was a painter, born in Surinam into a Jewish community that had been founded in the seventeenth century by one David Cohen Nassy. The painter from Surinam was first incarcerated by the Nazis in Belgium, where he was living at the outbreak of the war, but in 1942 was transferred to Internment Camp Lager VII at Laufen, Germany, and then to the neighboring Burg Tittmoning, an *Internierungslager* (internment camp) for officers and enemy civilians, Oflag VII-D, where he was provided with painting materials supplied by the Red Cross, and where he survived the war in relative comfort. Nassy had an American passport. Being American did not necessarily help if you were also black—some African-American soldiers were summarily executed. However, there was a greater likelihood of an American Jew being sent to the death camps than an American black. Nassy's Jewish name might have given him away, in which case he would probably have been murdered. As a black-skinned Jew and therefore as a conflation of Jew and black, Nassy posed a double threat to German racial purity, but paradoxically the camouflage of his black skin may have saved him. Another black Jew, in Nazi terms, was Soya K., a dancer; her father was a Cameroonian, her mother a German whose father was a baptized Jew. Despite persecution and being threatened with sterilization, Soya K. survived the war, spending the last year in prison in Prague (Rosenhaft.2015).[7]

In Nazi-controlled Europe, the unstable medieval and early modern discourses about the color of Jews had solidified into a more stable, conflated vision of Jew and black in which racial hatred of Jews and blacks assigned blackness to the principal racial enemy—the Jews. All Jews, except actual black Jews, now participated in this assigned blackness, through a kind of double vision, through dirt, blood, *Rassebild*, metaphor, or Rudolf Virchow's warning about the skin hidden beneath the sleeve, as propaganda cartoons and images, widespread opinion, and racial theories demonstrated. Of course, at the same time, it could be visually established that European Jews were not in fact black. The *Rassenwahn* that had engulfed Europe included the further paradox that passing themselves off as white, "camouflaged, cross-dressed, chameleon-like," in Céline's hate-filled words, was one of the Jews' principal crimes (Kestling.1998; Ehrenreich.2007; Plass.2013).

Notes

Prologue

1. It must also be noted that polygenesis was not the only avenue toward the racialization of Jews and blacks, as the sixteenth-century Iberian obsession with *limpieza de sangre* (purity of blood) shows. "Jewish" families that had converted to Christianity several generations before and had entailed frequent alliances with Iberian "Old Christian" families were still considered to have contaminated blood, as a good deal of recent work has shown (e.g., Biale.2007; Nirenberg.2013).

Chapter 1

1. The term "negro" was commonly and neutrally used in the eighteenth, nineteenth, and early twentieth centuries in English, Spanish, French, and German and it is thus used in this book where required. "Negro" is uncapitalized throughout. So are "black" and "white" where these words apply to groups of people. There is a good argument for capitalization in contemporary America (Robert S. Wachal. 2000. "The Capitalization of Black and Native American." *American Speech* 75.4. pp. 364-365). However the capitalized "Black" conveys a political sense of community and identity in the present time, which would be inappropriate, say, in eighteenth-century Africa or Europe and capitalized "White" strikes an even more stridently contemporary note. This book is about an earlier period and it would be anomalous to project contemporary sensitivities on to a different landscape.
2. Like Paracelsus, Bruno was a difficult man. Before long he threw out the images of the Virgin and saints that adorned his cell, was discovered with a closely annotated copy of a forbidden book—Erasmus's *Commentaries*—hidden in his latrine, and rebelled against his teachers, whom he accused of trying to make him "the slave of a foolish system of deceit."
3. In 1583, Bruno went to England; enjoyed a brief but close friendship with Queen Elizabeth I; was driven from Oxford after a controversial lecture, where his excitable manner, accent, and Neapolitan fashion of talking with his hands were ridiculed; and, according to recent research, perhaps became a spy (at the time the government was spending the fabulous sum of £12,000 a year on spies); and, as such, was instrumental in the execution of the Catholic Mary, Queen of Scots (Bossy.2002). Much of his teaching and writing attacked Catholic dogma. But during his wanderings he also got into serious trouble with the Calvinists (in Geneva) and the Lutherans (in their stronghold in Helmstedt in the duchy of Braunschweig-Wolfenbüttel).

4. See also: McIntyre.1903; Levy.1995.
5. The names "Julius Caesar" had been given to him by his soldier father along with Lucilio. He used Julius Caesar as his authorial style.
6. Commentary noting the similarity of apes to human beings had been around for a while. Comparisons between aged humans and apes are common in early Jewish sources—for example, *Midrash Tanchuma* (Pekudei 3):

   > In the seventh stage he resembles a monkey, who is different from all other creatures. He asks about everything; he eats and drinks like a youngster and laughs like a child. He returns to his childish ways in discernment but not in other things. Even his children and the men of his household mock him, curse him, and hate him. When he offers an opinion, they say: "Ignore him, for he is an old fool." He behaves like an ape in all situations and in whatever he says. Even the children laugh at him and mock him, and the wild birds can awaken him from his sleep.

7. "Come Calviniste et come Juif."
8. It became Williamsburg in 1699.
9. The full title was *The Negro's and Indians Advocate suing for their admission to the church, or, A persuasive to the instructing and baptizing of the Negro's and Indians in our plantations shewing that as the compliance therewith can prejudice no man's just interest, so the willful neglecting and opposing of it, is no less than a manifest apostacy from the Christian faith: to which is added, a brief account of religion in Virginia.* London: Printed for the author, by J.D. and are to be sold by most booksellers.
10. Some of the original debts were the result of a massive infrastructure project Baron Lahontan *père* had obsessively undertaken, trying to make the local river (the Gave de Pau) navigable from Pau down to the Atlantic at Bayonne, which often involved infringing on ancient fishing and other rights and the forced acquisition of land. The baron had to pay out greater and greater sums in compensation and the rest of the money went to the lawyers. In 1677 the family lost the château and lands.
11. Shortly afterwards, in *A New General Collection of Voyages and Travels* (1745), Thomas Astley (d.1759) the London publisher, commented on the implications of Atkins' theory:

    > He has taken Notice in his *Navy Surgeon* how difficultly the color is accounted for, and elsewhere declares, that although it be a little heterodox, he is persuaded the black and white Race have originally sprung from different colored first parents. With Mr. Atkins' leave, this is not to be a little heterodox but in a great Degree so; since that doctrine cannot subsist but by the Destruction of the Mosaiacal Account, which derives Mankind from one common Stock. And by the same rule that the Blacks had their peculiar Parents, every other Nation of a different colour must have had a particular father and Mother; and thus instead of confining the origin of the human Race to one single pair of Sexes, there will be introduced a great Number of original Creations. Indeed the Negroes themselves account for their Blackness in this Manner, if their Opinion may be of any Authority in the Case: For the Marabouts (as Labat observes) have a Tradition, that of Noah's three Sons, one was White, the other tawny, and the

third black; and that each of them had a Wife of his own colour, from whence proceeds the Difference among Nations in this Respect. (Atkins.1735; Ernst, Harris.999)
12. Voltaire's ready wit, waspish tongue, and willingness to take risks meant that he would have difficulties with the French and later other political and ecclesiastical authorities. In 1726, he was imprisoned in the grim fortress of the Bastille but shortly afterwards was offered the alternative of exile in England. After two and a half years he returned and wrote *Lettres Philosophiques*, which was published in Paris in 1734. Its distinctly pro-English tone, the fact that it had not been passed by the censor, and its criticism of the French court resulted in the book's being publicly burnt. Voltaire fled Paris to Cirey, in Champagne, where the Marquise du Châtelet, Voltaire's mistress, offered him asylum in her husband's partly derelict château. There he wrote *Traité de la Métaphysique*.
13. *Caffre* is the French form of English *Kaffir*, which is derived from the Arabic *kāfir* ("non-believer" or non-Muslim). It was used in English and other European languages to denote black Africans and by the twentieth century became a term of abuse, particularly in South Africa.
14. It is possible that M.L. was the physician and naturalist Martin Lister (1639–February 2, 1712) (Malcolmson.2016).
15. There have been Jews in India for well over a thousand years, and perhaps longer. There were four main Jewish communities in India in the early modern period: Jews living in the interior and particularly in the Mughal Empire; the so-called Baghdadi community, which was chiefly associated with the coastal trading towns of Surat, Calcutta, and Bombay; the Bene Israel of the Konkan coast in western India and Bombay; and the ancient community in and around the port town in Kerala. The existence of Jews in Cochin had been known among scholars in Europe since at least the sixteenth century, when Jesuit sources, such as the works of Alexander Valignano, referred to Cochin's Jews. As we have seen, there was even scholarly knowledge of the fact that some of these Jews were black, but this did not provoke any particular discussion. The community achieved greater visibility in 1665 when Rabbi Menasseh Ben Israel of Amsterdam cited the community in his famous petition to Oliver Cromwell. The Jews of Cochin would become vitally important in discussions about race over the last couple of decades of the eighteenth century but even more so after the publications of *Memoirs of the life and writings of the Rev. Claudius Buchanan, DD* (1817). (Wolf.1901; Fischel.1962; Katz, Goldberg.2005; Katz.2013; Parfitt.2017).

Chapter 2

1. Given that Jews were so often portrayed as black, it is possible that the figure in the Marnhull Orphrey is in fact a Jew, and there is perhaps the suggestion of a gray horn protruding from the mass of black curly hair on its head. I am grateful to Dr. Eric Zafran for information about anti-Jewish banners containing images of the head of a negro. It would seem that in this imagery too there is a conflation of Jew and black.

2. Constructions of blackness or explanations of blackness were not always negative throughout the late medieval or early modern periods. During the Renaissance there was often a nuanced approach to human pigmentation. The term "black" was employed descriptively as well as pejoratively, and variations in the skin color of Africans and other dark-skinned people were contemplated with interest, alongside other African physical characteristics. There were, indeed, sometimes assumed to be many good features of Africa and its populations. According to a long-running discourse that was prevalent during the fifteenth century, an earthly paradise based on the notions of Pliny (AD 23–79) and Ptolemy (AD c.100–c.170) and connected with the legends of Prester John and the ninth-century Jewish writer known as Eldad ha-Dani (Eldad the Danite), was to be found in sub-Saharan Africa. This association fed into the short-lived idea that west Africa was a land of health, wealth, wonders, and plenty.

In 1455 Alvise da Cadamosto (c.1432–1488), the Venetian slaver and explorer, set sail for Africa from Lagos in southern Portugal. Sailing down the arid coastline, eventually he reached the Senegal river, where he encountered the Azanaghi (Idzagen) people, whom he termed *berretini* (dark brown). He wrote:

> This river separates the Blacks from the brown people called the Azanaghi, and also the dry and arid land, that is, the above-mentioned desert, from the fertile country of the Blacks ... It appears to me a very marvelous thing that beyond the river all men are very black, tall and big, their bodies well formed; and the whole country green, full of trees, and fertile; while on [the north] side the men are brownish ... lean, ill-nourished, and small in stature.

Further north there were Arabs who were a lighter color brown, *bruni*. Cadamosto's unprejudiced and much-quoted assessment that the blacks were superior to the more "Caucasian" north African types, and the fine distinctions he drew between the colors of African populations, would have been unusual two centuries later.

Similarly, Leonardo da Vinci (1452–1519) interrogated the underlying reasons for different skin color with a degree of cool detachment. In his Notebooks he wrote: "The black races in Ethiopia are not the product of the sun for if a black gets a black with child in Scythia, the offspring is black; but if a black gets a white woman with child the offspring is gray. And this shows that the seed of the mother has power in the embryo equally with that of the father." His explanation for African blackness was that in Africa, where it was hot, negroes slept during the day and came out during the cool black of night, hence they themselves were black. Europeans on the other hand slept at night and spent their lives in the bright light of day, hence they were white. This idea, or a variant of it, was still alive at the height of the Enlightenment. Dr. Frank Nicholls (1699–1778), fellow of the Royal Society, and Gulstonian Reader at Oxford who "professed to teach anatomy, physiology and the general principles of pathology and midwifery in thirty nine lectures," imagined that the "blackness of the Ethiopian" was an attribute granted by God for a very good reason, and could be easily explained. Because of the great heat of Africa, the negro would be obliged to take cover in some dark place throughout the day and his "dark color would conceal him from the numerous ravenous beasts which infest those parts, when he was to fetch in his necessaries and provisions in the night-time." Early Dutch travel accounts such as those of Pieter van den Broecke (1585–1640) suggest that views of Africans were often ambiguous. Sometimes they were marked by repugnance and dislike, but also sometimes by fairness, generosity, and admiration. Educated Europeans of this period were also aware of differences between different groups of Africans. (See also White.1799; *British Medical Journal*.October 1868; Delumeau, O'Connell.2000; Cagle.2015.)

3. Going beyond the usual basic categories of Ethiopians or Egyptians he made a list of various ethnicities or clans drawn from classical authors and perhaps Augustine, which suggested the most important differences between groups of people was not their color but what they ate. Thus, there were the usual Troglodytes but also "root eaters" (*Ryzophagi*), "seed eaters" (*Spermophagi*), "eaters of fish" (*Ichthiophagi*), and "fruit eaters" (*Illophagi*). There was also some uncertainty about the actual color of Africans. Philippo Pigafetta in the middle of the sixteenth century described Africans as "of divers colors, as white, blacke, and a middle color beweene both: they are of a very good stature and have a good countenance."

4. This was not always the case: a sixteenth-century poem published in Basel argued that Africa had lost its preeminence as the "the mother of monsters" and had been replaced by Kraków.

5. The subtitle of Grégoire's book was *Recherches sur leurs facultés intellectuelles, leurs qualités morales et leur littérature: suivies de notices sur la vie et les ouvrages des nègres qui se sont distingués dans les sciences, les lettres et les arts* (Researches on their intellectual faculties, their moral qualities and their literature: followed by notes on the life and works of negroes who have distinguished themselves in science, literature and the arts.) The frontispiece carried a resounding line from the eighteenth-century celebrity and poet Mary Robinson, who like Grégoire was a keen opponent of slavery. "Whatever their tints may be," she wrote of blacks, "their souls are still the same."

6. Jean-Baptiste Labat (1664–1738).

7. Augustine noted that part of the punishment meted out to Cain was that he was condemned to "*gemens et tremens*" (groaning and trembling). In the Pseudo-Jonathan Targum to Genesis as in the Zohar, the Jewish mystical work, the idea was that God engraved a mark on the forehead of Cain in the form of one of the letters of the Tetragrammaton (YHWH) "so that anyone who would find him, upon seeing it on him, would not kill him." Later the mark was considered to consist of horrific lumps on the body, or horns sprouting from the top of the head. Later the mark was considered to be simply blackness (Friedman.2000; Horowitz.2006).

8. The idea that Saturn was the Jewish planet is also found in Jewish astrological texts such as Abraham Ibn Ezra's (c.1096–c.1164) *Sefer ha-Olam*.

9. The legends about the *Rote Juden* have been shown to be a conflation of discrete stories about the Lost Tribes, Gog and Magog, and multiple legends about Alexander the Great, known collectively as the Romance of Alexander, dating from the third century, which described how a low race of men had been trapped behind a wall by Alexander (Gow.1994).

10. I am indebted to Eric Zafran for drawing my attention to Gow's book.

11. *Plica polonica* is a rare affliction characterized by an uncontrollable matting of the hair.
12. Twenty years later Lord Byron could remark that the "English have at last compassionated their negroes," but the Jews had little if any chance of similar compassion or redemption "from mankind in general" (Katz.2016).

Chapter 3

1. The core area, while its boundaries fluctuated as a result of wars, was situated in the present-day Congo Republic but at different times it extended north into present-day Gabon and south into what is today the Cabinda exclave. Loango had a number of quite well-constructed towns and trading ports, including the large and important walled commercial city of Mbanza Loango. The German *Encyklopädie* of Johann Georg Krünitz (1728–1796) observed that the town stood "three English miles from the coast in a large plain" and was very cool "because of the many palm trees under which the houses are built. The streets are wide and long and are kept very clean. The king has his houses on the west side, and in front of the door there is open ground where he sits, whenever he holds a feast or a council of war." James Cowles Prichard (1786–1848), the British ethnographer noted in 1837 that the Loango capital, "at a distance from the coast, contains 15,000 inhabitants," and this was the seat of government and an administrative and religious hub.
2. In the sixteenth century Leo Africanus (1494–c.1554) wrote an informative few paragraphs about Loango. In the words of the translation by John Pory, *A Geographical Historie of Africa* (1600), the Loangans "have one supreme king . . . they traffique in Congo, and carry home from there salt and great shels to be used for coine (which are brought thither from the Isle of St. Tomé) in exchange for the clothe of the palm tree, and of Ivory." Between 1607 and 1610, Andrew Battell (c.1565–1614), the English traveler, visited Loango and brought back a detailed description of the social life of the kingdom along with an exciting day-to-day account of his own myriad adventures and misfortunes. Battell subsequently told his stories and impressions to the vicar of a neighboring village, Samuel Purchas (1577?–1626), and later to an unknown "transcriber." A Dutch sailor and merchant, Pieter van den Broecke (1585–1640), arrived in Loango in 1608 for the first of three visits. Upon landing he heard that the king of Loango had just impaled a Portuguese ship's master on an elephant tusk for having shot a Dutch trader. His Loango adventures, which appeared in print in 1634, gave a good deal of objective information about the country and was marked by a respectful attitude toward its people, less anchored in racial ideas of difference than in simple cultural curiosity. Another traveler, the Swiss barber-surgeon Samuel Brun (or Braun) (1590–1668), embarked on his first voyage to Loango and the Congo River in 1611 and left an account that was published in German in 1624 and subsequently in Latin. A monumental compilation on Africa including Loango, *Naauwkeurige Beschryvinge der Afrikaensche Gewesten*, followed in 1668 by the Dutch geographer Olfert Dapper (1636–1689), with a second edition eight years later, and translations

into French, English, and German. Dapper, who had already written about the existence of unicorns in Maine, and wrote of terrifying monsters in Loango, never left his comfortable study in the Netherlands and based his description of west Africa in part on material obtained from the Dutch West India Company. In total between fourteen thousand and eighteen thousand slaves were being exported out of Loango every year. Most of them had been captured within the Loango kingdom. Others had been seized in the distant interior and carried on boats to the coast via intricate waterways that years before, when there was little slave trading, had been developed for trade in ivory, elephants' tails, camwood, and copper. With the rapid increase in slavery, there was a parallel rise in social oppression, and people were enslaved within the kingdom for trifling reasons. The Maloango, Loango's ruler, played the competing trading nations against each other, and middlemen from the Vili ethnic group operated as brokers between local traders and European ship captains. This led to considerable fortunes being made, much of which was in the hands of African nobles (Prichard.1837; Martin.1972; Ischei.1997; Heywood.2007).
3. Literary monsters of various kinds abound in seventeenth-century travel and utopian writings such as Savinien de Cyrano de Bergerac's (1619–1655) *L'autre monde ou les états et empires de la lune* (The Other World or the States and Empires of the Moon) (1657) or Gabriel de Foigny's (c.1630–1692) *La Terre Australe connue* (The Southern Land, Known) (1676), which imagines an entire continent peopled by hermaphrodites, or Jonathan Swift's (1667–1745) *Gulliver's Travels*(1726), which describes, among others, the savage "Yahoos" (Weinstock.2016).
4. The word "monster" is derived from the Latin word "monstrum," which has the similar meaning of "monstrous creature" but also has the sense of demonstration or revelation. From Roman times on, the word implied more specifically unusual births that might be portents of the divine will. In the early modern period monsters were still seen as revealing something.
5. Often very ancient stories of monstrosities were transposed into observed contemporary realities, such as the denizens of the New World or chimpanzees. According to Edward Tyson's *Anatomy of a Pygmie Compared with that of a Monkey, an Ape and a Man* (1698), baboons were the "cynocephaly"—the dog-headed men of ancient Greek and Egyptian mythology, who had entered into Augustine's discussion of monsters. In his *Discourse on Inequality* (1755) Rousseau described the contemporary unease provoked by biological hybridity but complained that travelers to Loango were all too ready to make of the pongos "the same beings that ancients took for divinities under the name Satyrs, Fauns, Sylvans." Moreover, arch rationalist as he was, Rousseau insisted that in all probability, once the matter was properly investigated, the monstrous Loango pongos that so many travelers had described would be found to be "neither beasts nor gods, but men." That said, he devoted a great deal of space to the pongos and was not really certain how to categorize them. The pongo in a recognizably human form later went on to have something of a literary career: in *Brother John's Story* H. Rider Haggard wrote: "These Pongo are horrible wizards, a great and powerful people, who live by themselves amidst the swamps and mix with none. If the Pongo catch . . . folk of any other tribe, either they kill them or take them

as prisoners to their own land, where they enslave them or sometimes sacrifice them to the devils they worship." In Hilaire Belloc's *Pongo and the Bull* the British prime minister is given the ironic nickname "Pongo" because of his "pear-shaped trunk, the lengthy arms, and the insufficiency of the lower limbs" (Moran.1995; Rousseau.2012).

6. According to Father Girolamo Merolla da Sorrento (d.1697), writing in 1682, the embamba would regularly leap on a passerby, wrap itself around him, and press its fatal needle into his chest. The only remedy against this was to slice the creature in half as it attacked, and the men of Loango always carried a knife around with them for this very purpose. This creature had some features in common with another Loango monster known as the bomma, mentioned by Giovanni Antonio Cavazzi da Montecuccolo (1621–1678), the Italian Franciscan missionary, in his *Istorica descrizione de Tre Regni: Congo, Mantamba et Angola* (Bologna, 1637). The tail of the bomma was armed with a nail in the shape of a scythe, made of a very hard substance—*di una materia molto resistante*—and on both sides of its anus there was a sharp cutting tool, like pliers. These pliers were used by the bomma to slice up tougher pieces of human flesh prior to eating them.

7. He was arrested for his anti-revolutionary sentiments in 1808 and died in custody shortly afterward.

8. Pinkerton's translation of the book noted: "It must be monstrous, the prints of its claws are seen upon the earth, and formed an impression on it of about three feet in circumference. In observing the posture and disposition of the footprints, they concluded that it did not run this part of the way, and that it carried its claws at a distance of seven or eight feet one from the other." Prints this large could perhaps have been made by something like an elephant, but elephants, of course, do not possess claws.

9. Leo Africanus had laconically observed that men there were "like animals who held their wives in common and had no religion."

Chapter 4

1. The original manuscript has recently been published in a critical edition: Christian Georg Andreas Oldendorp.2000. *Historie der caribischen Inseln Sanct Thomas, Sanct Crux und Sanct Jan, insbesondere der dasigen Neger und der Mission der evangelischen Brüder unter denselben. Erster Teil: Kommentierte Ausgabe des vollständigen Manuskriptes aus dem Archiv der Evangelischen Brüder-Unität Herrnhut.* Berlin: Verlag für Wissenschaft und Bildung. See also: Oldendorp.1987. *A Caribbean Mission: A History of the Mission of the Evangelical Brethren on the Caribbean Islands of St. Thomas, St. Croix and St. John.* Ann Arbor, MI. Karoma Publishers.

2. It should be noted that post-war Africanists, including the few who have specialized in the Loango state (Phyllis Martin's *The External Trade of the Loango Coast* is an example) have made absolutely no mention of the black Jews of Loango. With the exception of the eccentric Jewish Enlightenment figure Ludwig Markus, who will be discussed later in the chapter, Jewish scholars engaged in the history and culture of the Jewish diaspora have had nothing to say about Loango's black Jews either. Some

of the black or dark Jewish communities elsewhere, who will come into our story, such as the Bene Israel of western India, the Beta Israel or Falasha of Ethiopia, and the black Jews of Cochin, have fared somewhat better, and scholarly societies, such as the Society for the Study of Ethiopian Jewry, and exhaustive bibliographies, such as the valuable one recently produced by Nathan Katz on the Jews of India (Katz.N.2013), as well as a mass of recent scholarship, have ensured that their role in the annals of Jewish life has been well recorded.

3. Earlier mentions of black or tawny Jews in India did not impact upon race discussions until the end of the eighteenth century.
4. *Allgemeine geographische Ephemeriden* was published by the *Landes-Industrie-Comptoir*, a body dedicated to social and economic development in Saxony-Weimar. The following year the *Comptoir* would create the important Geographical Institute in Weimar, which produced atlases, globes, travel maps, and journals.
5. Malte-Brun, a Danish geographer, was born Malthe Conrad Bruun at Thisted in Jutland. He adopted the style Malte-Brun once he moved to France after his banishment from Denmark in 1800.
6. The *casas da tinta*, or paint or dye houses, were traditional constructions used for a rite of passage known as *Tchikumbi*, which involved the ritual painting of girls prior to marriage. The British explorer Richard Burton (1821–1890 gave a graphic description of the *casas da tinta*

> where nubile girls are decorated by the Nganga, or medicine-man, with a greasy crimson-purple pigment and, preparatory to entering the holy state of matrimony, receive an exhaustive lecture upon its physical phases. Father Merolla tells us that the Congolese girls are locked up in pairs for two or three months out of the sight of man, bathing several times a day, and applying "taculla," the moistened dust of a red wood; without this "casket of water" or "of fire," as they call it, barrenness would be their lot. After betrothal the bride was painted red by the "man-witch" for one month, to declare her engagement, and the mask was washed off before nuptials. Hence the "Paint House" was a very abomination to the good Fathers.

I am grateful to Dr. Marina Pignatelli of the University of Lisbon for casting light on this issue.

7. Recent scholarship has suggested that the origins of the Jewish community of Ethiopia (Beta Israel or Falasha) should be seen in the context of religious and political processes that occurred in Ethiopia between the fourteenth and sixteenth century. During this period — one of great political and social turmoil—loosely affiliated groups of people referred to in the Ethiopian sources as *ayhud* (Jews) developed into an ethnic group that became known by the pejorative term *Falasha*. The term *ayhud* was generally used to refer either to political opponents of the Ethiopian Solomonic dynasty or to Christian heretics. The religion and ethnicity that emerged from these amorphous groups of rebellious and heretical *ayhud* were based on some form of Ethiopian Christianity. At its most orthodox, Ethiopian Christianity is a remarkably Judaic form of the Christian religion. It can be imagined that the forms celebrated by the rebellious and heretical *ayhud* were even more so. The term *Falasha* as a

description of this new group was only widespread from around 1500. Occasionally the term *Falasha* is used here in preference to the term *Beta Israel*, as this is the term used at the time (Parfitt.2017).

8. Landing in Marseilles, he was greeted with great enthusiasm by Buffon, who cited Bruce frequently in future editions of his *Histoire Naturelle*. In Paris he was received at the court of Louis XV (to whom he gave a valuable Geʼez manuscript) and was later given an audience by Pope Clement XIV. Soon after his arrival back in London (where he was received at court by George III), James Boswell (1740–1795) wrote a sarcastic piece on Bruce's travels for the *London Magazine*. The stories that tumbled from Boswell's pen were so unexpected and so apparently mendacious that Bruce was soon pilloried by the likes of Horace Walpole (1717–1797) and Samuel Johnson (1709–1784). Mortified, Bruce slunk back to his Kinnaird estates and started work on his *Travels*, which did little to rescue his reputation, in part because they presented an ethnography of an African nation in such a way as to make Africans seem improbably similar to Europeans.

9. When he wrote that "the court of London and the court of Abyssinia are, in their principles, one," he was treading on thin ice. His narrative, which was full of sophisticated and witty exchanges with Ethiopians, whom he obviously liked, in many respects destabilized the hierarchy of peoples that the Enlightenment naturalists had been so busy constructing.

10. Bruce lost his standing in London society, and for a while in Enlightenment circles generally, and became known as the "Abyssinian liar." Walpole claimed that during a dinner party someone asked Bruce if he had observed any musical instruments during his travels in Abyssinia. "Musical instruments?" said Bruce, and paused— "Yes, I think I remember one lyre." Another guest whispered to his neighbor, "I am sure there is one less since he came out of the country." Arthur A. Moorefield, "James Bruce: Ethnomusicologist or Abyssinian Lyre?" *Journal of the American Musicological Society* 28.3 (1975).

11. Once he moved to France he adopted the style Louis Marcus.

12. In an increasingly color-conscious Europe, Jews were increasingly eager to be seen as white. In order to avoid the racial color stigma arising from the coupling of Jews and blacks and in the old accusations that they were "black and ugly," Jews employed the stratagem of proclaiming their own whiteness in order to insert themselves in the dominant culture.

In the United States Jews were confronted with the same question: whether the Jews generally, long depicted as dark or black, were racially connected with Africa or Europe. Many Jews were embarrassed and belittled by the question, and until the middle of the twentieth century there was a distinct ambiguity about the perceived and self-perceived color of Jews, as there was of the color of the Irish and other groups. As a means of evading the conflation of Jews and blacks, Judaism itself was placed in direct opposition to blackness. An indignant article in the New York *Jewish Record* of January 23, 1863, noted: "We know not how to speak in the same breath of the negro and the Israelite. The very names have startlingly opposite sounds, one representing all that is debased and inferior in the hopeless barbarity and heathenism of six thousand years, the other, the days when Jehovah conferred on our fathers the glorious equality which led the Eternal to converse with them, and allow them to enjoy the communion of angels." In the face of continuous comparisons between blacks and Jews in the 1930s, the American rabbi Max Raisin (1881–1957) decreed bluntly that "negroes must not be likened to Jews. They never wrote a bible, did not give prophets and messiahs to the world." The distinctions American Jews drew between themselves and blackness were reflected in the way they distanced themselves from black Jews. In 1924, the Jewish writer Konrad Bercovici published an account of "Jewish Negroes—Abyssinian Jews, squat and long bearded, hooknosed *falashes*, real Jews" who were forced to live alongside blacks because other Jews did not want them in their neighborhoods. The lack of interest in black Jews on the part of white Jews spanned the period from the discovery of "Jews of all colors" toward the end of the eighteenth century to relatively modern times (Brodkin.1998; Ribak.2017).

13. This name was bestowed upon him by his friend the poet Heinrich Heine (1797–1856). Before his move to Paris, Markus had dealings with Heine through scholarly lectures organized around the *Verein für Cultur und Wissenschaft des Judenthums* (Association for Culture and Science of Judaism). Markus was something of a polymath. As Heine's biographer wrote of him:

    > He rummaged in all the departments of knowledge; he gulped down whole libraries, he ransacked the treasure-chests of all tongues, old and new . . . but from all his spiritual excursions he came ever back home to the story of the sorrows of the house of Israel—to Jerusalem's place of Golgotha, and to the dialect of his fathers, the tongue of Palestine—on which account he perhaps cultivated the Semitic languages with greater love than the rest. (Stigand.1875)

14. The first reference to the Bene Israel community of Maharashtra in western India is in a 1738 letter from a Danish missionary, J. A. Sartorius, who had been sent to Madras in 1730 by the Christian Knowledge Society. Sartorius wrote of communities of Jews called Bene Israel in "Surat and Rajapore." According to Sartorius these Jews (he does not specify which of the two communities) used the word "Shema" as "a formula of prayer and doctrine." He wrote that "they have not the books of the Old Testament nor do they understand Hebrew but Hindustani the language of the country where they reside . . . they practice circumcision as a part of their religion. They wear turbans and a long dress reaching to their feet, and long trousers, just as the Mohammedans do." As a result of outside Jewish influence the Bene Israel of Bombay started practicing a normative form of Judaism early in the nineteenth century (N.Katz.2013; Parfitt.2017).

15. The Abbé's stated source for the novel idea of "Jews of all colors" was not Büsching or Oldendorp but the journal of a Dutch learned society, (which some twenty years before had scooped the mathematical principles of the Sudoku puzzle). As the abbé wrote: "Voyez sur cet objet une dissertation curieuse, en hollandais, dans le tome VI des *Mémoires de la société de Flessingue, Verhandelingen vitgegeven door het zeeuwsch, genootschap der wetenschappen te Vlissingen*".

16. His source for this was not some recent book of travels, but the medieval Jewish traveler Benjamin of Tudela (1130–1173), who, in fact, had never seen the Falashas, as

they had not emerged as a group at this time. Nonetheless Benjamin was convinced, like many other people, that in Ethiopia there was a powerful black Jewish kingdom (Fauvelle-Aymar.2013).

17. *Geographische Nosologie oder Die Lehre von den Veränderungen der Krankheiten in den verschiedenen Gegenden der Erde: in Verbindung mit physischer Geographie und Natur-Geschichte des Menschen* (Geographical Nosology; or the doctrine of the transformation of diseases in different regions of the earth: in connection with physical geography and natural history of man). Stuttgart. Steinkopf, 1813.

Chapter 5

1. Quite appropriately he introduced his magnum opus, *Crania Britannica: delineations and descriptions of the skulls of the aboriginal and early inhabitants of the British islands* (1867), with Byron's lines about the skull—"This was once Ambition's airy hall, the dome of Thought, the palace of the Soul."
2. An account from 1841 tussled with the issue of how the "secretion" of pigment sometimes fails to happen,

    hence the anomaly of white negroes; and sometimes only in interrupted lines or patches, whence the anomaly of spotted negroes; and we even have a few rare cases of negroes in America, who, in consequence of very severe illness, have had the whole of the black pigmentation absorbed and carried off, and a white pigment diffused in its stead. In other words, we have instances of a black man being suddenly bleached into a white man.... Hence the unhappy race of Albinoes, and a whole pedigree of white negroes. (*The Christian Traveller*.1841)

3. Hitler, too, played with the fantasy of socially positive mass whitening. Attributing something of the success of British imperialism to the fact that the British were not interested in "washing the dirty linen of their subject people," Hitler observed in a dinner conversation that "we would like to rub a negro until he becomes white" (Hitler.2013 p.38).
4. Buchanan was born in a village near Glasgow of pious parents who had high hopes that he would take holy orders in the Church of Scotland. His early years were not promising. Having taken a degree in the ancient University of Glasgow, he devised a harebrained scheme, not revealed to his parents, to travel through Europe on foot, supporting himself by playing the fiddle. This bold enterprise came to nothing, but for several years he lived rough in London, sometimes having to pawn his clothes to sustain himself.
5. His descriptions of the immolation of widows (*suttee*); the Jagganath (which he called Juggernaut) rituals as a mindlessly dangerous, child-sacrificing, bloody cult; and the festival of *Churruck Puja*, where "men are suspended in the air by iron hooks passed through the integuments of the back," among other "degraded" Indian customs, and his insistence on the need to evangelize India, did much to transform British attitudes toward the ancient civilizations of the subcontinent (Altman.2017).
6. Mount Aurès, eastern continuation of the Saharan Atlas range.

7. D'Abbadie published his report as "Notice sur les Falachas" in the *Journal des Débats* of July 6, 1845. In November 1849, *The Jewish Chronicle* printed a letter from a correspondent who had interviewed d'Abbadie containing information about the Falashas.
8. The *Eclectic Review* commented, "We should not deem it necessary to notice this *queer* book, but for the purpose of warning the reader against any idea, which might be suggested by its imposing title, that it contains any useful or interesting discussion."
9. Hearing of his departure for the "Great Desert," the *Journal of the Royal Geographic Society of London* noted gloomily that "Mr. Richardson's enterprise is looked upon as foolhardy and desperate. He has been advised against it, but his resolution was not to be shaken. We very sincerely wish his daring enterprise may be crowned with that success of which perhaps we can hardly entertain any legitimate hope." On the Jews of the Sahara see Boum.2011.
10. Owen came from a family of relatively modest means. Before joining the Royal Navy he attended Lancaster Grammar School, where his teachers characterized him as "lazy and impudent." Samuel Smiles's great Victorian bestseller *Self-Help* noted his humble origins and observed approvingly that this "Newton of Natural History, began life as a midshipman, and did not enter upon the life of scientific research in which he has been so distinguished, until comparatively late in life." He went on to found the Natural History Museum and was appointed science tutor to Queen Victoria's children (the court was astonished to learn that tadpoles turned into frogs).
11. I have not been able to trace the source of this reference. John Beddoe speculated that it might have been the famous 1822 work by Silk Buckingham, *Travels in Palestine, through the countries of Bashan and Gilead, east of the river Jordan: incl. a visit to the cities of Geraza and Gamala, in the Decapolis* (London: Longman). However, it is difficult to see why he thought this, as the group Buckingham described was neither black, particularly "low," nor Jewish.
12. In his short life Waitz became a full professor of psychology and an honorary fellow of both the anthropological and ethnological societies of London; produced a two-volume critical edition of Aristotle's *Organon* and an important work on psychology, *Grundlegung der Psychologie*; and wrote his six-volume anthropological work *Anthropologie der Naturvölker* (1859–1864), perhaps the first substantive work of anthropology. It appeared in English in 1863, edited by the honorary secretary of the Anthropological Society of London, J. Frederick Collingwood.
13. In 1831 Dr. Pruner had participated in a scientific expedition to Egypt, where he was appointed professor of anatomy by the viceroy, Mehmed Ali (1769–1849).
14. Professor Kurt Sprengel (1766–1833), the German physician and botanist.
15. Elected a member of the French Academy of Sciences in 1852, three years later Quatrefages was appointed to the chair of ethnography and anthropology at the *Muséum national d'Histoire naturelle*, which had been founded in 1793.
16. The presence of black Jews in Timbuctoo, mentioned by Quatrefages, was fully attested in the travel literature of the day. By way of example, Joseph Dupuis (1789–1874), who had served as British consul and vice consul in Mogador and elsewhere, visited Kumasi in 1820. His 1824 travel account, which received favorable notices in London's *Monthly Critical Gazette* and elsewhere, was entitled *Journal of a Residence*

in *Ashantee Comprising Notes and Researches Relative to the Gold Coast, and the Interior of West Africa*. He observed that in early descriptions of the area there was supposedly a country called Yahoodee. However, he put the record straight and observed that

> Yahoodee simply implies Jews, the tribes of Jews, &c. which term the Moslems apply to the people of the Mosaic faith who inhabit the lower Atlas . . . They also apply the term Yahoodee to the Hebrew or Jewish tribes, *whether native Africans, or not,* who inhabit Marroa, some parts of Fillany, and the neighborhood of Timbuctoo. (Dupuis.1824)

17. See Chapter 7.

Chapter 6

1. A fellow of the Royal Society, White was famous for having mummified a female patient whose embalmed corpse he kept in an old clock case in his house in Sale, from shortly after her death in 1758 to 1813. The corpse became known as the Manchester Mummy.
2. Most improbably, in the summer of 1927, a show at the Berlin Zoo featured twenty-four "African Jews" playing hand drums and bagpipes. The chief draw was a beautiful "picture perfect" young African Jewess, Camilla, "possessing facial features of the nobility," who became the darling of Berlin. Perhaps the last Jewess to do so, as the first large-scale Nazi Party national congress took place in Nuremberg in August 1927. In his address to his followers, Hitler pointed to the threat of international Jewry and to the inferiority of negro blood. It is difficult to know what Hitler and his Nazis would have made of this troupe of African Jews who, in the same month, August 1927, had taken up residence in the Berlin Zoo, drawing great crowds and getting rave reviews for their musical performances. A Berlin daily enticed people to the show with the headline: "The beautiful Camilla and the dwarf Saïd." This Jewish dwarf served coffee while the beautiful Camilla quite simply took the city by storm. Berlin fell in love with the Jewish African Camilla—"no-one can argue," trumpeted one paper, "that the star of the troupe is Camilla" (Bruce.2017).
3. The skull collection is now to be found in the Academy of Natural Sciences of Drexel University, formerly the Academy of Natural Sciences of Philadelphia.
4. A somewhat convoluted case consisted of the allegedly Jewish origin of the population of Kashmir. The popular and prolific English writer and schoolmaster John Bigland (1750–1832), in *An Historical Display of the Effects of Physical and Moral Causes on the Character and Circumstances of Nations* (1816), was struck by the color of Kashmiris. For centuries travelers had been bringing back stories illustrating the supposedly Jewish origins of the people of Kashmir. One of Bigland's sources for this ethnological perspective was the great orientalist and adventurer George Forster (d.1792), a civil servant in the East India Company, on the Madras establishment, who was the first British traveler to journey from India through Central Asia and then on to Russia. In *A Journey from Bengal to England* (1798) he noted that when he encountered the "Kashmirians"—"a fair people . . . I imagined . . . that I had come among a nation of

Jews." For Bigland, at a time when the polemic surrounding skin color and what caused it was at its height, the detail concerning their fair skin color was critical. He used it as proof that naturally pale Jews, despite the burning heat of Kashmir, were able to maintain their skin color, as part of a "racial substance, in a completely unchanging state, for ever." His view was that the light color of Kashmiris was proof of the immutable racial structure of Jews (Forster.1798; Bigland.1816; Bruns.2011).

5. Nott also spoke about the Ten Tribes of Israel "almost lost by amalgamation" as they mixed over the centuries with other peoples—"and yet the uninformed are discovering them, not only in the remote corners of the Old but in the New World. The aborigines of America have been taken for the *lost tribes*, and California for the land of Ophir—both ideas equally ridiculous."

6. The son of a Swiss pastor, Agassiz had studied in the universities of Heidelberg and Munich, where he earned two doctorates, one in medicine and the other in philosophy. He first came to public attention as a result of his revolutionary work on glaciers in his native Switzerland, proving that the world had passed through an ice age, with respect to which great honors, if not financial rewards, were heaped on him. His subsequent move to the United States in 1846 was largely inspired by his desire to fund new research projects and pay off old debts. At Harvard he initially kept alligators and eagles in his back yard and from these humble beginnings went on to found what would be one of the largest zoological museums in the world—now called, after "the creator of American science" the Louis Agassiz Museum of Comparative Zoology. It is worth noting that a neighboring school also named after "the creator of American science" has removed his name in favor of the name of the school's first African-American headmistress, given his views about race, and it is difficult to imagine that the museum will fail in due course to follow suit. Similarly, there have been efforts to change the name of the Swiss mountain the *Agassizhorn*, named to mark his findings in glaciology.

7. The Chartist movement was a British working-class movement that grew out of the failure of the 1832 Reform Act to extend the franchise. It was ignited by the "People's Charter" of 1838.

8. Semien Mountains in northern Ethiopia.

9. Lake Tana, the source of the Blue Nile and Ethiopia's largest lake.

10. The Qemant are a small subgroup of the Agaw ethnic group, whose traditional religion has a number of Judaic features. See: Gamst, Frederic C.1969. *The Qemant. A Pagan-Hebraic Peasantry of Ethiopia*. New York. Holt, Rinehart and Winston; Leyew, Zelealem.2003. *The Kemantney Language*. Köln. Rudiger Koppe Verlag.

11. The Agaw or Agau are an ethnic group in Ethiopia.

12. His claim that the French aristocracy was racially superior to the rest of the French people on account of its Aryan origins did not receive the enthusiastic support in France he might have hoped for.

13. Numerous sightings were made until the twentieth century of allegedly Bedouin groups of Jewish origin in the lower Jordan Valley (Ben Zvi.1957).

14. J. B. Ginsburg, a missionary in Morocco of Jewish origin, worked for the London Society for Promoting Christianity Among the Jews.

244 NOTES

15. The full title: *God's Image in Ebony: Being a Series of Biographical Sketches, Facts, Anecdotes, etc., Demonstrative of the Mental Powers and Intellectual Capacities of the negro Race* (1854).

Chapter 7

1. Physiognomy had a particular influence on the sciences or pseudosciences of craniometry and phrenology, which had been developed by the anatomist Franz Joseph Gall (1758–1828).
2. "You assert that your mothers had no commerce with he-goats, nor your fathers with she-goats. But pray, gentlemen, why are you the only people upon earth whose laws have forbidden such commerce? Would any legislator ever have thought of promulgating this extraordinary law if the offence had not been common?" (*Dictionnaire philosophique*.1764).
3. Bernard Picart (1673–1733) published *Cérémonies et coutumes religieuses de tous les peuples du monde, représentées par des figures dessinées par B. Picart, avec des explications historiques*, which appeared between 1723 and 1743 in a number of languages and editions.
4. https://www.mutualart.com/Article/The-Artist-as-Ethnographer--CharlesCord/8B8607CA79F23996
5. See note at Edinburgh University online archives: https://archiveshub.jisc.ac.uk/search/archives/d0e2a699-72a9-30c6-9b65-76101dba49c3?terms=jews
6. The canon's belief that Jewish racial specificity survived frequent intermarriage with other "races" reflects the much earlier Catholic *limpieza de sangre* (purity of blood) arguments in sixteenth-century Spain. Jews who had converted to Christianity several generations before and had entailed frequent alliances with Iberian "Old Christian" families were still considered to have contaminated blood, as a good deal of recent work has shown (Biale.2007).
7. As Jacobs wrote:

    It will be observed that in the composite . . . containing the largest number of components (thirteen) the face has distinctly what is termed a Jewish expression, though it is full-faced. It follows that the peculiar expression known as Jewish cannot be due to the droop of the nose alone. The full lips, the heavy eyelids, and large irides have much to do with it. So far as the nose is concerned it is the flexibility of the alme, or wings of the nostrils, that are distinctive rather than its curvature . . . Of the fidelity with which they pourtray [sic] the Jewish expression there can be no doubt. Each of the eight composites shown might be taken as the portrait of a Jewish lad quite as readily as any of the components. In some cases, . . . the portraits are less Jewish than the composites . . . These facts are something more than curious; they carry with them conclusions of scientific importance. If these Jewish lads, selected almost at random, and with parents from opposite parts of Europe, yield so markedly individual a type, it can only be because *there actually exists a definite and well-defined organic type of modern Jews*. Photographic science thus seems to confirm the conclusion

I have drawn from history, that there has been scarcely any admixture of alien blood amongst the Jews since their dispersion. (Jacobs, 1886 p.53)

As Jacobs was an enthusiastic supporter of the doctrine of the purity of the Jewish race and its immutability over time, he was inevitably opposed to the idea that the Jews of Loango, the black Jews of the Sahara, the Falashas, Bene Israel, or Cochini Jews were racially Jewish. For him they were merely "Jews by religion but not by birth."

8. Gobineau was familiar with the literature describing Jews in remote parts of the world and here based himself, in part, on the travel writing of Joseph Wolff, who claimed to have discovered vast numbers of dusky "Rechabite" Jews, armed to the teeth, in southern Arabia (Wolff.1839).

9. At the height of the imperial age there was scarcely a more critical issue than that of the much-desired adaptability of Europeans to the rigors of foreign climes. One of the problems that beset British, French, and other colonial enterprises in Africa, India, and elsewhere was the high mortality rate experienced by European traders, administrators, and missionaries. In 1910 Maurice Fishberg (1872–1934), the Jewish-American physical anthropologist who specialized in the ethnology of the Jews, went as far as to say that this was the

most urgent problem which confronts modern statesmen, anthropologists, and sociologists ... Many claim that the European is not fit for this change, and that those who survive the difference in the physical environment, even if the new climate differs but little from that of the mother country, have to undergo a kind of transformation which effects their entire organism. (Fishberg.1911 p.17)

This grave impediment to imperial progress appeared to be a racial problem endemic in Europeans; Jews, however, seemed to be immune to it. "The Jews appear to be an exception in this respect," wrote Fishberg. "They live, thrive, perpetuate their kind, and preserve their identity under all varieties of climatic conditions" (Fishberg.1911 p.17). The existence of black and dark Jews at one end of the color spectrum was apparently proof of this valuable endemic trait. Richard Andree (1835–1912), the German ethnographer and geographer mentioned earlier in the chapter, noted:

The Jew is able to acclimatize himself with equal facility in hot and in cold latitudes and to exist without the assistance of the native races. He lasts from generation to generation in Surinam (Dutch Guiana) or in Malabar (India), tropical climates where Europeans, in course of time, die out, unless they are constantly re enforced by new immigration from the mother country. (Andree.1881 pp.70–71)

10. Spiller had some experience organizing undoubtedly well-meaning international conferences, as two years before he had organized the First International Moral Education Congress. From 1904 on he labored as the secretary of the London-based International Union of Ethical Societies, which colorless body preceded the Humanist movement. Apart from this and other duties, he wrote Humanist hymns, some of which were collected in *Hymns of Love and Duty for the Young* (1910).

Chapter 8

1. At one point Latham was director of the ethnological department of the Crystal Palace exhibition center.
2. Founded by Jean Louis Armand de Quatrefages de Bréau, Paul Broca and Louis-Adolphe Bertillon in 1875.
3. In his bestselling *Rural Rides* (1830), he observed that even dogs displayed "more [reasoning ability] than many a Negro that I have seen". He had anti-Semitic views too. Again, in *Rural Rides* he wrote of Jews with "hook-noses and round eyes," and elsewhere described them as extortionate usurers (Scherr.2003).
4. The term "Semitic" was coined in 1781 by August Ludwig von Schlözer of the famous Göttingen History school as a way of describing Arabic, Aramaic, Hebrew and other cognate languages.
5. After the Second World War, in the speeches of Malcolm X and other black activists the message was similar: what Europe had done to the Jews, America would end up by doing to the blacks.
6. According to Egon Freier von Eickstedt (1892–1965), the physical anthropologist who edited the Nazi *Zeitschrift fur Rassenkunde* (Journal of Racial Studies) from 1933–1945, Meiners was "the great innovator".
7. His ideas influenced Gobineau, Georges Vacher and Robert Knox.

Chapter 9

1. As Haddon wrote in 1898:

    The gross index is gotten by subtracting the number of red and fair-haired persons from that of the dark-haired, together with twice the black-haired. The black is doubled, in order to give its proper value to the greater tendency to melanosity shown thereby; while brown [chestnut] hair is regarded as neutral, though in truth most of the persons placed in B are fair-skinned, and approach more nearly in aspect to the xanthous [light] than to the melanous [dark] variety. The formula is: D + 2N-R-F = Index. From the gross index the net, or percentage index, is of course readily obtained. (Haddon. 1898 p.26)

2. Grosz was sometimes taken for a Jew and had an ambiguous, conflicted relationship with Jews, often portraying them as sadistic and deviant. His Jews are strangely colored. In one painting, a Jack the Ripper figure, which figure is also an Eastern European Jew, has a face that is sickly, dark, and yellow, intended here and elsewhere in his work to portray "disturbance and deviance" (White.2007).
3. The demonization of the Jewish billionaire George Soros for allegedly financing the immigration of Africans and others into Europe and the demonization of the Jewish refugee agency HIAS by the white supremacist who killed eleven Jews at the Tree of Life synagogue in Pittsburgh in 2018 because "HIAS likes to bring invaders in that kill our people" are of a similar nature. Moreover, white nationalists in the United States and elsewhere often link Jews and the threat of black/white race mixing,

as Jews allegedly are trying to bring about the genocide of the white race (King, Leonard.2016). The "Unite the Right" rally in Charlottesville in 2017 was a clear conflation of antisemitism and anti-black racism. Jews and blacks were held to be equally responsible for the dangers faced by white Americans.
4. The phrase is borrowed from the title of the 1999 book by Matthew Frye Jacobson, *Whiteness of a Different Color: European Immigrants and the Alchemy of Race* (Cambridge, MA: Harvard University Press).
5. In the United Kingdom in the 1970s this formula would be termed "political blackness."
6. Estimates of the black population of Nazi Germany range from 5,000 to 25,000.
7. Landra and his Vice-Director in the Italian Race Office, Lino Businco, were the Italian delegates. The Germans were represented by Dr. Walter Gross, Head of the Nazi Office of Racial Politics, and his Vice-Director, the physician and race expert Dr. Rudolf Frercks, author of *Deutsche Rassenpolitik* (Leipzig: Reclam, 1937).
8. The Marnhull Orphrey mentioned in Chapter 2 shows a black man, perhaps with a horn sprouting out of his head, beating Jesus. The black man is perhaps intended to be a Jew (there are no blacks mentioned in the story of the crucifixion) and a way of indicating that this really was a Jew was to provide him with a horn.
9. Henry Ford's antisemitic book *The International Jew*, culled from articles in the *Dearborn Independent*, was translated by *Hammer* and appeared in the summer of 1921 as *Der Internationale Jude*.
10. Ford dealerships throughout the country were expected to promote subscriptions to the *Dearborn Independent*, thus boosting its sales, which peaked at 700,000.
11. I am grateful to Professor Michael Alexander for bringing this article to my attention.
12. Richard Strauss composed a *festliches Vorspiel* for the exhibition, which he conducted at the opening.
13. I am grateful to Dr. Len Lyons for sharing his remarkable erudition on the history of jazz.

Chapter 10

1. His 1942 *Leitfaden der Rassenhygiene* (Primer for Racial Hygiene) called for "a complete solution to the Jewish question" (Hayes, Roth.2010).
2. Anthropologists, scientists, and doctors were later involved in the infamous "selections" carried out at the railway sidings at Auschwitz.
3. A fellow academic called Margarete Landé, who was referred to by Agnon and his wife as Mrs. Landé-Clauss.
4. Essentially, Clauss was interested in what people observed in the practice of race, and during the 1920s he wrote three books seeking to show that Husserlian phenomenology had made possible for the first time a rigorous conceptualization of race. His most important works were *Die Nordische Seele* (1923) (The Nordic Soul), *Rasse und Seele* (1926) (Race and Soul), and *Rasse und Charakter* (1936) (Race and Character).

In the 1930s and during the war he participated in race experiments and examinations using crude and barbaric anthropometric methods.

5. It should be noted that postwar Africanists, including the few who have specialized on the Loango state (Phyllis Martin's *The External Trade of the Loango Coast* is an example) have made absolutely no mention of the black Jews of Loango. With the exception of the eccentric Jewish Enlightenment figure Ludwig Markus, the "king of Abyssinia," Jewish scholars engaged in the history and culture of the Jewish diaspora have had nothing to say about Loango's black Jews either.
6. See footnote 2 Chapter 6.
7. https://encyclopedia.ushmm.org/content/en/article/josef-nassy

Bibliography

Abernethy, Arthur Talmage.1910. *The Jew a Negro: Being a Study of the Jewish Ancestry from an Impartial Standpoint*. Moravian Falls, NC: Dixie Publishing Company.

Abrahams, Israel.1961. *Jewish Life in the Middle Ages*. New York: Meridian Books.

Afro-American Encyclopaedia; Or, The Thoughts, Doings, and Sayings of the Race, Embracing Addresses, Lectures, Biographical Sketches, Sermons, Poems, Names of Universities, Colleges, Seminaries, Newspapers, Books, and a History of the Denominations, giving the Numerical Strength of Each. 1895. Nashville, TN, and Florida.

Agassiz, Jean Louis Rodolphe.1850. "The Diversity of origin of the Human Races." *Christian Examiner*. Boston.

Ahlbäck, Anders.2015. *The Overly Candid Missionary Historian: C.G.A. Oldendorp's Theological Ambivalence over Slavery in the Danish West Indies*. Leiden: Brill.

Alexander, Nathan.2018. "Atheism and Polygenesis in the Nineteenth Century: Charles Bradlaugh's Racial Anthropology." *Modern Intellectual History*. 16.3.

Allgemeine geographische Ephemeriden.1803. 11. Eds. Adam Christian Gaspari and Friedrich Justin Bertuch. Verlage des Landes—Industrie Comptoirs.

Altman, Michael J.2017. *Heathen, Hindoo, Hindu: American Representations of India, 1721–1893*. New York: Oxford University Press.

American Phrenological Journal and Repository of Science, Literature and General Intelligence. 1858. 27–28.

Andree, Richard.1881. *Zur Volkskunde der Juden*. Leipzig: Velhagen und Klasing.

Annegarn, Joseph.1834. *Handbuch der Geographie für die Jugend*. Munster: J. H. Deiters.

Armistead, Wilson.1848. *A tribute for the Negro; being a vindication of the moral, intellectual, and religious capabilities of the colored portion of mankind; with particular reference to the African race*. Manchester: William Irwin.

Atkins, John.1735. *A voyage to Guinea, Brasil and the West Indies; in His Majesty's ships, the Swallow and Weymouth: describing the several islands and Settlements, viz, Madeira, the Canaries, Cape de Verd, Sierraleon, Sesthos, Cape Apollonia, Cabo Corso, and others on the Guinea coast; Barbadoes, Jamaica, &c. in the West-Indies; the color, diet, languages, habits, manners, customs, and religions of the respective natives, and inhabitants. With remarks on the gold, ivory, and slave-trade; and on the winds, tides and currents of the several coasts*. London. printed for Caesar Ward and Richard Chandler, at the Ship, between the Temple-Gates in Fleet-Street, and sold at their shop in Scarborough.

Augstein, H. F.2016. *James Cowles Prichard's Anthropology: Remaking the Science of Man in Early Nineteenth Century Britain*. Leiden: Brill.

Bach, Raymond.1999. "Identifying Jews: The Legacy of the 1941 Exhibition, 'Le Juif et la France.'" *Studies in 20th Century Literature*. 23.1.

Bancel, Nicolas; David, Thomas; Thomas, Dominic.2014. *The Invention of Race: Scientific and Popular Representations*. London: Routledge.

Barbot, Jean.1746. *Description of the Coasts of North and South Guinea*. London: H. Lintot.

Bastian, Adolf.1874. *Die Deutsche Expedition an der Loango-Kuste*. Jena: Costenoble.

Battell, Andrew.1625. "The strange adventures of Andrew Battell of Leigh in Angola and the *adjoining* regions" in *Hakluytus posthumus: or, Purchas his pilgrimes, contayning a history of the world in sea voyages and land travells, by Englishmen & others.* Ed. Samuel Purchas. London: William Stansby for Henrie Fetherstone.

Battell, Andrew.1905. *The Strange Adventures of Andrew Battel of Leigh in Angola and Adjoining Regions.* Ed. Ernst Georg Ravenstein. London: Hakluyt Society.

Beddoe, John.1861. "On the Physical Characteristics of the Jews." *Transactions of the Ethnological Society of London.* 1.

Beddoe, John.1885. *Races of Britain: A Contribution to the Anthropology of Western Europe.* Bristol: Arrowsmith.

Beddoe, John.1893. *The Anthropological History of Europe, Being the Rhind Lectures for 1891.* London: A. Gardner.

Beke, Charles T.1845. "On the Languages and Dialects of Abyssinia and the Countries to the South." *Proceedings of the Philological Society.* 2.33.

Ben Zvi, Itzhak.1957. *The Exiled and the Redeemed.* Philadelphia: Jewish Publication Society of America.

Bendyshe, Thomas.1865. "The History of Anthropology." *Memoirs Read before the Anthropological Society of London.* London: Trübner and Company.

Berenbaum, Michael.1993. *The World Must Know.* Boston: Little, Brown and Co.

Berenbaum, Michael; Peck, Abraham.2002. *The Holocaust and History: The Known, the Unknown, the Disputed, and the Reexamined.* Bloomington: Indiana University Press in association with U.S. Holocaust Memorial Museum.

Bernhard. Patrick.2017. "Blueprints of Totalitarianism: How Racist Policies in Fascist Italy Inspired and Informed Nazi Germany." *Fascism: Journal of Comparative Fascist Studies.* 6.

Bernier, François.1684. "Nouvelle division de la terre par les différentes espèces ou races qui l'habitent." *Journal des Scavans.* Paris: Lambert & Cusson.

Biale, D.2007. *Blood and Belief: The Circulation of a Symbol between Jews and Christians.* Berkeley: University of California Press.

Biblical Repertory and Princeton Review. 1855. Philadelphia: James A. Peabody.

Bigland, John.1816. *An Historical Display of the Effects of Physical and Moral Causes on the Character and Circumstances of Nations, Including a Comparison of the Ancients and Moderns in Regard to their Intellectual and Social State.* London: Printed for Longman, Hurst, Rees, Orme, and Brown.

Bigland, John.1820. *A Compendious History of the Jews.* Derby: H. Mozley.

Bildhauer, Bettina; Mills, Robert.2003. *The Monstrous Middle Ages.* Toronto: University of Toronto Press.

Bindman, David.2011. "Frog to Apollo: A French Print after Lavater and Pre-Darwinian Theories of Evolution." *Print Quarterly.* 28.4.

Blackwood's Edinburgh Magazine. 1844. 56.

Bloom, Etan.2011. *Arthur Ruppin and the Production of Pre-Israeli Culture (Studies in Jewish History and Culture).* Leiden, Boston: Brill.

Blumenbach, Johann Friedrich.1865. *The Anthropological Treatises of Johann Friedrich Blumenbach.* London: Longman, Green, Longman, Roberts & Green.

Blunt, Wilfred J. W.2004. *Linnaeus, The Complete Naturalist.* London: Frances Lincoln.

Boaz, Rachel E.2012. *In Search of "Aryan Blood": Serology in Interwar and National Socialist Germany.* Budapest and New York: Central European University Press.

Bond, Dean W.2016. "A.F. Büsching and the Place of Geographical Knowledge in the German Enlightenment, c.1740–1800." PhD thesis: Department of Geography, University of Toronto.
Boodts, Shari.2019. "Did Augustine Believe in Monsters?" https://www.medievalists.net/2019/06/did-augustine-believe-in-monsters/
Bornstein, George.2011. *The Colors of Zion: Blacks, Jews and Irish from 1845 to 1945*. Cambridge, MA, and London: Harvard University Press.
Bossy, John.2002. *Giordano Bruno and the Embassy Affair*. New Haven, CT: Yale University Press.
Boum, A. "Saharan Jewry: History, Memory and Imagined Identity." *Journal of North African Studies*. 16.3.
Bowring, John, Sir.1877. *Autobiographical Recollections of Sir John Bowring*. London: H. S. King.
Brace, Charles Loring.1863. *The Races of the Old World*. New York: C. Scribner.
Brace, Charles Loring.2005. *"Race" is a Four-Letter Word: The Genesis of the Concept*. New York and Oxford: Oxford University Press.
Brace, Emma.1894. *The Life of Charles Loring Brace Told Chiefly in His Own Letters*. New York: Scribner.
Breitenbauch, Georg-August von.1786. *Vorstellung der vornehmsten Völkerschaften der Welt nach ihrer Abstammung, Ausbreitung und Sprachen*. Leipzig: J. E. Lange.
Brodkin, Karen.1998. *How Jews Became White Folks and What That Says About Race in America*. New Brunswick, NJ, and London: Rutgers University Press.
Brown, Robert.2016. *The History and Description of Africa and of the Notable Things therein Contained: written by Al-Hassan Ibn Mohammed al-Wezaz Al-Fasi, baptized as Giovanni Leeone, but better known as Leo Africanus. Done into English in the Year 1600 by John Porry*. Abingdon, UK: Taylor & Francis.
Browne, P. A.1850. "Microscopic Examination of the Pile of the Head of Albinos." *Proceedings of the American Association for the Advancement of Science*. 3–4.
Browne, Sir Thomas.1650. *Pseudodoxia Epidemica, Or, Enquiries Into Very Many Received Tenets, and Commonly Presumed Truths*. London: A. Miller.
Bruce, Gary.2017. *Through the Lion Gate: A History of the Berlin Zoo*. New York. Oxford University Press.
Bruder, Edith.2008. *The Black Jews of Africa: History, Religion, Identity*. New York: Oxford University Press.
Bruns, Claudia.2011. "Antisemitism and Colonial Racism" in *Racisms Made in Germany*. Ed. Wulf D. Hund. Münster: Lit Verlag.
Bruns, Claudia.2014. "Toward a Transnational History of Racism: Wilhelm Marr and the Interrelationships between Colonial Racism and German Anti-Semitism" in *Racism in the Modern World: Historical Perspectives on Cultural Transfer and Adaptation*. Eds. Manfred Berg and Simon Wendt. New York: Berghahn Books.
Bruns, Paul Jakob.1799. *Neue systematische Erdbeschreibung von Afrika*. Nurnberg: Schneider and Weigel.
Buchanan, Claudius.1812. *The works of the Rev. Claudius Buchanan, L. L. D., comprising his Christian researches in Asia, his Memoir on the expediency of an ecclesiastical establishment for British India, and his Star in the East, with three new sermons*. New York: Whiting & Watson.
Buffon, Georges Louis Leclerc de.1749–1789. *Histoire Naturelle, générale et particulière, avec la description du Cabinet du Roi*. Paris: Imprimerie royale (36 volumes).

Buffon, Georges Louis Leclerc de.1792. *Barr's Buffon. Buffon's Natural History, Containing a Theory of the Earth, a General History of Man etc.* Transl. J. S. Barr. London: Barr.
Bulletin de la Société de Géographie.1830. 13–14. Paris: Arthis-Bertrand.
Bulletins de la Société d'Anthropologie de Paris.1863. 1.4. Paris: Société d'Anthropologie.
Burleigh, Michael; Wippermann, Wolfgang.1991. *The Racial State: Germany 1933–1945*. Cambridge, UK: Cambridge University Press.
Burton, Richard.1864. "Notes on Waitz's Anthropology." *Anthropological Review*. vii. November.
Burton, Richard.1876. *Two Trips to Gorilla Land and the Cataracts of the Congo*. London: S. Low, Marston, Low, and Searle.
Burton, Richard.1898. *The Jew, the Gypsy and El Islam*. Chicago and New York: Herbert S. Stone.
Büsching, Anton Friedrich.1779. *Geschichte der jüdischen Religion, oder des Gesetzes: ein Grundriss*. Berlin: J. C. F. Eisfeld.
Büsching, Anton Friedrich.1780. *Magazin für die neue Historie und Geographie*. 14.
Cagle, Hugh.2015. "Beyond the Senegal: Inventing the Tropics in the Late Middle Ages." *Journal of Medieval Iberian Studies*. 7.2.
Calmet, Augustin.1812. *Calmet's Great Dictionary of the Holy Bible: Historical, Critical, Geographical, and Etymological . . .: with an Ample Chronological Table of the History of the Bible, Jewish Calendar, Tables of the Hebrew Coins, Weights and Measures . . .: Revised, Corrected, and Augmented, with an Entirely New Set of Plates*. London: Samuel Etheridge.
Campbell, Albert A.1942. "Note on the Jewish Community of St. Thomas, U.S. Virgin Islands." *Jewish Social Studies*. 4.2.
Campbell, John.1851. *Negro-mania; being an examination of the falsely assumed equality of the various races of men*. Philadelphia: Campbell and Power.
Capsali, Elijah.1975. *Seder Eliyahou Zouta*. Eds. A. Shmuelevitz, S. Simonsohn, and M. Benayahu. Jerusalem: Mekhon Ben Zvi.
Carlebach, Julius.1978. *Karl Marx and the Radical Critique of Judaism*. London: Routledge and Kegan Paul.
Carroll, Charles.1900. *"The negro a beast"; or, "In the image of God"; the reasoner of the age, the revelator of the century! The Bible as it is! The negro and his relation to the human family! . . . The negro not the son of Ham*. St. Louis, MO: American Book and Bible House.
Carroll, Charles.1902. *The tempter of Eve; or, The criminality of man's social, political, and religious equality with the Negro, and the amalgamation to which these crimes inevitably lead. Discussed in the light of the Scriptures, the sciences, profane history, tradition, and the testimony of the monuments*. St. Louis, MO: Adamic Publishing Co.
Cavazzi da Montecuccolo, G.1687. *Istorica Descrizeione de tre regni Congo, Matamba ed Angola situati nell'Etiopia inferiore occidentale e delle missioni apostoliche esercitatevi da religiosi cappuccino*. Bologne: Giacomo Monti.
Céline, Louis-Ferdinand.1942 (first published 1938). *L'école des cadavres*. Paris: Editions Denoël.
Celticus, Docteur [pseudonym].1903. *Les 19 tares corporelles visibles pour reconnaitre un juif*. Paris: Librairie Antisémite.
Chamberlain, Houston Stewart.1911. *The Foundations of the 19th Century*. London and New York: John Lane.

Charlton, Derran.2012. "Giordano Bruno: Mad, Bad and Dangerous to Know." *The Oxfordian*. v.14.
Chatterjee, Kumkum; Hawes, Clement.2008. *Europe Observed: Multiple Gazes in Early Modern Encounters*. Lewisburg, PA: Bucknell University Press.
Chidester, David.1996. *Savage Systems: Colonialism and Comparative Religion in Southern Africa*. Charlottesville: University Press of Virginia.
Chidester, David.2014. *Empire of Religion: Imperialism and Comparative Religion*. Chicago and London: Chicago University Press.
Chisick, Harvey.2016. "On the Margins of the Enlightenment: Blacks and Jews." *The European Legacy*. doi:10.1080/10848770.2015.1114214
Christian Traveller. Western Africa. Being an Account of the Country and Its Products; of the People and Their Condition; and of the Measures Taken for Their Religious and Social Benefit. 1841. London: C. Knight & Company.
Clarke, John.1849. *Short Vocabularies of Languages: and Notes of Countries and Customs in Africa*. Berwick-upon-Tweed: Daniel Cameron.
Cook, Ezra A.1922. *Ku Klux Klan Secrets Exposed: Attitude Toward Jews, Catholics, Foreigners, and Masons: Fraudulent Methods Used, Atrocities Committed in Name of Order*. Chicago: Ezra A. Cook.
Cook, Mercer.1936. "Jean-Jacques Rousseau and the Negro." *Journal of Negro History*. 21.3.
Crania Americana; Or a Comparative View of the Skulls of Various Aboriginal Nations of North and South America; To Which Is Prefixed an Essay on the Vareities of the Human Species. Illustrated with Seventy-Eight Plates and a Colored Map. 1840. Samuel George Morton. Reviewed in *The North American Review*. 51.108.
Crawfurd, John.1866. "On the Physical and Mental Characteristics of the Negro." *Transactions of the Ethnological Society of London*. 4.
Crawley, Ernest.1902. *The Mystic Rose: A Study of Primitive Marriage*. London: Macmillan & Co.
Critical Review, Or, Annals of Literature. 1783. 57. London: W. Simpkin and R. Marshall.
Curran, Andrew.2011. *The Anatomy of Blackness: Science and Slavery in an Age of Enlightenment*. Baltimore, MD: Johns Hopkins University Press.
Dahse, Johannes.1911. "Ein zweites Goldland Salomos: Vorstudien zur Geschichte Westafrikas." *Zeitschrift für Ethnologie*. 43.
Darrow, Jason.1846. *The New Light, Or, Discourses on the Christian Church, on the Evils of Sectarianism and on the True Manner of Becoming Christians*. Covington, KY: printed for the author at the office of the "Licking Valley Register."
Darwin, Charles.1871. *The Descent of Man, and Selection in Relation to Sex*. London: John Murray.
Dash, Mike.2012. "Hitler's Very Own Hot Jazz Band." https://www.smithsonianmag.com/history/hitlers-very-own-hot-jazz-band-98745129/
Davidson, Allan K.1990. *Evangelicals and Attitudes to India, 1786–1813: Missionary Publicity and Claudius Buchanan*. Oxfordshire: Sutton Courtenay Press.
Davies, Alan.1988. *Infected Christianity: A Study of Modern Racism*. Montreal: McGill-Queen's Press.
Davis, Christian.2012. *Colonialism, Antisemitism, and Germans of Jewish Descent in Imperial Germany*. Ann Arbor: University of Michigan Press.
Davis, Natalie Zemon.2006. *Trickster Travels: A Sixteenth-Century Muslim Between Worlds*. New York: Hill and Wang.

Davison, Carol M.2004. *Anti-Semitism and British Gothic Literature*. London: Palgrave Macmillan.
Delumeau, Jean; O'Connell, Matthew.2000. *History of Paradise: The Garden of Eden in Myth and Tradition*. New York: University of Illinois Press.
Denbow, James.1999. "Heart and Soul: Glimpses of Ideology and Cosmology in the Iconography of Tombstones from the Loango Coast of Central Africa." *Journal of American Folklore*. 112.445.
Dennett, Richard E.1905. "Bavili Notes." *Folklore*. 16.4.
Desmond, Adrian; Moore, James.2009. *Darwin's Sacred Cause: How a Hatred of Slavery Shaped Darwin's Views on Human Evolution*. Boston: Houghton Mifflin Harcourt.
Diderot, Denis; d'Alembert, Jean le Rond. *Encyclopedia of Diderot & d'Alembert. 1765. Collaborative Translation Project*. Translated by Pamela Cheek. Ann Arbor: Michigan Publishing, University of Michigan Library. Web. May 13, 2017. http://hdl.handle.net/2027/spo.did2222.0000.027. Translation of "Nègres blancs," *Encyclopédie ou Dictionnaire raisonné des sciences, des arts et des métiers*. 11. Paris. 1765.
Diderot, Denis; d'Alembert, Jean le Rond.1780. *Encyclopédie ou Dictionnaire raisonné des sciences, des arts et des métier* 22. Berne, Lausanne: Les sociétés typographiques.
Dodounou, Tsevi.2011. *Le mythe de l'albinos dans les récits subsahariens francophones*. Münster: LIT Verlag.
Dohm, Christian Wilhelm von.1781. *Über die burglicher Verbesserung der Juden*. Berlin: Nicolai.
Dorigny, Marcel.2003. *The Abolitions of Slavery: From Léger Félicité Sonthonax to Victor Schoelcher, 1793, 1794, 1848*. New York: Berghahn Books.
Dublin Review. 1845. 19.
Dupuis, Joseph.1824. *Journal of a Residence in Ashantee Comprising Notes and Researches Relative to the Gold Coast, and the Interior of West Africa . . . to which is Prefixed an Account of the Origin and Causes of the Present War*. 18. London: Colburn.
Du Quesne, Abraham.1696. *A New Voyage to the East Indies in the Years 1690 and 1691 being A full Description of the Isles of Maldives, Cocos, Andamants, and the Isle of Ascention; and all the Forts and Garrisons now in possession of the French, with an Account of the Customs, Manners, and Habits of the Indians. To which is added, A New Description of the Canary Islands, Cape Verd, Senegal and Gambia, &c. Done into English from the Paris Edition*. London: Printed for Daniel Dring at the Harrow and Crown near St. Dunstan's Church in Fleetstreet.
Edinburgh Gazetteer, or Geographical Dictionary Accompanied by an Atlas, 4. 1822.
Edinburgh Medical and Surgical Journal. 1828.
Efron, John M.1994. *Defenders of the Race: Jewish Doctors and Race Science in Fin-de-Siècle Europe*. New Haven, CT, and London: Yale University Press.
Efron, John M.2008. *Medicine and the German Jews: A History*. New Haven, CT, and London: Yale University Press.
Efron, John M.2015. *German Jewry and the Allure of the Sephardic*. Princeton, NJ: Princeton University Press.
Ehrenreich, Eric.2007. *The Nazi Ancestral Proof: Genealogy, Racial Science, and the Final Solution*. Bloomington: Indiana University Press.
Ehrmann, Theophil Friedrich.1811. *Neueste Kunde von Afrika: nach Quellen bearbeitet. Süd-Afrika und die afrikanischen Inseln*. Prague: Diesbach.
Eigen, Sara; Larrimore, Mark Joseph, Eds.2012. *The German Invention of Race*. New York: SUNY Press.

Eldridge, C. C.1996. *The Imperial Experience: From Carlyle to Forster*. London: Palgrave.
Ellingson, Ter.2001. *The Myth of the Noble Savage*. Berkeley: University of California Press.
Encyclopaedia Britannica—A Dictionary of Arts, Sciences and General Literature. 1898. London and New York: Werner Company.
Epstein, Steven.2001. *Speaking of Slavery: Color, Ethnicity and Human Bondage in Italy*. Ithaca, NY: Cornell University Press.
Erickson, Paul A.1986. "The Anthropology of Josiah Clark Nott." *Kroeber Anthropological Society Papers*. 65–66.
Erle, Sibylle.2010. *Blake, Lavater and Physiognomy*. Studies in Comparative Literature. Oxford: Legenda.
Ernst, Waltraud; Harris, Bernard.1999. *Race, Science and Medicine 1700–1960*. London and New York: Routledge.
Estes, Matthew.1846. *A Defence of Negro Slavery, as it Exists in the United States*. Montgomery: Press of the Alabama Journal.
European Magazine and London Review. 1783. London: Philological Society of London. 4.
Evangelical Review. 1859–1860. 11. Gettysburg: Neinstedt. 18.
Evans, Richard J.2016. *The Pursuit of Power: Europe 1815–1914*. New York: Viking.
Faber, Eli.1998. *Jews, Slaves, and the Slave Trade: Setting the Record Straight*. New York and London: New York University Press.
Fabri, Johann, E.1784. *Handbuch der neuesten Geographie für Akademien und Gymnasien Halle*. Halle: Hemmerdeschen Buchhandlung.
Fabri, Johann, E.1794. *Allgemeinnütziges Geschicht-und Staaten-Wörterbuch*. Wien: Ignaz Alberti.
Farrar, F.1865. "Fixity of Type." *Transactions of the Ethnological Society of London*. 3.
Farrar, F.1867. "Aptidudes of Races." *Transactions of the Ethnological Society of London*. 5.
Fauvelle-Aymar, François-Xavier.2013. "Desperately Seeking the Jewish Kingdom of Ethiopia: Benjamin of Tudela and the Horn of Africa (Twelfth Century)." *Speculum*. 88.2.
Feferman, Kiril.2007. "Nazi Germany and the Mountain Jews: Was There a Policy?" *Holocaust and Genocide Studies*. 21.1.
Ficalho, Conde de.1898. *Viagens de Pêro da Covilhã*. Lisboa: A. M. Pereira.
Figal, Sara Eigen.2010. *Heredity, Race, and the Birth of the Modern*. London and New York: Routledge.
Fischel, Walter J.1962. "Cochin in Jewish History: Prolegomena to a History of the Jews in India." *Proceedings of the American Academy for Jewish Research*. 30.
Fish, Bruce; Fish, Becky Durost.2001. *Angola, 1880 to the Present: Slavery, Exploitation, and Revolt*. Philadelphia: Chelsea House Publishers.
Fishberg, Maurice.1903. "Physical Anthropology of the Jews II.—Pigmentation." *American Anthropologist*. N.S. 5.1.
Fishberg, Maurice.1911. *The Jews: A Study of Race and Environment*. London: Walter Scott Publishing.
Forster, George.1798. *A Journey from Bengal to England, through the northern part of India, Kashmire, Afghanistan and Persia and into Russia, by the Caspian Sea*. London: Faulder.
Friedman, John Block.2000. *The Monstrous Races in Medieval Art and Thought*. New York: Syracuse University Press.
Fritsch, Theodor.1927. *The Riddle of the Jew's Success*. Leipzig: Hammer-Verlag.
Fritsch, Theodor.1931. *Handbuch der Judenfrage die wichtigsten Tatsachen zur Beurteilung des jüdischen Volkes*. Leipzig: Hammer-Verlag.

Fromont, Cecile.2014. *The Art of Conversion: Christian Visual Culture in the Kingdom of Kongo*. Chapel Hill: University of North Carolina Press.
Gardinier, David.1981. *Historical Dictionary of Gabon*. Metuchen and London: Scarecrow Press.
Garrett, Aaron.2000. "Hume's Revised Racism Revisited." *Hume Studies*. xxvi.1.
Geographical Journal. 1900. London: Royal Geographical Society.
Georg Forsters Werke. 1958. Berlin: Akademie Verlag. viii.
Gillette, Aaron.2002. "Guido Landra and the Office of Racial Studies in Fascist Italy." *Holocaust and Genocide Studies*. xvi.3.
Gilman, Sander.1985. *Difference and Pathology: Stereotypes of Sexuality, Race and Madness*. Ithaca, NY: Cornell University Press.
Gilman, Sander.1986. *Jewish Self-Hatred: Anti-Semitism and the Hidden Language of the Jews*. Baltimore, MD: Johns Hopkins University Press.
Gilman, Sander.1990. "The Jewish Body: A 'Footnote.'" *Bulletin of the History of Medicine*. 64.4.
Gilman, Sander.1992. "The Visibility of the Jew in the Diaspora: Body Imagery and Its Cultural Context." B. G. Rudolph Lecture in Judaic Studies, Syracuse University.
Gilman, Sander.1992. *The Jew's Body*. London: Routledge.
Gilman, Sander. 1993. *Freud, Race, and Gender*. Princeton: Princeton University Press.
Gilman, Sander.1994. "'The Jewish Nose: Are Jews White? Or, the History of the Nose Job" in *The Other in Jewish Thought and History: Constructions of Jewish Culture and Identity*. Eds. Laurence J. Silberstein and Robert L. Cohn. New York and London: New York University Press.
Gilman, Sander. 1995. *Franz Kafka, the Jewish Patient*. New York and London: Routledge.
Gilman, Sander. 1998. *Creating Beauty to Cure the Soul: Race and Psychology in the Shaping of Aesthetic Surgery*. Durham, NC: Duke University Press.
Gilman, Sander.1999b. *Making the Body Beautiful: A Cultural History of Aesthetic Surgery*. Princeton, NJ: Princeton University Press.
Gilman, Sander.2006. *Multiculturalism and the Jews*. New York and London: Routledge.
Gobineau, Comte Joseph Arthur de.1853. *Essai sur l'inegalité des races humaines par le comte de Gobineau*. Paris: Didot Frères.
Gobineau, Comte Joseph Arthur de.1983. *Oeuvres*. Paris: Gallimard.
Gobineau, Comte Joseph Arthur de.1915. *The Inequality of Human Races*. London: William Heinemann.
Goldenberg, David M.2003. *The Curse of Ham: Race and Slavery in Early Judaism, Christianity, and Islam*. Princeton, NJ: Princeton University Press.
Goldenberg, David M.2017. *Black and Slave: The Origins and History of the Curse of Ham*. Berlin: Walter de Gruyter.
Goldhagen, Daniel, Jonah.1996. *Hitler's Willing Executioners: Ordinary Germans and the Holocaust*. New York: Alfred A. Knopf.
Gothaische Gelehrte Zeitungen. 1779. Gotha: Carl Wilhelm Ettinger.
Gould, Frederick J.1923. *The Life-Story of a Humanist*. London: Watts & Co.
Gould, Stephen Jay.1996. *The Mismeasure of Man*. New York: W. W. Norton.
Gow, Andrew C.1994. *The Red Jews: Antisemitism in an Apocalyptic Age, 1200–1600*. Leiden: Brill.
Gray, John.1911. "John Beddoe, M.D., LL.D., F.R.S., F.R.C.P., Foreign Assoc. Anthrop. Soc., Paris; Corr. Member Anthrop. Soc., Berlin; Hon. Member Anthrop. Soc., Brussels and Washington, Soc. Friends of Science, Moscow." *Man*. 11.

Green, Jeffrey.1999. "'A Revelation in Strange Humanity': Six Congo Pygmies in Britain 1905–1907" in *Africans on Stage: Studies in Ethnological Show Business*. Ed. Bernth Lindfors. Bloomington: Indiana State University Press.

Green, Tobias.2005. "Further Considerations on the Sephardim of the Petite Côte." *History in Africa*. 32.

Green, Tobias.2009. *Inquisition: The Reign of Fear*. London: Macmillan.

Green, Warren.1984. "The Fate of the Crimean Jewish Communities: Ashkenazim, Krimchaks and Karaites." *Jewish Social Studies*. 6.2.

Greenblatt, Stephen.2017. *The Rise and Fall of Adam and Eve*. New York and London: W. W. Norton.

Greene, John C.1954. "Some Early Speculations on the Origin of Human Races." *American Anthropologist*. N.S. 56.1.

Grégoire, Henri B.1789. *Essai sur la régénération physique, morale et politique des Juifs*. Metz: L'imprimerie de Claude Lamort.

Grégoire, Henri B.1808. *De la littérature des nègres, ou Recherches sur leurs facultés intellectuelles, leurs qualités morales et leur littérature: suivies de notices sur la vie et les ouvrages des nègres qui se sont distingués dans les sciences, les lettres et les arts*. Paris: Maradan.

Grégoire, Henri B.1828. *Histoire des sectes religieuses qui sont nées, se sont modifiés, se sont éteintes dans les différentes contrées du globe, depuis le commencement du siècle dernier jusqu'à l'époque actuelle*. Paris: Baudouin.

Grenfell, Morgan.1680. *The Negro's and Indians Advocate, suing for their admission to the church, or, A persuasive to the instructing and baptizing of the Negro's and Indians in our plantations shewing that as the compliance therewith can prejudice no man's just interest, so the willful neglecting and opposing of it, is no less than a manifest apostacy from the Christian faith: to which is added, a brief account of religion in Virginia*. London: Printed for the author, by J.D.

Grill, Johnpeter Horst; Jenkins, Robert L.1992. "The Nazis and the American South in the 1930s: A Mirror Image?" *Journal of Southern History*. 58.4.

Güssfeldt, Paul; Falkenstein, Julius August Ferdinand; Pechuël-Loesche, Eduard.1879. *Die Loango-Expedition ausgesandt von der Deutschen Gesellschaft zur Erforschung Aequatorial-Africas, 1873-1876: ein Reisewerk in drei Abtheilungen*. Leipzig: P. Frohberg.

HaCohen, Ran.2018. "The 'Jewish Blackness' Thesis Revisited." *Religions*. 9.7. https://doi.org/10.3390/rel9070222

Haddon, Alfred.1898. *The Study of Man*. London: John Murray.

Hale, Sir Matthew.1677. *The Primitive Origination of Mankind: Considered and Examined According to the Light of Nature*. London: William Godbid.

Hall, John Charles.1850. "An Analytical Synopsis of the Natural History of Man" in *The Races of Man, and their Geographical Distribution*. Ed. Charles Pickering. London: H. G. Bohn.

Hall, Ronald E.2012. *The Melanin Millennium: Skin Color as 21st Century International Discourse*. Heidelberg, New York, and London: Springer.

Haller, John S.1970. "The Species Problem: Nineteenth-Century Concepts of Racial Inferiority in the Origin of Man Controversy." *American Anthropologist*. N.S. 72.6.

Hamilton Smith, Charles.1848. *The natural history of the human species: its typical forms, primeval distribution, filiations, and migration*. Edinburgh: W. H. Lizars.

Hargreaves, John D.1957. "Winwood Reade and the Discovery of Africa." *African Affairs*. 56.225.
Harris, Graham.2002. *Treasure and Intrigue: The Legacy of Captain Kidd*. Toronto and Oxford: Hounslow.
Harris, Marvin.2001. *The Rise of Anthropological Theory: A History of Theories of Culture*. Walnut Creek, CA: Rowan Altamira.
Harrison, Peter.2002. *Religion and Religions in the English Enlightenment*. Cambridge, UK: Cambridge University Press.
Harrison, Simon.2012. *Dark Trophies: Hunting and the Enemy Body in Modern War*. New York: Berghahn Books.
Hart, Mitchell.1995. "Picturing Jews: Iconography and Racial Science" in *Studies in Contemporary Jewry: XI: Values, Interests, and Identity: Jews and Politics in a Changing World*. Ed. Peter Y. Medding. New York and Oxford: Oxford University Press.
Hart, Mitchell B.2000. *Social Science and the Politics of Modern Jewish Identity*. Stanford, CA: Stanford University Press.
Hart, Mitchell.2007. "Maurice Fishberg and the Ambiguities of Jewish Identity." *AJS Perspectives: The Magazine of the Association for Jewish Studies*. 1.
Hart, Mitchell B.2011. *Jews and Race: Writings on Identity and Difference, 1880–1940*. Lebanon, NH: UPNE.
Harvey, David.2012. *The French Enlightenment and its Others: The Mandarin, the Savage, and the Invention of the Human Sciences*. New York: Palgrave.
Hayes, Peter; Roth, John K., Eds.2010. *The Oxford Handbook of Holocaust Studies*. Oxford: Oxford University Press.
Haynes, Stephen R.2002. *Noah's Curse: The Biblical Justification of American Slavery*. New York: Oxford University Press.
Heath, Andrew.2012. "'The Producers on the One Side, and the Capitalists on the Other': Labor Reform, Slavery, and the Career of a Transatlantic Radical." *American Nineteenth Century History*. 13.2.
Heintze, Beatrix.1999. "Ethnographic Appropriations: German Exploration and Fieldwork in West-Central Africa." *History in Africa*. 26.
Herbert, Sir Thomas.1638. *Some Yeares Travels Into Divers Parts of Asia and Afrique Describing Especially the Two Famous Empires, the Persian and Great Mogull . . . as Also, Many . . . Kingdomes in the Oriental India and Other Parts of Asia; Together with the Adjacent Iles . . . With a Revivall of the First Discoverer of America*. London: Iacob Blome and Richard Bishop.
Hertzberg, Arthur.1968. *The French Enlightenment and the Jews*. New York and London: Columbia University Press.
Hess, Jonathan M.2000. "Johann David Michaelis and the Colonial Imaginary: Orientalism and the Emergence of Racial Antisemitism in Eighteenth-Century Germany." *Jewish Social Studies*. N.S. 6.2.
Heywood, Linda M.; Thornton, John K.2007. *Central Africans, Atlantic Creoles, and the Foundation of the Americas, 1585–1660*. Cambridge, UK: Cambridge University Press.
Hildebrandt, Georg Friedrich.1803. *Lehrbuch der Anatomie des Menschen*. Braunschweig: Schulbuchhandlung.
Hitler, Adolph.1939. *Mein Kampf*. Translated and annotated by James Murphy. New York, London, and Melbourne: Hurst and Blackett Ltd. https://mk.christogenea.org
Hitler, Adolph.2013 (first ed.1953). *Hitler's Table Talk 1941–1944: Secret Conversations*. Eds. Hugh Redwald Trevor-Roper and Gerhard L. Weinberg. New York: Enigma Books.

Hochman, Leah.2014. *The Ugliness of Moses Mendelssohn: Aesthetics, Religion & Morality in the Eighteenth Century*. London: Routledge.
Holmberg, Eva Johanna.2012. *Jews in the Early Modern English Imagination: A Scattered Nation 1400–1700*. Burlington, VT: Ashgate.
Home, Henry, Lord Kames.2007. *Sketches of the History of Man Considerably enlarged by the last additions and corrections of the author*, edited and with an introduction by James A. Harris. Indianapolis: Liberty Fund.
Hondius, Dienke.2017. *Blackness in Western Europe: Racial Patterns of Paternalism and Exclusion*. London: Routledge.
Horowitz, Elliott S.2006. *Reckless Rites: Purim and the Legacy of Jewish Violence*. Princeton, NJ, and Oxford: Princeton University Press.
Hovelacque, Abel.1882. *Les Races humaines*. Paris: Léopold Cerf.
Hund, Wulf D.2015. "Simianization: Apes, Gender, Class, and Race." *Racism Analysis*. Yearbook 6. Berlin: Lit Verlag.
Hund, Wulf D.; Koller, Christian; Zimmermann, Moshe, Eds.2011. *Racisms Made in Germany*. Münster: Lit Verlag.
Hunt, James.1863. "On Ethno-Climatology; or the Acclimatization of Man." *Transactions of the Ethnological Society of London*. 2.
Hunt, James.1864. "On the Negro's Place in Nature." *Journal of the Anthropological Society of London*. 2.xv–lvi.
Hutton, Joseph E.1923. *A History of Moravian Missions*. London: Moravian Publication Office.
Innys, William and John.1734. *The Present State of the Republick of Letters*. 14. London: Printed for W. Innys at the West End of St Paul's.
Irmscher, Christoph.2013. *Louis Agassiz: Creator of American Science*. Boston and New York: Houghton Mifflin Harcourt.
Ischei, Elizabeth.1997. *A History of African Societies to 1870*. Cambridge, UK: Cambridge University Press.
Jackson, John P.; Weidman, Nadine.2014. *Race, Racism, and Science: Social Impact and Interaction*. Santa Barbara, CA: ABC-CLIO.
Jacobs, Joseph.1886. "On the Racial Characteristics of Modern Jews." *Journal of the Anthropological Institute of Great Britain and Ireland*. 15.
Jahoda, Gustav.2015. *Images of Savages: Ancient Roots of Modern Prejudice in Western Culture*. London: Routledge.
Jewish Herald and Record of Christian Effort for the Spiritual Good of God's Ancient People. 1848.
Johnes, Arthur James.1846. *Philological Proofs of the Original Unity and Recent Origin of the Human Race Derived From a Comparison of the Languages of Asia, Europe, Africa, and America Being an Inquiry How Far the Differences in the Languages of the Globe are Referrible to Causes Now in Operation*. London: John Russell Smith.
Johnson, Charles.1724. *A general history of the pyrates: from their first rise and settlement in the Island of Providence, to the present time*. London: T. Warner.
Johnson, Paul.1988. *A History of the Jews*. New York: Harper Perennial.
Jones, Adam.1983. *German Sources for West African History 1599–1699*. Studien zur Kulturkunde. 66. Wiesbaden: Franz Steijner Verlang.
Jordan, Winthrop D.2013. *White Over Black: American Attitudes Toward the Negro, 1550–1812*. Chapel Hill: UNC Press Books.

Kagan, Richard L.; Morgan Philip, D.2009. *Atlantic Diasporas: Jews, Conversos and Crypto-Jews in the Age of Mercantilism 1500–1800*. Baltimore, MD: Johns Hopkins University Press.

Kames, Henry Home, Lord.1774. *Sketches of the History of Man*. Edinburgh: Printed for W. Creech.

Kames, Henry Home, Lord.1807. *Memoirs of the Life and Writings of the Honourable Henry Home of Kames*. Edinburgh: Printed for W. Creech.

Kananoja, Kalle.2012. *Central African Identities and Religiosity in Colonial Minas Gerais*. Turku: Åbo Akademi University.

Kant, Immanuel.2007. *Anthropology, History, and Education*. Cambridge, UK: Cambridge University Press.

Kaplan, M. Lindsay.2007. "Jessica's Mother: Mediaeval Constructions of Jewish Race and Gender in *The Merchant of Venice*." *Shakespeare Quarterly*. 58.

Kaplan, M. Lindsay.2013. "The Jewish Body in Black and White in Medieval and Early Modern England." *Philological Quarterly*. 92.1.

Kaplan, M. Lindsay.2018. *Figuring Racism in Medieval Christianity*. New York: Oxford University Press.

Katz, David S.2016. *The Shaping of Turkey in the British Imagination, 1776–1923*. London: Palgrave Macmillan.

Katz, David S.; Israel, Jonathan Irvine.1990. *Sceptics, Millenarians, and Jews*. Leiden: Brill.

Katz, Nathan.2013. *Indian Jews: An Annotated Bibliography 1665–2005*. New Delhi: Manohar.

Katz, N.; Goldberg E.2005. *Kashrut, Caste and Kabbalah: The Religious Life of the Jews of Cochin*. New Delhi: Manohar.

Katz, Steven T. 1994. *The Holocaust in Historical Context: Holocaust and Mass Death Before the Modern Age*. New York: Oxford University Press.

Kestling, Robert W.1998. "Blacks Under the Swastika: A Research Note." *Journal of Negro History*. 83.1.

Kidd, Colin.2006. *The Forging of Races. Race and Scripture in the Protestant Atlantic World, 1600–2000*. Cambridge, UK: Cambridge University Press.

Kiewe, Heinz Edgar.1953. "Nigerian Sculpture of a Jewish Trader." *Jewish Quarterly Review*. 44.2.

King, Richard; Leonard, David.2016. *Beyond Hate: White Power and Popular Culture*. Abingdon, UK, and New York: Routledge.

Kleingeld, Pauline.2007. "Kant's Second Thoughts on Race." *Philosophical Quarterly*. 57.229.

Knobel, Marc.1988. "L'ethnologue à la dérive: George Montandon et l'ethnoracisme." *Ethnologie Française*. 18.2.

Knox, Robert.1850. *The Races of Men—A Fragment*. Philadelphia: Lea and Blanchard.

Koerner, Lisbet.2009. *Linnaeus: Nature and Nation*. Cambridge, MA, and London: Harvard University Press.

Kreppel, Jonas.1925. *Juden und Judentum von heute: übersichtlich dargest.; ein Handbuch*. Zürich: Amalthea-Verlag.

Krünitz, Johann Georg.1804. *Ökonomisch-technologische Encyklopädie, oder allgemeines System der Staats-, Stadt-, Haus- und Landwirthschaft, wie auch der Erdbeschreibung, Kunst- und Naturgeschichte: in alphabetischer Ordnung. Von Lilie bis Loango*: 79. Berlin: J. Pauli.

Kundrus, Birthe.2005. "From the Herero to the Holocaust? Some Remarks on the Current Debate." *Africa Spectrum*. 40.2.

L.P.1695. *Two Essays, sent in a letter from Oxford to a Nobleman in London, By L. P., M.A.* London: R. Baldwin.

Lackerstein, Debbie.2012. *National Regeneration in Vichy France: Ideas and Policies, 1930–1944*. London: Routledge.

La Gamma, Alisa.2015. *Kongo: Power and Majesty*. New York: Metropolitan Museum of Art.

Langton, Daniel.2014. "Jewish Evolutionary Perspectives on Judaism, Anti-Semitism, and Race Science in Late 19th Century England: A Comparative Study of Lucien Wolf and Joseph Jacobs." *Jewish Historical Studies*. 46.

Latham, Robert Gordon.1850. *The Natural History of the Varieties of Man*. London: John Van Voorst.

Laurentiis, Allegra de.2014. "Race in Hegel: Text and Context" in *Philosophie Nach Kant: Neue Wege Zum Verständnis von Kants Transzendental- Und Moralphilosophie*. Ed. Mario Egger. Berlin: De Gruyter.

Lavater, Johann Caspar.1827. *Physiognomy; or the corresponding analogy between the conformation of the features, and the ruling passions of the mind, tr. [and abridged] by S. Shaw*. London: Thomas Tegg.

Lavater, Johann Caspar.1853. *Essays on Physiognomy*. London: Thomas Tegg.

Lavater, Johann Caspar.1866. *Physiognomy, Or, The Corresponding Analogy Between the Conformation of the Features and the Ruling Passions of the Mind: Being a Complete Epitome of the Original Work of J.C. Lavater*. London: William Tegg.

Lawrence, Sir William.1819. *Lectures on physiology, zoology and the natural history of man*. London: J. Callow.

Lawrence, Sir William.1822. *Lectures on physiology, zoology and the natural history of man*. London: Benbow.

Lee, Debbie.2002. "Johnson, Stedman, Blake, and the Monkeys." *Wordsworth Circle*. 33.3.

Lemaire, Jacques Joseph.1695. *Les voyages du sieur Le Maire aux iles Canaries, Cap-Verd, Senegal, et Gambie*. Paris: J. Collombay.

Levy, Leonard Williams.1995. *Blasphemy: Verbal Offense Against the Sacred, from Moses to Salman Rushdie*. Chapel Hill: UNC Press.

Leyden, John.1817. *Historical Account of Discoveries and Travels in Africa*. 2. Edinburgh: Constable.

Liba, Moshe (with the assistance of Norman Simms).2003. *Jewish Child Slaves in São Tomé*. Wellington: New Zealand Jewish Chronicle Publications.

Limor, Ora; Stroumsa, Guy G., Eds.1996. *Contra Iudaeos: Ancient and Medieval Polemics Between Christians and Jews*. Tubingen: J. C. B. Mohr.

Lindemann, Albert S.1997. *Esau's Tears: Modern Anti-Semitism and the Rise of the Jews*. Cambridge, UK: Cambridge, University Press.

Lipton, Sara.1999. *Images of Intolerance—The Representation of Jews and Judaism in the Bible Moralisée*. Berkeley: University of California Press.

Lipton, Sara.2014. *Dark Mirror: The Medieval Origins of Anti-Jewish Iconography*. New York: Metropolitan.

Lis, Daniel.2009. "'Ethiopia Shall Soon Stretch Out Her Hands': Ethiopian Jewry and Igbo Identity." *Jewish Culture and History*. 11.3.

Lis, Daniel.2015. *Jewish Identity Among The Igbo Of Nigeria: Israel's Lost Tribe and The Question of Belonging in the Jewish State*. Trenton, NJ: Africa World Press.

Livingstone, David.1870. *Missionary Travels and Researches in South Africa: Including a Sketch of Sixteen Years' Residence in the Interior of Africa, and a Journey from the Cape of Good Hope to Loanda on the West Coast, Thence Across the Continent, Down the River Zambesi, to the Eastern Ocean*. New York: Harper & Brothers.

Livingstone, David N.2008. *Adam's Ancestors: Race, Religion, and the Politics of Human Origins*. Baltimore, MD: Johns Hopkins University Press.

Livingstone, David N.2015. "Finding Revelation in Anthropology: Alexander Winchell, William Robertson Smith and the Heretical Imperative." *British Journal for the History of Science*. 48.3.

Long, Edward.1774. *The History of Jamaica; or, General survey of the antient and modern state of the island: with reflections on its situation, settlements, inhabitants, climate, products, commerce, laws, and government*. London: T. Lowndes.

Lonsdale, Henry.1870. *A Sketch of the Life and Writings of Robert Knox, the Anatomist*. London: Macmillan.

Loomba, Ania; Burton, Jonathan.2007. *Race in Early Modern England a Documentary Companion*. New York: Palgrave Macmillan.

Lopez, Odorado.1597. *A Report of the Kingdom of Congo, a Region of Africa, and of the Countries that border round about the fame, &c. Drawn out of the writings and discourses of Odoardo Lopez, a Portingall, by Philippo Pigafetta. Translated out of Italian by Abraham Hartwell*. London: John Wolfe.

Lozny, Ludomir R., Ed.2011. *Comparative Archaeologies: A Sociological View of the Science of the Past*. New York: Springer Science & Business Media.

Lusane, Clarence.2003. *Hitler's Black Victims, The Historical Experiences of European Blacks, Africans and African Americans During the Nazi Era*. New York and London: Routledge.

Lynch, Hollis R.1971. *Blyden, Black Spokesman: Selected Published Writings of Edward Wilmot*. London: Frank Cass and Co.

Maciejko, Paweł.2006. "Christian Elements in Early Frankist Doctrine." *Gal-Ed*. 20.

Mackay, Hugh.2008. "'Lust's Dominion' and the Readmission of the Jews." *Review of English Studies*. N.S. 59.241.

MacMaster, Neil.2000. "'Black Jew: White Negro': Antisemitism and the Construction of Cross-Racial Stereotypes." *Nationalism and Ethnic Politics*. 6.4.

Malcolmson, Christina.2016. *Studies of Skin Color in the Early Royal Society: Boyle, Cavendish, Swift*. London: Routledge.

Malte-Brun, Conrad.1823. *Universal Geography, Or, a Description of All the Parts of the World, on a New Plan: Africa and adjacent islands*. Edinburgh: Adam Black.

Marcus, Ludwig. (Marcus, Louis) 1829. *Notice sur l'époque de l'établissement des Juifs dans l'Abyssinie*. Paris: Imprimerie royale.

Mark, Peter; da Silva Horta, Jose.2004. "Two Early Seventeenth Century Sephardic Communities on Senegal's *Petite Côte*." *History in Africa*. 31.

Mark, Peter; da Silva Horta, Jose.2011. *The Forgotten Diaspora: Jewish Communities in West Africa and the Making of the Atlantic World*. New York: Cambridge University Press.

Maroney, Eric.2010. *The Other Zions: The Lost Histories of Jewish Nations*. Lanham, MD: Rowman & Littlefield.

Martin, Phyllis M.1972. *The External Trade of the Loango Coast 1576–1870*. Oxford: Oxford University Press.

Maupertuis, Pierre Louis Moreau.1744. *Dissertation physique à l'occasion de Nègre Blanc*. A. Leyde.

McCord, Louisa Susanna Cheves.1995. *Political and Social Essays by Louisa Susanna Cheves McCord*. Ed. Richard C. Lounsbury. Charlottesville: University of Virginia Press.
McIntyre, James Lewis.1903. *Giordano Bruno*. London: MacMillan.
Melamed, A.2003. *The Image of the Black in Jewish Culture—A History of the Other*. London: Routledge.
Mellinkoff, Ruth.1981. *The Mark of Cain*. Berkeley: University of California Press.
Mellinkoff, Ruth.1993. *Outcasts: Signs of Otherness in Northern European Art of the Late Middle Ages*. Berkeley: University of California Press.
Merola, Girolamo.1682. *A voyage to Congo, and several other countries chiefly in Southern Africk*. London: H. Lintot and J. Osborn.
Metcalfe, Samuel L.1843. *Caloric: Its Mechanical, Chemical and Vital Agencies in the Phenomena of Nature*. London: Pickering.
Michaelis, Johann David.1769. *Spicilegium geographiae hebraeorum exterae: post Bochartum*. Göttingen: Vandenhoeck.
Miles, W. F. S.2013. *Jews of Nigeria: An Afro-Judaic Odyssey*. Princeton, NJ: Markus Wiener Publishers.
Miller, Christopher.1985. *Blank Darkness: Africanist Discourse in French*. Chicago: University of Chicago Press.
Millingen, John Gideon.1837. *Curiosities of Medical Experience*. London: Richard Bentley.
Missionary Review of the World. 1898. 21.
Misson, Maximilien.1699. *A New Voyage to Italy: With Curious Observations on Several Other Countries, As, Germany, Switzerland, Savoy, Geneva, Flanders, and Holland. New Voyage to Italy*. London: T. Goodwin.
Mitchel, Serels M.1997. *Jews of Cape Verde: A Brief History*. Brooklyn, NY: Sepher-Hermon Press.
Mitchell, David T.; Snyder, Sharon L., Eds.1997. *The Body and Physical Difference: Discourses of Disability*. Ann Arbor: University of Michigan Press.
Modern Part of an Universal History from the Earliest Accounts to the Present Time. 1781. London: C. Bathurst.
Mokhtari, Fariborz.2012. *In the Lion's Shadow: The Iranian Schindler and His Homeland in the Second World War*. Stroud, UK: The History Press.
Montandon, George-Alexis.1940. *Comment Reconnaître et Expliquer Le Juif?* Paris: Nouvelles Éditions Françaises.
Moorefield, Arthur A.1975. "James Bruce: Ethnomusicologist or Abyssinian Lyre?" *Journal of the American Musicological Society*. 28.3.
Moran, Francis III.1995. "Of Pongos and Men: 'Orangs-Outang' in Rousseau's 'Discourse on Inequality.'" *Review of Politics*. 57.4.
Morris-Reich, Amos.2006. "Arthur Ruppin's Concept of Race." *Israel Studies*. 11.3.
Morris-Reich, Amos.2006b. "Project, Method, and the Racial Characteristics of Jews: A Comparison of Franz Boas and Hans F. K. Günther." *Jewish Social Studies*. 13.1.
Morrow, Jeffrey L.2016. *Three Skeptics and the Bible: La Peyrère, Hobbes, Spinoza, and the Reception of Modern Biblical Criticism*. Eugene, OR: Wipf and Stock Publishers.
Morton, Samuel G.1839. *Crania Americana; or, a Comparative View of the Skulls of Various Aboriginal Nations of North and South America: to which is Prefixed an Essay on the Varieties of the Human Species*. Philadelphia: J. Dobson.
Morton, Samuel G.1844. *Crania Aegyptiaca; or, Observations on Egyptian ethnography, derived from anatomy, history, and the monuments*. Philadelphia: John Penington.
Mosse, George L.1978. *Toward the Final Solution*. New York: Howard Fertig.

Müller-Hill, Benno.1988. *Murderous Science: Elimination by Scientific Selection of Jews, Gypsies and Others, Germany 1933–1945*. Oxford and New York: Oxford University Press.

Münster, Sebastian.1655. *The Messias of the Christians and the Jewes: held forth in a discourse between a Christian, and a Iew obstinately adhering to his strange opinions, & the forced interpretations of scripture, wherein Christ the true savior of the whole world is described from the prophets and likewise that false and counterfeited Messias of the Jewes, who in vaine is expected by that nation to this very day, is discovered / written first in Hebrew, but now rendered into English by Paul Isaiah, a Jew born, but now a converted and baptized Christian. London The Messias of the Christians and the Jewes.* London: William Hunt.

Nautical Magazine: A Journal of Papers on Subjects Connected with Maritime Affairs. 1870. London: Brown, Son and Ferguson.

Nautical Magazine and Naval Chronicle for 1855. 2013. Cambridge, UK: Cambridge University Press.

New Gazetteer of the Eastern Continent: Or, A Geographical Dictionary: Containing, in Alphabetical Order, a Description of All the Countries, Kingdoms, States, Cities, Towns, Principal Rivers, Lakes, Harbors, Mountains, &c., &c. in Europe, Asia, and Africa, with Their Adjacent Islands. 1808. Ed. Jedidiah Morse and Elijah Parish. Boston: J. T. Buckingham.

New General Collection of Voyages and Travels . . . in Europe, Asia, Africa and America . . ., Also the Manners and Customs of the Several Inhabitants . . .: Consisting of the Most Esteemed Relations, which Have Been Hitherto Published in Any Language. 1745. London: Thomas Astley.

New York Journal of Medicine. 1844.

Newitt, Malyn D.1995. *A History of Mozambique*. Bloomington: Indiana University Press.

Ngoïe-Ngalla, Dominique.2010. *Au Royaume du Loango, les athlètes de Dieu*. Paris: Editions Publibook.

Nirenberg, David.2013. *Anti-Judaism: The Western Tradition*. New York: W. W. Norton.

Nott, Josiah Clark.1844. *Two Lectures on the Natural History of the Caucasian and Negro Races*. Mobile, AL: Dade and Thompson.

Nott, Josiah Clark.1850. *The Physical History of the Jewish Race*. Charleston, SC: Walker and James.

Nott, Josiah Clark.1850a. "An Examination of the Physical History of the Jews, in its Bearings on the Question of the Unity of the Races." *Proceedings of the American Association for the Advancement of Science*. 3.

Nott, Josiah Clark; Gliddon, George Robins.1854. *Types of Mankind or Ethnological Researches*. Philadelphia: Lippincott, Grambo & Co.

Ogilby, John.1670. *Africa: being an accurate description of the regions of Aegypt, Barbary, Lybia, and Billedulgerid*. London: Printed by T. Johnson for the author.

Oisteanu, Andrei.2009. *Inventing the Jew: Antisemitic Stereotypes in Romanian and Other Central-East European Cultures*. Lincoln and London: University of Nebraska Press.

Oja, Carol J.; Tick, Judith.2018. *Aaron Copland and His World*. Princeton, NJ: Princeton University Press.

Oldendorp, Christian Georg Andreas.1777. *Geschichte der Mission der evangelischen Brüder auf den caraibischen Inseln S. Thomas, S. Croix und S. Jan*. Barby: C.F. Laux.

Oldendorp, Christian Georg Andreas.1987. *History of the Mission of the Evangelical Brethren on the Caribbean Islands of St. Thomas, St. Croix, and St. John.* Ann Arbor, MI: Karoma Publishers.
Olson, James Stuart.1996. *The Peoples of Africa: An Ethnohistorical Dictionary.* Westport, CT: Greenwood Publishing Group.
Olson, Roger E.; Collins Winn, Christian T.2015. *Reclaiming Pietism: Retrieving an Evangelical Tradition.* Grand Rapids, MI: Wm. B. Eerdmans Publishing.
Ouellet, R.; Beaulieu, A.1990. *Œuvres Complètes.* Montreal: Les Presses de l'Université de Montréal.
Owen, Sir Richard.1859. *On the classification and geographical distribution of the Mammalia.... To which is added an appendix "on the Gorilla" and "on the extinction and transmutation of Species."* London: John W. Parker.
Palmié, Stephan.1995. *Slave Cultures and the Cultures of Slavery.* Knoxville: University of Tennessee Press.
Pankhurst, Richard.2005. "Racism in the Service of Fascism, Empire-Building and War: The History of the Italian Fascist Magazine 'La Difesa della Razza'" in *Auf Dem Weg Zum Modernen Athiopien. Festschrift für Bairu Tafla.* Eds. Stefan Brune and Heinrich Scholler. Munster: LIT.
Parfitt, Tudor.2000. *Journey to the Vanished City: The Search for a Lost Tribe of Israel.* New York: Random House.
Parfitt, Tudor.2002. *The Lost Tribes of Israel: The History of a Myth.* London: Weidenfeld and Nicolson.
Parfitt, Tudor.2003. "Descended from Jewish Seed: Genetics and Jewish History in India: The Bene Israel and the Black Jews of Cochin." *Journal of Indo-Judaic Studies.* vi.
Parfitt, Tudor.2003. "Hebrew in Colonial Discourse." *Journal of Modern Jewish Studies.* 2.2.
Parfitt, Tudor.2013. *Black Jews in Africa and the Americas.* Cambridge, MA: Harvard University Press.
Parfitt, Tudor.2017. "The Jews of Africa and Asia" in *The Cambridge History of Judaism.* 7. *The Early Modern World, 1500–1815.* Eds. Jonathan Karp and Adam Sutcliffe. Cambridge, UK: Cambridge University Press.
Parfitt, Tudor; Egorova, Yulia.2005. *Genetics, Mass Media, and Identity: A Case Study of the Genetic Research on the Lemba and Bene Israel.* London: Routledge.
Parfitt, Tudor; Trevisan-Semi, Emanuela, Eds.2005. *The Jews of Ethiopia: The Birth of an Élite.* London: Routledge.
Park, Mungo.1817. *Travels in the Interior Districts of Africa: Performed in the Years 1795 1796, and 1797 with an Account of a Subsequent Mission to that Country in 1805.* London: John Murray.
Patai, Raphael; Patai, Jennifer.1975. *The Myth of the Jewish Race.* New York: Charles Scribner.
Paterlini, Marta.2007. "There Shall Be Order: The Legacy of Linnaeus in the Age of Molecular Biology." *EMBO Reports.* 8.9.
Pearson, Hugh N.1817. *Memoirs of the Life and Writings of the Rev. Claudius Buchanan, D.D.* Philadelphia: Benjamin & Thomas Kite.
Pechuel-Loesche, Eduard.2007. *Volkskunde von Loango.* Stuttgart: Verlag von Strecker & Schröder.
Pennington, James William Charles.1841. *A Text Book on the Origin and History of the Colored People.* Hartford: L. Skinner.

Percival, Melissa.2003. "Johann Caspar Lavater: Physiognomy and Connoisseurship." *Journal for Eighteenth Century Studies.* 26.

Perin, Constance.1990. *Belonging in America: Reading Between the Lines.* Madison: University of Wisconsin Press.

Pickering, Charles.1850. *The Races of Man, and their Geographical Distribution.* London: H. G. Bohn.

Pigafetta, Filippo.1591. *Relatione del reame di Congo et delle circonvicine contrade, tratta dalli scritti e ragionamenti di Odoardo Lopez portoghese per Filippo Pigafetta.* Rome: Bartolomeo Grassi.

Pinkerton, John.1814. *A General Collection of the best and most interesting voyages and travels, digested by J. Pinkerton.* London: Longman, Hurst, Rees etc.

Plass, Hanno.2013. "*Der Welt-Dienst:* International Anti-Semitic Propaganda." *Jewish Quarterly Review.* 103.

Poliakov, Léon.1971. "Les idées anthropologiques des philosophes du Siècle des Lumières." *Revue française d'histoire d'outre-mer.* 58.212.

Poliakov, Léon.1974. *The Aryan Myth: A History of Racist and Nationalist Ideas in Europe.* New York: Basic Books.

Popkin, Richard.1987. *Isaac La Peyrère (1596–1676): His Life, Work, and Influence.* Leiden: Brill.

Pory, John.1600. *A Geographical Historie of Africa written in Arabicke and Italian by John Leo a More borne in Granada and brought up in Barbarie.* London: Georg. Bishop.

Prichard, James Cowles.1813. *Researches into the Physical History of Mankind.* London: John and Arthur Arch.

Prichard, James Cowles.1831. *The Eastern Origin of the Celtic Nations: Proved by a Comparison of Their Dialects with the Sanskrit, Greek, Latin, and Teutonic Languages. Forming a Supplement to Researches Into the Physical History of Mankind.* Oxford: S. Collingwood.

Prichard, James Cowles.1837. *Researches into the Physical History of Mankind: Ethnography of the African races.* London: Sherwood, Gilbert & Piper.

Proyart, Abbé.1776. *Histoire de Loango, Kakongo et autres Royaumes d'Afrique.* Paris: C. P. Berton.

Pulzer, Peter.1978. *The Rise of Political Anti-Semitism in Germany and Austria.* Cambridge, MA: Harvard University Press.

Purchas, Samuel.1614. *Purchas His Pilgrimage: or Relations of the World and the Religions observed in all Ages and Places discovered, from the Creation unto this Present.* London: Printed by William Stansby for Henrie Fetherstone.

Purchas, Samuel.1625. *Hakluytus Posthumus or Purchas his Pilgrimes, contayning a History of the World in Sea Voyages and Lande Travells, by Englishmen and others.* London: Printed by William Stansby for Henrie Fetherstone.

Qureshi, Sadiah.2011. "Robert Gordon Latham, Displayed Peoples, and the Natural History of Race, 1854–1866." *Historical Journal.* 54.1.

Randles, William Graham Lister.2013. *L'ancien royaume du Congo des origines à la fin du XIXe siècle.* Paris: Éditions de l'École des hautes études en sciences social.

Rasmussen, Daniel.2011. *American Uprising: The Untold Story of America's Largest Slave Revolt.* New York: Harper-Collins.

Ratzel, Friedrich.1898. *The History of Mankind* London: Macmillan and Co.

Ravenstein, Ernest George.1900. *The Voyages of Diogo Cão and Bartholomeu Dias, 1482–88.* London: W. Clowes and Sons.

Raynal, Guillaume; Thomas, Abbé.1770. *Histoire philosophique et politique des établissemens & du commerce des européens dans les deux Indes.* Amsterdam: E. van Harrevelt.
Reade, William Winwood.1863. *Savage Africa: being the narrative of a tour in equatorial, southwestern, and northwestern Africa; with notes on the habits of the gorilla; on the existence of unicorns and tailed men; on the slave trade; on the origin, character, and capabilities of the negro, and on the future civilization of western Africa.* London: Smith, Elder.
Reid, J. M.1968. *Traveller Extraordinary: The Life of James Bruce of Kinnaird.* London: Eyre and Spottiswoode.
Religious Magazine; Or, Spirit of the Foreign Theological Journals and Reviews. 1830. 4.
Renschler, Emily S.; Monge, Janet.2008. "The Samuel George Morton Cranial Collection: Historical Significance and New Research." *Expedition.* 50.3.
Resnick, Irven M.2012. *Marks of Distinctions: Christian Perceptions of Jews in the High Middle Ages.* Washington, DC: Catholic University of America Press.
Reynolds, David S.2008. *Waking Giant: America in the Age of Jackson.* New York: Harper Perennial.
Ribak, Gil.2017. "'Negroes Must Not Be Likened to Jews': The Attitudes of Eastern European Jewish Immigrants Toward African Americans in a Transnational Perspective." *Modern Judaism—A Journal of Jewish Ideas and Experience.* 37.3.
Richardson, James.1848. *Travels in The Great Desert of Sahara, in the Years of 1845 and 1846 containing Narrative of Personal Adventures, During A Tour Of Nine Months Through the Desert, amongst the Touaricks and Other Tribes Of Saharan People; Including A Description Of The Oases And Cities Of Ghat, Ghadames, And Mourzuk.* London: Richard Bentley.
Robertson, John M.1915. *A Short History of Freethought Ancient and Modern.* London: Watts and Co.
Roem, Nils.2005. *Jewish Scholarship and Culture in Nineteenth-Century Germany: Between History and Faith.* Madison: University of Wisconsin Press.
Rosenhaft, Eve.2015. "Black Germans and the Holocaust." Lecture delivered at the International Slavery Museum, Liverpool, on January 17, 2015. https://www.liverpoolmuseums.org.uk/ism/resources/Blacks-Germans-and-the-Holocaust-(January-2015).pdf
Rousseau, Jean-Jacques.2012. *The Major Political Writings of Jean-Jacques Rousseau: The Two "Discourses" and the "Social Contract."* Chicago: University of Chicago Press.
Rowland, Ingrid.2008. *Giordano Bruno: Philosopher/Heretic.* New York: Farrar, Straus & Giroux.
Roy, J. -Edmond.1895. "Le Baron de Lahontan." *Délibérations et Mémoires de la Société Royale du Canada.* Ottawa: John Durie et fils.
Ruppin, Arthur.1913. *The Jews of Today.* New York: Henry Holt.
Sagaert, C.2013. "L'utilisation des préjuges esthétiques comme redoutable outil de stigmatisation du juif: La question de l'apparence dans les écrits antisémites du XIXe siècle à la première moitié du XXe siècle." *Revue d'anthropologie des connaissances.* 7.4.
Salesa, Damon Ieremia.2011. *Racial Crossings: Race, Intermarriage, and the Victorian British Empire.* Oxford: Oxford University Press.
Sanders, Edith R.1969. "The Hamitic Hypothesis; Its Origin and Functions in Time Perspective." *Journal of African History.* 10.4.
Sayre, Gordon M.2000. *Les Sauvages Américains: Representations of Native Americans in French and English Colonial Literatures.* Chapel Hill: University of North Carolina Press.

Schechter, Ronald.2003. *Obstinate Hebrews: Representations of Jews in France, 1715–1815*. Berkeley: University of California Press.

Scheck, Raffael.2006. *Hitler's African Victims: The German Army Massacres of Black French Soldiers in 1940*. New York: Cambridge University Press.

Scherr, Arthur.2003. "'Sambos' and 'Black Cut-Throats': Peter Porcupine on Slavery and Race in the 1790s." *American Periodicals*. 13.

Schleunes, Karl, Ed.2001. *Legislating The Holocaust: The Bernhard Loesoner Memoirs and Supporting Documents*. New York and London: Routledge.

Schneider, Richard J.2016. *Civilizing Thoreau: Human Ecology and the Emerging Social Sciences in the Major Works*. New York: Camden House.

Schön, James Frederick; Crowther, Samuel.1843. *Journals of the Expedition up the Niger in 1841*. London: Hatchard and Son.

Schorsch, Jonathan.2004. *Jews and Blacks in the Early Modern World*. Cambridge, UK: Cambridge University Press.

Schorsch, Jonathan.2005. "Blacks, Jews and the Racial Imagination in the Writings of Sephardim in the Long Seventeenth Century." *Jewish History*. 19.1.

Sciences in Enlightened Europe. 1999. Eds. William Clark, Jan Golinski, and Simon Schaffer. Chicago: University of Chicago Press.

Segal, Judah Benzion.1983. "White and Black Jews at Cochin, the Story of a Controversy." *Journal of the Royal Asiatic Society of Great Britain and Ireland*. 2.

Seth, Suman.2014. "Materialism, Slavery, and The History of Jamaica." *Isis*. 105.

Shelford, April G.2013. "Race and Scripture in the Eighteenth-Century French Caribbean." *Atlantic Studies Global Currents*.10.1.

Schutjer, Karin. 2015. *Goethe and Judaism: The Troubled Inheritance of Modern Literature*. Evanston, IL: Northwestern University Press.

Siegel, Brian.1996. "Anthropology and the Science of 'Race.'" *Anthropology Publications*. Paper 6.

Simmons, John G.2002. *Doctors and Discoveries: Lives that Created Today's Medicine*. New York: Houghton Mifflin Harcourt.

Simpson, William.1843. *A Private Journal Kept During the Niger Expedition*. London: John Shaw.

Skott, Christina.2014. "Linnaeus and the Troglodyte: Early European Encounters with the Malay World and the Natural History of Man." *Indonesia and the Malay World*. 42.

Smith, Justin E. H.2013. "'A Series of Generations': Leibniz on Race." *Annals of Science*. 70.3.

Smith, Justin E. H.2015. *Nature, Human Nature, and Human Difference: Race in Early Modern Philosophy*. Princeton, NJ: Princeton University Press.

Sonderegger, Arno.2009. "Anglophone Discourses on Race in the 19th Century: British and African Perspectives." *Stichproben. Wiener Zeitschrift für kritische Afrikastudien*.16.9.

Sòrgoni, Barbara.2002. "Racist Discourses and Practices in the Italian Empire Under Fascism" in *The Politics of Recognizing Difference: Multiculturalism Italian-Style*. Eds. Ralph Grillo and Jeff Pratt. Aldershot, UK: Ashgate.

Soyer, François.2007. *The Persecution of the Jews and Muslims of Portugal: King Manuel I and the End of Religious Tolerance (1496–7)*. Leiden and Boston: Brill.

Spiller, Gustav.1911. *Papers on Inter-racial Problems communicated to the First Universal Races Congress held at the University of London July 26–29*. London: P. S. King.

Staum, Martin S.2003. *Labeling People: French Scholars on Society, Race, and Empire, 1815–1848*. Montreal: McGill-Queen's Press.
Staum, Martin S.2011. *Nature and Nurture in French Social Sciences, 1859–1914 and Beyond*. Montreal: McGill-Queen's Press.
Steinweis, Alan E.2008. *Studying the Jew: Scholarly Antisemitism in Nazi Germany*. New York: Harvard University Press.
Stern, Fritz. 1979. *Gold and Iron: Bismarck, Bleichröder and the Building of the German Empire*. New York: Vintage Books.
Stiefel, Barry L.2014. *Jewish Sanctuary in the Atlantic World: A Social and Architectural History*. Columbia: University of South Carolina Press.
Stigand, William.1875. *The Life, Work, and Opinions of Heinrich Heine*. London: Longmans, Green.
Stow, Kenneth.2017. "The Catholic Church and the Jews" in *The Cambridge History of Judaism. The Early Modern World, 1500–1815*. Eds. Jonathan Karp and Adam Sutcliffe. Cambridge, UK: Cambridge University Press.
Strehle, Stephen.2013. *The Dark Side of Church/State Separation: The French Revolution, Nazi Germany, and International Communism*. New Brunswick, NJ, and London: Transaction Publishers.
Strickland, Debra Higgs.2003. *Saracens, Demons, & Jews: Making Monsters in Medieval Art*. Princeton, NJ: Princeton University Press.
Stuurman, S.2000. "François Bernier and the Invention of Racial Classification." *History Workshop Journal*. 50.50.
Sweet, James H.2003. *Recreating Africa: Culture, Kinship, and Religion in the African-Portuguese World, 1441–1770*. Chapel Hill: University of North Carolina Press.
Taguieff, Pierre-André, 2008. *La Judéophobie des Modernes: Des Lumières au Jihad mondial*. Paris: Odile Jacob.
Tang, Chenxi.2008. *Modernity: Geography, Literature, and Philosophy in German Romanticism*. Stanford, CA: Stanford University Press.
Taylor, Bayard.1863. *The Lands of the Saracen or, Pictures of Palestine, Asia Minor, Sicily, and Spain*. New York: G. P. Putnam.
Thomas, Hugh.2015. *The Slave Trade: The Story of the Atlantic Slave Trade 1440–1870*. London: Hachette.
Thompson, Carl.2007. *The Suffering Traveller and the Romantic Imagination*. Oxford: Clarendon Press.
Trachtenberg, Joshua.1983. *The Devil and the Jews: The Medieval Conception of the Jew and Its Relation to Modern Antisemitism*. Philadelphia: Jewish Publication Society of America.
Travels of Sir John Mandeville: The Version of the Cotton Manuscript in Modern Spelling. 1900. London and New York: Macmillan and Co.
Trevisan Semi, Emanuela.1987. *Allo Specchio dei Falascià. Ebrei ed Etnologi Durante il Colonialismo Fascista*. Firenze: Giuntina.
Trevisan Semi, Emanuela.1989. "L'oscillation ethnique: le cas des Caraïtes pendant la seconde guerre mondiale." *Revue de l'Histoire des Religions*. 206.4.
Trevisan Semi, Emanuela.1990. "The Image of the Karaites in Nazi and Vichy France Documents." *Jewish Journal of Sociology*. 33.2.
Trevisan Semi, Emanuela. Ed.2016. *Conversioni all'Ebraismo*. Rome: Bonnano Editore.
Tristram, Henry Baker.2012[1860]. *The Great Sahara: Wanderings South of the Atlas Mountains*. Cambridge, UK: Cambridge University Press.

Tuckey, James Hingston.1818. *Narrative of an Expedition to Explore the River Zaire, Usually Called the Congo, in South Africa, in 1816 Under the Direction of Captain J. K. Tuckey: To which is Added, the Journal of Prof. Smith, Some General Observations on the Country and Its Inhabitants and an App.: Containing the Natural History of that Part of the Kingdom of Congo Through which the Zaire Flows.* London: Murray.
Tudor, Alyosxa.2014. *From [al'manja] with love. Trans_feministische Positionierungen zu Rassismus und Migratismus.* Frankfurt a.M.: Brandes & Apsel.
Twain, Mark.2010. *Autobiography of Mark Twain.* Berkeley, Los Angeles, and London: University of California Press.
United States Democratic Review. 1842. 11.
Universal Magazine of Knowledge and Pleasure: Containing News, Letters, Debates, Poetry, Musick, Biography, History, Geography . . . and Other Arts and Sciences; which May Render it Instructive and Entertaining to Gentry, Merchants, Farmers, and Tradesmen. To which Occasionally Will be Added, an Impartial Account of Books in Several Languages, and of the State of Learning in Europe; Also of the Stage, New Opera's, Plays, and Oratorio's. 1790. 87.
Usque, Samuel.1965. *Consolation for the Tribulations of Israel.* Ed. Martin A. Cohen. Philadelphia: Jewish Publication Society.
Vansina, J.2007. "On Ravenstein's Edition of Battell's Adventures in Angola and Loango." *Africa.* 34.
Villault, N. Sieur de Bellefond.1669. *Relation des costes appelées Guinée; avec la description du pays, moeurs et façons de vivre des habitans.* Paris: D. Thierry.
Vincent, A.1985. "The Jew, the Gipsy and El-Islam: An Examination of Richard Burton's Consulship in Damascus and His Premature Recall, 1868–1871." *Journal of the Royal Asiatic Society of Great Britain and Ireland.* 2.
Voegelin, Eric.1997. *Race and State.* Baton Rouge and London: University of Missouri Press.
Vogt, Peter.2009. "Count Zinzendorf's Encounter with Judaism and the Jews. A Fictitious Dialogue from 1739." *Journal of Moravian History.* 6.
Voltaire.1734/1957. *Traité de Métaphysique.* Manchester: Manchester University Press.
Voltaire.1879. *Œuvres Complètes De Voltaire: Nouvelle Édition.* Paris: Garnier Frères, Libraires-Éditeurs.
Waitz, Theodor.1863. *Introduction to Anthropology.* London: Longman.
Walckenaer, Charles Athanase.1828. *Histoire générale des voyages ou Nouvelle collection des relations de voyages par mer et par terre: Premiers voyages dans l'océan Atlantique méridional, sur toute la côte occidentale d'Afrique, depuis le cap Lopez-Gonzalvo jusqu'au Cap Negro; Livre XV: Observations des premiers voyageurs sur les royaumes de Loango, de Congo, d'Angola, de Benguella et des pays voisins.* Paris: Lefèvre.
Wallace, A.1864. "The Origin of Human Races and the Antiquity of Man Deduced from the Theory of 'Natural Selection.'" *Journal of the Anthropological Society of London.* 2.
Walvin, James.1993. *Black Ivory: History of British Slavery.* London: Fontana Press.
Warburton, Eliot.1844. *The Crescent and the Cross: Romance and Realities of Eastern Travel.* London: Henry Colburn.
Webster, Jeremy.2006. "The 'Lustful Buggering Jew': Anti-Semitism, Gender, and Sodomy in Restoration Political Satire." *Journal for Early Modern Cultural Studies.* 6.1.
Weinberg, Gerhard.Ed.2003. *Hitler's Second Book: The Unpublished Sequel to Mein Kampf.* New York: Enigma Books.
Weingart, P.1989. "German Eugenics Between Science and Politics." *Osiris.* 5.

Weinreich, Max.1999. *Hitler's Professors: The Part of Scholarship in Germany's Crimes Against the Jewish People*. New Haven, CT: Yale University Press.

Weinstock, Jeffrey Andrew, Ed.2016. *The Ashgate Encyclopedia of Literary and Cinematic Monsters*. London: Routledge.

Weissblei, Gil.2016. "The Curious Friendship Between S. Y. Agnon and a Future Nazi Criminal." *Ha-Aretz*, March 27.

White, Charles.1799. *An account of the regular gradation in man, and in different animals and vegetables and from the Former to the Latter*. London: C. Dilly.

White, Michael.2007. "The Grosz Case: Paranoia, Self-Hatred and Anti-Semitism." *Oxford Art Journal*. 30.3.

Whitman, James Q.2017. *Hitler's American Model: The United States and the Making of Nazi Race Law*. Princeton, NJ: Princeton University Press.

Wiedemann, Felix.2009. "Der doppelte Orient Zur völkischen Orientromantik des Ludwig Ferdinand Clauss." *Zeitschrift für Religions und Geistesgeschichte*. 61.1.

Wilson, John Leighton.1847. "An Ethnographic View of Western Africa." *Biblical Repertory and Princeton Review*. 27.

Wilson, John Leighton.1856. *Western Africa: Its History, Condition, and Prospects*. London: Sampson Low.

Wiseman, Nicholas Patrick.1842. *Twelve Lectures on the Connection Between Science and Revealed Religion: Delivered in Rome*. London: C. Dodman.

Wistrich, Robert S.2013. *Demonizing the Other: Antisemitism, Racism and Xenophobia*. London: Routledge.

Wolf, Lucien, Ed.1901. *Menasseh ben Israel's mission to Oliver Cromwell: being a reprint of the pamphlets published by Menasseh ben Israel to promote the re-admission of the Jews to England, 1649–1656*. London: Macmillan.

Wolff, Joseph.1839. *Journal of the Rev. Joseph Wolff*. London: James Burns.

Woodward, John.1696. *Brief instructions for making observations in all parts of the world as also, for collecting, preserving, and sending over natural things: being an attempt to settle an universal correspondence for the advancement of knowledge both natural and civil*. London: Printed for Richard Wilkin at the King's Head in St. Paul's Church-Yard.

Wright, Thomas.1906. *The Life of Sir Richard Burton*. London: Everett & Co.

Wulf, Joseph.1983. *Musik im Dritten Reich—Eine Dokumentation*. Gütersloh: Ullstein.

Young, Jason R.2011. *Rituals of Resistance: African Atlantic Religion in Kongo and the Lowcountry South in the Era of Slavery*. Baton Rouge: LSU Press.

Young, Robert J. C.1995. *Colonial Desire: Hybridity in Theory, Culture and Race*. London: Routledge.

Zafran, Eric.1979. "Saturn and the Jews." *Journal of the Warburg and Courtauld Institutes*. 42.

Zimmerman, Andrew.1999. "Anti-Semitism as Skill: Rudolf Virchow's 'Schulstatistik' and the Racial Composition of Germany." *Central European History*. 32.4.

Zimmermann, Moshe.1986. *Wilhelm Marr: The Patriarch of Antisemitism*. New York and Oxford: Oxford University Press.

Index

For the benefit of digital users, indexed terms that span two pages (e.g., 52–53) may, on occasion, appear on only one of those pages.

Figures are indicated by *f* following the page number

Abel (the biblical), 10–11
Abernethy, Arthur Talmage, 174–75, 177–79
abolitionism, 36, 102
Abrabanel, Isaac ben Judah, 45–46
Abraham (the biblical), 21, 111, 164
Abriss der Sitten und Gebräuche aller Nazionen, oder kurze Darstellungen der merkwürdigsten menschlichen Wohnpläze, Beschäftigungen und Gewohnheiten in den fünf Theilen der Welt (Outline of the Manners and Customs of all Nations, or Brief Representations of the Strangest Human Dwelling places, Occupations and Manners in the five Regions of the World) (Lang), 73
Abyssinian Jews, 71–72, 73, 81, 113, 117
An account of the regular gradation in man, and in different animals and vegetables and from the Former to the Latter (White), 99
Adam (the biblical), 1, 2, 5, 7, 10–11, 12, 13 14, 17, 20, 21, 78–79, 86–87, 103
Adam, H. G., 129
Africans, Native Americans origins compared, 13–14. *See also* blacks
The Afro-American Encyclopaedia, 97–98
Afro-Germans, 184
Agassiz, Jean Louis Rodolphe, 23–24, 101, 113–15, 243n6
Agau, 113
Agnon, S. Y., 220–21
Alchabitius (Al-Qabisi), 42–43
Alexander VII, Pope 12

Alexander the Great, 233
Allgemeine geographische Ephemeriden (Ehrmann), 65
Allgemeiner Handatlas (Andree), 144
The American Cyclopædia, 57–58
American School (of Anthropology), 101, 102, 114
Anacletus II, 43
An Analytical Inquiry Into the Principles of Taste (Knight), 62
"Analytical Synopsis of the Natural History of Man," Hall, 88
Andree, Richard, 69, 144–45, 152–53, 226
animal-human relations, 27–28, 57–58, 59
animal species, 25
Annegarn, Joseph, 67
antisemitism. *See also* racism-antisemitism conflated
  black-Jew fusion in constructing, 181, 182, 183
  expulsion and resettlement option, 169–70, 172
  German national racial study supporting, 180–81
  historical, 158–59
  physical characteristics in, 192
  proponents of, historically, 166
  skin color in, 158–59
  study of, ix
antisemitism of reason, 206
"Aptitudes of Races" Farrar, 102–3
Arendt, Hannah, 162, 164–65
Aristotle, 56
Armistead, Wilson, 88–89
Astley, Thomas, 37, 40

Atkins, John, 14–15
Augustine, St., 57, 61
Augustine of Hippo, 1–2, 4–5, 6, 11, 23

Baartman, Sara, 162–63
Bagatelles pour un massacre (Céline), 182
Baldaeus, Philip, 72
Ballin, Hans, 222
Barnum, P. T., 162–63
Barrère, Pierre, 41
The Bass Saxophone (Škvorecký), 203–5
Bastian, Adolf, 11, 92, 144, 226
Bateson, William, 183
Battell, Andrew, 59–60
Bauer, Bruno, 172
Bauer, Elvira, 186–88, 187f
Baumgarten, Siegmund, 222
Bazan, Heinrich Banniza von, 208
Beddoe, John, 118–22, 151, 152, 177–79
Beke, Charles Tilstone, 112–13
Bernier, François, 21–24, 162–63
Bertillon, Alphonse, 94–95
Bertillon, Louis-Adolphe, 94–95, 214
Bertin, George, 143–44
Best, George, 3, 41
Beta Israel (see also Falasha)
The Bible View of Slavery (Raphal), 95–96
Bigland, John, 137
Blackamoors, 43–44, 50
black blood, 54–55, 170, 191
black cruelty, 31, 32, 37, 129
black Jewish face, the, 145–46
black Jews
    of Abyssinia, 81
    blacks, commonality with, 106–7
    of Cochin (*see* Cochin)
    creation of the, 131
    European, 226–27
    existence of, 142
    of the great desert, 91
    heresy of, 110
    in Nazi Germany, 226–27
    of Palestine, 92
    proof of existence, 120
    public display of, 242n2
    purity of the, 108
    race theory, impact on, x
    racial impurity, 110–11, 112–13, 126–27, 130–31
    white Jews into, 67–68
    white Jews vs., 97–98
black Jews, skin color
    caloric theory of, 83–84
    causes of, 130
    climate theory of, 82–83, 84, 85, 156
Black Jews in Africa and the Americas (Parfitt), 168–69
black Jews of Loango
    authenticity of, 65–66, 68–69, 80, 85–86
    blackness of, 62, 74–75
    characteristics of, 69
    color mutability, 67–69, 72, 74–75, 76–77, 78–80, 84
    color spectrum, 73
    described, 64
    impact of discovery of, 64–65, 75
    intermarriage, 153
    Jewish interest in, 70–71
    Jewishness of, 226
    origins, 66, 68–69, 70, 71–72, 73–74
    phenotypes of, 145
    physiognomy, 69, 146
    racial impurity, 145
    racial mutability, 76–77, 78–80
    reality disputed, 67
    as real Jews vs. converts, 73–74
    reputation, origins of, 56
    transformation from white to black, 72
    whiteness transformed, 116
blackness
    beliefs associated with, 31–32
    color spectrum of, 74–75
    determining and identifying, 191, 207
    transforming into white, 17–18, 32, 45–46, 78–79, 84, 88
    transforming into yellow, 88–89
blackness, explanations for
    Biblically based, 2–3, 13, 18, 33, 38–39
    climate/environment, 38, 74–75, 82–83, 84, 85, 156, 172–73
    degeneracy, 67–68
    disease, 50
    disputed, 38
    medical, 41
    scientific, 39–41

sin and cruelty, 32
technical, 34–35
black race
   origins, 7, 8, 17, 19–20, 27, 38
   ranking, 33–34
blacks
   colonial desire for and fear of, 173, 174
   elimination of the, 186
   in European society, 34–35
   intelligence of, 105
   othering of, 33–34, 50, 113–14, 117, 123
   public display of, 34, 59–61, 103, 162–63
   regeneration of the, 36
   rights of, 35
   uniqueness of, 109–10
   voting rights, 101
blacks, characterized as
   animals, 37, 51, 165
   cannibals, 167
   cunning, 49
   diseased, 184
   ignorant, 41, 49
   innately inferior, 36–37
   monstrous, 167, 172
   odorous, 161
   primates, 125, 160–61, 172–73
   sexual/sexually depraved, 27, 34, 57–58, 59, 172–73, 184, 195
   thieves and liars, 49
   ugly, 33, 167–68
blacks, characterized by
   adaptability, 125, 127, 128, 152
   physical characteristics, 33, 167–68
   physical constitution, 37
   physiognomy, 134, 136, 137, 141–42, 143, 147
blacks-Jews conflation, elements of. *See also* black Jews of Loango
   ability to transform to European, 177, 178f
   American legal system in the, 191–92
   ancestry, 50
   in art, 181–82
   blood, 170–71, 177–79, 186
   colonization, 169–70
   construct, hatred in the, 172
   cultural specificity-primitivism in, 159
   development of, 175

   disease, 50
   essential characteristics, 50
   fear of cross-breeding, 183–84
   genocide, 162, 164–65
   hate within the, 158
   historical thinking on, ix–x
   Hottentots, 162–64
   by Morton's theory, 105–6
   by Nott's theory, 106–7
   odor, 161
   in origins, 159–60
   othering, 158
   persistence of belief in, 177–79
   physical characteristics, 53–54, 157–58, 160–61, 166–68, 172, 181–83, 186–89
   physiognomy, 142, 144, 145–46
   political emancipation denied, 52
   as primitives, 172
   racial characteristics, 171
   racial origin, 174–75
   racism, 168–69
   sexuality/depravity, 174, 175, 195
   Third Reich, 157
   threat posed (racial danger), 183, 184
   undesirability, 50
   in the Western imaginary, 168–69
blacks-Jews differences, studies of, 52
black skin, causes of. *See* blackness, explanations for
   climate/environmental, 82–83, 84, 85, 156
black-white duality, 31, 53–54
Blake, William, 133–34
The blessed Jew of Marocco: or, A Blackmoor made white (Calvert), 46
Blumenbach, Johann Friedrich, 3, 17 18, 20, 23–25, 62, 122, 135, 137, 151, 159, 169–70
Boas, Franz, 154, 206, 209–10
Boaz, Rachel, 219
Boemus, Johann, 56
Bormann, Martin, 222
Bory de Saint-Vincent, Jean Baptiste, 100
Boudin, Jean-Christian, 152
Bowdich, Thomas Edward, 70
Bowring, John, 122
Brace, Charles Loring, 90–91
Breitenbauch, Georg-August von, 73–74

Brereton, William, 44
Brettschneider, Marla, 168–69
Brief Instructions for Making Observations in All Parts of the World (Woodward), 39–40
Broca, Paul, 214
Broecke, Pieter van den, 59, 232–33n2
Brosse, Guy de la, 59
Browne, Thomas, 33, 38–39, 46–47, 56
Bruce, James, 70
Brücher, Heinz, 210–11
Bruno, Giordano, 5–9, 10, 13–14, 22–23, 31, 48, 99, 105–6, 114
Bruns, Claudia, 175, 189–91
Bruns, Paul Jakob, 70, 157–58
Buchanan, Claudius, 81, 82, 108, 112, 240n4
Buffon, Georges Louis Leclerc de, 24, 25–27, 28–29, 45, 78, 83, 99, 134
Burke, Luke, 24
Burke, William, 137–38
Burleigh, Michael, 205
Burton, Richard, 100, 102, 122, 124, 128–29, 161–62, 225
Büsching, Anton, 67–68, 73, 82
Buttes, Henry, 45

Caesarius of Heisterbach, 46–47
Caffres, 18
Cain (the biblical), 10–11, 17–18, 38, 39, 109–10
Caldani, Leopoldo Marco Antonio, 88–89
Calmet, Antoine Augustin, 2–3
Caloric: Its Mechanical, Chemical and Vital agencies in the Phenomena of Nature (Metcalfe), 83–84
Calvert, Thomas, 46
Campbell, John, 116–17, 140, 166
Camper, 134–35
Canaan (the biblical), 2–3
Caput Bonae Spei Hodiernum Das ist vollstandige Beschreibung des Africanischen Vorgeburges der Guten Hofnung (Kolben), 164
Carlyle, Thomas, 57
Carroll, Lewis, 122–23
Le Cat, Claude-Nicolas, 67

Céline, Louis-Ferdinand, 177–79, 182, 189, 227
Chamberlain, Houston Stewart, 170–71, 214, 224
Chamberlain, Joseph, 104
Christian Researches in Asia (Buchanan), 82
A Christian Turn'd Turk (Daborne), 46
Churchill, Winston, 186–88
The City of God (Augustine of Hippo), 1–2
Civil War, American, 101–2, 157–58
Clarke, John, 66
Clauss, Ludwig Ferdinand, 220–21
Clement VIII, 7–8
climate determinism, 78, 82–83, 84, 85, 87, 89, 92, 93–95, 96–98, 156
climate determinism, effect on
  black Jews' skin color, 82–83, 84, 85, 156
  blackness, 38, 74–75, 82–83, 84, 85, 156, 172–73
  Jewish skin color, 12, 87, 111–12, 118, 119–20, 121
  skin color, 78, 82–83, 84, 85, 87, 89, 92, 93–95, 96–98, 172–73
climate determinism in monogenesist theory, 76, 156
Cobbett, William, 166
Cochin, black and white Jews of, 72–74, 81–82, 83, 87, 93–94, 95, 108, 156
Cohn, Norman, 127–28
Collingwood, J. F., 124
coloreds, 191–92
color mutability
  black Jews of Loango, 67–69, 72, 74–75, 76–77, 78–80, 84
  disease explaining, 17–18
  environmentally caused, 78, 93–94
  faith and, 46
  preoccupation with, 67–69
  racial significance, 88
  sin and cruelty causing, 32, 45–46
Comment Reconnaître et Expliquer le Juif? (How to recognize and explain the Jew) (Montandon), 161–62, 215–16
Conolly, John, 103
Cook, James, 27
Cordier, Charles Henri Joseph, 136

Crania Aegyptiaca; or, Observations on Egyptian ethnography, derived from anatomy, history, and the monuments (Morton), 105
Crania Americana; or, a Comparative View of the Skulls of Various Aboriginal Nations of North and South America: to which is Prefixed an Essay on the Varieties of the Human Species (Morton), 105
Crawfurd, John, 122, 124, 134, 161
Cromwell, Oliver, 72
cruelty
  black, 31, 32, 37, 129
  Jewish, 49–50
Curiosities of Medical Experience (Millingen), 82–83
Curran, Andrew, 34–35, 60
Cursor Mundi, 32
Cuvier, Georges, 20, 23–24, 86, 162–63
Cuvier, Nicolas Frédéric, 23–24

d'Abbadie d'Arrast, Antoine Thomson, 84–86
Daborne, Robert, 46
da Gama, Vasco, 162–63
Dapper, Olfert, 57, 59–60
Darrow, Jason, 37–38, 172–74
Darwin, Charles, 8, 102, 113–14, 122, 125–26, 131–32, 142–43, 149–50, 211
Das Buch Paragranum (Paracelsus), 4–5
Das Judenthum in der Fremde (Bauer), 172
Das Jüdische Komplott (The Jewish Plot) (Parole der Woche) (Slogan of the Week) series), 186–89, 189*f*
Das Rassenrecht in den Vereinigten Staaten (Race Law in the United States) (Krieger), 191
Davis, Joseph Barnard, 76–77, 105
De Admirandis Naturae Reginae Deaeque Mortalium Arcanis (On the Wonderful Secrets of Nature, the Queen and Goddess of Mortals) (Vanini), 8
Dearborn Independent, 200–2
The Defense of the Race (*La Difesa della Razza*), 197–200, 198*f*, 199*f*, 201*f*

De innumerabilibus, immenso, et infigurabili (Of the innumerable, the immense and the unfigurable) (Bruno), 6
De La Littérature des Nègres (Grégoire), 36
Der Jude als Rassenschänder (The Jew as Race Defiler) (Plischke), 204*f*
Der Jude als Rasseschänder: eine Anklage gegen Juda und eine Mahnung an die deutschen Frauen und Mädchen (*The Jew as Race Defiler*: An Indictment of Judah and a Reminder to German Women and Girls) (Plischke), 186–88
Der Jude als Weltparasit (The Jew as World Parasite) (Reiffer & Schwarzburg), 222–24, 225, 226
Der Judenspiegel (A Mirror to the Jews) (Marr), 165–66
Der Mythus des zwanzigsten Jahrhunderts (The Myth of the Twentieth Century) (Rosenberg), 212
Le Dernier Métro (Truffaut), 221–22
Der Stürmer (Streicher), 193, 194*f*, 202
"Der Talisman" Relink, 204*f*
Der Weg zum Siege des Germanenthums über das Judenthum (The Victory of Jewry over Germandom) (Marr), 165–66
The Descent of Man (Darwin), 122, 131–32
Deslondes, Charles, 37
Desmoulins, Louis-Antoine, 24, 100
De Umbris Idearum (On the Shadows of Ideas) (Bruno), 5–6
Devir, Nathan, 168–69
d'Holbach, Baron, 49
Diderot, Denis, 38–39, 57, 61
Die Grundlagen des neunzehnten Jahrhunderts (The Foundations of the Nineteenth Century) (Chamberlain), 170
Didymus the Blind, 31
Die Juden als Rasse (The Jews as a race) (Judt), 152–53
Die Juden der Gegenwart (The Jews of Today) (Ruppin), 153
Die Judenfrage als Racen-, Sitten-und Culturfrage (The Jewish Question as a Racial, Moral, and Cultural Question) (Dühring), 192–93

Die Rehobother Bastards und das Bastardisierungsproblem beim Menschen (The Bastards of Rehoboth and the Problem of Miscegenation in Man) (Fischer), 183
Die Verbreitung der Juden in der Welt—Statistische Beiträge zu den Fragen der Zeit [The Distribution of Jews in the World— Statistical Contributions to the Questions of the Time]) (Zander), 225
La Difesa della Razza (The Defense of the Race), 197–200, 198f, 199f, 201f
Diseases of the East (*Krankheiten des Orients*) (Pruner), 93–94
Dissertation on the physical cause of the color of Negroes (*Dissertation sur la cause physique de la couleur des Nègres*) (Barrère), 41
Dissertation physique à l'occasion du nègre blanc (Maupertuis), 60
Dissertation sur la cause physique de la couleur des Nègres (Dissertation on the physical cause of the color of Negroes) (Barrère), 41
"The Diversity of Origin of the Human Races" Agassiz, 114
Dr. Celticus, 135, 151, 160, 161–62, 167–68, 218
Drummond, Blair, 28
Du Bois, W. E. B., 154
Dühring, Eugen, 192–93
Dyets Dry Dinner (Buttes), 45

Eastern Life (Martineau), 135–36
Efron, John, 82
Egorova, Yulia, 170
Ehrenreich, Eric, 219
Ehrmann, Theophil Friedrich, 65–66
Eichmann, Adolf, 224–25
Einstein, Albert, 206
Eldad the Danite, 44
Eliot, T. S., 181
embamba, 58
empachas, 58
Enoch (the biblical), 7
Entartete Musik: Eine Abrechnung (Ziegler), 203f

Entartete Musik exhibition, 202–3
Eric or Little by Little (Farrar), 141
Eschenbach, Wolfram von, 34
Essai sur la régénération physique et morale des Juifs (Grégoire), 52–53
Essai sur l'inégalité des races humaines (Gobineau), 150–51, 159
Essay on the causes of the variety of complexion and figure in the human species etc. (Smith), 30
Estes, Mathew, 167–68
Ethiopian blacks, 7
Ethiopian Jews, 70, 71, 225
Ethnographic Parallels and Comparisons (*Ethnographische Parallelen und Vergleiche*) (Andree), 144
Ethnographische Parallelen und Vergleiche (*Ethnographic Parallels and Comparisons*) (Andree), 144
The Ethnology of the British Colonies and Dependencies (Latham), 159
Etymologiae (Isidore of Seville), 2
eugenics, 183–84
European Jews, 156–57, 226–27
Eve (the biblical), 1, 2, 7, 17, 20, 21, 86–87, 103
"Evolution and Permanence of Type" Agassiz, 114
evolutionary theory, 131
"An examination of the Physical History of the Jews in its bearing on the Question of the Unity of the Races" Nott, 111
"The Eye of the Negro" Kollock, 135–36

Fabricius, Johann Andreas, 12–13
Falashas 112–13, 117, 225
Falkenstein, Julius, 226
The Fardle of Facions (Waterman), 33
Farrar, Frederic William (Dean Farrar), 102–3, 141–42
Fascism, 195–96
Final Solution, 186
Fischer, Eugen, 183–84, 214, 216–18, 220
Fishberg, Maurice, 154, 181, 208–9
Fliethmann, Elfriede, 219
Folklore of the Jews (*Volkskunde Der Juden*) (Andree), 69, 144–45

Ford, Henry, 200–2
Forster, Johann Georg Adam, 27
Forster, Johann Reinhold, 27
The Foundations of the Nineteenth
 (Century, Die Grundlagen des
 neunzehnten Jahrhunderts)
 (Chamberlain), 170
Fragmente— Sur les Lignes d'Animalité
 (Lavater), 133–34
France, 35, 36, 185–86
Freisler, Roland, 191–92, 222–23
French colonies, 36, 37
Freud, Sigmund, 62
Fritsch, Theodor, 177–79, 192–93, 205

Gall, Franz Joseph, 76
Galton, Francis, 149–50, 183
Gassendi, Pierre, 21
General history of the Pyrates, 14
genetics, 183–84
Genetics, Mass Media, and Identity (Parfitt
 & Egorova), 168–69
genocide, 162, 164–65
Geographical Nosology (Geographische
 Nosologie) (Schnurrer), 74–75
Géographie mathématique, physique et
 politique (Malte-Brun), 68–69
Géographie mathématique, physique et
 politique (Mentelle), 68–69
Geographische Nosologie (Geographical
 Nosology) (Schnurrer), 74–75
George III, 135
Gershwin, George Jacob, 203–5
Geschichte der jüdischen Religion (History
 of the Jewish Religion) (Büsching), 73
Geschichte der Mission der Evangelischen
 Brueder auf den Caraibischen
 Inseln St. Thomas, St. Croix, St.
 Jan (A History of the Mission of
 the Evangelical Brethren on the
 Caribbean Islands of St. Thomas, St.
 Croix and St. John) (Oldendorp), 64
Giddon, George R., 24, 101
Gilman, Sander, 41–42, 45, 156, 157–58,
 189, 208–9
Girtanner, Christoph, 57–58
Gliddon, George Robbins, 106–7, 109, 149
Globke, Hans, 212, 221–22

goat, the, 47–48, 135, 160, 174
Gobineau, Joseph Arthur de, 118, 123,
 150–51, 159, 165–66, 167, 171, 214
Goethe, 143–44
Goethe, Johann Wolfgang von, 162
Goldbeck, J. C., 89
"Golgotha" Morton, 148
Gould, Stephen Jay, 105
Grant, Madison, 184
Great Desert, the black Jews in, 91
The Great Sahara— Wanderings
 South of the Atlas Mountains
 (Tristram), 120–21
Greenblatt, Stephen, 9
Grégoire, Henri Jean-Baptiste (Grégoire,
 Abbé), 36, 41, 52–53, 62, 68,
 78–79, 82
Grenfell, Morgan, 12–13
Grossstadt (Metropolis) (Grosz), 181–82
Grosz, George, 181–82
Grundriss der Geschichte der Menschheit
 (Outline of the History of Mankind)
 (Meiners), 167
Gulliver's Travels (Swift), 14
Günther, Hans F. K. (the "Race Pope"),
 208–9, 211–12, 213, 214, 216–18, 225
Güssfeldt, Paul, 226
Gwilym, Dafydd ap, 80

HaCohen, 42, 51
Haddon, Alfred Cort, 143–44, 160, 209–10
Haeckel, Ernst, 210–11, 218
Hale, Mathew, 18–19
Hall, John Charles, 87–88
Ham (the biblical), 2–3, 13, 33, 38–39, 117
The Handbuch der Geographie für die
 Jugend (A Geography Manual for
 Young People) (Annegarn), 67
Handbuch der Judenfrage die wichtigsten
 Tatsachen zur Beurteilung des
 jüdischen Volkes (Handbook of
 the Jewish Question— the Most
 Important Facts for the Evaluation of
 the Jewish People) (Fritsch), 177
Hare, William, 137–38
Harrison, James, 103
Hart, Mitchell, 210
Heraclitus, 31

Herbart, Johann Friedrich, 92
Herder, Johann Gottfried, 10, 52
Herskovits, Melville J., 209–10
Hildebrandt, Georg Friedrich, 74
Hippocrates, 30, 42
Histoire de Loango, Kakongo et autres royaumes d'Afrique (A History of Loango, Kakongo, and Other African Kingdoms) (Liévin-Bonaventure Proyart), 59
Histoire Naturelle, générale et particulière avec la description du Cabinet du Roi (Buffon), 25
Histoire philosophique et politique des établissemens & du commerce des européens dans les deux Indes (Raynal), 38–39
Historical Display of the Effects of Physical and Moral Causes on the Character and Circumstances of Nations (Bigland), 137
History of Jamaica (Long), 27
History of the Jewish Religion (*Geschichte der jüdischen Religion*) (Büsching), 73
A History of the Mission of the Evangelical Brethren on the Caribbean Islands of St. Thomas, St. Croix and St. John (*Geschichte der Mission der Evangelischen Brueder auf den Caraibischen Inseln St. Thomas, St. Croix, St. Jan*) (Oldendorp), 64
Hitler, Adolph, 184–86, 192–93, 196–97, 200, 205, 206, 212, 213, 218, 220, 221, 222, 223
Hitler's Table Talk 1941–1944: Secret Conversations (Hitler), 205
Hodges, Edward Richmond, 120
Holocaust, 164–65, 219
homo sapiens, 24–25, 26, 27
homo troglodytes, 24–25
Hooton, Earnest Albert, 209–10
Hottentots, 162–64
Hotze, Henry, 122–23, 150–51
Hovelacque, Abel, 135, 160
How to recognize and explain the Jew (*Comment Reconnaître et Expliquer le Juif?*) (Montandon), 62, 182–83, 215–16

Hugh of Lincoln, 130
Hulsius, Antonius, 12
human zoos, 34, 59–61, 103, 162–63, 242n2
Humboldt, Alexander von, 210–11
Hume, David, 36–37, 83
humoral theory, 42
Hunt, James, 122–25, 152
Hunter, John, 24, 61, 62
Husserl, Edmund, 221
Huxley, Julian Sorell, 209–10
Huxley, Thomas, 122–23

The Index, A Weekly Journal of Politics, Literature, and News; Devoted to the Exposition of Mutual Interests, Political and Commercial, of Great Britain and the Confederate States of America (Hotz, ed.), 123
Indian Mutiny, 103
Isidore of Seville, 2
Israel, Menasseh ben, 11
Istorica descrizione de Tre Regni: Congo, Mantamba et Angola (Montecuccolo), 58
Italy, World War II, 195–96
Itinerario de Ludovico de Varthema Bolognese (Varthema), 47

Jackson, John, 168–69
Jacobs, Joseph, 149–50
Jacobson, Matthew Frye, 192
Jäger, Gustav, 218
Japheth (the biblical), 2–3
Jean-Baptiste Margat de Tilly, 18
Jefferson, Thomas, 57–58
Jerome, 31
Jesenska, Milena, 181
"Jeux de la Nature et Monstres," Diderot, 57
The Jew, Judaism, and the Judaization of the Christian Peoples (*Le Juif, le Judaïsm et la Judaïsation des peoples chrétiens*) (Mousseaux), 212
The Jew, the Gypsy and El Islam (Burton), 128
The Jew and France at the Palais Berlitz (*Le Juif et la France au Palais Berlitz*) (Montandon), 182–83

INDEX   281

The Jew a Negro: Being a Study of the Jewish Ancestry from an Impartial Standpoint (Abernethy), 174
The Jew as World Parasite (*Der Jude als Weltparasit*) (Reiffer & Schwarzburg), 226
Jewish blackness, 42–43, 45–46
Jewish cruelty, 49–50
Jewish culture, 159
Jewish diaspora, 124
Jewish face, the, 133, 134–36, 143–44, 145–46, 192
Jewish groups of color, 153
Jewish homeland, 153
On Jewish Illnesses (*Von den Krankheiten der Juden*) (Wolf), 51
The Jewish Plot (*Das Jüdische Komplott*) (Parole der Woche) (Slogan of the Week) series), 186–89, 189f
Jewish race
   black blood of the, 157, 159
   existence of, 158–59, 209
   origins, 7, 8, 10, 11, 159–60
   purity of the, 86–87, 106–7, 109–11, 115–17, 121–22, 125, 127, 144–45, 147–51, 153–55, 156
   racial unity, 153
   strands of the, 160
Jewish type, 153
Jews. *See also* blacks-Jews conflation, elements of
   adaptability, 124–25
   admission into the kingdom, 9–10
   blackness assigned to, 227
   conversion, effects of, 46–47
   elimination of the, 186
   European, whiteness of, 118
   expulsion and resettlement option, 169–70, 172
   material improvement, downsides of, 53
   meretricious representation of, 53
   othering of, 50, 109–10, 113, 119, 127–29, 147–48, 152, 157–58
   political rights, 36
   racial differences, explaining, 41–42
   regeneration of the, 36
   somatic blackness, 44
   species of, 157
   types of, 177–79, 181–82
   Voltaire on difference of, 16
Jews, characterized as
   adaptable, 151–53
   bestial, 173, 175
   chameleons, 177–79, 188–89, 191
   cunning, 49, 149–51
   dangerous and violent, 48–49
   diseased, 50, 51
   as goats, 135, 160, 174
   ignorant, 49
   inferior, 43
   invisible, 177–79, 189
   mongrel, 177
   monstrous, 47–48, 49, 167, 173, 175
   mortal threat to Christendom, 43–44
   negroid parasites, 192–93
   odorous, 9–10, 46–47, 135, 161–62, 218
   primates, 51, 160, 181
   sexual/sexually depraved, 44, 135, 175, 192–93, 194f
   social vampires, 49
   ugly, 45–46, 167
Jews, characterized by
   black and putrid blood, 42–43
   color, 41–42, 43, 44, 45
   indistinct reasoning, 44
   physical and moral character, 52–53
   physical characteristics, 45–46, 167
   physiognomy, 133–36, 137, 138–41, 142–44, 147–51, 154
   two kinds of noses, 160
Jews, identifying
   badges for, 41–42
   color for, 41–42
   difficulty in, 207–10
   hair and skin color in, 180–81, 192, 195–96
   Italy, World War II, 195–96
   Third Reich, 180–81, 211–14, 215–16, 218, 219–22, 223, 224–26
Jews, skin color
   Africanization of Jews in, 158
   color spectrum, x, 73–74, 82, 88, 90, 92, 93–94, 118–19, 177–79
   consensus on, 156
   importance of, 156–58
   Nazi propaganda concerning, 222–23

Jews, skin color, causes of
    Biblically based, 18
    climate/environment, 87, 111–12, 118, 119–20, 121, 147
    dirt / sunburn, 51
    disease, 50, 51
The Jews: A Study of Race and Environment (Fishberg), 209
Jews of many colors principle, 130
The Jews of Today (*Die Juden der Gegenwart*) (Ruppin), 153
Johnes, Arthur James, 80
John II, 93–94
Johnson, Paul, 171
Journey in West Africa including the Exploration of Senegal (*Voyage dans L'Afrique Occidentale comprenant l'exploration du Sénégal etc.*) (Raffenel), 93
Judaism, physical manifestation of, 46
Juden Stellen Sich Vor (Jews Introduce Themselves) (Rupprecht), 189–91, 190f
Judeophobia, 183
Judt, J. M., 152–53
Le Juif, le Judaïsm et la Judaïsation des peoples chrétiens (The Jew, Judaism and the Judaisation of the Christian peoples) (Nott), 127–28
Le Juif, le Judaïsm et la Judaïsation des peoples chrétiens (The Jew, Judaism, and the Judaization of the Christian Peoples) (Mousseaux), 212
Le Juif et la France au Palais Berlitz (The Jew and France at the Palais Berlitz) (Montandon), 182–83
Julie, ou la nouvelle Héloïse (Rousseau), 35–36

Kafka, Franz, 181
Kames, Lord, 28, 29–30, 31, 59, 62, 83, 99
Kant, Immanuel, 20, 24, 26–27, 49
Kaplan, M. Lindsay, 42, 43
Karaites, 224
Karsenty, Mme., 215
Keith, Arthur, 161
Kershaw, Ian, 212
Kingsley, Charles, 122–23
Kirk, Robert, 44
Klinkosch, Joseph Thaddäus, 88–89
Knight, Richard Payne, 62, 78–79
Knox, Robert, 96–97, 100, 104, 124, 137–40, 148–49, 158, 159, 165–66, 167
Kolben, Peter, 164
Kollmann, Josef, 210–11
Kollock, Charles, 135–36
Krankheiten des Orients (Diseases of the East) (Pruner), 93–94
Krieger, Heinrich, 191
Krünitz, Johann Georg, 61–63
Ku Klux Klan, 195

Lamekh (the biblical), 18
Landé, Margarete, 220–21
Landra, Guido, 196–97
Lang, Friedrich Carl, 73
Lapouge, Vacher de, 214
Lassalle, Ferdinand, 171
Latham, Robert Gordon, 159
Laurentiis, Allegra de, 29
Lavater, Johann Kaspar, 133–35
Lawrence, William, 86–87, 137
Layard, Austen Henry, 138–39, 148–49
L'école de Cadavres (School of Corpses) (Céline), 177–79
Lectures on Physiology, Zoology, and the Natural History of Man (Lawrence), 86
Leeuwenhoek, Antonie Philips van, 40
Lefébure, Gabriel, 137
Leibniz, Gottfried Wilhelm, 23
Leonardo da Vinci, 232n2
Les Nouveaux Voyages de Mr. le Baron de La Hontan dans l'Amérique Septentrionale (Louis-Armand de Lom d'Arce), 13
Les Races humaines (Hovelacque), 135, 160
Lessing, Gotthold Ephraim, 49–50
Lettre à Philotine (La Peyrère), 12
Leviathan (the biblical), 7
Liévin-Bonaventure Proyart, Abbé, 59
Lincoln, Abraham, 101
Linnaeus, Carl, 20–21, 23–25, 26, 27, 28, 29
Loango. *See also* black Jews of Loango
    described, 234–35n2
    hybrids of, existence of, 55

monstrous races of, 27
terrifying creatures of, 57–60
white Negros of, 59–62
writings on, 61–62
Lombroso, Cesare, 195–96
Long, Edward, 27–28, 49
Lopez, Duarte, 59
Lösener, Bernhard, 207–8
Lost Tribes of Israel (Parfitt), 168–69
Louis-Armand de Lom d'Arce, Baron La Hontan, 13
Louis II de Bourbon, 11, 12
Louis XIII, 59
L.P., 19

Machado, Francisco, 50
MacMaster, Neil, 158, 168
Maillet, Benoît De, 16
Malfert, Auguste, 17–18, 38, 41
Malte-Brun, Conrad, 68–69, 72, 100
Mandel, Georges, 185–86
Manifesto della Razza (Race Manifesto), 195–96
Man's Place in Nature (Huxley), 123
Markus, Ludwig, 70–72
Markuse, Max, 184
Marnhull Orphrey, 31, 32f
Marr, Wilhelm, 158–59, 161, 165–66
Martineau, Harriet, 135–36, 151
Marx, Karl, 171
Maupertuis, Pierre-Louis Moreau de, 60, 162–63
Mechelen, Archbishop of, 12
Meckel the elder, Johann Friedrich, 41
Meiners, Christoph, 27, 167, 169–70
Mein Kampf (Hitler), 184, 192–93, 196, 213, 221
Melamed, A., 41–42
The Melting Plot (Zangwill), 154
Mémoires de Trévoux (Jean-Baptiste Margat de Tilly), 18
Mémoire sur l'origine des Nègres et des Américains (Note on the Origin of the Negroes and Americans) (Malfert), 17
Menasseh ben Israel, 72
Men Before Adam (La Peyrère), 10
Mendel, Gregor Johann, 183
Mendelssohn is on the Roof (Weil), 222

menstrual blood, 45–46
Mentelle, Edme, 68–69
Messias Christianorum et Judaeorum (The Messias of the Christians and the Jewes) (Münster), 44
The Metaphysic of Man; or, the Pure Part of the Physiology of Man (Goldbeck), 89
Metcalfe, Samuel, 83–85
Methushael (the biblical), 18
Michaelis, Johann David, 169–70
Miles, William, 168–69
Millingen, John Gideon, 82–83
A Mirror to the Jews (*Der Judenspiegel*) (Marr), 165–66
The Mismeasure of Man (Gould), 105
Misson, François Maximilian, 45, 46–47
Mondnacht (Moonlit Night) (Grosz), 181–82
monogenesist theory. *See also* Prichard, James Cowles
  acceptance of, 24–25, 29
  antislavery movement and, 102
  Biblical story supporting, 2–3
  climate determinism in, 76, 156
  defined, 1
  discredited, 99, 100
  evidence of, 107
  Jews' belief in, 2
  mutability of physiognomy in, 137
  persistence of, 1
  proponents of, 2, 6–7, 23, 30, 86–88, 91
  questioning, 3–4
monsters
  characteristics of, 25
  classification of, 57
  existence of, 57
  race mixing in creating, 57
monstrous race(s)
  African, 56
  blacks charactized as, 167, 172
  Christian images of the, 47–48
  considered human, 1–2
  Jews characterized as, 47–48, 49, 167, 173, 175
  Khoikhoi (Hottentots), 162–64
  origin of the, 38
  Rutland Psalter, 47–48
  Western speculation over, 27–28

Montaigne, 83
Montandon, George-Alexis, 161–62, 182–83, 214, 215–16, 218, 223–24
Montecuccolo, Giovanni Antonio Cavazzi da, 58
Montesquieu, 83
Moonlit Night (*Mondnacht*) (Grosz), 181–82
Moors, 43–44, 50
The Moral and Intellectual Diversity of Races (Nott & Hotze), 150–51
Morton, Samuel George, 24, 101, 105–7, 148
Moses, 171
Mosse, George Lachmann, ix, 53–54
Mountain Jews, 224–25
Mousseaux, Gougenot des, 127–28, 212
mulattos, 28, 61–62
Münster, Sebastian, 44
music, 200–5, 203f
Muslims, 43
The Myth of the Twentieth Century (*Der Mythus des zwanzigsten Jahrhunderts*) (Rosenberg), 212

Napoleon, 37
Nassy, David Cohen, 226–27
Nassy, Joseph, 226–27
"Of National Characters" Hume, 36–37
Native Americans, 13–14, 18, 34, 97, 103, 110
Natural History of Man (Prichard), 77–78, 84–85
Natural History of The Human Species: Its Typical Forms, Primeval Distribution, Filiations, and Migrations (Smith), 115
The Natural History of the Varieties of Man (Latham), 159
natural selection, 125–26, 142–43
Natürliche Schöpfungsgeschichte (The History of Creation) (Haeckel), 210–11
Naval Surgeon (Atkins), 14–15
Nazi Germany
American model of racism used in, 212–13
anti-Jewish racial legislation, 212
Aryan classification system, Italians in the, 196–97
Aryan superiority, belief in, 210–11
blacks and black Jews in, 226–27
blacks in, 185–86
holocaust, 219, 222–24, 226–27
Jewishness, identifying, 211–14, 215–16, 218, 219–22, 223, 224–26
national racial study, 180
negrification of, 192–93
polygenist racial theory, 224
race defined in, 206–10, 211–14, 216–18, 222
racial legislation, 191–92
racial policies, legitimizing, 218–19, 220, 221
racial purity, threats to, 192–95, 194f, 197–200, 201f
racism-antisemitism conflated, 197–205, 198f, 199f, 201f, 203f, 204f
science excellence in, 206
Negromania: Being an Examination of the Falsely Assumed Equality of the Various Races of Men (Campbell), 116
Negrophobia, 183
The Negro's and Indians Advocate (Grenfell), 13
Neubauer, Adolf, 44
Neue Erdbeschreibung (Büsching), 67
Neues und vollständiges geographisches Lexikon für Kaufleute und Geschäftsmänner (New and Complete Geographic Dictionary for Merchants and Businessmen) (Schedel), 67
New and Complete Geographic Dictionary for Merchants and Businessmen (*Neues und vollständiges geographisches Lexikon für Kaufleute und Geschäftsmänner*) (Schedel), 67
New Division of the Earth by the Different Species that Inhabit it (*Nouvelle division de la terre par les différentes espèces ou races qui l'habitent*) (Bernier), 21, 24
A New General Collection of Voyages and Travels (Darrow), 37–38

INDEX 285

New Journey in the Land of the Negroes (*Nouveau Voyage dans le Pays des Nègres*) (Raffenel), 93
The New Light, Or, Discourses on the Christian Church, on the Evils of Sectarianism and on the True Manner of Becoming Christians (Darrow), 172
New Voyage to Italy (Misson), 45
Nicholls, Frank, 232n2
Nightingale, Florence, 118
Nineveh and its Remains. A narrative of an expedition to Assyria (Layard), 138–39
Noah (the biblical), 2–4, 27, 38
Non-existent pre-Adamite, or, a confutation of a certain somebody's vain and Socinianizing dream, by which an anonymous author, using the Holy Scriptures as a pretext, endeavored not long ago to expound to the imprudent that there were men in the world before the first Adam (Hulsius), 12
Nott, Josiah Clark, 24, 76–77, 95, 96, 101, 104–5, 106–13, 127–28, 147–49, 150–51
Nouveau Voyage dans le Pays des Nègres (New Journey in the Land of the Negroes) (Raffenel), 93
Nouvelle division de la terre par les différentes espèces ou races qui l'habitent (New Division of the Earth by the Different Species that Inhabit it) (Bernier), 21, 24
Nouvelles Editions françaises entitled Comment Reconnaître et Expliquer le Juif? (How to Recognize and Explain the Jew?) (Montandon), 182–83

"Observations Intended to Favour a Supposition That the Black Color (As It Is Called) of the Negroes Is Derived from the Leprosy" Rush, 18
"Occasional Discourse on the Negro Question" Carlyle, 57
"Occasional Discourse on the Nigger Question" Carlyle, 57
Oekonomische Encyklopädie, 61–62, 64
Oficial, Yosef b. Nathan, 45–46

Ohne Lösung der Judenfrage keine Erloesung des deutschen Volkes (Without a Solution to the Jewish Question there will Be no Redemption for the German People) (Streicher), 186–88, 188f
Oldendorp, Christian Georg Andreas, 64–66, 67–68, 70–71, 72, 73–74, 75, 79, 82
Omnium gentium mores (Waterman), 33
one-drop concept, 54–55, 191, 192–93
original sin, 11
"The Origin of Human Races and the Antiquity of Man deduced from the theory of 'Natural Selection'" Wallace, 126, 142–43
On the Origin of Species by Means of Natural Selection, or the Preservation of Favoured Races in the Struggle for Life (Darwin), 102
othering
  of blacks, 33–34, 50, 113–14, 117, 123
  blacks and Jews, elements of conflation, 158
  of Jews, 13, 17, 50, 109–10, 113, 119, 127–29, 157–58
Outline of the Manners and Customs of all Nations, or Brief Representations of the Strangest Human Dwelling places, Occupations and Manners in the five Regions of the World (*Abriss der Sitten und Gebräuche aller Nazionen, oder kurze Darstellungen der merkwürdigsten menschlichen Wohnpläze, Beschäftigungen und Gewohnheiten in den fünf Theilen der Welt*) (Lang), 73
Owen, Richard, 91, 119–20, 241n10

Paracelsus (Philippus Aureolus Theophrastus Bombastus von Hohenheim), ix, 4–5, 6, 99, 213
Parfitt, Tudor, 168–69
Parole der Woche (Slogan of the Week) series, 186–89, 189f
The Passing of the Great Race (Grant), 184
Paterlini, Marta, 24–25
Paul, St., 10–11

Paxman, Jeremy, 127
Pechuël-Loesche, Eduard, 226
Peed, James, 120–21
Persian Jews, 224–25
La Peyrère, Isaac, 9–12, 17, 31, 46, 99, 105–6
Pezzl, Johann, 51
Phillips, Philip, 148–49
phrenology, 105
physical anthropology
　polygenesist theory and, 108–9
　proving race, 181
　proving racial origin, 105, 136, 152–53, 154, 158
　uses of, WW II, 159
"On the Physical Characteristics of the Jews" Beddoe, 151
Physical Ethnography of the African Races (Prichard), 79
The Physical History of the Jewish Race (Nott), 127–28
Physiognomische Fragmente zur Beförderung der Menschenkenntnis und Menschenliebe and, in English, Essays on Physiognomy designed to Promote the Knowledge and Love of Man (Lavater), 133–34
physiognomy
　black, 134, 136, 137, 141–42, 143, 147
　Jewish, 133–36, 137, 138–41, 142–44, 147–51
　mutability of, 137, 138–41, 142–43
Picart, Bernard, 135–36
Pickering, Charles, 23–24, 87–88
Pigafetta, Filippo, 58
Plato, 31
Plischke, Kurt, 186–88, 204f
Ploetz, Alfred, 166
Poliakov, Léon, ix, 162
Polish Jews, 51
Polygenesist theory
　beginnings, 99
　consequences forewarned, 92–93
　defined, 1
　evidence of, 100–1, 105–7, 118–19
　to explain racial differences, 76, 90–91, 99–100
　Jewish skin color explained, 156–57
　mutability of physiognomy, 137

　physical anthropology proving, 108–9
　proponents of, 4–9, 13–17, 18–20, 27–28, 29–30, 99–101, 105–6, 108–10, 114–17 (*see also specific proponents*)
　racist arguments for, 101–3, 105–6, 177
　scientific, 125–26
pongos, 57–58, 59, 235–36n5
Popkin, Richard, 5, 10
Porgy and Bess (Gershwin), 203–5
Pouchet, Félix-Archimède, 149
Prae-Adamitae (La Peyrère), 10, 11, 12
pre-Adamism, 4, 9–13, 17
Presentation of the Most Distinguished Peoples of the World (*Vorstellung der vornehmsten Völkerschaften der Welt*) (Breitenbauch), 73–74
Present State of the Cape of Good-Hope, or, A Particular Account of Several Nations of the Hottentots: Their Religion, Government, Laws, Customs, Ceremonies, and Opinions; Their Art of War, Professions, Language, Genius (Kolben), 164
Prichard, James Cowles, 6, 23–24, 51, 76–79, 80–82, 84–85, 86–87, 91, 100, 104–5, 108–9, 110, 112–13, 119, 122, 126, 159
primates
　blacks compared to, 27, 57–58, 59, 125, 160–61, 172–73
　Jews compared to, 51, 181
　sex, primate-human, 27–28, 57–58
The Primitive Origination of Mankind (Hale), 18–19
The Principles of Sociology (Spencer), 62
Programma quo divisionem herniarum novumque hermiae ventralis speciem proponit (Klinkosch), 88–89
Pruner, Franz Ignaz (Pruner Bey), 93–95
Pseudodoxia Epidemica or Vulgar Errors (Browne), 38–39, 46–47
Purchas, Samuel, 3
Purchas His Pilgrimage (Purchas), 3
Purchas His Pilgrimes (Purchas) 11
pygmy Jews, 47–48

Quatrefages de Bréau, Jean Louis Armand de, 94–95, 96–97, 100, 146, 156, 214

race
    determining, 179–80, 219–20
    existence of, 211
race defilement, 192–93
race madness, 177, 183
race pollution, 194f
race(s)
    black vs. white, 26–27
    categorizing the, 22–24
    color basis for dividing the, 22–23, 31
    environmentally caused, 29–30
    hierarchy of the, 26–27, 86–87,
        92–93, 105–6
    invention of, 21
    models of difference, 26–27, 28
    mutability of the, 76–78, 80–81, 87–89,
        90–91, 141–42
    number proposed, 23–24, 122, 214
    observations explaining the, 21–22
    phrenology of, 76
    taxonomy of the, 22–23
races, hierarchy of, 34–35
The Races of Man (Pickering), 87–88
Races of Men (Knox), 158
The Races of Men— a Fragment
    (Knox), 137–38
The Races of the Babylonian Empire
    (Bertin), 143–44
The Races of the Old World (Brace), 90
Racial Science of the Jewish People
    (*Rassenkunde des jüdischen Volkes*)
    (Günther), 211–12
racism, anti-black, 172
    American model of, 165, 166, 191–92,
        195, 212–13
    basis of, 54
    empire justified through, 103
    German, 164–65
    legal and political changes, 35
    modern, beginnings of, 3–4
    polygenesis and, 101–3, 105–6
    study of, ix, 1
racism-antisemitism conflation. *See also*
    antisemitism
    basis of, 162
    in Europe, 166
    Fascism in the, 195–96
    genocide, 162, 164–65

    illustrated, 197–200, 198f, 199f, 203f
    Italy in the, 195–97
    Marx in the, 171
    in music, 200–5, 203f
    Nazi Germany, 193–95, 197–205, 198f,
        199f, 201f, 203f, 204f
    racial purity, threats to, 197–200, 201f,
        203f, 204f
Raffenel, Anne, 93
Ramses-Meiamoun, 141
Rapell des Juifs (La Peyrère), 9
Raphal, Morris, 95–96, 146
Rassenkunde des jüdischen Volkes (Racial
    Science of the Jewish People)
    (Günther), 211–12
Ratzel, Friedrich, 171, 214, 226
Ravenstein, Ernst Georg, 69
Raynal, Abbé, 38–39
Reade, William Winwood, 66, 143
Reche, Otto Carl, 218, 219–20
Reclus, M. Elisée, 97
Red Jews, 44
Reicher-Sosnowski, Michał, 224
Reiffer, Emil, 223–24
religion, physical manifestation of, 46
Relink, Karel, 204f
*Researches into the Physical History of
    Mankind* (Prichard), 76–78, 80
Retzius, Anders, 100
Richardson, James, 91–92
The Rise and Fall of the Third Reich
    (Shirer), 212
Robespierre, 82–83
Robinson, Mary, 233n5
Roosevelt, Franklin D., 173, 186–88
Rosenberg, Alfred, 212, 213
Rosenberg, Alfred Ernst, 210–11, 216–18
Rousseau, Jean-Jacques, 35–36, 57–58
Rozet, Claude Antoine, 88–89
Rüppell, Wilhelm Peter Eduard Simon,
    88–89, 117
Ruppin, Arthur, 153, 156
Rupprecht, Philipp (Fips), 178f,
    189–91, 190f
Rush, Benjamin, 18

sacred race, origins, 7
Saint-Hilaire, Geoffroy, 162–63

Saint Pierre, Bernadin de, 35
Samuel, Rabbi, 46
Sandoval, Fray Prudencio de, 50
Sardari, Abdol Hossein, 224–25
Scheck, Raffael, 186
Schedel, Johann Christian, 67
Schnurrer, Friedrich, 74–75
Schorsch, Jonathan, 50
Schwarzburg, Erich, 223–24
The Searchlight, 195
In Search of "Aryan Blood" (Boaz), 219
Second Book (*Zweites Buch*) (Hitler), 200
segregation, justifying, 12–13
Selbstmörder (Suicide) (Grosz), 181–82
Semler, Johann Salomon, 222
Septimius Severus, 31
sex
 interracial, 28, 34
 primate-human, 27–28, 57–58
sexuality/sexual depravity
 blacks and Jews, elements of conflation, 175, 195
 blacks characterized by, 27, 34, 57–58, 59, 172–73, 184, 195
 Jews characterized by, 3, 44, 175, 192–93, 194f
On the Shadows of Ideas (*De Umbris Idearum*) (Bruno), 5–6
Shem (the biblical), 2–3
Shirer, William, 212
sin, 11, 32, 45–46
Sketches on the History of Man (Buffon), 28–29
skin color
 German national racial study on, 180
 origin of, 78
 racial darkening, 78–79
skin color, elements affecting. *See also* black skin, causes of
 black blood, 54–55
 caloric theory, 83–84
 climate/environment, 78, 82–83, 84, 85, 87, 89, 92, 93–95, 96–98, 172–73
Škvorecký, Josef, 203–5
slave rebellion, 37
slavery
 in France, 35, 36
 the French colonies, 36, 37
 justifying, 12–13, 17, 34–35, 37, 95–96, 136, 165–66
 opposition to, 35–36
slaves, characteristics assigned, 36
slave trade, 37
Smith, Charles Hamilton, 115–16, 147
Smith, Justin, 6
Smith, Samuel Stanhope, 20, 30
Sömmering, Samuel Thomas von, 41
Soros, George, 246–47n3
Soya K., 226–27
Sparwenfeld, Johan Gabriel, 23
species
 defining, 25
 varieties vs., 20–21
Spencer, Herbert, 62
Spiller, Gustav, 154
Sprengel, Kurt, 68–69
Stalin, Joseph, 186–88
Steinweis, Alan, 222
St. John, Henry, 1st Viscount Bolingbroke (Bolingbroke), 16–17
Stow, Kenneth, 48
Streicher, Julius, 186–88, 188f, 193, 194f, 202
Strickland, Debra Higgs, 47–48
Stuckart, Wilhelm, 212
Studies in Jewish Statistics: Social, Vital and Anthropometric (Jacobs), 149–50
"The Study and Uses of History" St. John, Henry, 16–17
The Study of Man (Haddon), 160
Suicide (*Selbstmörder*) (Grosz), 181–82
Swift, Jonathan, 14
Systema Naturae (Linnaeus), 24–25

Taft, Hessy, 222
Tasso, Torquato, 56
Taylor, Bayard, 147, 151
Telliamed, ou entretiens d'un philosophe indien avec un missionnaire français sur la diminution de la mer (*Telliamid,* or Conversations between an Indian philosopher and a French missionary on the diminution of the sea and the creation of the land) (Maillet), 16
The Bastards of Rehoboth and the Problem of Miscegenation in Man

(*Die Rehobother Bastards und das Bastardisierungsproblem beim Menschen*) (Fischer), 183
The History of Creation (*Natürliche Schöpfungsgeschichte*) (Haeckel), 210–11
Theilhaber, Felix, 184
The Jewish Question as a Racial, Moral, and Cultural Question (*Die Judenfrage als Racen-, Sitten-und Culturfrage*) (Dühring), 192–93
The Jews as a race (*Die Juden als Rasse*) (Judt), 152–53
Third Reich. *See* Nazi Germany
Times Atlas of the World, 144
Totem and Taboo (Freud), 62
Towards the Final Solution (Mosse), ix
Trachtenberg, Joshua, 48
Traité de la couleur de la peau humaine en général, de celle des nègres en particulier et de la métamorphose d'une de ces couleurs en l'autre, soit de naissance, soit accidentellement (Treatise on the color of human skin in general, on that of Negroes in particular and of the transformation of one of these colors into another, either through birth or by accident (Le Cat), 67
Traité de la Métaphysique (Voltaire), 15, 17
Trau keinem Fuchs auf grüner Heid und keinem Jud auf seinem Eid (Trust No Fox on His Green Heath and No Jew on His Oath) (Bauer), 186–88, 187*f*
Travels in the Great Desert: including a Description of the Oases and Cities of Ghet Ghadames and Mourzuk (Richardson), 91
Travels to Discover the Source of the Nile, in the years 1768, 1769, 1770, 1771, 1772 and 1773 (Bruce), 70
Treatise on the color of human skin in general, on that of Negroes in particular and of the transformation of one of these colors into another, either through birth or by accident (Le Cat (*Traité de la couleur de la peau humaine en général, de celle des nègres en particulier et de la métamorphose d'une de ces couleurs en l'autre, soit de naissance, soit accidentellement*), 67
A Tribute for the Negro (Armistead), 88
Tristram, Henry Baker, 120–22
True Discourse of the Late Voyages of Discoverie (A Best), 3
Truffaut, François, 221–22
Trust No Fox on His Green Heath and No Jew on His Oath (*Trau keinem Fuchs auf grüner Heid und keinem Jud auf seinem Eid*) (Bauer), 186–88, 187*f*
Turks, 50
Twain, Mark, 37
Two Essays sent in a Letter from Oxford to a Nobleman in London. The First Concerning Some Errors about the Creation, General Flood, and the Peopling of the World. The Second Concerning the Rise, Progress and Destruction of Fables and Romances (L.P.), 19
Types of Mankind: Or, Ethnological Researches: Based Upon the Ancient Monuments, Paintings, Sculptures, and Crania of Races, and Upon Their Natural, Geographical, Philological and Biblical History, Illustrated by Selections from the Inedited Papers of Samuel George Morton (Gliddon & Nott), 106, 107

Über die verschiedenen Rassen der Menschen (Of the Different Races) (Kant), 26–27
unity of humankind doctrine, x, 7, 23, 25, 30, 76–77
unity of the universe doctrine, 5–6

Vacher de Lapouge, Georges, 167
Valignano, Alexander, 72
Vanini, Lucilio (Julius Caesar Vanini), 8, 9, 31, 48, 99, 105–6
varieties, species vs., 20–21
Varthema, Ludovico di, 47
Verschuer, Otmar von, 214, 215
Victoria, Queen of England, 141

The Victory of Jewry over Germandom (*Der Weg zum Siege des Germanenthums über das Judenthum*) (Marr), 165–66
Virchow, Rudolf, 179, 180, 206, 210–11, 227
Vitalis, Orderic, 43
Volkskunde Der Juden (Folklore of the Jews) (Andree), 69, 144–45
Voltaire, 15–17, 30, 31, 36, 49, 61, 135, 173
Von den Krankheiten der Juden (On Jewish Illnesses) (Wolf), 51
Vorstellung der vornehmsten Völkerschaften der Welt (Presentation of the Most Distinguished Peoples of the World) (Breitenbauch), 73–74
voting rights, 101
Voyage dans L'Afrique Occidentale comprenant l'exploration du Sénégal etc. (Journey in West Africa including the Exploration of Senegal) (Raffenel), 93
Voyage to Guinea (Atkins), 14–15
A Voyage to Guinea, Brasil and the West Indies (Atkins), 14–15

Waddington, Samuel Ferrand, 89–90
Wagner, Richard, 170, 222
Wagner, Robert, 186
Waitz, Theodor, 92–94, 130, 146–47, 241n12
Walker, John, 30
Wallace, Alfred Russell, 125–26, 142–43, 144, 151–52, 211
Walter, Bruno, 200
wandering Jew motif, 49
Warburton, Eliot George, 133
Wastl, Josef, 219
Waterman, William, 33
Weber, Max, 20
Weil, Jiří, 222
Weissenberg, Samuel, 208
West, Benjamin, 135
White, Charles, 99–100, 156–57
white Jews
 black Jews vs., 97–98
 of Cochin, 82, 83, 93–94, 95, 108, 146, 156
 immutable purity, 87, 95–96, 112
 into black Jews, 67–68
 of Loango, 67
 purity of the, 108
 racial types proved by, 29
 whiteness of, 146
white Negros, 59–62, 78
whiteness
 determining, 180–81
 transformation into black, 17–18, 43, 45–46, 61, 67–68, 74, 80–81, 88, 89–90, 92, 96–97, 118
white race, origins, 7
Whitman, James Q., 191
Williams, Raymond, 181
Wippermann, Wolfgang, 205
Without a Solution to the Jewish Question There Will Be No Redemption for the German People (*Ohne Lösung der Judenfrage keine Erloesung des deutschen Volkes*) (Streicher), 186–88, 188f
Wolf, Elcan Isaac, 51
women, 22–23, 27, 139–40
Woodward, John, 39–40
world, origination of the. *See* monogenesist theory; polygenesist theory; pre-Adamism
Wright, Thomas, 129–30

Young, Robert, 132

Zander (*Die Verbreitung der Juden in der Welt—Statistische Beiträge zu den Fragen der Zeit* [The Distribution of Jews in the World—Statistical Contributions to the Questions of the Time]), 225
Zander, Friedrich, 225
Zangwill, Israel, 154–55
Ziegler, Hans Severus, 202–3, 203f
Zimmerman, Andrew, 179–80
Zimmermann, Eberhard August Wilhelm von, 68–69, 83
Zweites Buch (Second Book) (Hitler), 200

Printed in the USA
CPSIA information can be obtained
at www.ICGtesting.com
BVHW040146310723
668003BV00001B/1